DISCOS

and

DEMOCRACY

DISCOS

and

DEMOCRACY

CHINA

IN THE

THROES

OF

REFORM

Orville Schell

ANCHOR BOOKS
DOUBLEDAY
NEW YORK LONDON TORONTO SYDNEY AUCKLAND

AN ANCHOR BOOK
PUBLISHED BY DOUBLEDAY
a division of Bantam Doubleday Dell Publishing Group, Inc.
666 Fifth Avenue, New York, New York 10103

ANCHOR BOOKS, DOUBLEDAY, and the portrayal of an anchor
are trademarks of Doubleday, a division of Bantam Doubleday
Dell Publishing Group, Inc.

Discos and Democracy was originally published by Pantheon Books,
a division of Random House, Inc., in 1988. The Anchor Books
edition is published by arrangement with Pantheon Books.

Portions of this book originally appeared in *The Atlantic*,
May 1988, and *Mother Jones*, June 1988.

Earlier versions of "The Limo-ization of Beijing" and
"A Dictionary Time Capsule" appeared in the *New York Times
Travel Section*, May 25, 1986, and *New York Times Book Review*,
June 7, 1987, respectively.

Library of Congress Cataloging-in-Publication Data
Schell, Orville.
Discos and democracy : China in the throes of reform /
    Orville Schell. — 1st Anchor Books ed.
        p.   cm.
Reprint. Originally published: New York : Pantheon
    Books, c1988.
Bibliography: p.
        1. China—Politics and government—1976– I. Title.
[DS779.26.S34   1989]
951.05—dc19   89-30241
                        CIP

ISBN 0-385-26187-X
PRINTED IN THE UNITED STATES OF AMERICA
FIRST ANCHOR BOOKS EDITION 1989
2   4   6   8   9   7   5   3

*For William Shawn, who first
encouraged me fifteen years ago
to start this ongoing narrative
of events in China*

Contents

||||||||||||||||||||||||||||||
•—— Acknowledgments ——————————————•

Good editors are the unsung partners of writers. There could hardly be a more hardworking, brilliantly insightful, ruthlessly critical, but profoundly constructive and encouraging editor in the business than Tom Engelhardt. My deepest thanks go to him for the care and long hours he lavished in helping to bring this book into being.

I wish also to thank Estelle Silbermann for her copy editing, Jeffrey Apter for a very conscientious job of proofreading, Li Cheng for his help in research and fact checking, Song Jia and Liu Baifang for their help in translating, and John Service, Andrew Nathan, Perry Link, and Carolyn Wakeman for the time they spent going over the manuscript, and Fang Lizhi and Liu Binyan for going over their respective chapters. I would also like to acknowledge the *Atlantic Monthly* for sending me to China; the Center for Chinese Studies at the University of California, Berkeley, where much of the library research was subsequently done; and the MacDowell Colony, where I was a fellow while writing a portion of this book.

Orville Schell
January, 1988

DISCOS

and

DEMOCRACY

Back to the Future

In February, 1987, when I arrived back in Beijing after five months away, the demonstrations that had filled the streets of China's cities with protesting students demanding democracy and freedom had just ended. The country, having enjoyed an unprecedented political thaw that summer and spring, was now gripped by a strong Maoist counter-reaction every bit as chilling as the winter weather itself.

Unsure where to begin by way of unraveling the confusing events of the past few months, I went out to Beijing University to have a look around; for it was there at China's pre-eminent university, known as Beida, that many of the demonstrating students had grouped before taking to the streets in protest. All that remained of those tumultuous days, however, were a few tattered wall posters and a sprinkling of students who had not yet returned home to celebrate Chinese New Year. Even though it was freezing cold, I strolled around the campus for an hour or so trying to find something specific—I had no idea what—that would help me conjure up those chaotic days when thousands of students rallied here to march on Tian'anmen Square, the political and spiritual center of the country.

I was just about to leave when, in the distance, the massive gray statue of Chairman Mao, which still keeps its lonely vigil at Beida, caught my eye. It struck me as somewhat of a paradox that it still stood not just on the campus of China's foremost institution of higher learning, but out in front of the university library. For it had been Mao Zedong, after all, who had once said, "If you read too many books, in the end they will petrify your mind," and he who had also proclaimed, "The more educated you are, the more reactionary."

Not quite sure why I felt drawn to this gargantuan Maoist relic, I walked over and sat down shivering on its pedestal to contemplate the irony of its presence; the incongruity of this enormous socialist icon still rising over the Beida campus in the new "New China" of Deng Xiaoping.

Irony and incongruity, as they have since "Liberation" in 1949, abound in China today, often mocking the very notions of a "people's republic," not to speak of a Communist party obsessed with the appearance of doctrinal consistency and orthodoxy. To an observer, the sense of the contradictory and the absurd has, if anything, become more pronounced since Deng Xiaoping came to power in 1977 and at the historic Third Plenum of the Eleventh Party Central Committee in December, 1978, proclaimed his new policies of opening China's door to the outside world and of economic liberalization, while at the same time insisting that his country was hewing to a socialist line. In fact, in the years since, so many contradictions have arisen between China's old Maoist identity and its new reformist self that the country has sometimes seemed locked in a state of self-induced cultural and political schizophrenia.

Sitting on Mao's pedestal, where just a few weeks ago students had decried their lack of freedom of speech, written wall posters championing democracy, and publicly burned Party newspapers to protest their distorted reports of the demonstrations, I clapped my bare hands together in the bitter cold to keep them from aching and began studying the huge figure towering over me. I was surprised to find that it was rendered not in bronze, marble, or even stone, but in that most proletarian of building materials, concrete, as if its makers had wished to underscore for eternity Mao's unity with "the broad masses of workers, peasants, and soldiers."

Looking up at him, I saw that his bare, grainy hands were clasped resolutely behind him and that his posture was perfectly upright, as if in defiance of the icy cold wind that seemed to be blowing the sculpted folds of his cement overcoat back in a ripple behind him. On his head was one of those squat, short-brimmed caps that had become his most indelible sartorial hallmark. There was about his lips the faintest suggestion of a smile, while his eyes gazed stalwartly out across the frozen brown lawn toward the gray brick classrooms beyond.

It was late in the afternoon, and only the occasional bundled-up student hurried past. My teeth were literally chattering, and I had just decided to leave when, glancing up at Mao's face one last time, I allowed my eyes to follow his stony gaze outward across the lawn; and there on the wall of a distant building I saw the barely discernible outlines of a few faded Chinese characters. Curious, I walked over, to discover that they were actually parts of whole quotations from Mao himself, which had been emblazoned on these walls twenty years ago at the height of the Great Proletarian Cultural Revolution. Painted over hurriedly as political lines changed and the high tide of Maoist revolutionary fervor ebbed, they were only now slowly reappearing like figures from a mist.

Then, as I looked carefully around, I saw to my amazement that all the surrounding buildings were in fact covered with these still partially obscured revolutionary exhortations. Under the combined effects of sun and rain, they were re-emerging now from oblivion, the way erosion will sometimes bring long-buried fossils back to the surface of the earth after millions of years of interment.

Moving nearer to the first building, I tried to read these blurred glyphs. But paint still so obscured large parts of each quotation that attempting to decipher them was like listening to a distant radio station whose reception keeps fading out at crucial moments.

"The big landlord class and the reactionary section of the intelligentsia . . ."; ". . . petit-bourgeois ideology, anti-Marxist ideology will . . ."; "All erroneous ideas, all poisonous weeds . . ." I could make out no more than a few fragments from each.

But at another nearby building, whose walls had been more exposed to the elements, whole quotations had reappeared through the layers of paint and now stood out boldly on the encrusted walls like those works of Jasper Johns that are filled with numbers, letters, and words.

"To make trouble, be defeated, make more trouble and be defeated again until it is destroyed—this is the logic of American imperialism."

"The question of suppressing counter-revolutionaries is one of a struggle between ourselves and the enemy, a contradiction between ourselves and the enemy."

"A revolution is not a dinner party, or writing an essay, or painting a picture, or doing embroidery; it can not be so refined, so leisurely and gentle, so temperate, kind, courteous, restrained, and magnanimous. A revolution is an insurrection, an act of violence by which one class overthrows another."

"Riding roughshod everywhere, U.S. imperialism has made itself the enemy of the people of the world and has increasingly isolated itself. Those who refuse to be enslaved will never be cowed by the atom bombs and hydrogen bombs in the hands of the U.S. imperialists. The raging tide of the people of the world against the U.S. aggressors is irresistible. Their struggle against U.S. imperialism and its lackeys will assuredly win greater victories."

I left Beida feeling as if I were re-emerging from the depths of an archaeological dig. Having come to find evidence of China's recent movement toward democracy, I had instead stumbled into a reliquary of China's old revolution, a revolution that, like a disembodied spirit, still hovered over the campus and, indeed, in ways that only became discernible in the coming months, over the country as a whole.

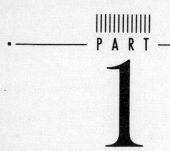

PART

1

DON'T BE

AFRAID

OF

DEMOCRACY

||||||||||||||||||||
A Dictionary
Time
Capsule

That previous summer of 1986, before the students began to demonstrate, China seemed far away indeed from Chairman Mao and all
that he had stood for. As I sat at home in my study puzzling through
piles of newspaper reports and documents describing a country
seemingly hell-bent on transforming almost every aspect of life overnight, I would from time to time focus with welcome relief on the
patterns of color the bindings of the China books on my shelves
formed. Over the months and years, as China changed confusingly,
they at least had remained immovable monuments, their titles as
deeply ingrained in my memory as the Great Helmsman's quotations
once were in the memories of all Chinese who lived through the last
decade of his tumultuous tenure as China's supreme ruler. There was
a vein of yellow and green spines where the volumes of Chinese fiction
were gathered on the higher shelves above my desk; to their right and
below, splashes of orange and red where books on China's Great
Proletarian Cultural Revolution resided; and a band of crimson where
my collection of "Little Red Bibles," containing Mao's most recitable
quotes, lay in repose. To the left there was a drab wasteland of white,
brown, and gray—documents from the various plenums and sessions
of People's Congresses and Central Committees of the Chinese Communist Party. And just above my desk were the blues and greens of
the Chinese dictionaries, encyclopedias, and other reference works.
    Over time these configurations became as fixed in my mind as the
ocean and the hills outside my windows. The placement of each book
was as known to me as the keys of a piano are to a pianist. Even in
the dark I could reach up and pluck any book I wanted from its place
with as much ease as a virtuoso striking the right note on a keyboard.

They made a reassuring backdrop for my study of a country that had fallen into the habit of changing every few months more than most others do in a decade.

One of the most frequently used books on my shelves was *A Chinese-English Dictionary*, a copy of which perches right above my desk between *Roget's Thesaurus* and *The New Columbia Encyclopedia*. It had been compiled in China by the Beijing Foreign Languages Institute and was published by the Commercial Press in 1981. This large green volume, with its gold-embossed binding, had become such a familiar presence in my study that once, when a friend borrowed it, the gap on the shelf made me feel as if a beloved piece of furniture had been removed from the room.

Surely there is nothing more emblematic of a particular historical period than its characteristic language. As China had been changing, so had its language, in ways sometimes confusing but always illuminating. Like shadows on the wall of reality, words in China have often been a uniquely important gauge of the shifting inner political state of the country, frequently difficult to plumb by any other means. Since so many struggles over the last three decades have been over the possession and meaning of words—for instance, what did it mean at a given moment to be revolutionary, leftist, bourgeois, democratic, patriotic, or capitalist (definitions that even today continue to shift with the changing imperatives of ever-fluctuating Party lines)—a dictionary was inevitably far more than just a compendium of meanings.

Indeed the 976 pages of entries in *A Chinese-English Dictionary* spoke in the militantly socialist and Maoist language that by 1986 seemed to defy almost a decade of rapid social change. Compiled during the last half of the Cultural Revolution, it was redolent of that kind of defiant Maoist phraseology that then characterized almost all Chinese writing and that still tenaciously endured in some deeply rooted aspect of Party officialese, just as Mao's quotations still survived on the walls of Beida. On the very first page the compilers of the dictionary declared: "*A Chinese-English Dictionary* was begun in 1971 according to a directive from our Great Leader Chairman Mao Zedong under the benevolent care of our beloved Premier Zhou Enlai, and was finished under the guidance of our brilliant Chairman Hua Guofeng's great strategic decision to grasp class struggle as the key link in running the country."

Even when I had nothing to look up, I oftentimes found myself browsing aimlessly through this repository of Maoist language, copying down bits of old socialist rhetoric and quotations from Mao himself the way one might rummage through a box of postage stamps in search of gems from a bygone era.

Fengxian Risk, hazard, danger: "Those who wage revolution fear no danger."

Shouxian Of first importance: "Who are our enemies? Who are our friends? This is a question of the first importance for the revolution."

Shisi To pledge one's life: "To be ready to die in defense of red political power."

Xie Evil, heretical: "To hit at the evil influence of capitalism," or, "Corrupted by evil ideology, he took to evil ways."

Sixin tadi To be dead set on or against: "Only a handful of people were dead set on following the anti-Party clique."

Gen Root: "Only by sticking to the socialist road can we do away with the root cause of poverty," or, "He made the mistake, but its source lay with the class enemy."

Such language was once so indelibly a part of China that the country seemed almost unimaginable without it. But no sooner had this dictionary been published than the reforms, which Deng Xiaoping began initiating in late 1978, started radically to alter the face of the country. By the mid-eighties China had begun to shift underneath its language the way a foundation heaved up by the freezing and thawing of the ground sometimes moves beneath a house. Words and phrases such as capitalist roader, counter-revolutionary, poisonous weed, running dog of American imperialism, self-criticism, bourgeois elements, and even comrade, which had once seemed as eternal as the Great Wall itself, had vanished and were replaced by a whole new vocabulary: bonus, disco, private enterprise, washing machine, wealth, credit card, lipstick, entrepreneur, necktie, stocks and bonds, public relations, bankruptcy, foreign investment, profit, and the appellations Mr. and Mrs. As language struggled to keep pace with the rapid changes of the real world, expressions that during Mao's time had been considered too dangerously bourgeois even to utter in private started to appear publicly in print. By spring, 1986, a whole second wave of reform began as the Party itself called for changes in China's political structure, making such words as democracy, two-party system, checks and balances, and human rights common parlance. So different in tone and subject matter were the stories that now appeared in the Chinese press that whenever I turned to my dictionary, it seemed more and more out of synch with the times.

The *Guangming Daily*, a newspaper favored by China's intellectuals, began running commentaries that made such surprising statements as, "The correct method [of finding truth] is to let people air their views, discuss, and even debate freely."

The *People's Daily*, the official organ of the Chinese Communist Party, announced that it would begin to run a column on bridge by American expert Allan Trask and Chinese-American, Catherine Wei.

The *Beijing Daily*, the conservative city-run paper, touted a newly opened, privately run credit cooperative in the capital that it proudly proclaimed would "break the monopoly of state-run banks."

The *Yangcheng Evening News*, a liberal Canton daily, heralded the opening of a new "international golf club" in the Zhuhai Special Economic Zone, lamenting that the incomplete facilities still did not entitle it to an "A rating."

The *China Daily*, China's English-language newspaper, ran a headline proclaiming DON'T WORRY, GET RICH, BO YIBO ASSURES BUSINESSES.

The *Liberation Army Daily*, the official organ of the People's Liberation Army, reported that a renowned Chinese scientist believed that flying saucers were a "natural phenomenon."

The *China Youth News*, published by the Central Committee of the Communist Youth League, announced approvingly that new businesses specializing in renting fashion models ("pretty girls" and "stalwart young men") for advertisements were opening up in Canton.

That summer, whenever I turned to *A Chinese-English Dictionary* to look something up, I felt as if I were entering the time-warped universe of one of those reprinted turn-of-the-century Sears Roebuck mail-order catalogues filled with churns, wood stoves, and hand-cranked water pumps.

Looking up *kaipi* ("to start up, to usher in") from the article about the upcoming bridge column in the *People's Daily*, I found the citation: "The birth of the Communist Party ushered in a new epoch in Chinese history."

Looking up the word *minjian* ("among the people") from the *Beijing Daily* account of the opening of a new local credit cooperative, I stumbled across a citation for an adjacent compound that read, "The reactionary government fed on the flesh and blood of the people."

From the headline that told of the rash of new modelling agencies that had just sprung up in Canton, I checked *chuxian* ("to appear, to emerge, to arise, to present") and found it illuminated by the citation, "The construction site presented an exciting scene of each one vying with the other in the socialist emulation campaign."

Among the entries for the words "democracy" and "democratic" (*minzhu*), I found the entry, "Democratic parties (those bourgeois and petit-bourgeois parties that have accepted the leadership of the Chinese Communist Party and joined the revolutionary united front)." Under *gai*, as in *gaige* ("to reform, change, transform"), I found the entry, "If we don't combat revisionism, the whole of China will change its color."

But after the student demonstrations in December, 1986, the rhetoric of the press suddenly regained a political stridency, and my dictionary, in turn, reacquired a certain unexpected semantic relevance. I was reminded, then, that while its definitions had seemed out of touch with Deng's "new" China, it had in actuality maintained its own kind of lonely witness to an aspect of the Chinese political persona that, although temporarily obscured, was still far from passé. I was also reminded of the ways in which the meaning of words themselves changed in China—how words like "conservative" and "reformer" invariably had a relative rather than an absolute meaning in the context of its ever-shifting political lines. Reading the newly militant headlines about the need to re-establish the primacy of "Party leadership," the "dictatorship of the proletariat," and the urgent need to stamp out "bourgeois liberalization" and "wholesale Westernization," I suddenly felt grateful to my dictionary for having so insistently served as a reminder of this authoritarian aspect of China, which superficial reforms were unlikely to erase. I realized that each time I had taken it from the shelf, opened its green binding, and let my fingers run down its columns of characters and compounds, far from plunging me back into a useless reliquary of the past, it had actually been speaking in a language still current on one side of China's divided political personality. In its insistent way, far from being irrelevant, it had been administering a corrective antidote against exactly the kind of historical amnesia that often grips socialist countries.

When, for instance, authorities at the Commercial Press began slipping loose-leaf versions of a corrected preface (minus the socialist encomiums to old Party leaders) into each new volume of the dictionary, it was tempting to accept their revisionism, particularly during the high tide of the reformist thaw in 1986, at face value; to believe that China had at last moved irrevocably beyond its past. But as the aftermath of the student demonstrations soon showed, there was still a part of China deeply anchored in the era of Chairman Mao. Like those species of arctic animals whose mottled summer coats become white in the wintertime, China, too, had a notable capacity for sudden changes in political appearance that left the creature beneath far less altered than one might imagine.

However, unlike Party propaganda tracts that can be quickly replaced, chapters of history books that can be hastily re-edited, or photographs of officials that can be discreetly airbrushed, the innards of a dictionary are far too complex to be altered by minor revisionist surgery; and, once widely distributed, a dictionary cannot be readily recalled from service, because any alternative would take years to prepare.

And so volumes of *A Chinese-English Dictionary* rest like time capsules in libraries like my own. Although sometimes they may seem to be speaking from the vantage point of a distant and incongruent past, they are also forms of living memory that continue to tell of a certain reality, even when propagandists try to change the meaning of words and when new leaders find it temporarily expedient to adopt new political lines.

Like all historical documents, such books are reminders that society's political characteristics are deep-rooted; that while they may sometimes seem to have been radically altered or even to have disappeared, very often they have only gone underground, where they endure like dormant genes waiting to manifest themselves again at some later date.

In the first few months of 1987, far from looking obsolete, *A Chinese-English Dictionary* began to seem almost clairvoyant. As much of its terminology came back in vogue, I resolved that in the future, as long as it clearly defined the words I wished to look up, I would not care if it did so using the roseate but frightening language of Chairman Mao's Revolution. For I had been reminded that far from distorting their meanings, this dictionary actually imbued them with a fuller significance by reminding me of this other dimension inherited from China's only partially interred past.

|||||||||||||||||||

• ———— Don't Be ——————————————— •
Afraid of
Democracy

In September, 1986, shortly after I arrived back in China on one of my several trips that year, I picked up the *China Daily* to be met not by a headline proclaiming the superiority of socialism or the dangers of "bourgeois liberalization" from the West, but by one that said, "Don't Be Afraid of Democracy." The article itself, which discussed a recent commentary that had appeared in the *Workers' Daily*, far from being propaganda for the kind of limited "socialist democracy" under the aegis of the Communist Party that had been in common parlance even during Mao's tenure, spoke of democracy in a much broader and more Western sense.

"Do words such as 'democracy,' 'freedom,' and 'human rights' mean to you just bourgeois liberalization?" it began, somewhat in the vein of a commercial for a household cleanser. "They do to some, [who] argue that there is danger that these words may lead people astray from our Party's leadership and from our socialist cause."

After effusively praising Western concepts of democracy as "progressive steps in the advance of history" that "represented the righteous interests of the people," the author of the *China Daily* article went on forcefully to advocate that such ideas "be recognized by us today," because although "some of us tend to be doubtful about the value of political slogans or structures that belonged to the bourgeoisie . . . there is always something worth learning and assimilating from bourgeois political systems."

Acknowledging that Western democratic systems and the philosophies on which they were based had already exercised a "far-reaching impact" on China, the article went on to say that "the appearance of the election system and the state Constitution [in China] have derived much from bourgeois key words like democracy and human rights."

The article concluded by proclaiming that "under today's circumstances—when China is opening its door wider to the outside—we must be flexible in adopting what is acceptable and positive from other nations, and try to communicate with the world in a language that not only contains the word 'revolution,' but also many others like 'democracy,' 'freedom,' and 'human rights.' "

From the perspective of Maoist China, this article and its accompanying headline had something of the shock effect the *New York Times* would have if it editorialized in favor of a one-party state under the dictatorship of the proletariat, a shock that was only slightly mitigated by the fact that I was sitting not in Beijing's dour Friendship Hotel eating Chinese food, but in the Great Wall Sheraton Hotel, enjoying a croissant and a cup of cappuccino.

As it turned out, it was only one of thousands of news articles, speeches, essays, and commentaries that had begun to appear in China as part of a radical program to extend Deng Xiaoping's eight-year-old reform movement from the country's economy to its political structure. At no time since December, 1978, when at the Third Plenum of the Eleventh Party Central Committee Deng had called for the "liberation of thought" and declared that "modernization" rather than "large-scale turbulent class struggle" was to become the nation's new priority, had China been so open and relaxed. Indeed, during the summer and fall of 1986 the tide of reform had been flowing so rapidly that the idea of Mao Zedong (never mind what he had stood for) seemed to have been swept out of the immediate consciousness of most Chinese and into history, where he seemed to occupy a place as remote as Qin Shihuang, China's first emperor.

By the early nineteen-eighties disruptive political "campaigns," which had once swept back and forth across the country with devastating regularity, had been decreed a thing of the past. "Verdicts" had been "reversed" on millions of Chinese who had been stigmatized as members of the "five black categories" (capitalists, landlords, rich peasants, counter-revolutionaries, and rightists and bad elements). Intellectuals who had long languished at the bottom of the social pyramid suddenly found themselves not just "rehabilitated" but on a swift elevator ride to the top of a society that was being newly designed both around and for them. Now called "advanced elements of the working class" rather than counter-revolutionaries and capitalist roaders, they were suddenly considered by the Party elite fit not simply to participate in the daily life of their country but to contribute to its governing.

Production rather than politics had been put "in command," to borrow a famous Maoist phrase. Communal farming had been abolished in favor of private farming. The centralization of and Party control over industry had been relaxed, giving managers unprecedented new powers over decision-making at the local level. Bonuses and other economic incentives had superseded spiritual exhortations such as "serve the people" as acceptable devices to encourage workers to produce. Private enterprise, once anathema to Chinese socialism, was actively being encouraged as a means of "invigorating" the economy and putting China's unemployed millions to work. Even private property was making a comeback. Houses and apartments were bought and sold on the open market, and there was an active market in "utilization rights" to rural land. This land, although still technically owned by the state, had by 1987 acquired the de facto status of private property through long-term leases to individual farm families which were bought and sold like deeds.

Almost everywhere one looked, evidence of a new, albeit often chaotic, energy and individualism abounded. In almost every city and town, streets that previously had been ominously emptied of private enterprise were now cluttered with peddlers, privately managed shops, stores, and free markets. Cities had been transfigured by high-rise apartments, which first sprang up in downtown areas and then quickly marched out across surrounding agricultural fields to make a new Chinese suburbia. The rural economy had been transformed by fairs and open markets, not to speak of its own construction boom in private housing, so that often towns and villages proved unrecognizable to those returning after only a few years' absence.

For the first time in almost thirty years, people were beginning to focus on private rather than public life. The family rather than the collective had again, as in pre-liberation China, become the main social unit of everyday existence. Even courtship and romance experienced a renaissance as the Party itself, after decades of frowning on such decadence, sanctioned personal relations as a legitimate human pastime. With Mao's notion of making individual sacrifices for the greater common good of society rapidly dimming, there was a recrudescence of the notion of—at least a newly expressed desire for—personal enjoyment and leisure. Amusement parks, dance halls, golf courses, video-game parlors, fashion shows, pop concerts, roller rinks, beauty salons, bowling alleys, coffee houses, and myriad other new forms of recreational entertainment proliferated.

As controls over art and literature eased, there was a flowering of new writing unequalled since the nineteen-thirties. Artists, long circumscribed by the conventions of socialist realism and revolutionary romanticism, began exhibiting boldly abstract painting; composers started to produce avant-garde musical scores and rock and disco groups dominated the popular music scene. Theater groups produced experimental dramas and Western plays and musicals; and a new generation of young film directors began to experiment with scripts and cinematic techniques that would have been totally unacceptable only a few years earlier.

Even the way people looked and dressed had changed radically. China, once among the least style-conscious countries in the world, had suddenly become aware of the world of design. (One village in Shandong province was even celebrated in the official press because every peasant was said to own a Western suit and tie.) Its aesthetic sensibility, so brutally defoliated by the notion of art as politics, had begun to re-emerge, so that over the last few years one had the eerie sense of watching a black and white photograph slowly becoming tinged with color as if by some miraculous new developing process. Not only did splashes of primary color reappear in people's dress but in the decoration of almost every aspect of life. Flower beds, once decried and often destroyed as symbols of self-indulgence, dotted the urban landscape. Streets dividers, once barren stretches of dirt and weeds, began to bloom with color. Balconies on apartment buildings were turned into miniature gardens. There was no more appropriate symbol of the manifold ways in which China had come alive than the way in which privately owned flower companies reappeared and prospered.

An old Party slogan, "However small the matters of Party and State, they are important. However important the matters of the individual, they are small," had been displaced by a new ethic, which put emphasis on the individual and the enjoyment of the self.

As the "open door" policy went into effect, China, which had formerly faced so aggressively inward, turned more and more outward for everything from technology and culture to management and capital. The transformation of people's lives, which included a new wide-eyed glorification of Western mass culture, was more than matched by China's economic opening to the West, so that even the once forbidden words "Western capitalism" soon acquired a seductive luster.

Countless delegations went abroad on trade and fact-finding missions. Tens of thousands of Chinese students went to foreign colleges and universities to study, while emigrants, with the help of overseas relatives, poured out of China to take up residence abroad.

In through China's revolving door spun a veritable horde of tourists, businessmen, adventurers, journalists, foreign experts, and scholars. New diplomatic relations, cultural exchange programs, foreign investment projects, and expanding trade relations during the first half of the decade seemed to know no limit. Though few people spoke any longer of "revolution," China was actually changing faster now than it ever had under the aegis of Chairman Mao. Often, however, in those changes one saw little more than a distorted and often bizarre funhouse mirror image of its former self. In fact, if one had drawn up a list of those things for which Mao's China had once stood, and then played the child's game of "opposites" by writing down their antithesis beside them, one could have quite blindly arrived at a fairly accurate description of Deng's new China without the expense and effort of actually going there.

Even the means of identifying China's complex network of political factions had been affected by this process, so that to the newcomer their labels often gave an erroneous impression of the real forces that were at work behind each group. For instance, old-line Maoists, who had once been known as radicals and who still yearned to see China's Communist Revolution continue, had paradoxically been dubbed conservatives. There was, in fact, nothing conservative about these hard-liners, except that they wished to return to the radical vision of China as an egalitarian, centralized, self-reliant socialist country as envisioned by Mao Zedong in the nineteen-fifties. Those Party leaders who now took a more conventionally Western, even technocratic, view of politics and economic change had oddly come to be referred to as reformers, when in actuality their political viewpoints were in many ways rather conservative—much closer, in fact, to those of Ronald Reagan (who had himself taken to calling China the "so-called Communist China") than to those of Karl Marx. Their reformist label derived simply from their wish to modernize their country and distance it from its Maoist past. To make matters even more confusing, these reformist leaders often referred to their hard-line or conservative Maoist adversaries as being influenced by leftism, while the hard-line or conservative Maoists themselves took to referring to the reformers as being under the influence of rightism. This confusion of terminology made the twists and turns of Chinese politics almost impossible for casual observers to unravel, and lent the whole Chinese political scene a curious Alice-in-Wonderland quality where everything was in reality something other than it seemed. The complexities of the political debate and factional struggle will be discussed in greater detail in the following chapters, but for now it may be helpful for the reader to think not in terms of conservatives and reformers, but in terms of Maoist hard-liners and Westernizers, or liberal reformers.

But during the fall of 1986 even the very visibility of these Westernizers or liberal reformers was deceptive. For against the riptide of changes they were promoting, those hard-line Party members who believed in the old revolutionary precepts and were still powerful continued to struggle to keep China attached to its Maoist moorings lest it be completely carried away by the force of liberal reform. Hard-liners like Deng Liqun, former propaganda chief and present Central Committee Secretariat member; Peng Zhen, Political Bureau member and Chairman of the National People's Congress; Chen Yun, the conservative economic planner and Standing Committee member of the Political Bureau; Hu Qiaomu, Political Bureau member and former secretary of Mao Zedong; and Wang Zhen, Vice-Chairman of the Central Advisory Commission—names one would hear over and over again in the coming months—were deeply wary of the pace and scope of the changes they observed in China as well as nostalgic for the ardor and idealism of Mao's earlier revolution. While younger liberal members of the Party heralded economic incentives, a commodity economy, market mechanisms, price reform, and reform of the political structure, these older hard-line Maoist leaders continued a discourse in the rhetoric of the bygone revolution on five-year plans, centralized control, evil winds, socialist spiritual civilization, and spiritual pollution.

That September of 1986, while so many Chinese publications were calling for democracy and political change, *Red Flag*, the Party's main theoretical organ and a political bastion of the hard-line faction, ran an article that, like a single dissonant chord in an otherwise tonal score, reminded Chinese—if they needed reminding, given thirty years of twists and turns in Party policy—that the fate of reform in China was still by no means a settled matter. The article, by the octogenarian hard-liner Wang Zhen, marked the tenth anniversary of Mao Zedong's death and the publication of a new version of his *Selected Works*. In a style redolent of the past, Wang wrote, "To my mind, the best way to commemorate Comrade Mao Zedong is to earnestly study and propagate Mao Zedong Thought, to draw wisdom and strength from its valuable spiritual wealth, and to guarantee the success of the building of socialist material and spiritual civilization. . . . China has a civilization of close to five thousand years. The Chinese nation has a revolutionary tradition and spiritual wealth worthy of our pride, of which the most valuable part is Mao Zedong Thought."

Wang's paean to Mao was an indication in these very liberal times of the vast aquifer of Maoist sentiment in China just beneath the surface of the Chinese Communist Party, if not Chinese society as a whole. In fact, as it turned out, Wang's article was also evidence that as early as the summer of 1986 hard-liners were marshalling their strength to thwart liberal efforts to spell out a bold and clear plan for political reform at the upcoming Sixth Plenary Session of the Twelfth Central Committee of the Communist Party of China, which was to be convened on September 28.

The *Red Flag* article, however, was only one of many signs suggesting that there were more points of tension for the Party to battle over. It was evidence of the ongoing, if sub-rosa, struggle for control of the Party between hard-liners like Wang Zhen and liberal reformers like Party General Secretary Hu Yaobang, Premier Zhao Ziyang, and propaganda chief Zhu Houze—a struggle that was at this particular time beginning to come to a head over key Party appointments to be filled at the upcoming Thirteenth Party Congress, which was finally convened in October, 1987. This competition was only a continuation of an ongoing "two-line struggle" that had pitted leadership factions against each other for decades, whatever their political positions at a given moment, and that had been responsible for the way in which Chinese politics had swung continuously from "left" to "right," oscillating between what the Chinese refer to as the tendency toward either "expanding" (*fang*) or "contracting" (*shou*) the boundaries of what was politically permissible.

Bridging these factions as an economic liberal reformer but as a political hard-liner was Deng Xiaoping. Eighty-two years old, on the Long March with Mao and other veteran revolutionary leaders, twice fallen from power during the Cultural Revolution, Deng was one of the few charismatic older leaders who shared common chords with both factions. By force of his revolutionary stature, political acumen, and close ties with the Army as well as the Party, Deng had usually managed to keep inter-Party debates largely submerged and behind the closed doors of the Central Committee. Sometimes, though, in carrying out his delicate balancing act, Deng would suddenly tilt precariously away from the side of the liberal reformers, and then, sensing a preponderance of power now on their own side, the hard-liners would make a lunge for greater control (as they had in 1983–84 when they had used a campaign against spiritual pollution to launch a broadside attack against reformist policies in general). In the past, however, Deng had always managed miraculously to restore the Party's precarious equilibrium before the whole political balancing act fell completely out of kilter.

Sometimes, perhaps even at Deng's urging, a hard-line leader would suddenly speak up in the midst of what otherwise seemed to be a sea of sentiment about liberal reform, offering a sober reminder that if some were enamored of capitalist-style economics and more Western forms of democracy, others—who knew how many or what their potential power?—were still enamored of Chairman Mao. For instance, just the previous September the veteran central economic planner Chen Yun had used all the right code words to ruffle the feathers of liberal reformers at the Chinese Communist Party National Congress by telling the delegates, "There are now some people, including Party members, who have forsaken socialist and communist ideals and turned their backs on serving the people. In pursuit of their own selfish gain, they put 'money above all else,' without regard to the interests of the state and people, even to the extent of violating the law and discipline. . . . These problems can be attributed to the relaxation of ideological and political work and the decline in the function and authority of departments in charge of such work."

Like a strong undertow that pulls with a deadly but invisible force, the hard-liners and their supporters (many of whom had entered the Party during the Cultural Revolution, when the criterion for membership had been "redness" rather than expertise) still exerted considerable if unseen power against the efforts of liberal reformers in and out of the Party who even in the halcyon days of 1986 represented something closer to a series of contradictory tendencies than a single monolithic political movement. Just as centuries earlier the bitter factional struggles among the powerful eunuchs who served the emperors remained obscure to those outside the Forbidden City, so in the fall of 1986, despite occasional eruptions of clearly delineated conflict, it was not easy to fathom the depth of division between leadership factions in the Chinese Communist Party. In fact, the crescendo of calls for greater political reform and democracy in Chinese political life and yet deeper reforms in China's Soviet-style economic system had so drowned out these conservative voices that it was tempting to assume that the Maoist hard-liners had ceased to exist as a serious political force in the top echelons of the Party. For a brief historical moment one might have sustained the illusion that China was rushing unfettered into a new and previously unimaginable future.

||||||||||||||||||||
The Liberal Reformers Speak Out

Until the spring of 1986, reform, even though it had been the dominant line in Party circles, had been applied in a relatively practical manner in Deng's China. It meant restructuring the country's economy and opening it up to the outside world, the impact of which, in every aspect of life from farming and education to business and tourism, was nothing short of monumental. Nonetheless, if China's economic system had been dramatically transformed (sometimes in ways unpredictable and not always pleasing to the reformers themselves), its archaic centralized political structure had remained largely untouched since it had been set up under the tutelage of Stalinist Russia in the early nineteen-fifties. That structure, it was clear, inhibited exactly the kind of individual initiative and freewheeling energy that liberal reformers had come to view as essential to vibrant economic growth; especially if, to enjoy such growth, China must rely on precisely that class of intellectuals and technocrats that it had so demeaned and abused for being insufficiently red during the last two decades of political upheaval. In no small measure, then, the call for democracy and more freedom of expression, unparalleled since Mao declared in 1956, "Let a hundred flowers bloom and a hundred schools of thought contend," was both an appeal and a concession to Chinese intellectuals. It was calculated to mobilize their enthusiasm, support, and participation in the Party's new program of economic development by granting more freedom.

What initially looked like an updated version of Mao's Hundred Flowers Movement had started rather discreetly in the spring of 1986 as Deng Xiaoping began dropping clues pointing toward a broadening reform movement to come. On March 28, 1986, he had told the Prime Minister of New Zealand that during China's seventh five-year plan reforms should spread to politics, education, and science. Several days later, when he met with the Prime Minister of Burma, he said that the "reform of the urban economy was actually [part of] an overall reform." And when on April 19 he met with a group of millionaire Hong Kong businessmen, he pointedly spoke in terms of China's need for "larger reforms."

In April, at a national conference of provincial governors, Deng announced that state-run enterprises below the provincial level would no longer operate "under the leadership of the Party committees." This was a decision of momentous political significance, since it was calculated to free lower-level industries from the suffocating embrace of the Party. At the same time, with classic—one might say labyrinthine—indirection, Deng resurrected ideas from a speech he had given in August, 1980, to an expanded session of the Political Bureau of the Chinese Communist Party Central Committee, and now had it recertified by the present Political Bureau as a revived textual canon. Entitled "The Reform of the Leadership System in the Party and the State," it was, for a Party leader, a savage attack on the Party's own ossified, stultifying structure.

"As far as the leadership and cadre system of our Party are concerned, the major problems are bureaucracy, overconcentration of power, patriarchal methods, life tenure in leading posts, and privileges of various kinds. Bureaucracy remains a major and widespread problem in the political life of our Party and state. Its harmful manifestations include the following: standing high above the masses; abusing power; divorcing oneself from reality and the masses; spending a lot of time and effort putting up an impressive front, indulging in empty talk, sticking to a rigid way of thinking; being hidebound by convention; overstaffing administrative organs; being dilatory, inefficient, and irresponsible; failing to keep one's word; circulating documents endlessly without solving problems; shifting responsibility to others, and even assuming the airs of a mandarin, reprimanding others at every turn, vindictively attacking others, and suppressing democracy. . . ."

Not content with this devastating list of particulars, Deng had in

1980 also elaborated some views on political reform in a more general way: "The slogan of strengthening the Party's unified leadership has resulted in the excessive concentration of power, inappropriately and indiscriminately in the Party Central Committee, which, in turn, concentrates its power in the secretaries, particularly the first secretary, who takes command and sets the tune for everything. In the end, unified Party leadership is reduced to nothing but the leadership of a single person."

Like a commander lobbing the opening shot of a fusillade, Deng in resurrecting this speech signalled that others might also open fire at China's rigid political structure. That April and May, as a whole series of events were held to commemorate the thirtieth anniversary of the Hundred Flowers Movement, other Party leaders suddenly began to speak up. Lest the Chinese people have any doubts that this new thaw was official policy, newspapers throughout the country quoted Deng as having said, "What a political party fears is its inability to hear the voice of the people. For a party, the most dreadful thing is the people's silence."

It is important to note, however, that as much as Deng believed China needed to "democratize" in order to modernize, he never wavered on one point: Such democratization must be carried out under the leadership of the Chinese Communist Party as prescribed in the Four Cardinal Principles (to uphold socialism, the people's democratic dictatorship, the leadership of the Communist Party of China, and Marxism–Leninism–Mao Zedong Thought) he had already enshrined in the Constitution. As he had explained in a 1985 speech, "While propagating democracy, we should make a strict distinction between socialist democracy and bourgeois democracy and individualist democracy. We should integrate democracy for the people with dictatorship over the enemy. We should integrate democracy with centralism, the legal system, discipline, and the Party leadership." It was within this controlled context, and this context alone, that Deng signalled a period of democratic "expansion."

At one of the April ceremonies commemorating the Hundred Flowers Movement, Hu Qili, the fifty-seven-year-old member of the Political Bureau and a protégé of the second most powerful figure in China, liberal Party General Secretary Hu Yaobang, sounded a clarion call for "the creation of a democratic, harmonious, and mutually trusting environment." At a May Day speech the next month, Hu Yaobang himself joined the chorus when he described modernization not just as an economic phenomenon but as a "comprehensive, far-reaching revolution" that ought to affect "people's thoughts and concepts, spiritual state, [and] ways of thinking." On May 31, he spoke again of the need for China to engage in an "overall reform process" that would touch both on "ideology and superstructure."

Zhu Houze, head of the Propaganda Department, another of Hu Yaobang's protégés, also began speaking out in a way that was strikingly bold for a man of his position but was clearly calculated to play to China's new modernizing elite of intellectuals.

In a speech published in the Party journal *Outlook* (*Liaowang*) analyzing the relationship between discipline and the need for creative freedom in art and literature, Zhu said, "As our country has not yet outstripped the world's most advanced capitalist countries in many different fields, it is difficult not to wonder whether we can believe in socialism and communism, and whether the social, economic, and political problems we face can be solved better than by the ways found by capitalist countries." Then, after some obligatory rhetoric about the need to adhere to the Four Cardinal Principles as general concepts, he went on to admit that China still confronted the "problem of choosing a political road to follow."

For China's chief of propaganda even to intimate that China's political direction was still unchosen was a startling admission, to say the least, and a clear signal to China's intellectuals that such free thinking was now in order on China's road to modernization. Zhu seemed, after all, to be saying that it was all well and good to keep the Four Cardinal Principles around as a kind of socialist comfort blanket, but that the real question of what kind of political system China should adopt was still up for grabs.

In August, Vice-Premier Wan Li, another staunch reformer in Deng's regime, and like Hu Qili a member of the Political Bureau, gave a speech entitled "Rendering the Decision-making Process Democratic and Scientific Is an Important Task of the Reform of the Political System." In it, he once again reaffirmed the Party's commitment to "loosening the bonds" on China's intellectuals and letting "a hundred flowers bloom and a hundred schools of thought contend." But he also called for something new in China—the creation of a "political environment marked by democracy, equality, and consultation." Indeed, he argued that the "style of subjectivism, opinionatedness, and authoritarianism in past decision-making must make way for the spirit of research and study, democratic discussion, and collective leadership.

"In a modernizing society, science and democracy are inseparable," he went on. "Without democracy, there can be no respect for knowledge, human talent, or creativity. . . . We have not yet established a rigorous system and procedure for making policy. We do not yet have an adequate support system, consultancy system, appraisal system, supervision system, and feedback system for that purpose." As a result, Wan continued, "there is no scientific way of testing the soundness of a policy decision . . . and [without changes] our socialist system will remain imperfect and the national economy will not be able to develop continuously and steadily."

Meanwhile Party General Secretary Hu Yaobang, on a trip to Europe in June, had surprised members of the Italian Communist Party by telling them that "Marxism is not an immutable dogma, and it must be constantly enriched and developed in the course of practice." When he arrived in Great Britain, he declared, "No progressive philosophical thought should become a dogma. It should instead be a spiritual force that ceaselessly inspires people to search and create. It should evolve in step with the development of actual conditions."

As with most past political movements set in motion by signals from top Party leaders, it took China's intellectuals a few months to assess the seriousness of the Party's intentions. It was all well and good for the Party to call for democracy and greater freedom of expression, but there were few who did not vividly recall how the original Hundred Flowers Movement in 1956 had ended in the bitter Anti-Rightist Campaign of 1957, or how Mao, after coaxing intellectuals to speak out, had gloated at the time over having "enticed the snakes out of their caves."

But the calls for greater freedom were so forceful, so explicit, and so widespread among leading Party figures that they soon generated feelings of hope and optimism among Chinese intellectuals anyway. By the summer of 1986 a great debate over the meaning and direction of democracy in China had begun.

|||||||||||||||||||||||||||||||||||||

·— The Great Debate ——————————————·
on Political Reform
and Democracy

During this past century China may have proved itself one of the most revolutionary societies on earth, but since their "liberation" in 1949, in many ways the Chinese have been one of the least rebellious people. Mass political upheavals have rarely arisen spontaneously from the bottom of society but through the inspiration and urgings of leaders at the very top of the Party. Burdened with thousands of years of a Confucian culture that put an overwhelming emphasis on order, hierarchy, and maintaining an obedient and correct relationship with superiors and leaders, the Chinese after 1949 evinced the same timid respect for Chairman Mao that they had once shown their emperors. In 1956, only after Mao had given permission to launch the Hundred Flowers Movement, did intellectuals begin to speak out; and, in 1966, only after he himself finally called upon them to "bombard the headquarters" of the Party, did Red Guards become rebellious and begin the Cultural Revolution.

Thus, it seemed in character that only after Party leaders began to speak out about the need for political reforms, in the spring of 1986, did China's intellectuals come politically to life. It was as if a main switch had been thrown, sending a current along unused lines to a whole network of long-darkened lights. Universities, departments of the government, and publications seemed to flash on, suddenly sponsoring seminars and meetings to discuss political reform. Literary and political *shalong*, or salons, became the rage. Writers and intellectuals long silent on such subjects spoke out, while newly founded independent student organizations blossomed on campuses and invited speakers of every kind to address enthusiastic gatherings. But what started as an echo of the views of liberal technocrats in the Party leadership soon acquired a vibrant life of its own; until, for the first time in twenty years, China enjoyed a real political debate focusing on the place of democracy in Chinese society.

Nowhere was this new openness more obvious than in the official media, suddenly filled with discussions of such previously taboo subjects as human rights, the separation of powers in government, political pluralism, checks and balances, and even freedom of speech and of the press itself. The *People's Daily*, no less, became dotted with commentaries (a genre of official writing often penned anonymously by high-ranking leaders) that made it read more like the op-ed page in a United States daily than a Party mouthpiece.

As early as May, one of these commentaries called for making the new "double hundred policy" ("Let a hundred flowers bloom and a hundred schools of thought contend") more than "an empty slogan." Doubtless this reflected the Party's desire to overcome the understandable apprehensions of intellectuals that this most recent bout of liberalization would soon suffer the same fate as its namesake. "In reality the 'double hundred policy' is a general policy through which to implement political democracy in the fields of ideology and culture," the paper asserted. "For thirty years our country's positive and negative experiences have proved that this is the only correct general policy for the development of science and the flourishing of culture. The fundamental reason this general policy has not been smoothly implemented in the past is the lack of political democracy. Hence the key to solving this problem lies in developing socialist democracy and genuine political democracy. . . ."

As Qin Jianxun, editor of the liberal Shanghai-based *World Economic Herald*, explained, China needs "a total reform, a total revolution. . . . [It needs] unprecedented shocks to political, economic, and social life, as well as to people's ideas, spiritual states, life-styles, and thinking methods."

Even in faraway northwestern China, the parochial *Ningxia Daily* exulted that "the severe winter that was strangling democratic activities has passed and . . . the spring of democracy . . . has come." It went on to note that "the phenomenon whereby people might easily get killed at any turn of events has become a thing of the past . . . and, instead, an atmosphere in which everyone is equal before truth, and an environment in which everyone is relaxed and harmonious, has gradually been created in its place."

Encouraged by Party promises that there would be no persecution of those who made intellectual inquiries about other political systems (as there had been in the aftermath of the Hundred Flowers Movement in 1957), a few bold Chinese even began to question openly the sanctity of Marxism–Leninism–Mao Zedong Thought itself and to challenge its role as the sole arbitrator of political truth in China. Such assurances also precipitated a resurgent interest in such Western political thinkers as Aristotle, Machiavelli, Rousseau, Locke, and Adam Smith.

Wang Ruoshui, a political theoretician who had been dismissed from his position as deputy editor at the *People's Daily* in 1983 for an article expounding on Marxism as "humanism," was emboldened enough to write in his old paper that "Marxism is but one school in the history of human thought. It can neither end the [search for] truth nor monopolize truth."

So free-ranging did the dialogue become that there were even reports of delegates at Party-sponsored symposia openly advocating the introduction of a multi-Party system in China, an idea that had not publicly been raised since the crackdown against the rightists thirty years earlier.

With the media publicly printing such subversive thoughts, an observer could easily overlook certain important realities, namely, that China was still a Communist state in which the Party continued to claim absolute control, and that there was still no consensus as to what political reform or democratization actually meant.

What fueled the interest of more Westernized urban intellectuals in political reform was quite different from whatever the most liberal of Party leaders thought they were encouraging. Whereas many intellectuals, particularly those who had been abroad in recent years, were coming to believe in freedom and democracy as values in their own right, most Party officials, even those who were reform-minded, tended to view democracy as a practical means toward very specific ends, namely modernization, economic well-being, and perhaps future parity with the world's great powers. In this sense, they were part of a long reformist tradition in China that, when it had sought democratization at all, had viewed it as a utilitarian device for releasing the kind of productive power necessary to "build the nation." Chinese reformers over the last century and a half had almost always been impressed by the Promethean energy and the urge toward experimentation in the industrialized West. After comparing China to the West, many had concluded that the source of this energy lay in the democratic nature of Western societies. They believed that freedom, human rights, and political participation were the primal forces of and a secret key to Western dynamism, and so had come to appreciate them as potential triggering devices rather than as abstract ideals that should be hallowed and protected by the state as the natural rights of every citizen.

From the official Chinese perspective, the dangerous side of these rights and this dynamism was, of course, the unbridled individualism and the potential chaos they seemed to loose upon the world. As a result, any according of rights that could not be directly justified as a means of stimulating production and materially strengthening the country did not interest China's earliest Qing Dynasty reformers any more than it did China's Marxists a hundred years later. Like their Qing Dynasty precursors, China's latest proponents of modernization had painfully concluded that their economic reforms could not be fully realized without a complementary dose of political reform of a democratic nature, one that would free up the creative and productive energies of the country's educated class.

A June article in the *Guangming Daily* alluded to this enduring connection between modernization and democratization by quoting an Eastern European economist as saying, "If you reform the economic system without reforming the political system, your economic reform will fall between two stools; it will not gain vitality and at the very least will be subject to many constraints."

"Developing a high degree of socialist democracy is an urgent demand of economic structural reform," wrote a columnist in *Outlook*. "This is because reform demands that we enliven our thinking, carry out bold exploration, pool the wisdom of the masses . . . and select the best plans in a democratic way. . . . It is appropriate to say that the extent of the success we score in [economic] reform will be determined by the extent of development in the socialist democratization we have promoted."

It was clear from the beginning that the Chinese Communist Party looked on democratization more as a vitamin supplement than as a complete meal. So while many Chinese intellectuals privately acknowledged that socialism had failed China and that China's only salvation could be through Western-style democracy, even in the politically open climate of 1986, few dared advocate it publicly. Most, still fearful of overstepping the unspoken boundaries to any dialogue in China, were careful to make the proper obeisance to the new, albeit more liberal line.

As one Chinese friend, who came from a well-known, reform-minded family, laughingly put it, "You can always tell a Chinese democrat. He's the indirect one, the one who will never come right out and ask to be free just to be free, but will always try to justify it in other terms. He will say, 'Please give me a little more freedom so that I can serve the state better and help make China rich and powerful.' That way they hope no one will be offended and the illusion of Communist supremacy can continue even while democracy is proclaimed."

Scholars, long constrained in their research by Party control, were among the first to speak out not just about the need for more academic freedom in China, but about the indissoluble relationship between academic and political freedom. In May, the *People's Daily* laid out the connection with remarkable candor: "If a person is constantly anxious when putting pen to paper or giving a lecture, and constantly worrying which of his formulations will go beyond the bounds of what is considered to be an academic problem to become a political problem, then he has no choice but to keep his mouth shut. . . . If we agree . . . to draw distinctions between academic and political problems, that is equivalent to saying that we have agreed—or at least given our tacit assent—to the assertion that academic problems can be discussed but political problems cannot. If citizens do not have the right to air their views on politics, then politics remains a forbidden zone, and people will still unavoidably warn each other that 'disaster comes from careless talk,' and will try to avoid 'incriminating themselves by what they say.' What kinds of masters of the state will they be? Then will not the concept of 'high-level democracy' be simply nothing more than idle theorizing?"

China's first "White Paper on Science and Technology," which was released in Beijing in September, 1986, put the dilemma this way: "Scientific research is a kind of creative mental work. Scientists and technologists should be able to enjoy freedom to think, study, and debate. They should also have the right to stick by and to publish their own opinions, to criticize and answer criticism. Respect for academic freedom is an expression of respect for people's democratic rights and for human intellectual creativity. It is not up to administrators to conclude what is right and wrong in academic fields. . . . Right and wrong can be determined only through free discussion and the test of practice. . . . Leaders should listen to scientists and technologists and encourage them to think and debate freely. Before decisions are made, scientists and technologists should be praised if they offer different opinions. It should be absolutely forbidden to criticize opinions as being 'not in line with the Party.' . . . To guarantee freedom is not only the duty of leaders, but of all scientists."

That November, as the movement for democratization reached its zenith, Xu Liangying, a research fellow at the Institute of Natural Sciences at the Chinese Academy of Sciences, boldly proclaimed that "academic freedom must be protected and ensured politically by a democratic system. . . . The disputes between Marxist and non-Marxist ideologies should only be settled through free discussion. . . ."

Making a clearly admiring reference to Western democracy, Xu then noted that in the West, "provided the law is not violated, people are allowed to freely express their opinions and set forth their ideas without being persecuted. By doing this, [Western democracies have] discarded the autocratic idea that 'heresies' are as frightful as fierce floods and savage beasts, and they have put an end to the uncivilized practice of burning people alive like Bruno [Giordano Bruno, tried for heresy and burned at the stake in Rome in 1600] and torturing people like Galileo."

The notion that there can be no academic freedom without political freedom may sound obvious to a Westerner, but to a Chinese Party leader for whom freedom was at best an emollient to be dispensed in discreet dosages to remedy specific maladies, this connection was not at all self-evident. Along with the new official willingness to relax controls, there remained a deep-seated wariness, hardly less among liberal Party reformers than Maoist Party hard-liners, that the dispensing of new freedoms to academics would only incite other groups to clamor for their share of "bourgeois freedom." And that wariness was justified. In practice, it proved quite impossible to arrogate freedom to scientists for research purposes while withholding it from, say, writers. As someone might unwittingly inherit an enormous and complex family of relatives by the simple act of marrying, so the Party by embracing certain limited notions of freedom had opened the door to myriad other claims.

As the dialogue continued, it quite naturally expanded. Bolder thinkers began to wonder out loud how a limited degree of democracy could flourish in China disconnected from its larger context of Western political systems and philosophies with which the very notion of democracy was indivisibly bound. Even in Party terms, were not such institutions as checks and balances, free elections, and the separation of powers the real source of the Western dynamism that China now sought in its quest for rapid economic development? Could China truly gain wealth and power simply by borrowing a few bits and pieces from Western notions of political participation? And were not these various individual features of democracy so intimately bound up with the larger systems from which they came that, like living organs transplanted from one host to another, they might by themselves cause a powerful immune reaction to set in? So wondered the most daring of China's intellectuals.

It was an old dilemma that went back to the Qing Dynasty, when scholar-officials had first unsuccessfully attempted to borrow science and technology and then limited forms of democracy from the West, and to graft them onto their Confucian system of values and government. These "self-strengtheners," as they were known during the latter part of the nineteenth century, tried to differentiate between acceptable "practical things" (*yong*), like science and technology, and unwelcome "spiritual things" (*ti*), like culture and values. They adopted the slogan "Use Chinese learning for matters pertaining to spiritual essence, and use Western learning for matters pertaining to practical use" ("*Zhongxue weiti, Xixue weiyong*"). The issue then, as in 1986, was whether or not China could borrow "Western learning" without corrupting or negating the "spiritual essence" of its own culture.

As sensitive as their Confucian forefathers to any imputation that their system had failed, China's liberal reform leaders had in the fall of 1986 nonetheless come to feel confident and strong enough to risk the thought of encroaching on China's "spiritual essence" to further modernize their country. In an article written that October in the *People's Daily*, for instance, the writer Li Xisuo seemed to suggest the futility of trying to hew to a *ti-yong*-like formulation, claiming that borrowing practical things from the West would not succeed as a modernizing strategy without also adopting a whole new "ideological foundation or scientific theory as a guiding principle."

"When society is at a critical point during radical change, archaic ideas seriously fetter people's minds and prevent the awakening of their consciousness," he wrote, making one wonder if he was not equating "archaic ideas" with communism. "Ideological emancipation then becomes a pre-condition of political transformation," he went on. "The scope and extent of ideological emancipation determine the scope and extent of political transformation, often making all the difference between success and failure." Although Li typically left vague what explicit kind of "ideological transformation" he might recommend, he did imply that, like one falling domino knocking down another, a continuing lack of a new ideology would only imperil political reform, and that a lack of political reform would in turn imperil even those economic reforms already successfully launched.

Whether or not he was right, a domino effect was indeed operating in China, though not quite the one Li had in mind. Each voice speaking up was indirectly encouraging the next, until an almost deafening hubbub of democratic pronunciamentos spilled out beyond both Party expectations and Party control.

Writing in an August edition of the *World Economic Herald*, the Shanghai-based political scholar Lu Weiping claimed, for instance, that it was "illogical" to try to adopt such things as Western science and management techniques without also adopting some of those political institutions that nurtured and supported them. Lu pointed out that Karl Marx himself had said, "Before seizing power, proletarians must learn to make use of the legislative assemblies, constitutions, and laws of the capitalist class." He concluded with the distinctly un-Maoist idea that "it is also hard to envision proletarian democracy without representative institutions."

In an equally bold article that appeared in the *Workers' Daily* that August, commentator Wu Guoguang claimed matter-of-factly that since there was now little dispute over the need for democracy in China, the real question was how to bring it about. His answer was simple: People could only learn how to exercise their democratic rights through the process of democracy itself. Warning of the traditional tendency to rely on "vaguely benevolent emperors," Wu claimed that the Chinese were "unsophisticated" about democracy "precisely because there has been no democratic tradition" allowed in the country.

Reading more like a lost section of *The Federalist Papers* than a piece in the Party-controlled press, an article in the *Economic Daily* declared: "Political democratization seeks to preserve popular participation in politics, management by the people, and regulation by the people, that they may comprehensively enjoy guaranteed rights and standing within their own country. The government should sincerely uphold equality, freedom, the airing of dissenting views, participation in the government, voting rights, recall, creativity, referendum, and other related political rights to aid the nation from drifting toward autocratic dictatorship. If political democracy is to be achieved, politics must remain open."

With a title that might have come straight out of a New Age magazine from California, a commentary in the July *People's Daily*, "Encourage Everyone to Give Voice to His Innermost Feelings," amounted to an impassioned cry for freedom of speech: "As the saying goes, 'What the heart thinks, the tongue must speak.' Our words reflect our true thinking, so we cannot but come out with what is on our minds. Whether our Party in power can hear the true voice of the people or not will have a great bearing on the success or failure of its cause. Whether the people are willing to speak their minds or not hinges on their confidence in our Party and is a sign marking the level of development of socialist democracy."

Another commentary in early September criticized China's former political climate, in which people who wished to discuss political issues were "terrified" into silence and made to feel as if they were "committing a great offense." It unreservedly called for a new freedom so that those who wished to discuss politics would not be made to feel that they were "committing a great offense and were politically questionable." It asserted: "All power belongs to the people. The people administer the affairs of the country according to provisions of the law, through various channels and in various forms; citizens enjoy freedom of speech and press. All this has been solemnly described in the Constitution, which vests in every citizen the sacred and inalienable right to air his or her views on political issues and to discuss and argue over them."

An October commentary continued in this unusual vein: "Man's history has proven that the confrontation of different theories is an effective means of finding the truth. . . . The principle of 'more debates, less criticism' is expected to win extensive consent since it will help to eliminate the evil legacy of ideological persecution and paranoia while normalizing criticism. We hope that leading officials will not interfere in debates that are carried out within the framework of the Constitution and that they will not abuse their positions to muzzle people."

By fall, such outspoken political opinions seemed almost to be taken for granted, though certain new topics, when broached in the press, still had the power to shock. In early November, for instance, the New China News Agency sent out a dispatch that declared, " 'People should keep their noses out of other people's personal affairs and respect their right to privacy,' a Beijing-based newspaper warned today. A commentary in the *Workers' Daily* noted that 'the right of privacy' originated in Western countries, but it is about time the concept was applied in China."

What left me incredulous about this piece of reportage was that in twenty-five years of following Chinese affairs, I had never heard or seen any public reference to the notion of the right of privacy in

China. Quite the contrary, the Chinese Communist Party had made it its business to put its nose into other people's affairs by every means possible: spying, an elaborate system of informants, interrogation, forced self-criticisms and confessions, all of which ended up in an individual's *dang'an*, or dossier, which trailed a person like a shadow until death. The idea that the Party might now be willing to retract its "nose" appeared, as the year drew to a close, another encouraging sign in the grand mosaic of changes seemingly transfiguring China.

One might have thought that at least the Institute of Marxism–Leninism–Mao Zedong Thought at the Chinese Academy of Social Sciences would have had someone on duty ready to refute the many heresies appearing in the press before China spun completely out of its old Maoist orbit; but, quite to the contrary, even Su Shaozhi, the director of the institute, who over recent years had gained increasing notoriety for the way he had been rethinking the theory of Marxist developmental stages, had been infected by the contagious idea of democratization. "The basic problem is that the people's right to [freedom of] speech and its right to participate in politics and decision-making have not been sufficiently established," he said. "All these democratic rights have long been written down in the Constitution, but are missing from the rules of our [day-to-day] system."

Although China was a country where cynicism about politics had evolved to a very advanced stage, in the second half of 1986 I heard surprisingly few people react with sarcasm to what was happening. Optimism and enthusiasm were the most noticeable hallmarks of the state of mind of those intellectuals with whom I came in contact. For the moment, a seemingly boundless energy for reform and a remarkable tolerance for changes of every kind made one wonder whether China might be the first Communist state to democratize itself from within.

As a *People's Daily* column by Zhang Mingshu rhapsodically proclaimed in November, "The establishment of a highly democratic socialist political system is indispensable to the country's modernization. The reform of Chinese society should be neither an economic recital nor even a political and economic duet. It should be a majestic symphony featuring economic, political, ideological, and cultural reforms."

|||||||||||||||||||
Bankruptcy
Comes to
China

Democracy was not the only new idea generating provocative headlines in 1986. It seemed as if every time I talked with a friend or opened a newspaper I ran across some jolting new development in China's rush toward modernity. One area that was a dizzying source of arresting occurrences was the Chinese economy, which since it had begun to be reformed in 1979 seemed bent on turning itself not only inside out, but upside down as well.

"A Living Buddha Goes into Big Business" read a June headline for a New China News Agency dispatch, datelined Lhasa, which told of the conversion of a Tibetan *trulku* (the reincarnation of a spiritually enlightened being) into an entrepreneur. "He's already cast off the earthly fetters of sorrow, suffering, and illusion and has attained spiritual fulfillment," said the dispatch. "Now Qacha Qamba Chilia, a living Buddha from a local monastery, has also become the general manager of the first corporation set up by Buddhists here."

"Private Business Creates More Jobs" declared an August *China Daily* headline above an article on a meeting of the All-China Self-Employed Laborers Association, at which it was announced that the number of private businessmen and workers in China's cities and towns had grown almost sixfold over the last five years. (The number of self-employed people in Beijing alone was reported to have grown four hundred times since the reforms encouraging private enterprise were initiated in the early eighties.)

"Army Unveils a Beauty Spot" announced yet another headline over an article recounting how the People's Liberation Army, with an eye toward profit, had entered China's booming cosmetics trade by developing a beautifying cream called Flying Rosy Clouds Brand 8403, a product praised at one science and technology fair as the "queen of cosmetology."

During those free-for-all months of 1986 perhaps the most implausible headline about economics I saw was "Bankruptcy Improves Businesses." The August New China News Agency dispatch told how Yuan Mu, Deputy General Secretary of the Central Financial and Economic Leading Group (headed by Premier Zhao Ziyang), had announced that an experimental bankruptcy law had just been put into operation in the cities of Taiyuan, Wuhan, Shenyang, and Chongqing. Mr. Yuan was quoted as saying that such a law would "eliminate backward companies through competition," a phenomenon that, in spite of socialist China's commitment to the working class, he referred to as "progressive."

After offering what under the circumstances seemed ingenuous assurances that China would remain socialist, Yuan went on to ask, "Why shouldn't we make use of the advanced science, technology, management, and forms of organization created by the capitalist system if they can serve socialism after we have modified them? Why should we protect those companies that cannot keep on going because their equipment and technology are completely out of date?"

One might have thought that the reply to Yuan's last question would have been obvious, namely, that one of the distinguishing features of China's avowedly Marxist government had been its willingness, through state ownership, to protect the workers of companies that lost money from unemployment. After all, Article 12 of the Chinese Constitution guaranteed full employment, stipulating that Chinese have the right, as well as the duty, to work. Evidently, though, protection of workers' jobs was not Yuan's exclusive or even main concern. He was more interested in finding ways of lessening the onerous financial obligations the state had incurred by being forced endlessly to prop up unprofitable enterprises. And little wonder. By 1985, almost a quarter of all state enterprises were losing money, forcing the government to subsidize them massively to the tune of 48 billion yuan a year, or approximately 20 percent of the state's annual income.*

If there was one distinguishing feature of China's economic reform program since 1979, it was the tendency of the central government to withdraw from the day-to-day running of the country's micro-economic life and to turn such responsibilities back over to local authorities,

---

* At the end of 1987, although inflation continued apace, one U.S. dollar was equal to just under four Chinese yuan.

units of production, and even individuals. This was viewed as a way of beginning to extract the state from its overwhelming economic responsibilities and crippling financial burden as the central management force of the whole economy. For instance, in the countryside under Deng's new "responsibility system" (which took responsibility from the state and devolved it to the actual local units of production), the rural People's Communes, once the hallmark of collectivized Chinese agriculture, had been dismantled and the land repartitioned to individual families to be farmed privately on long-term leases. Other agricultural resources such as forestry, aquaculture, and livestock production had also been decollectivized and turned back to individuals to be managed privately. Rural areas, which had once been completely reliant on the state for the purchasing, selling, and distribution of goods, now blossomed with new cooperative and private enterprises set up by ambitious peasant entrepreneurs eager to follow the Party's new slogan, "To Get Rich Is Glorious."

In the cities, the government began taking more and more decision-making power from the central ministries that had once planned every aspect of China's industrial economy and turning it over to factory managers. In some cases, whole factories that had been unprofitable under state management were leased or simply given to local workers and managers to run on their own. The government, unable efficiently to manage living space for hundreds of millions of people, even began to back out of the housing business, once the almost complete dominion of the state, as nouveau riche peasants in the countryside built their own homes, and enterprises in the city, eager to make money, began constructing apartment units for sale to wealthy private individuals.

By 1986, the Chinese economy had so changed in direction and character that even though the "means of production"—land in rural areas and heavy industry in the urban areas—were still technically owned by the state, it was little more than a euphemism to refer to China's system as socialist. While the notion of bankruptcy in China might take some getting used to, it was in many ways just one more logical extension, albeit a more extreme one, of the leadership's pre-existing policies.

Like the ugly older sister trying to wedge her ungainly foot into Cinderella's glass slipper, a writer in a November issue of the *Workers' Daily* tried to reconcile bankruptcy with the constitutionally guaranteed right to employment this way: "If an enterprise is announced to be broke, will workers of this enterprise lose their right to work? Will this go against the spirit of the Constitution? Obviously not. First, the workers of the bankrupt enterprise lose only one employment opportunity within a certain time, but they do not lose the right to get another job, because other employment opportunities are available to them." What the article seemed to be implying was that as long as the state had not taken away a worker's right to work, it did not matter if he lost his job.

Less than two weeks later, I ran across a headline in the *China Daily* that announced, "Bankruptcy System Will Be a Success." The article itself, translated from *Outlook*, took one more chip out of the decades-old notion of China as the ultimate welfare state. "The publication of a bankruptcy law has become inevitable as reform of the economic structure develops in strength," it said matter-of-factly, as if, from the Marxist point of view, a bankruptcy law in China was as historically inevitable as the withering away of the state.

Chao Siyuan, who headed the drafting committee for the new bankruptcy law, put the matter more bluntly. "The main purpose of the law is to smash the 'big pot' economic system that is deeply rooted in state-owned enterprises" and that has "failed to give play to the advantages of the socialist system." Asked why the idea of bankruptcy had upset so many people, Chao answered, "First, most Chinese have a misunderstanding of the word 'bankruptcy.' In the past we often said, 'The scheme of imperialism went bankrupt,' which means in political terms that it suffered a thorough defeat. But the sense of the term bankruptcy as used in law and economics is little known to Chinese, so they see bankruptcy as a monster and feel nervous about it. Second, bankruptcy is a deadly threat to the old economic system of 'eating from the same big pot.' Everyone knows that the old system is like opium; all hate it, but few want to throw it away. We often complain of the sullen faces of shop assistants in state-owned businesses, but few people want to smash the system. They say, 'Oh, no! It's the lifeblood of socialism!' "

For many Party reformers, the idea of a bankruptcy law had come to seem like a logical consequence of a responsibility system that allowed enterprises to sink or swim according to their own profits and losses. In this context, bankruptcy looked like a heaven-sent blessing, the perfect tool both for giving marginal industries new incentives to become self-sufficient and for jettisoning those mired hopelessly in red ink that ate so deeply into the state budget.

The inevitability of a permanent, nationwide bankruptcy law seemed more of a reality when on August 3 the Shenyang Municipal Government, taking advantage of its status as one of the guinea pig cities in China's experimental "chapter 11 revolution," actually declared the Shenyang Anti-Explosion Equipment Factory "too sick to be cured." Its property and assets were unceremoniously put up for auction, and in September its workers were let go with six months of severance pay at 75 percent of their former salaries.

In June, 1986, the Sixteenth Session of the Sixth Standing Committee of the National People's Congress (NPC) began to debate drafts for a nationwide bankruptcy law. But like the Party leadership, the committee members soon found themselves bitterly divided between two very different visions of China's economic future. The debate over the advisability of permanently enshrining the concept of bankruptcy as part of Deng's new socialist canon raged on within the NPC for almost half a year. Not even a monumental eight-day joint session of the NPC's Law Committee, the State Economic and Financial Affairs Commission, fifty NPC Standing Committee members, plus "responsible people" from twelve provincial and municipal People's Congresses could break the deadlock.

Discussing bankruptcy was one thing, but adopting a national bankruptcy law quite another. Supporters argued that China could no longer bear the unlimited liability of so many unprofitable enterprises without risking bankruptcy itself. Critics countered that "conditions for enforcing the law" were not yet "ripe" and that it was dangerous to take such precipitous action before more fundamental issues like the control of prices (which had been rising due to shortages) and giving factory managers more power (so that they might plausibly be held accountable for the bottom lines of their enterprises) had been worked out.

In early September, only after months of debate, did the Law Committee of the NPC compromise and recommend that a provisional law be adopted. Even then, the elderly chairman of the congress, Peng Zhen, balked. Alluding to fears shared by other hard-liners that once the law was passed, local governments might suddenly and indiscriminately start cleaning their ranks of unprofitable factories, thereby creating economic chaos, he continued to express apprehension over "the immaturity of conditions for a full-scale law at the present."

On December 2, just as the students were beginning to demonstrate, the Eighteenth Session of the NPC's Standing Committee finally voted on adopting the Trial Enterprise Bankruptcy Law, and by the time ballots were counted, in true Chinese democratic centralist fashion the measure had passed by 101 to 0, with nine abstentions, abstentions having become, it seemed, China's most exalted form of electoral dissent.

Immediately, China's propaganda organs went into action, creating a public relations agent's dream of PR for the new law. Articles appeared in almost all media outlets in China extolling this marvelous new step forward into Chinese socialism. The next day, for instance, using the kind of inverted logic with which earlier Confucian reformers had rationalized their borrowings from the West during the Qing Dynasty, the *Workers' Daily* declared that the law's purpose was "not to make enterprises bankrupt, but to increase their vitality." It went on to note that "the provisions in the bankruptcy law on straightening out enterprises that apply for bankruptcy indicate our wish for these enterprises to make every possible effort to restore their vitality through consolidation to avoid going bankrupt."

Gu Ming, director of the State Council's Economic Legislation Research Center, which had helped draft the law, offered his own brand of rationalization by claiming in essence that nothing had changed but some terminology. "Enterprises may still go bankrupt at the socialist stage; this is an unavoidable fact. What we refused to accept in the past was simply the term 'bankruptcy.' It just did not sound right to us. But actually, by allowing the very small number of enterprises that have wasted the country's resources to go bankrupt, and by stopping them from suffering losses year after year, we can protect the country's property and assets. Apart from this, the enforcement of a bankruptcy law can help enterprises transform pressure into a driving force, and can help them rouse themselves to reorganize their work. . . ."

Treating the concept of bankruptcy as if it were a bracing new Taoist elixir of immortality capable of single-handedly assuring China a bright socialist future, Gu rhapsodically went on, "I believe that enforcement of the bankruptcy law will provide a great shock, a push forward to all those enterprises that lose several billion yuan a year, and that it will enable the masses to supervise enterprise leaders, make people less bureaucratic, lead to technological advances, speed up technical transformation and exchanges, create closer cooperation between people holding different posts, [and] help us give play to the superiority of socialism. . . ."

Even though China's new law was a provisional one, it had

established the legitimacy of the notion of bankruptcy in a people's republic, and in doing so had laid to waste one more myth about the invulnerability and superiority of China's socialist system. In fact, sometimes in those fall months of 1986 it seemed as if Chinese socialism was on a roller-coaster ride to oblivion, for it was hard to imagine how the People's Republic of China could theoretically embrace many more ideas and institutions like bankruptcy without bankrupting itself ideologically.

|||||||||||||||||
·——— Socialist ———·
China's
Big Board

By the middle of 1986, the Chinese government was beating a rapid retreat not only from failing industries but from many other previously self-imposed economic responsibilities. One of the main areas of responsibility from which it was backtracking was its onerous role of being the country's main source of investment capital. By 1985, it had launched a major retrenchment program based on the assumption that the country's enterprises should become more self-reliant. As the journal *Outlook* described the situation in the fall of 1986, "Last year's tightening up of the money supply provided a great stimulus to individual fund-raising. For under the conditions of this retrenchment, many large enterprises that were previously well supplied with capital [from the government] now found themselves in financial difficulty."

However, weaning state-owned enterprises and local governments away from reliance on the public dole was easier said than done. If the state was going to make subsidies harder to come by, if bank loans were inadequate to meet the huge demands for new capital, and if foreign loans and joint ventures were still so fraught with complexities and restrictions that they were beyond the grasp of most state-owned enterprises and local governments, where would desperate managers and officials find new sources of capital to carry out China's much-vaunted program of modernization? Without such new sources of capital, which also provided access to new forms of foreign technology needed to upgrade backward plants, many crucial Chinese enterprises were clearly going to founder. Had the government simply pulled back without approving some new sources of investment capital, China's economic development would have come to a grinding halt, leaving the country with no chance whatsoever of reaching parity with the developed West by the year 2000 as Deng Xiaoping had promised.

"Economic reform had hit a snag. How could businesses get together enough money to invest in large-scale projects, and how could the government's role be played down?" asked a *China Daily* columnist in November, 1986. "The solution was to switch the main body of investment from the government to free enterprise by allowing banks and money markets to play their part." And how in a free enterprise system did "money markets play their part" to generate investment capital? Through the sale of stocks and bonds to other enterprises and private investors.

Selling shares and interests in its means of production was a stunning idea for a socialist country that had always prided itself on state ownership. But given the general direction that China's liberal reformers wished to see the economy move in, there seemed little alternative; and who could say, in any case, that a stock and bond market was any more out of character than a bankruptcy law? After all, bankruptcy opened an avenue for the government to get rid of some of the deadwood in China's economy, while the issuance of stocks and bonds at least gave surviving enterprises a means of reviving themselves.

The sale of securities by capital-hungry enterprises had actually begun on an ad hoc basis early in 1984, after the Party Central Committee had issued a document permitting rural units to raise funds by selling shares to investors. Even though the leadership had not initially intended to include urban enterprises and industries in this new fund-raising scheme, the idea soon found favor in the cities as well as in the countryside. Before the government quite realized what was happening, and before the Party had been able to hold any kind of real debate about the appropriateness or advisability of a socialist people's republic selling ownership shares in its enterprises, the idea of stocks and bonds had swept the country.

Whereas bonds at least did not, strictly speaking, constitute shares of actual ownership in a given enterprise, stocks did. This raised a thorny theoretical dilemma for the Party: How could a country with a socialist economy countenance the privatization of its enterprises? The impatience of some reform leaders to see China develop as rapidly as possible may have inclined them to accept the resurrection of capitalist-style financial markets as a fait accompli. But those hardliners who had, for instance, balked at the idea of a bankruptcy law were at least as wary of seeing the dilution of state ownership through the sale of stocks and bonds. Having spent their whole lives struggling for a very different kind of revolution, they viewed assaults on state ownership of the means of production (even though it was being carried out in the name of economic development) with something less than enthusiasm. As devout Marxists, their circumspection was certainly justified. Seductive as financial markets might appear as a means of generating quick capital for investment-hungry businesses, the idea of selling stocks and bonds did raise fundamental questions about the evolving nature of China's "socialist" economy. For instance, Li Guoguang, one of China's foremost economists, expressed fears that if shares became concentrated in the hands of certain groups of people, China might again develop a class of "coupon clippers," living, in effect, off the exploited labor of others.

The ambiguity and confusion of this developing situation was highlighted in July, 1986, by the curious position in which Beijing's Tianqiao Arcade Department Store found itself. In 1984, the store had reorganized itself as the Tianqiao Company Ltd. and had pioneered the sale of stock in order to open branches in outlying provinces. Bypassing the normal process of asking the state for investment capital, the store began selling shares of stock first to its employees and then to the public at large. But when the directors applied for a new business license, government officials became nonplussed by how to categorize the company for registration purposes. By this time it was neither a state-owned, a collectively owned, or a privately owned enterprise, but rather a mixture of all three. It thus defied any of the bureaucracy's old categories. After much head scratching, and before a business license could finally be issued, the city had to create a special designation for this new kind of store. Moreover, the initial stock sale was so successful, and subsequent business so good, that in 1986 the company decided to make a second offering.

By 1987, thousands of other Chinese enterprises had followed the lead of Tianqiao Company Ltd. and in a new kind of mass movement began issuing shares of their own in an unregulated and often haphazard manner.

Shenyang, the capital of Liaoning province and the homeland of Chinese bankruptcy, was one of the cities in China most in need of new capital to revitalize its aging industries. "How could Shenyang possibly have gotten the rich infusion of capital that it longed for?" asked a September article in the liberal newspaper the *Economic Daily*, which had described the Manchurian city as economically "anemic." "Well, where there is life there is hope. In 1984 about a dozen small enterprises that had been unable to procure capital to finance technological innovation got the idea of making bonds available for purchase by their own employees. In no time they had collected 4 million yuan. This unexpected bonanza set the industrial and political leaders of Shenyang into motion."

By the middle of 1986, the city boasted 114 state-owned and 338 private-collective enterprises that had already issued shares and bonds totalling some 354 million yuan. This—and similar situations in other large cities—added up to a vibrant, chaotic, and largely unregulated new securities market. Enterprises hungry for investment capital were of course thrilled by the turn of events, but the massive hemorrhage of private money into these securities (money that might otherwise have gone into state banks, where the rate of forced saving had until 1987 been about 35 percent, double that of any other Communist country) contributed to a growing Party debate about whether or not such financial instruments violated Marxist ideology, and what the government's position should be in regard to them.

In truth, since the idea of selling stocks and bonds had already spread widely, there was little for the national government to do but to offer its de facto approval and try and benefit somehow from the situation. Liberal reformers, already disposed to relaxing the Party's grip on the economy, soon began to openly advocate officially sanctioned stock and bond markets where shares could not only be bought and sold but also traded under government supervision.

"Let businesses and individuals have a piece of the cake," suggested Beijing University economics professor Li Yining, who in Chinese financial circles had come to be known as China's stock guru. "Only this will ensure that our enterprises do not become the adjuncts of government departments. Since the state will go on owning large chunks of the concerns, the socialist nature of China will not be jeopardized."

On August 3, 1986, the government officially relented and authorized the city of Shenyang to become the first city in the People's Republic of China to open an officially sanctioned securities market since 1949.

Only two bond issues and no stocks were initially offered for sale on the Shenyang exchange through a minuscule cashier's window at the Shenyang Trust and Investment Corp. When it was announced that as a bonus incentive to clients the exchange was also going to run a lottery with prizes ranging from an apartment to 200 yuan in cash, local investors came running.

"We have reached a watershed in the history of socialist development," proclaimed Hua Sheng, a researcher at the Chinese Academy of Social Sciences. "Not even Hungary and Yugoslavia, which in many ways are ahead of China in the introduction of market mechanisms, have dared tinker with the contentious issue of ownership."

Although the Shenyang exchange was meant to help bring order to the unregulated selling of securities in the city, at first it appeared to have relatively little effect. Private securities dealers, far from disappearing, began to congregate informally in the streets, alleys, and doorways around the exchange itself to promote their own offerings to investors eager, one way or another, to get in on the new bond-selling bonanza.

"Some officials were so distressed that they suggested a ban on these activities," reported the *Economic Daily* in September. But lamely claiming that such private dealers were "an inevitable outcome of the official exchange," and that in any case "a lot of people live far away from the city and find it inconvenient to go to the exchange during business hours"—and doubtless keeping in mind the city's interest in helping local enterprises find much-needed investment capital—the town fathers finally decided to allow private dealers to continue operating in the environs as an informal supplement to the official exchange.

Like Shenyang, Shanghai, which had hosted a very active stock market before 1949, had, by 1986, also become the site of an increasingly active private market for what were sometimes euphemistically called socialist securities. By the fall, 1,480 collective enterprises had already privately issued shares worth more than 225 million yuan, and 700 city-run enterprises had issued shares worth approximately 900 million yuan. On September 26, 1986, municipal Shanghai leaders, endeavoring to bring some order to their burgeoning financial markets, went one step beyond Shenyang and opened the first stock exchange of the People's Republic of China. Whereas the Shenyang exchange only issued bonds, the Shanghai exchange issued both bonds and stocks, thus raising the troublesome question of private ownership of the means of production in an even starker form.

However, investors seemed hardly bothered by such theoretical niceties. Early that morning, hundreds of investors carrying bundles of bills lined up in front of the Jingan Branch of the People's Bank of China and its subsidiary, the Shanghai Trust and Investment Company, to wait for the doors of the exchange to open. After a thirty-seven-year hiatus, buyers appeared as eager as ever; in this case they were purchasing stocks in the Feile Sound Equipment Corporation and the Yanzhong Industrial Corporation, the first two of over fourteen hundred companies applying for government approval to go public on the new exchange.

By nine-thirty, one half hour after the new stock exchange had opened, all 700 shares of Feile stock and most of the 450 Yanzhong shares had been sold. By the end of the day, there was nothing left for disappointed Shanghai investors to buy, raising the question: Why, when there were obviously so many investors eager to buy stocks and bonds, and when there were so many companies eager to go public, had there been so few stocks for sale on the official market? "We are responsible to the shareholders," replied Wang Yuchun, the bank manager. "We would never allow a company on the exchange that might go bankrupt."

"Some people equate stocks with capitalism," said the president of the Yanzhong Industrial Corporation, which already had 18,220 shareholders from earlier private stock transactions and was now considering investing with a Philippine partner in the purchase of a McDonald's fast food franchise for Shanghai. "My idea is that it is a good way to apply socialism to developing our economy. If I hadn't sold shares, that money would not have been available for the company."

At the very end of September, four days after the Shanghai Exchange had opened, officials in Beijing—ever competitive with their southern rival—announced that they, too, would soon have an exchange of their own. But for now, all they could offer was some news: The Liyuan Chemical Company Ltd. had been the first enterprise in the city approved for a stock issue. Stock and some bonds worth 3 million yuan were to be sold to state-run businesses, collectives, and even individuals. In October, Vice-Mayor Sun Fuling announced that when the Beijing market finally did open, it would be part of a larger and more ambitious financial scheme. This included not only plans to dilute the ownership of select, large-scale, state-run enterprises by selling stock to investors, but also plans to wean a host of medium-size state-run enterprises away from government sponsorship by leasing them back to private and collective management. The Beijing Municipal Government was eager, said Sun, to carry out these reforms as part of the Party's call to liberate enterprises from the stifling embrace of government bureaucracy. Ever mindful of his duty as a Party member to maintain at least a facade of belief in state ownership, Sun hastily added that the Chinese government would continue to own at least 51 percent of the proposed joint-stock firms. Although no Beijing exchange was consecrated in 1987, new markets did open in Harbin, Guangzhou, Tianjin, Ningbo, and Wuhan, with several more planned in other large Chinese cities.

When one thinks of stock exchanges, one almost automatically conjures up images of wealth, moguls, and grand pillared buildings, as well as hectic trading floors roiling with frenzied buying and selling. However, the exchanges in China were still a far cry from their capitalist progenitors. In Chongqing, the capital of Sichuan province, for instance, I visited a bond market located in the lobby of a downtown branch of the Bank of China. Physically quite similar to the Shenyang and Shanghai exchanges, it helped put this new Chinese institution in perspective.

Out in front, on the corner of Nationalities and May Fourth streets, a large placard had been erected. "You Are Welcome to Purchase Bonds Issued by the Bank of China," it said; below, it announced the sale of one-year 9 percent bonds, in 100 and 500 yuan denominations, whose purpose was "the accumulation of more capital to speed up the Four Modernizations." (Impressed by the ease with which investment capital could be raised for development through the sale of bonds, the various levels of Chinese government had themselves stepped up efforts to get into the bond business.) Curious to see what the whole process of becoming a Chinese coupon clipper was like, I decided to go in with a friend and buy a bond.

In the gloomy bank lobby, under a chandelier shaped like a giant octopus whose outstretched tentacles held white glass globes, we lined up with ten or fifteen other people before a single wooden desk. There, two sullen-looking women sat before piles of fatigued 10 yuan notes banded into one-hundred-bill packets. Since China's largest denomination note was at that time 10 yuan (it is now 50 yuan) and since personal checks were almost unheard of, all large purchases had to be paid for with these ungainly bricks of cash. In this sense, even with its new securities exchanges, China was still much closer to a frontier economy than to one furnished with the sophisticated financial institutions of the industrialized world, where customers with traveller's checks, credit cards, and bank drafts conduct instant transactions by computer.

As we waited, the two women counted off blocks of currency like clerks at a horse-track betting window, stuffed them into a simple wooden drawer that drooped from underneath the table, and then issued wallet-size bond certificates to investors. The only sound in the room was the clicking of scores of abacuses and the grinding of several lilliputian-size air conditioners, which strained hopelessly away against the humid air.

This Chongqing bond market was admittedly a far cry from New York's Big Board, but as crude as it was, its symbolism was enormous. Simply by putting its official imprimatur on the concept of stocks and bonds, and by allowing securities exchanges to open in China at all, the Party had indeed created what the *Economic Daily* referred to as "a breakthrough experiment in financial reform . . . an event that made the whole world take notice."

The first belated government efforts to create official stock and bond exchanges as well as to formulate new rules to regulate these pioneering markets were largely ex post facto attempts to bring a burgeoning, freewheeling new sector of the economy under some semblance of state control. The government was concerned not only that massive amounts of new investment might elude the state planning process and, by overheating the economy, help aggravate an inflationary situation, but also that most Chinese, including many of those lining up with such enthusiasm to invest at the official exchanges (never mind the people who had been buying on the private market), had little conception of what they were getting into, indeed, hardly even knew what a stock or a bond was.

In fact, many investors confused the purchase of shares with making deposits in savings accounts. For instance, upon hearing that by buying bonds they could gain up to a 15 percent return annually (7.2 percent interest plus a 7.8 percent maximum dividend), potentially twice the 7.5 percent ceiling on savings account interest rates, they clamored for a piece of the action. But many of these eager incipient capitalists did not have the vaguest comprehension of the risk of investing in a company. Few were aware, for instance, that particularly with fly-by-night companies whose stocks or bonds were sold after hours in the streets, a buyer could easily stand to lose everything. Although the government was struggling to keep up, regulations were lagging sorely behind expanding markets, and by 1987 China was still a long way from having an efficiently operating Securities and Exchange Commission.

"China, in the process of experimenting with this new stock system, lacks the relevant regulations and laws to guide such matters as the proportion of dividends given to shareholders and the settlement terms if an enterprise goes bankrupt," admitted an October article in the *China Daily*. It went on to note glibly that the extraordinary changes in China's economic system were "disturbing to some people and exciting to others."

One person who was clearly excited by what was happening in the Chinese world of investment was the chairman of the New York Stock Exchange, John J. Phelan, Jr. Along with nearly two dozen senior American investment and commercial bankers, Phelan arrived in Beijing on November 10. His advent in the People's Republic was not a little reminiscent of the Pope, accompanied by a flock of cardinals, landing in a remote Third World country to bless a struggling local Catholic church. For several days the pinstripe-suited Americans met in the Mongolian Room of the Great Hall of the People with some three hundred latter-day Chinese counterparts. There, a mere stone's throw from Mao Zedong Memorial Hall, where the body of the Chairman still lay in state, they discussed stocks, banking, investment, capital accumulation, and insurance.

As Chen Muhua, State Councillor and President of the People's Bank of China, said in her opening remarks to participants of this first China–United States Symposium on Financial Markets, the occasion "is a chance for us to gain experience from the United States in developing our stock and securities markets, and ultimately in promoting our banking business." One publication described the occasion as a chance for China to share the experiences of an "elder brother" in this brave new world of capitalist high finance.

"You're going to see an enormous amount of growth in this area if the trend continues," observed Phelan before leaving for home. "They have an insatiable need for capital. They have to get more money into the mainstream."

It had been precisely this "insatiable need for capital" that had been responsible in the first place for the spontaneous development of the unofficial securities markets in China that the government was now trying to bring to heel. As had so often been the case during this topsy-turvy period of economic reform, actual changes in the economic structure of the country had often led rather than followed policy, so that the government frequently found itself in the somewhat embarrassing position of running along behind the flow of events, trying to rationalize radical changes with policy statements and regulations long after they were accomplished realities. Chen Yun, a Political Bureau Standing Committee member and hard-liner who still believed in the virtues of centralized socialist planning and who took a circumspect view of this new world of autonomous high finance that was developing in China, had referred to this kind of system-within-a-system as a bird cage economy, meaning that China was, in effect, raising capitalist birds inside a socialist bird cage. The question on many people's minds, which few Chinese actually seemed to wish to confront head-on, was, "When would these capitalist birds grow too big and break out of their socialist cage?"

Whenever I asked liberal reformers how China's previous commitment to a highly centralized, rigidly controlled, Marxist economy could be squared with this more freewheeling laissez-faire system, I invariably met with demurrals. While a few older party cadres still struggled to rationalize these radical changes in Marxist terms, most younger cadres (many of whom had been abroad to study) seemed not only uninterested in the contradiction from a theoretical perspective, but not a little irritated at being reminded of China's continued insistence that it was a socialist country. In their rush to a new future, they brushed aside China's socialist past as if this aspect of their country's persona was a bothersome, somewhat embarrassing detail they now wished everyone would forget. What interested them was managing and using the exciting new financial instruments of bankruptcy and stocks and bonds to create maximum productive power. In this sense, they were the true heirs of Deng Xiaoping's pragmatism.

Like someone who begins putting up a kitchen shelf and, without quite intending to, knocks down a wall, builds another room, and then, still without any architectural drawings, finally, bit by bit, ends up remodelling the whole house, China's economy was being rebuilt in a very piecemeal fashion. But what the design of this new economy was ultimately going to look like, how all these financial institutions borrowed from other economic systems were going to fit together to create a new and operable whole, remained an imponderable, so that sometimes it seemed that the whole process of economic reform would end up as nothing more than a chaotic jumble of spare parts, each adopted from elsewhere to solve a specific problem, but with no internal consistency. China, which for so long had touted itself as the domain of the world's pre-eminent visionary thinkers, now seemed devoid of any vision at all, indeed even of any model. Perhaps the dilemma of the liberal reformers was simply that while they did not quite know where they were going, they knew where they no longer wished to remain, and hoped that simple motion might help them discover a new system as they went. In addition, fears of rousing the hard-line Maoists often seemed to stifle open official discussions by reformers of new models for China's economic future. If these older revolutionaries were often powerless to halt the erosion of the economic system in which they believed, they could at least drag their feet on the ideological front, and, playing on the fact that officially the Party still continued to claim China as a socialist country that based itself on the teachings of Marxism–Leninism–Mao Zedong Thought, they could still stifle public discussion of new kinds of economic theory and systems. And it was here in the world of theory that the liberal reformers seemed most willing to give ground, perhaps hoping to effect a kind of trade-off with their hard-line adversaries in which theoretical concessions would in turn allow them a freer hand in the dominion of practice. This less than explicit compromise allowed the old hard-liners to dream their socialist reveries, while giving tacit permission to the reformers to ram through such path-breaking practical changes as the bankruptcy law and the regulations that now allowed for officially sanctioned stock and bond markets. It had, however, the liability of depriving the reformers, as well as China, of a public stage on which to think out loud and formulate a comprehensive and understandable vision of China's economic future. Indeed, it sometimes seemed that the liberal reformers, such as the coterie of young economists and political theorists that Premier Zhao Ziyang had gathered around him at his Institute for Structural and Economic Reform, knowing that any efforts to reconceive the fundamentals of China's economic system would be too politically provocative, had decided instead just to gnaw away as inconspicuously and quietly as possible at the foundations of the country's socialist economy like so many termites. Perhaps they hoped that such a strategy would allow them to weaken it to the point where it would ultimately topple of its own accord before anyone got around to labelling what they were doing as the theoretical heresy that it actually was.

||||||||||||||||||||||||||||||||||
· — Building Friendship ——————————————— ·
Through
Golf and Guns

Crucial in China's drive to modernize, as Deng Xiaoping saw it, was advanced foreign technology, which could only be bought from abroad with hard currency. In the drive to acquire such currency, one of the most readily available sources was tourism. To encourage and accommodate an increasing number of foreign visitors, the Chinese government had made a concerted effort to improve the tourist environment and infrastructure of the country. Previously closed areas such as Mongolia, Tibet, and Xinjiang were reopened for travel; scores of Western-style hotels were inaugurated; fleets of Japanese-made taxis and tourist buses appeared; new jet aircraft were purchased; docking facilities for cruise ships were upgraded; and new first-class trains were put into service. By 1986, almost 1.5 million foreign tourists and over 20 million Chinese from overseas poured into China (compared to less than a quarter of a million foreigners and a million and a half overseas Chinese in 1978), earning the government well over $1 billion U.S. Even so, the 1986 percentage increase in tourism was substantially less than that of the annual average over the previous few years, a worrisome matter for government officials ever more desperate for foreign currency. Increasingly aware that tourists were attracted not just to historic sites, but also to other kinds of recreational facilities, the Chinese began a push to build a whole new host of tourist-related projects: theme parks, bowling alleys, golf courses, seaside resorts, amusement parks, and other kinds of entertainment spots, the likes of which no Chinese on the mainland had seen in decades.

One of the first landmarks in this "recreationalization" of China appeared in the summer of 1984 when the luxurious $3.2 million Zhongshan Hot Springs Golf Club in Zhuhai, Guangdong province, opened for business. This lavish and spectacularly set new golf club, the first of its kind to open in China since 1949, was designed by the renowned American golf pro Arnold Palmer and was part of a joint venture between China and a group of Hong Kong investors headed up by millionaire Henry Fok. It represented a link symbolically no less crucial than the bankruptcy law or the securities exchanges in the web of institutions that China was now setting up to raise funds for its ever more decentralized and capital-hungry economy. But unlike the bankruptcy law and the securities exchanges, which were lodged within Chinese society itself, this network of tourist facilities was to a large extent beyond the reach of everyday Chinese. In fact, in its separation from Chinese life, it was hauntingly reminiscent of that earlier network of foreign concessions in the old treaty ports, which had once dotted China's coastline. This new network of posh and expensive clubs, restaurants, resorts, and hotels was once again making it possible for foreign travellers to visit China, indeed to travel from one end of the country to the other, without ever having to come into contact with the reality of the society itself.

The Zhongshan Hot Springs Golf Club was typical of this new aggregate of ventures in its foreign design, its foreign financing, and its dedication to providing ease and pleasure to foreigners in China. It featured a plush clubhouse, a Western bar and restaurant, and a resort complete with a health club, swimming pool, stables, disco, and a department store that even included an antique shop. The complex was located an hour from the border of the Portuguese colony Macau, up against the Laoshanwei hills, where, while shooting down a fairway, one could pause to admire picturesque Chinese peasants plowing their rice fields with water buffalo. As George Chow, a Hong Kong citizen employed by Henry Fok to supervise operations at the new course, observed to *New York Times* correspondent John Burns, "For now, I think it's all a little strange to them [the local peasants], these foreigners walking around hitting a ball with a stick."

The Zhongshan Hot Springs Golf Club did not really come of age until October, 1986, when it hosted eighty-eight golfers from fifteen countries in the First China Open Amateur Men's Golf Championship, a sporting event sponsored by the newly established Golf Association of the People's Republic of China and Thomas Cook Financial Services in Hong Kong. Of the nine Chinese contestants in the championship, all had previously caddied the course to pick up money for their peasant families, whom they still helped in nearby fields during the busy harvest and planting seasons. While they hardly constituted an indigenous Palm Springs-like golfing world, these nine youths, none older than twenty-two, were the first representatives of any post-1949 generation to tee off in China. As the magazine *China Sports* proudly explained, when they began playing, "they had practically nothing to start with . . . even the golf clubs had to be brought in from abroad. . . . [But] with good physical qualities and capable of enduring hardship, they made rapid progress, [so that] most of them can now play a par-72 course in 80."

Even though they did not place well in their first championship match, Peter Tang, their coach from the Royal Hong Kong Golf Club, claimed nonetheless to be impressed with their progress. "I always tell them to do what they can, and never mind how well their rivals are doing. As it is, they are still too young and inexperienced to stand the pressures of a big tournament. . . . What they need is psychological training. . . . With more mental disciplining, I'm sure they will catch up with the best of Asia in four or five years."

Like so many other foreign things recently adopted by China, golf spread with surprising speed. By 1987 the Zhongshan Hot Springs course was no longer the only links in China, and Zhao Ziyang, the new General Secretary of the Chinese Communist Party, had even taken up the sport at the newly opened Beijing International Golf Club. An eighteen-hole, 72-par, $19.4 million course jointly run by the local Changping County Economic Relations and Trade Corporation and the Japan Golf Association, it was officially opened by Vice-Premier Wan Li in August, 1986. In his seventies, Wan was reported to have missed the first two balls before finally connecting for a disappointing ten-yard drive. Located in the valley north of the capital, where the emperors of the Ming Dynasty had once been elaborately buried, its modern clubhouse, restaurant, hotel, and bar were hardly more than a good wood shot away from an imperial tomb. This proximity angered some critics, who feared for the cultural despolation of this historically significant area. Other officials, worried about the severe water shortage in the Beijing area, expressed concern lest the mammoth project drain the water table to irrigate the golf course's fairways and greens, thus harming local farming and causing ecological damage. Even within China's tourist industry itself there were some officials who were skeptical about the advisability of building golf courses, because they questioned whether golf could really be a motivating factor in bringing tourists to China.

"The growing trend among group international visitors is to schedule shorter stays in Beijing . . . and most come to see things Chinese, not the same things they can see at home," Zhu Qixin, Deputy Director of the Management Office of the Beijing Municipal Administration of Tourism, said of the project in 1985. But whatever the merits of his criticism, the project itself proceeded apace.

More curious was the absence of any critique of golf from a Marxist perspective. No one seemed even faintly bothered by the embarrassing fact that, at least during the first few months the course was open, almost all the golfers who came to play were foreign. Since it was the chosen sport of a stratum of international society that included wealthy and powerful foreign industrialists, politicians, and corporate CEOs— whom the Party itself once referred to scornfully as "big capitalists"— one might have thought that some Chinese custodian of Marxist purity would have pointed out the distinctly unsavory "class character" of golf as an institution. But to my knowledge, no such analyses were ever made of golf in China—or, for that matter, of the rapidly expanding foreign-only tourist network now webbing the country. Instead, as with the radical reforms of the economy, the Chinese leisure and recreation revolution hit the country without either an accompanying framework of ideology to justify it or any convincing critique to oppose it. In fact, the process, once started, seemed to acquire a logic of its own, one so inherently powerful that it grew exponentially in a realm of its own that often appeared beyond anyone's comment or control.

To take but one example, the golf course and club were, it turned out, the least of what local officials had planned for the Ming Tombs valley. Twenty other recreational projects were also on the drawing board, including lodging facilities, swimming pools, a ski hill, an amusement park, and even a race track and equestrian center named after the Mongol Emperor Kublai Khan, whose dynasty, ironically enough, had been overthrown by the Mings. Moreover, this whole new leisure-time universe was to be served by an overhead rail connection to Beijing.

But perhaps the strangest, most inventive manifestation of China's new preoccupation with recreation for foreigners was the North China International Shooting Academy, which opened for business near Beijing in 1987. Far from being an academy, this unusual tourist spot was really nothing more than a highly priced firing range, where foreigners could wile away a few hours blazing at targets and blowing things up, though not without considerable expense, payable in hard currency. Even those involved in the manufacture of deadly firearms, it seemed, were not immune from the scramble for foreign exchange. As a brochure for the range explained in broken English, the North China International Shooting Academy was "set up in accordance with China's currency policy of 'Enliven [sic] the domestic economy and open to the outside world.'" According to the New China News Agency, the range was designed to give foreign patrons "a chance to play with exotic weapons." In fact, probably few other shooting ranges in the world provide such a wide variety of exotic weapons for their trigger-happy patrons. The academy, an organization that was under the jurisdiction of the State Council's Ministry of Machine Industry (formerly the First Ministry of Ordnance), offered everything for the recreational pleasure of the foreign guest from pistols, sniper rifles, and AK-56 submachine guns, to 14.5 mm anti-aircraft guns and anti-tank rocket launchers.

One beautiful, sunny fall day I visited the academy, located about a half hour's drive outside of Beijing in Changping county, not far from the Great Wall. Near the town of Nankou, my taxi turned in through a large cement gate guarded by soldiers armed with rifles and bayonets. When they saw that the cab contained a foreigner, far from ordering us to halt, they simply waved us by. As we glided unescorted through what looked like a military installation, China as I had first come to know it over a decade ago suddenly flashed back into my mind. I recalled how during the Maoist era one would have been severely chastised just for taking a photo of a soldier in the street, never mind cruising unescorted around an Army base in a city taxi on the way to a military arsenal to play with Chinese weapons.

My head was still swimming with the incongruity between China's recent past and present as my taxi finally arrived at a nondescript two-story concrete building. Here I was met at the curb by an academy representative who evinced the same sort of eagerness for a customer one might expect from a salesman at an American used-car lot.

When I informed him that I had come to shoot rather than just to look around, as many reporters had evidently been doing, he enthusiastically squired me into a spotlessly clean room (identified by a placard as the Drinking Room), decorated with an oil painting of a European Alpine scene, vases of plastic flowers, a promotional academy calendar featuring a Renoir painting of a cherubic young girl, and a cooler full of Coca-Cola. In these unlikely surroundings, he handed me a shooting application form and a price list for the use of each weapon, including ten rounds of ammunition. As I studied the unfamiliar fare of firearms, I felt a little as I often do when handed a complex menu in a strange language at an ethnic restaurant: light 7.62 mm submachine gun Type 85 ($25), 7.62 sniper rifle Type 79 ($35), 14.5 mm anti-aircraft machine gun ($120), and a 76 mm salute gun ($325).

I was just working my way down this unusual bill of fare when a videotape blinked on a TV monitor standing just beneath the Alpine painting. "Please accept our most cordial welcome. . . . We hope that your experience here will give you a happy memory," said a cartoon figure in stilted English as classical piano music rippled in the background and pictures came on of happy foreigners firing contentedly away with sundry automatic weapons at targets made up to look like the rough outlines of humans.

"Friendship brings together all of us of different colors and different languages," continued the video narrative as an inferno of flame from an exploding anti-tank rocket blasted a small shed to smithereens. "Your coming gives us happiness. . . . If you want to keep a record of this experience, our video service is glad to help you. . . . To serve you warmly is our pleasure."

When the video was over, I signed up to fire twenty 7.62 mm rounds (costing approximately $37 U.S.) from a lightweight Type 81 machine gun. I was then ushered over to a souvenir stand, where I picked up a shovel-billed cap like those worn by American golfers, but embroidered with the Chinese characters for the North China International Shooting Academy, and a machine-gun tie clip. After a quick visit to the range's "museum," which displayed cases of all kinds of weapons from discreet gold- and silver-inlaid pistols to an enormous anti-aircraft gun complete with a seat like a lawn tractor's, we went upstairs to the firing area.

I had been so engrossed in the video and the museum that I had not even noticed the absence of any sounds of firing weapons, but once upstairs at the firing booths that looked out to the Western Hills, I suddenly realized that beside the soft sighing of a gentle breeze, there was complete silence.

"How has business been?" I asked Lu Fugen, the academy's operations manager.

"Oh, so so," he replied noncommittally while loading some shells into a round clip under my Type 81 machine gun, which sat perched on its tripod before us.

"Which nationality frequents the range most often?"

"Oh, all kinds of foreign guests."

"Like who?"

"Oh, mostly Japanese friends," he replied with a rueful look, pointing down toward my weapon as if by talking with him I had been neglecting my real duties here at the academy.

I hunched over my machine gun, squinted down the barrel at the silhouette target in the distance, and squeezed off my first short burst of automatic weapons fire (which stitched the ground to one side of the target with a little line of exploding dust). There was, I thought, something bitterly ironic in the fact that foreigners—particularly the Japanese, who had once occupied much of China—could now return to shoot off machine guns, play golf, and sell cars, refrigerators, and televisions, more or less at their own pleasure and purely for profit. In fact, in September, 1985, students in Beijing had staged street demonstrations against what they had called the second Japanese occupation, by which they meant Japan's growing economic domination of markets in China. While their demonstration had quickly been put down by Chinese police, it had raised the very sensitive issue of China's new and increasingly complex, if not outright subordinate relationship with the more powerful industrialized nations of the outside world. Although Chinese leaders, including Deng Xiaoping himself, tirelessly proclaimed China's need to "learn from abroad" and to make "foreign learning serve Chinese goals," the issue of once again being or even seeming to be occupied by privileged foreigners was in the long run as potentially inflammatory as any confronting the Chinese leadership.

I left the shooting academy feeling somewhat triste, wondering about the advisability of shooting ranges for foreigners, but also hoping that business would pick up for the academy after they had finalized plans to make available mortars and tanks (which would presumably be driven out of range of the anti-tank rocket launchers) for the added recreational pleasure of their clients.

For now, the pressures to modernize—even to give the appearance of modernization—were clearly overpowering considerations of this subtle but dangerous historic tension point caused by foreign privilege in China. By May, 1987, when Beijing's second links, the $3 million Chaoyang Golf Club, opened just outside the city, near Unity Lake, it seemed clear that golf kultur and special preserves for foreigners were in China to stay for a good, long time. Even though the project was a Sino-Japanese joint venture (operated by the China Sports Service Company and the Beijing Corporation of Agriculture and Industry's East Wind Farm in conjunction with the Kosaido Development Co. Ltd and the Toko Bussan Co. Ltd.), virtually all the club members were foreign, with 60 percent being Japanese. "The club is meant to provide Beijing golf lovers with a place to practice their sport and to socialize," said the Japanese deputy general manager, Ryozaburo Ono.

By 1987 ten similar projects were also under construction in other Chinese cities, including a thirty-six-hole course outside of Shanghai, which in the nineteen-thirties had boasted as many as five golf clubs at one time.

Until the last few years, the idea of such leisure-time activities as legitimate pastimes even for visiting foreigners had been almost unheard of. The Chinese Communist Revolution, which stressed sacrifice and hard work, left little room for types of enjoyment that smacked in any way of self-indulgence. Mao's severe egalitarianism, coupled with his notion that one's primary duty was to serve others rather than oneself, militated against the idea of recreation as a form of individual enjoyment. Before Mao's death, even China's sports stars had been assigned to regular work units, where they were expected, at least in theory, to toil like ordinary people. For most Chinese, the most rarefied form of recreation imaginable would have involved seeing one of a limited number of "revolutionary" movies, plays, and operas, or perhaps taking a Sunday walk in the park.

As Western influences began to pour into China and Deng Xiaoping's reforms put more and more discretionary income into Chinese pockets, these Maoist values crumbled. People were clearly starting to think more and more about themselves. Rather than waiting for a distant and uncertain socialist utopia to arrive, they wanted to know how they might find some pleasure in the here and now.

But because China was so eager to earn as much foreign exchange as possible, and because Chinese themselves could not afford high levels of leisure consumption, virtually all first-class recreational facilities were designated for foreigners. And, in most cases, Chinese were not allowed admittance, even if by chance they did happen to have the requisite hard currency.

In the free-for-all climate of 1986, as long as a project could be justified as contributing to socialist production (a notion that had a lot to do with production and very little with socialism, and that Deng had codified by such utterances as "The purpose of socialism is to make the country rich and strong"), the government and the Party seemed only too willing to avert their Marxist gaze from obvious political contradictions. But even though this foreigners-only leisure infrastructure rarely welcomed local Chinese, it had a profound influence on how Chinese were coming to see the world. Many Chinese, of course, worked in these facilities. Others had the opportunity to see them on specially arranged tours, while many more were influenced simply by the aura of exclusive wealth and forbidden luxury that these modern, Westernized oases generated. Paradoxically, their suggestive power was often only reinforced by their inaccessibility. Left to imagine their interiors from the outside, and all that might possibly go on inside them, ordinary Chinese frequently imbued them with more glamour and excitement than was their due. This was indeed the stuff of which Western, materialist, even anti-Marxist dreams were born.

Moreover, the Party seemed naively to presume that the presence of luxury resorts, golf courses, and firing ranges for foreigners would not profoundly affect the socialist ethics and values of the Chinese who worked there or otherwise came in contact with them, never mind the country as a whole. Nine peasant caddies learning how to play golf in Guangdong may not have seemed very significant to reform-minded Party officials in Beijing concerned with maintaining China's foreign currency reserves, modernizing the country, and integrating the country's newly Westernized elite into cosmopolitan culture and the world market system. But the experiences of those nine adolescents were emblematic of the way in which whole new segments of Chinese society were beginning to be involved with and even fascinated and seduced by the outside world. And who could blame them? Once China's doors were thrown open to the capitalist and materialist West and Japan, it would have been unrealistic to expect the Chinese alone to resist the temptations of all their accompanying symbols of wealth, ease, and power, things that had proved so enormously gripping almost everywhere else in the world.

||||||||||||||||||||

The
Limo-ization
of Beijing

From the inside of a twenty-three-foot-three-inch-long blue-black Fleetwood Brougham Cadillac stretch limousine equipped with a five-liter V-8 engine, vinyl roof, white-wall tires, air-conditioning, tinted push-button windows, color television, AM-FM radio, dual refrigerators, bar stocked with Gorham crystal glasses, lace antimacassars on the backs of the red plush seats, and a chauffeur in a new blue uniform with bright brass buttons, China's Maoist past seemed far away indeed. In fact, pulling out of the Great Wall Sheraton Hotel in Beijing, where the Union Car Rental Company, an offshoot of the China International Trade and Investment Corporation, had just opened for business with a fleet of twenty new Cadillacs and twenty-six Mercedes-Benzes, and turning down North Donghuan Road through the flow of crowded buses, bicycles, trucks, donkey carts, and curious pedestrians, one hardly felt one was in China at all, but rather in the soft seat of a Cinerama theater watching a filmed travelogue of the Orient. As the noisy, dusty world of Beijing slid silently by the shining metal hull to the accompaniment of nothing more than the soothing hum of the air conditioner, the familiar Cadillac emblem on the hood seemed like a contemporary version of the figureheads carved on the bows of the great sailing ships that once fueled the opium trade between China and the West.

Unlike in the days when Beijing did not even have taxis roaming its streets, now one could tour the city and its environs or be whisked in cool noiseless comfort to the Great Wall or the Summer Palace inside a *Ka-di-la-ke* simply by ringing an extension on the hotel phone. "Now that China has adopted a policy of 'opening to the outside,' we want to be able to provide the best cars and the best drivers possible for our foreign VIP guests," Wang Shaojun, the company's young assistant general manager, told me over a cup of coffee. "To do this, our head, Mr. Rong Yiren [who comes from a prominent and wealthy pre-1949 Shanghai family], decided to import these cars. Our intention was to become something like Avis. But since there are still problems in China with foreigners driving their own cars without Chinese licenses, for now we must provide chauffeurs.

"Formerly people might not have been able to accept these kinds of things and might have become angry," she added in response to my question about the role of luxury cars in post-Mao China. "But now everything has changed and we're more open-minded. We believe China should develop and look to the future on all fronts."

Since Beijing was still far from accustomed to such high-class livery, and since the city had just recently become swamped with taxis, business for Union Car Rental had been somewhat slow in coming. As recently as two years ago, when a serious taxi shortage left throngs of angry Western tourists and businessmen stranded and cursing outside their hotels, a car rental service would have had no trouble finding clients regardless of cost. But now that the city's taxi fleet had swollen to epic proportions (there were 14,000 cabs in Beijing by the end of 1986 compared to only 11,000 in New York City), Union Car Rental had stiff competition. Nonetheless, a certain segment of China's visitors, perhaps accustomed to such pampering at home, found the idea of such limousines all the more irresistible in socialist China.

"Your own Alexander Haig has reserved a car for his upcoming trip," I was told, with a mixture of hope and pride, by Wu Wei, an eager young woman who worked behind the Union Car Rental counter attired in a black Western-style suit and bow tie. "We think that many other American VIPs will also like our cars, because they will make them feel as if they were back home."

Who can say exactly what it is that has kindled such a passion for limousines among contemporary Americans. But whatever urgency they evince at home about manifesting their power, status, and prestige through automobiles, by mid-1986 it was clear that they had also begun to bring it with them to Beijing. Now that China had changed so much, what CEO of a Western multinational would still feel comfortable arriving for a banquet at the Great Hall of the People in a Toyota cab, much less one of the old hospital-green Shanghai sedan taxis that still plied the streets in ever dwindling numbers? What foreign businessman trying to hammer out a difficult new joint-venture agreement with an immovable Chinese counterpart might not dream of arriving in a glistening new stateside limo at the No. 2 Beijing Steam Turbine Factory, in hopes of thereby gaining a little needed face and jolting the comrades into making an important concession? And what retired high-ranking public official returning to Beijing for the first time as a private citizen to raise the flag for his new consultancy firm would not feel that his sagging ego might be nourished back to health if he were swept into the city from the airport inside twenty-three feet three inches of Detroit-made tinted glass and high-gloss steel?

Indeed, Cadillac and Mercedes-Benz limousines were only the newest additions to a whole new layer of luxury travel services recently come to China for wealthy foreigners and top Party members. Deluxe first-class German-made train cars were already available on certain rail lines. Luxurious air-conditioned cruise ships had long since been plying the China coast and the Yangtze River. First-class hotels were opening in most large Chinese cities. Club Med had a resort on Kunming Lake at the Summer Palace outside Beijing and would soon complete construction on its full-service club in Shenzhen, across the border from Hong Kong. Curious about what had happened to the Maoist slogan of "self-reliance," which had once been painted on almost every wall, chimney, and billboard in China, I asked Assistant Manager Wang what had become of all the old Red Flag limousines that had been made domestically and once represented the ultimate degree of luxury in China. With their wooden dashboards, curtained rear windows, and chrome characters for Red Flag written in Mao's own hand and affixed to their rear trunks, these locally produced automotive leviathans, the exclusive perks of China's top leaders and visiting foreign dignitaries, had once cruised the streets of Beijing without competition from foreign interlopers.

"Red Flag cars are somewhat backward," Assistant Manager Wang replied unenthusiastically. Then, brightening only a little, she continued, "They've stopped making the old models. But I hear that they're now trying to design something more up-to-date that will include mechanical parts from your Lincoln company."

It was hardly surprising, of course, that Red Flag limos were becoming as extinct as portraits of the Chairman himself, for alongside the newly arrived Fleetwoods and Mercedeses, they did indeed look like behemoths, throwbacks to another age. While Mao still lived, however, I had enjoyed watching as they whisked high-ranking officials, hidden behind curtains, through the nearly carless streets of Beijing to what then seemed to me to be mysterious, forbidden destinations.

In a land that was supposed to have purged itself of all distinctions of rank and privilege, those limousines were among the few publicly visible symbols of a social privilege that endured and even flourished among the Party elite at the height of the Great Proletarian Cultural Revolution. Indeed, as those strangely forbidding conveyances sped by, it was possible even then to imagine feeling a gust of Imperial China blow past with them. The hauteur of those cadres (their Maoist slogans notwithstanding) harked back to a time when high officials and members of the imperial family made no pretense of being at one with the masses and would pass through the streets of their capital in curtained sedan chairs guarded by huge attending retinues.

One spring night in 1986, as I took a shortcut home through the hotel's underground parking garage, I happened upon several of the old socialist war horses parked lifelessly off to one side on slowly deflating tires. Covered with the dust that blows onto Beijing each spring from the steppes of Mongolia, these relics by now seemed almost interred in their parking spots.

That night as I slept in my room eight floors above the abandoned cars, I dreamt of home in California and the giant condors, which like Red Flag limousines are also an ungainly but very native species brought to the edge of extinction by the modernizing world around them. And in that dream I distinctly saw several battered old condors, silhouetted against the cobalt-blue sky, staring down at gleaming rows of predatory Cadillac Fleetwoods.

In the morning, when I went downstairs to eat my Western breakfast, and later as I drove away from the ultra-modern hotel in a new Japanese taxi through streets choked with traffic, past scores of new high-rise buildings, this image still burned brightly in my mind. Besides the mixture of confusion and exhilaration I had been feeling about China's new openness, I was more aware than ever of a sense of growing unease about the rapidity of change that I saw happening everywhere around me.

PART 2

BODYBUILDING

AND

BIKINIS

||||||||||||||||
A Vacuum

Each time I arrived in Beijing, I was reminded of the bitter truth that China's capital was one of the most characterless and ugly cities in the world. From the heavy, kitsch, Soviet-inspired buildings to the Hollywood Babylon-style edifices of China's own socialist-heroic period and the cellblock-like apartment houses of more recent vintage, all have had an ungainly look of aesthetic poverty to them. So relentless had the Party been in expunging from the city what was ancient—including its once imposing walls, its religious shrines, its outdoor markets, its teahouses, and serene old courtyard residences—that now little remains except some mummified and gaudily restored temples and kitschy replicas of traditional buildings. Yet the capital's former reputation as a city steeped in history and culture still somehow survives its dispiriting modern reality.

The Chinese have had a more complex relationship with their ancient culture than any other society I know. Once infatuated with the very notion of antiquity and recklessly proud of their several millennia of continuous culture and civilization, young Chinese intellectuals turned on that civilization with an unparalleled vengeance during the first half of this century, when it seemed that it was this very culture that had rendered their country impotent and unable to stand up to the predations of the industrialized West and Japan.

The Communists, too, tapped into this deep current of cultural nihilism, and when they came to power launched campaign after campaign against "remnants of China's feudal past." Behind their relentless war against the "old society," which they viewed as having exploited the masses of common people for thousands of years, was a misguided attempt to crystallize a new identity around a very new notion of China as a revolutionary socialist society. This Party-sponsored loathing of China's traditional self, which found its most extreme expression in the so-called Cultural Revolution when Red

Guards launched an orgy of destruction against anything and anyone tainted by the past, was followed by a second great self-devouring when Mao finally passed from the scene. Filled with self-doubt over the chaos and violence that it had visited on the Chinese people, the Party began to repudiate whole aspects of its revolutionary Maoist persona as well, so that by the mid-eighties what it meant to be a citizen of the People's Republic of China was once again up for grabs.

Just as they left a sense of cultural emptiness in cities like Beijing, these repeated paroxysms of cultural and political self-immolation left China not only intellectually and spiritually confused, but also extremely vulnerable to all sorts of outside influences. Perhaps there is no more apt metaphor for the way in which the Party had exposed the Chinese people to foreign cultural invasion than its ordering in the nineteen-fifties of the destruction of Beijing's ancient protective City Wall, a forty-foot-high twenty-five-mile-long rampart that was as wide on top as an avenue. In its place now stands a freeway, the No. 2 Loop Bypass.

China, so long closed to the "pernicious" influences of the capitalist world, had under the Party's aegis paradoxically become a kind of cultural vacuum. Rather than giving China the strength to resist incursions from without, it only tended to make the country more vulnerable. The Party was, of course, aware of the problem, although unable to comprehend and unwilling to fully confess its own role in the destruction of Chinese culture and its people's national identity. It frequently spoke fearfully of the dangers of spiritual pollution, bourgeois liberalization, and wholesale Westernization, as if the outside world were a vast reservoir of pathogenic cultural bacteria waiting to attack and infect China. The metaphor was apt but incomplete. China was indeed at risk, not simply because there were contaminating cultural bacteria at large, but because its own cultural immune system had been so compromised that without closing its doors and putting the country back into quarantine (as many hard-liners no doubt would have liked), most of its people were unable to defend themselves against even normal risks of infection.

In spite of all its pride, bluster, and rhetoric about being a "great nation" and a "great people" with a "glorious past" and a "bright future," China in truth no longer had, as an antidote, a homegrown model to provide it with a cultural identity, and thus cultural resistance. All that an aging leadership could offer to stem the tide of foreign influence, which quite naturally rushed in, was Marxism–Leninism–

Mao Zedong Thought, a now weary and threadbare corpus of ideas, repudiated so many times in practice by the Party itself that none but the most naive could place much faith in it. Party calls to preserve the best from the East while borrowing from the West missed two elemental facts: The Western consumer package, from discos to democracy and from videos to capitalism, was knit together into such a tight, complex, indivisible, and sophisticated whole that even far more self-assured societies than China had difficulty separating it into its component parts before rejection or adoption. As it was, as soon as one aspect of this package entered China, the rest inexorably filtered in behind it through China's "open door." In addition, there was very little that China had to offer in creating the kind of new, balanced synthesis that Party theoreticians dreamed about when they thought of saving face by taking the best from both East and West. It was a humiliating situation for the country's leaders, all the more so since it had been the Party itself that was largely responsible for the destruction of China's former identities.

With so little to oppose it, pop and consumer culture from abroad rushed into China with a vengeance. Worship of things "foreign" (*yang*) may not have reached the fever pitch of Mao adoration, but there was a slavish aspect to the new infatuation with all those things that now came pouring in from abroad: refrigerators, cars, tape players, and televisions from Japan; food, cosmetics, and fashion from Europe; films, music, and democracy from the United States.

||||||||||||||||||||||

· —— Bodybuilding —————————— ·
and Bikinis

While walking through a free market in Beijing's Haidian district one day, I spotted an unusually large throng of people crowding around a private vendor whose stall consisted of a plastic drop cloth spread out on the dirty sidewalk. Since none of the other stalls in the market were doing much business, I was curious to find out what commodity had such drawing power.

Moving closer, I saw that a mustachioed youth in a trench coat was proffering packets of color postcards to a raucous group of young males.

"Just six yuan for all ten poses! Come and get 'em!"

Edging into the crowd, I found to my astonishment that he was selling glossy color photos of Chinese women wearing brightly colored bikinis.

"Where do they come from?" I asked the vendor, to the great merriment of the onlookers, who started cheering and catcalling.

"The cards come from Guizhou in southwest China, but the girls come from some Chengdu bodybuilding competition," he replied with a salacious grin. "Better buy some. They're going fast!"

Unburdening myself of six yuan, I retreated down the street with a friend to study my purchase more carefully. Had they not had "Ruler of Heaven Bodybuilding Championship, Chengdu" printed on their flip sides, there would have been no reason to identify these women as anything but amateur pinup girls. In fact, what was most noticeable about these female "bodybuilders" (*jianmei yundong yuan*) was not their impressive musculature but their lack of it. Adorned with lipstick, rouge, headbands, and earrings, they had assumed suggestive poses that made it clear they intended to show off their nakedness as much as their pecs and biceps.

In the following weeks as I roamed around the streets of Beijing, one of the world's most sexually conservative cities, it became clear that those postcards were no isolated manifestation of Chinese prurience. Private newsstands, which had appeared in recent years on many busy street corners, held a bountiful harvest of sports and bodybuilding magazines featuring both Western and Chinese muscle men and women. At one crowded outdoor stand, for instance, a new magazine called *Bodybuilding and Beauty* displayed a cover photo of the well-oiled torso of Sylvester Stallone (who had become a Chinese hero after his film *First Blood* was inexplicably chosen by Chinese film authorities to play at local movie theaters). He was posed beside his young Scandinavian wife, Brigitte Neilsen, who wore a risqué cutaway leotard and a well-moussed new-wave hairdo. The magazine's table of contents listed such articles as "The Philosophy of Maintaining Your Health," "Plastic Surgery," "Bodybuilding for Women over Fifty," and "Clothing, Makeup, and Beauty."

At a second newsstand, with another crowd pressing in around it, I found among a plethora of pop culture magazines the premier issue of *World Sports Outlook*. The magazine's gaudy cover featured a photo of the two winners of the International Mixed Pairs World Championship: Kevin Lawrence (Ke-wen Lao-lun-si in Chinese), wearing a bulging G-string, and Diana Daniels (Dai-an-na Da-ni-si) in a diminutive bikini. Bursting with health, glistening muscles rippling, this occidental god and goddess smiled while clasping each other, as if at any moment they might dance right off the cover into the mesmerized crowd of Chinese onlookers. The inside cover featured a blond Hollywood starlet, a scant gold bikini straining against her ample breasts, and a small free weight in each hand. A caption explained that she was able to maintain her "beautiful body proportions" through regular workouts.

The rest of the magazine was filled with other bulging and glistening bodies. Except for a few entrants from Singapore, Japan, and Taiwan, all were Caucasian. Only at the back of the magazine did Chinese from the People's Republic make their debut in a series of smaller and significantly less lustrous photos.

"Because bodybuilding is compatible with the psychology of people's love of beauty as well as being an effective method to build healthy and handsome bodies, it will flourish [in China] as an adjunct to the rising standard of living, and it will become an ever broader and deeper phenomenon," noted an accompanying text.

As I walked through the streets of Beijing, and later Shanghai, it seemed that every newsstand had come alive with near naked bodies. Even magazines that had little or nothing to do with health or fitness had begun to include photos of bodybuilders. Being the main kind of public nakedness evidently tolerated by the official censors, bodybuilding was being exploited much in the same way that Western magazines exploit swimsuit issues to attract the attention of readers. Sports magazines could quite naturally garnish their covers with the figures of lithe young female gymnasts or swimmers in scant attire, but journals of reputed literary merit had also taken to featuring pretty young women, often in provocative poses.

"Look at the magazines on sale . . . and you will find that most of their covers carry pictures of pretty girls," complained an article in *Liberation Daily*. And it's not just a matter of "nice faces," the article went on to note with displeasure. They even show "women's naked bodies . . . in the bath or sleeping nude," and then caption them with "seductive headlines like, 'I Love Nude Models.'" One thing the

Liberation Daily failed to mention was that a startling number of these *déshabillé* seductresses were foreign rather than Chinese.

Farmer, purportedly an agricultural magazine, sported a cover shot in one issue of a voluptuous long-haired Western girl wearing lipstick, earrings, dark glasses, and a minuscule red string-bikini. Behind her lurked a depraved-looking oriental man in a chartreuse beret who was sticking his tongue out suggestively and rolling his eyes salaciously as he ogled her body.

Commodities of China featured not a photo of some domestic product, as one might have expected, but a busty blond-haired woman in a form-fitting white dress and scarlet earrings who stared with narcissistic absorption into a hand mirror.

Overseas Literary Digest, which specialized in articles on and translations of foreign literature, also regularly used cover photos of chic Western fashion models. One particularly memorable issue featured a Caucasian woman in a white caftan-like gown standing in the snowbound arctic tundra surrounded by a team of huskies; another showed a close-up of a blond woman with heavily made-up, sultry eyes, who seemed to be proffering her slightly parted ruby lips for readers to kiss.

"Ever since women were allowed to wear bikinis at a national bodybuilding contest, magazine editors have felt largely 'emancipated' to use big close-ups of women in bikinis as cover pictures," lamented the *Liberation Daily*. "This has become somewhat out of place. Although people love to see pretty women . . . something must be wrong when all kinds of magazines about films, sports, literature, life, and education carry them without any relative reason."

The problem with such appeals to a Chinese sense of decorum was that in the new world of economic reform, they clashed with the bottom-line mentality of the responsibility system. Having been weaned off state subsidies and forced into the uncertain world of self-reliance, where profit and loss made the difference between a successful and a bankrupt magazine, publishers and editors were more and more mindful of what made publications sell; and in China, where the only officially acceptable disrobed women were bodybuilders, a major industry soon grew up to exploit photos of them.

Bodybuilding itself was not, however, all prurience in China. In the mid-eighties a movement of body-conscious youth had begun to emerge in reaction to the sense just then affecting many Chinese that it was no longer taboo or dangerous to focus on the self. This in turn created a demand for exercise programs on television, aerobics classes, and private exercise gyms. One of the pioneers of this fitness movement was a man named Yuan Guohui from Guangdong province, who in 1983 was reported to have raised enough money to open China's first privately owned health club and bodybuilding gym. Not content with this milestone accomplishment, soon thereafter he set about raising an additional 40,000 yuan of private capital to hold a privately sponsored weight-lifting tournament.

In 1984, as more and more regional bodybuilding competitions were organized, Central Television and the magazine *New Sports* produced a TV special entitled "The Road to Bodybuilding" that stunned viewing audiences with the sight of young Chinese flexing their musculatures like so many apprentice Arnold Schwarzeneggers. In true Hollywood spin-off tradition, the TV show soon spawned a book of the same title which proved to be successful enough to run through a second edition.

However, it was not until 1985 that the magazine *Women in China* took the decisive step of organizing the country's premier women's bodybuilding team. That same year, when officials convened in Gothenburg, Sweden, China was voted the one hundred twenty-eighth member of the International Federation of Bodybuilders. But only in November, 1986, when China held its Fourth National Hercules Cup Invitational Bodybuilding Tournament in Shenzhen (the Special Economic Zone just across the border from Hong Kong), did bodybuilding really come of age in the People's Republic. This was the first time in China's history that such a large and well-publicized bodybuilding tournament had included both male and female as well as foreign contestants: 228 competitors (57 of whom were women) on 47 teams from both China and Hong Kong.

The head judge in the women's competition endeavored to de-emphasize the female entrants' musculature by saying, "We shouldn't be overly critical about the ladies' muscular development because they have small frames and more fat on their bodies than their male counterparts. Taking their physical features into consideration, scores should be given in the following order of priorities: 1) Balance. 2) Proportions. 3) Musculature. 4) Lines and posing."

As it turned out, most of the six thousand people in the audience were not there to appreciate female "muscular development" anyway. The posing itself was described by one Chinese writer as "a great treat" for spectators, who, according to a local paper, greeted the bikini-clad women with an "outburst of deafening cries, shrieks, and catcalls," which so embarrassed them that they "slowly bowed their heads."

The winner of the all-around men's individual title was He Yushan, a worker from Beijing who belonged to the Chinese railway system's Locomotive Team. But his victory was almost completely overshadowed by the competition in the women's events, in which Chen Jing, a cyclist from the Chengdu Acrobatic Troupe in Sichuan province, took the honors, receiving high marks in the Chinese press for her "beautiful feminine features, good muscle proportion, fine posing technique, and stage charisma." Later, she and her bodybuilder husband, Leng Gaolun, teamed up for some joint posing, for which they won first place in the mixed division title.

Because of the "bikini controversy," the event received a tidal wave of publicity in China. Even Party-controlled papers took the opportunity to spice up their pages with photos and articles on the controversy. The tournament itself attracted so much interest from journalists that sponsors decided to exploit their unprecedented situation by charging reporters an application fee of 10 yuan ($3 U.S.), as well as an entrance fee of 200 yuan. ($60 U.S.), more than double the monthly salary of most workers. When they were deluged with protests, a tournament spokesman replied curtly, "If you don't want to pay, simply don't come. We haven't invited you in the first place."

The cool reception that tournament officials offered the media and the stiff fees they imposed had little effect on journalistic attendance. As the *China Daily* observed, "Even some reporters who do not specialize in sports news have come to take a look." In the end, three hundred members of the press from over one hundred media organizations showed up, triple the number that had ever attended any previous sporting event in China.

The decision to allow bikinis to be worn at this event certainly made good business sense, but it was not one that had come easily. For months the issue had been hotly debated in official circles. Rumors had it that this controversy had gone all the way to the Central Committee in Beijing. Just as with the touchy issue of bankruptcy that had been resolved by passing a provisional law, officials finally decided to approve bikinis on an experimental basis only. Six weeks before the event, Xu Jia, a spokesman for the Chinese National Sports Commission, told a reporter from the Hong Kong–based newsmagazine *Asiaweek* that the Shenzhen competition would be a "test case." Said Comrade Xu: "We will monitor popular reaction to the competition before deciding whether bikinis will be in."

In fact, if China wanted to compete internationally in bodybuilding, there was no choice, for under the rules of the International Federation of Bodybuilders, to which China now belonged, women entrants would be disqualified without bikinis. As in so many other areas of endeavor, in facing the cosmopolitan world, Chinese Party officials found no comfortable middle ground to stand on, no simple accommodation for its socialist reluctance. When permission was finally granted by the authorities to take this momentous step toward sartorial minimalism, the official Chinese press described the event as a great "blow against feudalism." But if it was a blow against anything, it was against precisely those things for which China had so defiantly stood for the last three and a half decades.

What made the advent of female bodybuilders in bikinis so subversive to the system was not so much the fact that a few scantily clad women appeared in public view, but that their appearance seemed emblematic of both the way people had begun to redirect the focus of their lives from society as a whole to their individual selves, and how disturbing the results could prove for the Party. For among those things that could be said to represent the antithesis of the Maoist ethic, the zeitgeist of bodybuilding was certainly high on the list.

"Serve the people," perhaps the most familiar slogan of Mao's China, had exhorted people to think first about hard struggle, sacrifice, and service rather than self-expression, never mind self-indulgence. The Chinese Communist "new man" or "new woman" was not supposed to stand out as an individual either intellectually or physically, but was to merge into the collectivity of society as a group player, as one of the masses. To cultivate the distinctiveness of one's own individual consciousness bespoke an entirely different private world of concern; to cultivate the individual human body and put it on public display asserted the primacy, even the glorification, of the self. However, just as the idea of wealth and freedom had begun to catch on among young people in China, so the notion of glorifying one's physical self had gained new, probably irreversible momentum. Moreover, this impulse was in no small measure stimulating China's new consumer economy, and making the cosmetics and beauty care, interior decoration and fashion industries among its most rapidly growing sectors. So what actual choice did Party reformers have but, as with bankruptcy and the new stock exchanges, to swallow the unpalatable social results along with the economic effects they desired? At this point in China's development, the lack of hard currency and products to buy still made the jump from a few million men ogling a few bikinied bodies to a whole nation of fashionable bikini-clad women a remote possibility. But the idea of transforming oneself, whether politically, spiritually, financially, or physically, without waiting for society to transform itself first through revolution, was now a notion firmly rooted in Chinese society, a notion that could result in some very strange and extreme forms of expression.

||||||||||||||

· —— Cosmetic —————————————— ·
Surgery

In early September, 1986, while walking just outside the Beijing Zoo, I noticed a printed handbill on a public bulletin board that showed two seemingly identical photographs of a pretty young woman in a turtleneck sweater. Walking over to look at it, I saw that under the first photo a caption read, "Before the Operation," and under the second photo another caption read, "After the Operation." A bold red headline to one side proclaimed, "Eye Jobs Done Quickly While You Wait! Get Fixed in One Trip! No Need to Take Time Off from Work." A handwritten note added, "We also do nose jobs, get rid of wrinkles, and remove acne scars." At the bottom of the handbill was an address in the East City district.

I had been aware for several years that young Chinese women, usually eager to look more Western in appearance, had, like women in other Asian countries whose cultures had been dominated by Western standards of beauty, begun to indulge in cosmetic surgery. In the past, what I had heard about cosmetic surgery had always made it sound like a quasi-underground business, not because it was technically illegal, but because fixing as it did on an individual's appearance, and smacking so literally of wholesale Westernization, it ran totally against Maoist—or even Nationalist—conceptions of Chinese pride and identity. And yet, here in 1986, on a busy street corner in the middle of the capital, was a public advertisement for eye and nose jobs to make Chinese youths look more foreign.

The next day, a Chinese friend and I found the "clinic," located off a narrow footpath between two ramshackle Beijing courtyard houses just outside the boundaries of the old city. Upon entering the alleyway, we encountered several seedy-looking youths in rumpled Western suits and soiled neckties whose efforts to affect macho poses were temporarily marred by the fact that their noses were swathed in enormous white bandages. Loitering outside a low doorway, they looked at us with unenthusiastic suspicion as we approached.

Stooping to enter, we found ourselves in a waiting room no bigger than the interior of a large American car. Two plain-looking young women sat vacantly on a wooden bench under a "beauty calendar" featuring a tall blond Western model whose breasts were as prominent as her nose and who stared out with sultriness across the water of an azure-blue swimming pool into the cheerless room beyond. Like the flame of a welding torch in a darkened space, the colors around her fairly glowed against the drab sheets of inexpensive and already yellowing paper with which the waiting room wall had been covered. The young woman who sat just below the calendar, twisting a hand-kerchief nervously in both hands, had a pale face that because of surgery was as grossly swollen as the calendar girl's overly voluptuous breasts.

The other young woman was paging through a dog-eared album of faded color photos that, like those Charles Atlas ads that used to contrast 98-pound weaklings with Herculean muscle men, showed before and after shots of patients who had had their noses successfully elevated and their almond-shaped eyes widened and embellished with epicanthic folds.

Just then, the door to an adjacent room opened and out stepped a man in a white surgical cap and gown that, although clean, was gray with age. He was Dr. Song Tongshu (a pseudonym), a soft-spoken elderly man with an almost wistful air who, once he got over the surprise of finding a foreigner in his waiting room, invited us into the privacy of his equally small operating room, which was furnished with only a cabinet, two stools, a floodlight, and an operating chair that looked like it might have come from a turn-of-the-century barber shop.

"Before I retired, I worked at the Beijing Plastic Surgery Hospital," he replied courteously when I asked him about his background. "Now

I am in private practice and am licensed by the government to work here by myself. It is all part of the new responsibility system that allows people to start their own businesses."

When I asked him what services his small, and seemingly primitive, clinic provided, he explained that he could remove acne scars (25 yuan), create epicanthic folds, and widen eyes (35 yuan), or raise noses (50 yuan) right there in his clinic. "But for patients who wish to have their breasts enlarged, their thighs or fanny reduced, or their legs lengthened, we must go to the hospital," he said matter-of-factly.

Stunned at the thought that any doctor, much less one from a small private clinic in a Beijing back alley, could lengthen someone's legs, I inquired of Dr. Song how this operation was performed. Extracting a pen and pencil from a drawer in the cabinet behind him, he began with utter equanimity a drawing showing how the shin bone could be sawed in half to create a slip joint that in turn would be slid an inch or two apart before being reset so that the bone could knit back together again.

The thought of people so unhappy with the length of their legs that they would consider having them sawed in half to create a presumably more Western height was horrifying. When we asked Dr. Song why anyone would want to do such a thing, he shrugged and said, "Nowadays everyone is so concerned with how they look." When we pressed him to elaborate on his thoughts about this new sense of urgency not only to look more beautiful but also more Western, he began to demur and to show a certain edginess.

"Actually," he said apologetically but civilly, "I do not really want to talk about it. Many young people come here, but it is still a somewhat sensitive issue."

By this time several new patients had arrived in Dr. Song's waiting room, and not wishing to take up any more of his time, we thanked him and stepped out of his office through a phalanx of silent patients who, with their various bandages, looked like so many battle casualties.

Walking out through Dr. Song's small waiting room past this gallery of bandaged Chinese faces, it was strange to recall that when Westerners first arrived en masse in China during the eighteenth and nineteenth centuries, Chinese had found them disturbingly large, hairy, smelly, and uncouth. Typical descriptions of these first sightings emphasized their beaklike, ugly noses and their unseemly, round, even deformed eyes. Their clothing was described as uncommonly tight and strange. Still believing sublimely in the superiority of their own values and culture, Chinese had initially dismissed not just the foreigners themselves but their very looks. But now it was another matter. Without a Chinese model—even a Maoist one—for how to act and look, young Chinese seemed to be wandering without direction, guided by nothing more than vague dreams of beauty and fulfillment through more Western looks.

No sooner were we back on a main street than I spotted a second advertisement for yet another plastic surgery clinic. "Good Beauty News!" it proclaimed. "The famous eye surgeon Dr. Wu Bushan has left his job to open a private business at 29 Longtoujing Street in the Xicheng district." The ad went on to list the names of some movie actresses and dancers whom he claimed as his patients. In fact, many Chinese professionals are leaving their low-paying jobs with state enterprises to go into business for themselves. As of the beginning of 1988, approximately 4.6 million, or one-fifth, of all doctors and nurses in China were working in privately run practices.

Turning around, I noticed that we were being watched by an old man with a stubbly beard who was selling fruit on the sidewalk nearby. Catching my eye, he smiled slyly. Gesturing toward the bulletin board on which the ad appeared, I asked him jokingly if these doctors were reliable. "Well, if they didn't do a good job," he said, "they wouldn't be able to put up their ads, would they?" He laughed skeptically.

Not sure whether or not he was putting me on, I asked if he knew anyone who had had cosmetic surgery.

"Who, me?" He guffawed and pointed at his distinctly flat nose. "You've got to be kidding!"

"Well, why would young Chinese want to undergo such painful operations?" I asked.

"You don't know the answer to that? Isn't that the way you Americans are? Your eyes have double folds and you've got big noses, don't you? Isn't that considered much more beautiful?"

"Well, I don't know," I hedged diplomatically. "Do *you* think they are more beautiful?"

"Oh. There's a big difference between what we old-timers like and what these young people think is beautiful," he replied in his burry Beijing accent. "Look at me. I just wear normal old clothes, but for young people fancy clothes are never good enough. They don't want to fit in any more; they just want to stand out. Before they feel complete, they have to put on all these shocking clothes and make themselves up as if they were going out onstage."

"Would you ever consider an eye job?" I asked, laughing.

"Me? I'm Chinese! Perish the thought!" He waved his hand in front of his face as if to fan away the repugnant idea. "If I got an eye job my children would all laugh at me."

"What about your children? Would they ever do a thing like that?"

"No! Absolutely not," he replied, his face suddenly darkening. "My children would never dare do such a thing. Anyway, I'm always watching them. It's only young hooligans *[liumang]* or the sons and daughters of the big Party cadres that do such things, and that's just because they have the money. They want to be like foreigners. But we old Chinese are different. Change our eyes or our noses? It's laughable! That's just not the Chinese way."

It appeared, however, that at least for many of China's urban youth the Chinese way had changed. Cosmetic surgery, as I soon found out, was hardly just a Beijing fad. In spite of Dr. Song's reticence about discussing the subject, by the mid-eighties the practice had spread to many Chinese cities. All over China young people were reaching out for new ways of making themselves beautiful, as the idea of personal good looks replaced the old Maoist concept that a person should be judged by his or her political attitude and good works. Indeed, appealing images of personal good looks often had much more to do with Western than Chinese styles, for any Chinese sense of aesthetics that had managed to survive the first half of the twentieth century had been ruthlessly scorched out as "bourgeois" during Mao's tenure, so that now few Chinese had any ingrown sense of what beauty meant.

Several months later, in March, 1987, the *China Daily*, reporting on a dispatch from the Shanghai-based *Liberation Daily*, noted, "No longer worrying about a full belly and a warm back, more and more Chinese are paying attention to their looks." According to the article, since 1980 more than ten thousand people had gone to the No. 9 People's Hospital in Shanghai for elective cosmetic surgery. As if waiting to buy tickets to see a popular music group, most had had to line up the night before to assure themselves a slot on the popular hospital's busy schedule. For the hospital, now concerned with its own profits and losses under the responsibility system, this steady stream of cash-on-the-barrel patients seeking cosmetic surgery was a lucrative source of income.

So closely had the notion of physical beauty come to be associated with Western criteria that more and more young people—whether they dared act on it or not—yearned to look foreign. It was no accident that many of China's new movie stars and pop singers came either from mixed parentage, like the Shanghai heartthrob Fei Xiang, or at least had confusingly Eurasian-looking features.

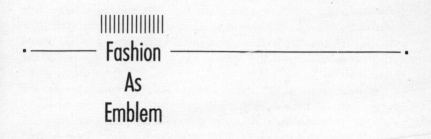

Fashion As Emblem

In no single area of life had the foreign so visibly taken hold in China as in the world of fashion. When I had first arrived in Beijing in the mid-seventies, the sartorial universes of the People's Republic and the outside world were so starkly divergent that one might almost have imagined that one was encountering a separate species. The ubiquitous cotton Mao suit (a style of dress originally adopted by the founder of the Chinese Republic, Sun Yat-sen, to replace the scholar's robe of the Qing Dynasty) came in regimental blue, gray, and khaki, had two pockets and a high collar, and was usually worn in tandem with one of those bulldog-nose brimmed caps made famous by Chairman Mao. An unwritten dress code prescribed that only cadres above a certain rank could wear dark-blue or charcoal-gray suits made out of polyester or wool, and that they could demonstrate their more exalted status by adding two extra pockets, much in the way United States military officers indicate higher rank by adding more bars and stripes. The universality of these repetitive colors and styles gave a superficial sense of sameness to the Chinese people, which only made the changes in fashion that followed Deng Xiaoping's rise to power all the more shocking to outside observers.

In fact, once liberated from their old sartorial prohibitions, so enthusiastically did young Chinese take to the world of fashion that soon Mao suits were piling up unsold on department store shelves.

Observing this rapidly changing scene, I sometimes had the impression of watching one of those films in which blossoming flowers shot in time-lapse photography seem to open in a few seconds when projected back at full speed. Each time I returned to China I found the stores selling, and the streets filled with, a whole new generation of styles. Had someone collected and exhibited the garments of each successive year, the display would have looked something like a high school science chart of the evolutionary process in which lower and amorphously shaped forms of aquatic life bud fins and tails, poke their heads cautiously out of the water, climb up on land, abandon their gills, sprout miniature feet, and then, with scales turning to hair, stand upright and lumber off the edge of the page toward the era of the Homo sapiens.

For young women, the first sign of this fashion renaissance was the reappearance of dresses, skirts, and smart sun hats, accompanied by a fad for permanents, calf-length nylons, sunglasses, and makeup. Designer jeans, turtleneck sweaters, and jogging shoes soon arrived on the scene, sold to local distributors through the back door by Chinese factories that had either set up joint ventures with foreign companies or contracted with foreign clothiers to make garments of the most contemporary design for sale abroad. (Foreign clothing companies found China's labor and raw material costs to be very competitive on the world market.)

As more and more made-for-export clothing began to infiltrate the country, China underwent one of the most precipitous, rapid fashion revolutions of any country in this century, one affecting people of all ages. Party cadres, many of whom were still reluctant to let go of their somber Mao suits, suddenly popped up in bright blue and gold Nike running shoes. Beneath their baggy jackets, dowdy-looking middle-aged women began to appear in stylishly patterned sweaters embroidered in English with such words as "modern" or "love." And bearded octogenarians, out in the streets to air their songbirds, could be seen not in traditional cotton-padded jackets but in flashy new ski parkas and even pre-faded denims.

Initially, as China began to emerge from Maoism, many domestically designed clothes were more evocative of the forties than the eighties because the design departments of garment factories were still in the grip of an older generation for whom clothing as self-expression meant fading memories of life before Liberation. It did not take long, though—given travel, television, movies, videos, and visitors from elsewhere—for younger Chinese to catch on to the design currents of consumer youth culture in the outside world. In the wintertime, instead of the thick khaki-colored overcoats with synthetic fur collars that both men and women had once worn, women began to emerge in brightly colored parkas and knitted hats and scarves. These, in turn, gave away to down-filled maxi-parkas and calf-length-high leather boots. In the springtime women changed into figure-hugging blouses, T-shirts, miniskirts, tight leather trousers, and even an occasional pair of hot pants and heels.

Compared to these radical developments in women's fashion, the changes in men's apparel were relatively sedate but nonetheless noticeable. By the early eighties, the Mao suit had evolved into a Chinese version of the Western suit, a garment every bit as curious and unique to China as the panda. These Chinese "Western suits" (*xizhuang*) almost always came in the same monotonous gray or gray-blue colors and were so styleless that they looked as if they had been fitted for hunchbacks, not ordinary people. It is true that just like their Western counterparts they included trousers, a jacket, and were almost always worn with a necktie, but there the similarity ended. The jackets drooped off the shoulders and hung straight down, giving the appearance that only one basic size was produced and simply adjusted for various body lengths by cutting off or adding material at the bottom. The trousers also had such a featureless bagginess that had they not had flies, which served as direction finders, it would have been hard to tell front from back. While obviously intended to convey an impression of modernity, the design—or lack of it—left these suits so at war with the shape of the human body that to a Western eye they actually looked stylistically retrograde compared to the relative nattiness of the Mao suits they replaced. Nonetheless, such suits quickly acquired great cachet and were soon de rigueur for anyone with upwardly mobile pretensions in Deng's new entrepreneurial society. By the mid-eighties it was not an uncommon sight in Chinese cities to run into street vendors in Western (sometimes even three-piece) suits and ties. In the countryside, it was not unusual to encounter peasants dressed in Western suits and ties riding down dirt paths on bicycles loaded with chickens, ducks, and produce. Even China's highest-ranking Party leaders began appearing for Central Committee meetings and Party Congresses dressed in this new form of foreign haberdashery.

By the second half of the decade, these approximations of Western business suits finally evolved to the point where they actually began to acquire suggestions of flair and styling such as new kinds of fabric, fitted waists, and double vents. In fact, a small vanguard of Chinese who had an opportunity to travel began to buy their clothes abroad, and thus to set a whole Western sartorial standard. It was even reported that Premier Zhao Ziyang himself was partial to shopping at Brooks Brothers.

The selection of footwear, which had formerly consisted of little more than traditional-style cotton shoes, khaki-colored high sneakers, or black leather oxfords, also suddenly began to evolve and grow. In a few short years, shoes that had formerly looked like miniature bathtubs grew sleek and narrow, sprouted heels, and began to change color. This evolution of Chinese footgear was accompanied by what can only be described as a stylistic mutation, namely men's shoes with high heels, which created the unlikely spectacle of sidewalks full of Chinese youths wobbling around elevated two or three inches off the ground. A particularly strange variant was the high-heeled sandal—which came in both leather and plastic—and which, when worn by China's street toughs, who strived for a definitely macho look, had the unintended, and not uncomical, effect of making them appear distinctly effeminate.

To the casual observer there was perhaps no more obvious manifestation of China's rapid change than the variety of new clothing designs that one saw in the streets and the multitude of fashion shows that were being held all across China by factories and trade corporations eager to sell their wares. By 1987 the evolution of fashion had advanced to such a point that it was often difficult to tell which Chinese youths were local and which were overseas compatriots from Hong Kong, Macau, Singapore, the United States, or even Taiwan.

But fashion was just one of the many ways in which China was beginning to merge into a global pop-based consumerism.

||||||||||||||||||
· ———— Letting a ————————————————————— ·
Hundred
Periodicals
Bloom

In 1986 nowhere were the effects of China's openness more evident than in the way new magazines and periodicals of every imaginable sort cropped up for sale on the streets of its cities. The relaxed political climate created a welcome latitude for writers of experimental poetry, short stories, essays, journalism, history, and other kinds of nonfiction such as the new genre of writing known as "literary reportage" (*baogao wenxue*) that flourished during this period and that was so ideally suited to the early eighties. Lying somewhere between journalism and fiction, it combined a strong component of investigative reporting with certain kinds of fictional license. Its investigative aspect allowed writers maximum latitude to take advantage of the increasingly open political climate to expose and comment on sensitive contemporary social and political issues previously considered off limits; yet its literary aspect (which was usually less pronounced) allowed a writer to take such liberties as reconstituting dialogue or changing names to avoid official retribution. Genres of writing such as literary reportage had helped revitalize popular interest in reading newspapers and periodicals in China because for the first time in two decades writers were able to articulate real grievances felt by the common man and to discuss society in a more or less truthful fashion.

By the end of 1986, according to the Chinese Writers' Association, some 5,240 periodicals were being published in China, including 560 serious literary journals such as *Modern Times* (*Dangdai*), *Shanghai Literature* (*Shanghai Wenxue*), *Reading* (*Dushu*), *People's Literature* (*Renmin Wenxue*), *Literature Review* (*Wenxue Pinglun*), *Poetry* (*Shi Kan*), *Prose Monthly* (*Sanwen*), and *Literary Reportage* (*Baogao Wenxue*), which published serious, and sometimes very bold, pieces of fiction and nonfiction. But the bulk of China's new publications consisted of pulp magazines with nary a literary or political pretension. These catered to a taste for romance, sex, violence, intrigue, crime, fashion, the supernatural, and the martial arts.

Compared to old-style revolutionary periodicals with their picture-less covers and blank backs, these exotic new competitors fairly glowed with glitzy photos of beautiful young models, depictions of lurid crimes, or shots of action-packed sporting events. Like the Mao suits that were piling up unbought in warehouses, older publications that tried to hew to a political line were ill equipped to compete with these lively, often trashy interlopers. Indeed, if the Party had applied the logic of its own responsibility system to such state-sponsored publishing ventures as the theoretical organ *Red Flag*, it would doubtless have been declared bankrupt long before the Shenyang Anti-Explosion Equipment Factory.

What was initially most striking about this new crop of popular tabloids was not their boldly adversarial views but rather the way in which they avoided politics, as it is defined in China, altogether. Not only was their subject matter patently apolitical, but their language had no suggestion of the kind of Party officialese in which all periodicals had once been written. Left with only a stack of these new publications as evidence, one would be hard pressed to guess that China still purported to be a revolutionary socialist country run by a Communist Party with a Party-controlled press. In fact, by the beginning of 1987 the publishing scene had changed so radically, and so many new periodicals were appearing, that the Party was no longer able to keep track, much less control, of the situation. State-owned publishing houses that found themselves unable to earn a profit by putting out politically correct or even serious works of writing took to publishing on the side a whole new class of mass market books and periodicals of little redeeming social importance, just to make money. Moreover, while in the past all publishing had been done by registered, state-owned companies, now numerous fly-by-night underground publishers were springing up, infinitely complicating control problems for the government. To get around the law requiring all books and periodicals to bear the registration numbers of their publisher, these underground printers sometimes simply forged the names and identification numbers of state-owned companies onto their illegal press runs in order to throw government inspectors off their trail.

As early as 1985 the *Workers' Daily* had decried the profusion of "profit-seeking tabloids that attract readers mainly by publishing filthy stories, describing violence, swindles, and obscenities. . . ." But since increasing sales was fast becoming the name of the game, publishers continued to vie with each other by printing magazines containing ever more sensational articles and more lurid covers. Besides emphasizing the imagery of such favorite traditional Chinese topics as the martial arts, tales of the supernatural, crime, and romance, publishers also began to rely heavily on foreign imagery for their graphics. This strategy was successful because foreign television programs, movies, pop music, and magazines had all helped create a stark distinction between what was from *guonei* (literally "inside the country") and from *guowai* ("outside the country"). Whatever was from outside the country had by then gained an irresistible cachet for many Chinese.

In Shanghai, for instance, I ran across a magazine called *Police Digest* whose cover featured not a Chinese policeman but a Teutonic blond young man in a tailored military uniform with a sleek but menacing-looking police dog at his side. During the Maoist era a general circulation magazine about the Chinese police would have been unthinkable. Police work of any kind, particularly that of the Public Security Bureau, had always been considered "internal" (*neibu*), a subject about which most Chinese barely dared whisper even to their closest friends. Yet here was a whole magazine consecrated to the subject, and far from touting the dedication and heroism of the Chinese constabulary, its draw was an anonymous Western police officer and his Germanic hound. Even more surprising, rather than recounting tales of socialist police heroism and rectitude, it told stories of robberies, sexual assaults, and murders, all depicted in the goriest detail.

At a small Beijing newsstand operated by a Chinese policeman who was evidently moonlighting, I was intrigued to find several issues of a magazine called *Motorcycle*. The first, from 1985, had a cover shot of two rather ordinary policemen in shapeless khaki uniforms and undistinguished-looking military-style caps sitting on a single very unglamorous Chinese-made military motorcycle with sidecar. They were staring straight ahead with what could only be called expressions of socialist rectitude.

The cover shot of a 1987 issue, which had been published in the wake of a Chinese motorcycle craze, had quite a different look. In this issue a debonair young man of Eurasian appearance sat sidesaddle astride a bright orange Honda dirt bike in an open field wearing a multicolored racing suit, black leather gloves, and orange boots. Cradled in his arm was a white visored helmet plastered with "Honda Racing Team" stickers in English. Unlike his baggy socialist predecessors, he gazed stalwartly toward the horizon with the cool nonchalance of a true biker.

Such hard-core Western imagery was by no means limited to pulp magazines. By the end of 1986, new-style greeting cards featuring saccharine photos of fuzzy kittens and towheaded Caucasian babies on manicured lawns were for sale everywhere. Christmas cards depicting smiling European families frolicking under Christmas trees or winter scenes more evocative of Austria and Norway than the Yangtze River valley were in vogue. What the Chinese called "beauty calendars," featuring anything from reproductions of the Sistine Chapel to shots of Brooke Shields, Sophia Loren, Susan Anton, and other Western film stars, had become the rage. So ubiquitous were they that the *Beijing Daily* even printed a letter from one irritated man who complained that nowhere could he find a calendar with traditional Chinese paintings on it.

This wholesale adoption of what was kitschiest and tackiest in modern Western pop culture almost gave the older kitsch and tackiness of Mao memorabilia from the sixties and seventies a certain authentic, if bizarre, retrospective charm—those cigarette lighters emblazoned with Mao quotes, posters of red-cheeked socialist maidens holding golden sheaves of grain to their bosoms, or the uniquely hybrid calendar and poster art of the time in which industrial smokestacks or high-tension wires peeked through mountain mists or from behind sprays of plum blossoms set in traditional Chinese landscapes. But all the socialist bluster of that period—the "high tide" of Chinese socialism—could not hide China's yearning to be seen as strong, modern, and industrial rather than weak, backward, and agrarian. In an all too familiar way, China's more recent wholesale adoption of Western images and iconography reflected the flip side of the same yearning. Only this time the images expressed a longing for a borrowed, bright, clean, modern, and exciting life of the sort that the West had come to symbolize.

Like life in China, which these seductive Western images only thinly masked, the bright covers of most of the new tabloids offered no more than a meager outer layer of color and gloss around the monotonous pages of cheap newsprint within, where even the fashion magazines became drab and monotonous. Here, where the color gave way to black and white, where the foreign models gave way to local ones, where up-to-date foreign fashions gave way to those the Chinese themselves had produced in an effort to imitate the West, one entered a painfully less luminous, often even tawdry, universe in which not one but two cultures had been displaced.

As understandable as it was, the recurrent use of these foreign images was troubling, for if, historically speaking, Chinese had been sensitive to anything in Sino-Western relations, it was the imputation of their inferiority. Seeing so many Western beauties now staring out from newsstands made one wonder what had become of that long-standing Chinese sensitivity to such an obvious worship of things foreign; what had become of China's once relentless vigilance in opposing exactly these kinds of very seductive symbols of Western beauty, wealth, and power that had so frequently in the past been viewed as humiliating by Chinese of almost every political persuasion.

Wandering the streets of Beijing and Shanghai looking at this latest crop of Westernized magazines and tabloids, it was easy to forget that Mao's Revolution had in no small measure been a reaction to wounds that China's worship of things foreign had inflicted on its pride; that it had been a response to the way in which these powerful alien emblems had demeaned and weakened China, which had already been deeply humiliated by years of foreign economic and military invasion, and which still valiantly struggled to maintain a sense of its own greatness.

|||||||||||||||||||

·——— Mao, ———————————·
Freud, and
Iacocca

At the Fourth National Congress of the Chinese Writers' Association, which opened at the end of 1984, Hu Qili, representing the Central Committee of the Chinese Communist Party, gave a surprising speech. "Literary creation is a form of spiritual labor," he told delegates. "The fruit of this labor is marked by the writer's individual character. It requires full exercise of individual creativity, perception, and imagination, as well as deep understanding, creative views, and distinctive artistic skills. Therefore creative writing must be free. That is to say, the writer must be able to think for himself with his own head, have full freedom to choose subjects, themes, and the modes of artistic expression, and have full freedom to express his or her own thoughts and feelings."

For writers, publishers, and readers alike, this speech, which came from the highest levels of the Party, was a promise of deliverance, and it presaged two years of almost unprecedented literary freedom. One of the most concrete signs of the Party's new liberal attitude toward publishing was the multitude of new publications and private book and periodical stands that began to appear.

Wusi Avenue (May Fourth Avenue) was named after the movement that began on May 4, 1919, in Beijing and subsequently triggered a sweeping attack all across the country against traditional Chinese culture and politics as the cause of China's political weakness and backwardness. Now it had become one of the main places in Beijing where private book and periodical vendors congregated to set up shop. Consisting of nothing more than a few boards laid across sawhorses or the back platforms of bicycle carts, these book stands were often unlicensed and their proprietors led a nomadic existence, coming and going like wisps of smoke, depending on the political climate and the fervor of the police. When the political situation was relaxed, one could buy a surprising variety of new, secondhand, and even out-of-print books not available elsewhere in the city. Indeed, the selection of publications offered at these stalls was often as bizarre and varied as the political climate itself. The only kinds of books one rarely encountered were the multivolume sets of selected works of the various "great leaders" of the Communist world—Mao, Deng, Liu Shaoqi, Zhou Enlai, Marx, Lenin, Engels, Stalin, even North Korea's Kim Il Sung and Romania's Nicolai Ceausescu. These were still part of the stock-in-trade of the state-run New China Bookstores, where they could usually be seen spread out unimaginatively in window displays, quickly yellowing in the sun, their pale, artless bindings covered with a telltale film of grit and dust. So hard was it to sell these Party-sponsored collections of dogma that one would sometimes encounter huge piles of them stacked like surplus building materials in back storage areas of these stores. In fact, by 1986, so déclassé had this particular genre of publishing become that, to make way for more salable titles, employees at one state-run bookstore in Chongqing had unceremoniously dumped piles of Chairman Mao's selected works into a filthy corner, where they awaited oblivion like so many old newspapers.

While the bookstalls on Wusi Avenue rarely carried Party propaganda, they were also by no means as comprehensive in their stock as the larger stores. But it was endlessly fascinating to wander past them and see what they did have, because, unlike their state-run competitors, these private vendors always tried to sell what was in vogue. Indeed, there was no better place in Beijing to put one's finger on China's literary pulse.

One day as I walked down the avenue, I kept a running list of the titles I saw. At the first stall I found the familiar bearded visage of Sigmund Freud looking up from a translation of *Creativity and the Unconscious*, and next to it a copy of *A General Introduction to the Theory of Psychoanalysis*. The works of Freud, a man whose theories about the unconscious mind were still not officially accepted by the state medical establishment as relevant to the treatment of mental illness in China, had made their return debut around 1985 and had been enjoying enormous popularity ever since. So it was not surprising that at another stall, later that day, I spotted a translation of Karen Horney's *Self-Analysis*, as well as an edited selection of Carl Jung's writings. Nor was it surprising that, at a time when the individual self was being elevated in stature in the world of sports, fashion, economics, and politics, intellectuals and writers, too, should become ever more concerned with the workings of the individual human psyche.

In fact, in these last few years, China's writers had all but abandoned socialist realism and revolutionary romanticism to begin exploring, albeit hesitantly and often crudely, the psychological dimensions of human life and interpersonal relationships. After so many years of being unable to read works by the likes of Freud, Horney, and Jung, it was hard to imagine what Chinese readers might now make of their very complex discussions of, and disagreements about, the nature of the human psyche, not to speak of such phenomena as the libido, repression, and guilt. Nonetheless, where once Chinese fiction (sometimes actually written collectively by committee) had been filled with sagas of class struggle and battles with spies and imperialist enemies from afar, it was now increasingly filled with tales of inner struggle—of love versus duty, fantasy versus reality—and tragic accounts of personal relations destroyed by the ravages of politics.

At the second stall a young man in a leather jacket presided over examples of another genre of book publishing equally indicative of China's recent preoccupation with the private rather than the public side of life. *A Handbook for the Life of Modern Women*, a marriage manual whose cover displayed an ingenue in a sexy black dress, a pearl choker, and a strange black hat topped with plastic daisies, got right into the trenches of private life, discussing dating, makeup, boy-girl relationships, feminine hygiene, marriage, and sexual relations. Also for sale was a manual entitled *Knowledge About Sex*, which was filled with explicit line drawings and offered counsel on such subjects as "The Physiology of the Male Sex Glands," "Sexual Maturity, Love, and Marriage," and "Sexual Life and Hygiene After Marriage." The existence of these and similar volumes reflected the fact that after years of exhorting Chinese to serve the people and lead exclusively political lives, the Party had now relented and implicitly sanctioned the notion of serving oneself as well. By doing so, it had, however, inadvertently acknowledged that pleasure, enjoyment, and even a certain quotient of self-indulgence were now permissible.

Such handbooks, however retrograde by present-day American standards, filled an enormous void in China. There had literally been no corpus of thought, group of experts, or set of writings available to help ordinary Chinese deal with the crisis created by these dimensions of their personal existence. Over and over I heard from friends heartbreaking stories about anguished courtships filled with sexual ignorance and fear that almost inevitably led to confusing, horrendous marriages. In fact, it would not be too extreme to say that one of the most tragic legacies of Mao's Revolution was its complete inability to understand and its refusal to acknowledge that no social order, much less a utopian one, can be built without some comprehension of people's interior emotional needs.

In spite of their popularity, many of the practical guides to human relations that did now get official approval for publication in China were frustratingly elusive on the questions young Chinese most wanted to ask. Worse yet, what advice was offered often proved so off-base as to be comical, since writers of these guides were frequently as ignorant on their subject as the youths they were purporting to advise. However, these handbooks were as close as China had come yet to frank, open discussions of these previously taboo subjects, so people bought and read them with great interest anyway.

Ironically, right next to this curious assortment of handbooks on the inner self lay the works of four Western authors not noted for their interest in interior life: *Leaders* by Richard M. Nixon, *The Third Wave* by Alvin Toffler, *Iacocca: An Autobiography* by Lee Iacocca, and *Ronnie and Nancy: A Very Special Love Story* by a writer named Bill Adler. Available in translation, these books sometimes seemed to be almost as ubiquitous in Chinese cities during 1986 as Mao's Little Red Book had been twenty years earlier.

At the next stall, run from the back of a bicycle cart by an older man, I found Chinese translations of Nietzsche, Jesus, Montaigne, and Machiavelli, the first of a new series of volumes on "the hundred great thinkers of the West," which was being edited by a group of young scholars headed by Chen Ziming, a research fellow at the Institute of Philosophy at the Chinese Academy of Social Sciences. At a gathering to celebrate the new series (which was scheduled to publish volumes by Sartre and Schopenhauer next), the liberal director of the academy's Institute of Political Science, Yan Jiaqi (whose own *Ten-Year History of the Cultural Revolution* ran afoul of the Chinese censors), sarcastically said that if Chinese had been able to read Machiavelli, they might have rebelled long ago against the idea of trying to find a benevolent ruler to be their saviour. "They would have known that a good system would work far better than a good head of state."

At another stall, sprinkled in among copies of Tang Dynasty poetry, the works of the Han Dynasty historian Sima Qian, and a book on Italian Renaissance art, I discovered an abridged English-language edition of *Wuthering Heights*, Arthur Hailey's *Hotel*, and a collection of short stories that included Henry James's "The Beast in the Jungle," Joseph Conrad's "The Secret Sharer," and Ralph Ellison's "King of the Bingo Game."

About a block farther down the street, at a stall almost completely surrounded by browsers, I spotted a single dog-eared copy of a book being passed from hand to hand by prospective buyers. It was *The Ugly Chinaman*, a work by the sixty-eight-year-old Taiwan-based Chinese writer Bo Yang. A reflection on Chinese cultural arrogance and backwardness, *The Ugly Chinaman* was then the talk of Beijing intellectual circles, even though—or perhaps it would be more accurate to say just because—it had been banned.

"How is it possible for such a great people and great nation to have degenerated to such a state of ugliness?" Bo had written elsewhere. "Not only have we been bullied around by foreigners; even worse, for centuries we've been bullied around by ourselves—from tyrannical emperors to despotic officials and ruthless mobs."

Bo Yang, who was born in the city of Kaifeng in Henan province on the mainland but now lives in Taiwan, had been accused of being a Communist agent by the Guomindang, who imprisoned him for nine years in Taiwan, and now had been officially derided on the mainland and had his books banned for purportedly having insulted and humiliated the Chinese people.

"I have discovered that God has predestined people like me for jail, whether jail be in Taiwan or on the Chinese mainland," he wrote wryly in *The Ugly Chinaman*. "But why does speaking the truth lead to such unfortunate consequences? My answer is that this is not a problem attributable to any individual, but rather to Chinese culture as a whole."

Viewing Communists and Nationalists alike as chips off the same block, Bo criticized them both for making China ugly, weak, and despotic by denying the Chinese people freedom and democracy. His biting criticism of those characteristics Chinese had always proudly held to be part of their unique cultural heritage meshed perfectly with the inquiring, even self-doubting mood that had been gripping China's intelligentsia since their crisis of belief in post-Mao China of the late nineteen-seventies.

There had been at least five editions of Bo's book printed on the mainland before the Chinese government finally banned it. But even after the banning, copies kept appearing at bookstalls like those on Wusi Avenue, as small provincial publishers, smelling profits to be made, began printing bootlegged editions and selling them through underground distribution networks. The only difference between the pre- and post-ban books was the price. Halfhearted government efforts to expunge it from the Chinese literary scene had only ended up making it more urgent for those who had not already read it to do so. In the new Chinese economic world of market mechanisms, such Party-induced demand allowed small booksellers to add on to a book's price what they referred to as a "risk fee." This was a surcharge that the vendors claimed was warranted as insurance against any possible losses they might sustain as a result of confiscation by raiding authorities. In some cases the risk fee could be substantial. Take Yan Jiaqi's *Ten-Year History of the Cultural Revolution*. After its banning in 1986, the Tianjin People's Press found itself stuck with 200,000 unbound copies moldering in inventory. But inventive staffers well aware of the value Party censorship immediately conferred on a book, particularly one on the Cultural Revolution, began smuggling thousands of copies out of the warehouse, stitching them together at home, and surreptitiously selling them to underground distributors. By the time the books hit the streets at stalls like those on Wusi Avenue, they were selling at ten times their original price.

In earlier years, when notions of what constituted revolutionary literature were clearer and private bookstalls unthinkable, state-run publishing houses and bookstores alike had a very definite idea of what they could and could not publish and sell. Most of them attended an annual meeting organized by the Party's Propaganda Department at which general guidelines were laid out for publishers, much in the same way economic plans and quotas were set for industrial enterprises and rural communes. Moreover, since all publishing houses were subsidized by the state—which also controlled the sale of paper and printing presses—publishers were far more concerned with putting out books that would reflect "correct thought" than books that would sell. For in the often illogical world of Chinese socialism, any book that sold well just created more work for the enterprise and its employees, while a book that was correct politically but did not sell well disturbed no one and helped bookstore managers build up a good fund of correct political karma with the Party.

The consequences of such a system were that bookstore shelves became stuffed with hortatory novels (*Bright Sunny Skies*), propagandistic plays (*Comrade, You Have Taken the Wrong Path!*), model operas (*The Red Detachment of Women*), poems (mostly by Chairman Mao), endless dreary documents on the Party's current political line, and enormous series of the works of the aforementioned big socialist leaders. Many of the bookstores also had an "internal" section, in which they could corral any off-center publications like so many wild horses. Here Party regulars could buy certain confidential works, official tracts and documents not meant for general distribution, and a few unsanitized books from abroad that were not supposed to be made available to the gullible public.

By the early nineteen-eighties, however, ideological questions were in such a state of flux and confusion, boundaries between what was correct and incorrect had grown so blurred, and censors had been thrown so off balance that publishing houses found themselves with a new, previously unimaginable freedom. What got published had become more a question of what editors wished to publish and less a matter of what the Party required. And yet, just as it was difficult to be clear about what kinds of private financial dealings were legal in the context of such a rapidly changing economic situation, so it became tricky for publishers to know just when and how far they could step over the line from orthodoxy to unorthodoxy. For many this ideological vagueness created a perplexing uncertainty, but for others it was a license to run free and to push the system as far as they could for political or financial gain.

While the Propaganda Department in Beijing, which had lower-level branch offices throughout China, had general responsibility for setting guidelines and overseeing what was published in China, editors at the publishing enterprises themselves usually made the day-to-day decisions on what actually went to press. According to the "three-tiered inspection system" (*sanshenzhi*), decisions on whether to publish a manuscript or an article usually went through three stages of review. An article was first submitted to an editor, and if passed by him, went up to the managing editor, and then finally to the editor in chief. Since these men were almost invariably Party members, and since all of them carefully read the official press and were thus keenly aware of Party policy and where the continually expanding and contracting margins of permissible political and literary dissent lay, they usually blocked any piece of writing that might be considered maverick before it was published.

But as the boundaries of permissibility became at once wider and less distinct, controversial pieces of writing like Bo Yang's *The Ugly Chinaman* began to slip through this system of institutional self-censorship and appear in print. It was only then that officials in the Propaganda Department or even high-ranking Party leaders might move to have a book explicitly banned.

That fall, the explosive growth of new newspapers, books, magazines, cards, and calendars showed no sign of abating. For instance, a survey at the Journalism Institute of the Chinese Academy of Sciences claimed that between 1980 and 1985 the number of newspapers in China had more than doubled to 1,177, and that in 1986 alone the number had again increased by more than 300. By 1987 not only had the numbers of new publications swollen to epic proportions but their contents seemed to have burst the bounds of the internal censorship system and of Party control as well. Many times in the past when the Party had launched campaigns against bourgeois decadence or spiritual pollution, publishing had been an early target of attack. Although everyone knew such hard-line Maoist forces still held a large but undetermined amount of power within the Party, it was hard to see much evidence of their controlling hand while prowling the bookstalls on Wusi Avenue during the fall of 1986.

Socialism Is Good

One lovely fall day in 1986 as I walked with a friend in the shade of the sycamore trees along the sidewalk of West Changan Boulevard, the big clock in the antenna tower of the Telegraph Building struck noon. But instead of simply tolling out the midday hour, it pealed forth the first few bars of the Maoist anthem "The East Is Red" on an electronic carillon.

> *The East is Red, the sun has risen.*
> *China has produced a Mao Zedong.*
> *He seeks happiness for the people*
> *He is the great saviour of the people.*

Hearing those few familiar bars of music momentarily plunged me back into the China I had known while Mao still lived. Then this revolutionary war-horse of a tune had blasted relentlessly from public address systems and radio stations all across China. Yet in the past five or six years, I now realized, I wasn't aware of having heard it even once, or for that matter having heard any of the other revolutionary songs that had once quite literally been the background Muzak to everyday life in China.

The next day I asked my friend, who used to be a member of a song and dance propaganda troupe, to dig up for me some of the old revolutionary songbooks of that time. Leafing through them was like taking a time machine back to that era when political idealism, innocence, and collectivism rather than cynicism, skepticism, and individualism were the animating principles of Chinese life. The naiveté of the lyrics of those songs were a reminder of that bygone era when people either believed in the Party or were cowed enough by revolutionary peer and Party pressure to accept its pronunciamentos as articles of faith. How else but through faith or fear could anyone have kept a straight face while singing, "All Commune Members Are Sunflowers," "Youthful Soldiers with Exalted Spirits," "Socialism Is Good," "Eternally Follow Chairman Mao," or "The Screws of the Revolution Will Never Rust"?

There was no mention of despair, heartbreak, love, or, God forbid, lust in those songs. They were utterly dedicated to the Party, the Revolution, new China, socialism, and Chairman Mao. Those rather than the self, wealth, or individual expression were their hallmarks, as well as the hallmarks of the age. "Study Chairman Mao's Works and Listen to Chairman Mao's Teachings," for instance, begins:

> *The works of Chairman Mao are like the red sun.*
> *Every word shimmers like gold.*
> *They make radiant the hearts of six hundred million people,*
> *And the enthusiasm they express for labor is ten*
>   *thousand leagues high.*
> *Communism is the source of our great idealism,*
> *And the army of the people is a power that is forever invincible.*
> *The work of making revolution is everlasting.*

The song "Socialism Is Good" begins:

> *Socialism is good, socialism is good!*
> *In socialist countries the status of the common people is high.*
> *Counter-revolutionary cliques are destroyed.*
> *The emissaries of imperialism are forced to run away with their tails*
>   *tucked between their legs.*
> *The masses of the whole country unite,*
> *And surge forward in a high tide to build socialism.*
> *Socialism is good, socialism is good!*

What effect these old revolutionary songs had had on the generation that came of age singing them, and what influence of theirs still lingered on as China now headed off hell-bent on a new course was hard to know, but by the nineteen-eighties children no longer sang them, record shops no longer carried them, and even officially run radio stations no longer bothered to play them. They had become as much the province of history as the *Book of Changes* and the *Analects* of Confucius. In fact, the only time I had recently heard them sung had been when Chinese friends had jokingly warbled a snatch or two remembered from their childhoods, as if they were engaged in the equivalent of a trivia game, or when a wag would sing a bowdlerized line or two as a form of ironic low comedy. For instance, instead of these lines from the "The East Is Red,"

> *The Chinese Communist Party is like the sun.*
> *Wherever it shines, there it is light,*
> *And there the people are liberated,*

jokesters, to spoof the constant flip-flopping of the Party line, sang:

> *The Chinese Communist Party is like the moon.*
> *At the beginning and middle of the month,*
> *It plays a different tune.*

When in 1975, while working in the Shanghai Electrical Machinery Factory, I had been awakened each morning by the deafening roar of "The East Is Red" from outdoor speakers that covered every square inch of the factory grounds with sound like interlocking fields of machine-gun fire, it was just the beginning of a long day of political bombardment. On billboards, the radio and television, in magazines, newspapers, comic books, films, and operas, all that one heard and saw were rouged children and rotund Mao-suited singers, faces radiant with socialist enthusiasm, bellowing out their didactic political paeans to Chairman Mao and crooning their saccharine arias about bumper harvests and the glories of serving the people. The relentlessness and ubiquity of these revolutionary songs withered the spirit and obliterated all peace of mind. Their invasive quality made private thought almost an impossibility.

So it says quite a bit that by the beginning of 1987 I was beginning to feel something like nostalgia for this extinct musical form. It was not that I had liked either the songs' lyrics or music, but that what had replaced them, often taking over the same radio stations and PA systems, was an even more unendurable kind of background music. It was in fact an utterly bizarre smorgasbord of Western pop, Cantonese rock and roll, classical favorites, top-twenty tunes, Taiwanese love ballads, country and western tunes, syrupy pop laments recounting Chinese versions of heartbreak and desire, and a specifically Chinese form of easy listening that was known as "light music." Like a camera missing all the middle-range f-stops, China seemed unable in music, even more than in other cultural areas, to find some comfortable middle ground between shutting out and letting in outside influences.

Although in a sense this new musical fare did combine the Chinese and the Western, it did so in a screwball and artless way that proved a far cry from the idealized synthesis for which Party leaders tirelessly propagandized, and on which they had theoretically based their open door policy. China's new musical fare could perhaps best be compared to the sort of Chinese-American cooking of an earlier era of Sino-American cultural miscegenation that, taking the worst from East and West, evolved such inedible mutant dishes as chop suey and chow mein. By almost any standards, Westernized Chinese popular music was a form of artistic retrograde motion, one area where the emphasis of the Maoist hard-liners on the dangers of spiritual pollution paradoxically had a clearly focussed and appropriate meaning.

Whatever their differences, these new musical forms and their socialist predecessors had one similarity, namely their pervasiveness. This new musical fare, too, was an inescapable aspect of life, emanating, as it did, from trains, taxis, restaurants, hotels, shops, airports, and sometimes ghetto blasters left playing in public like faulty fire hydrants spewing water into the gutter. Having gotten rid of one kind of musical pollution, China had only replaced it with another. What made enduring this bastardized mishmash even more intolerable was the recognition that while listening to "The East Is Red" and its kindred revolutionary songs had been a form of inescapable punishment, at least it had been an involuntary one inflicted on people by the Party. This new music, however, was being inflicted on the people by the people themselves.

The only respite came when, after a succession of love songs and elevator music, one might suddenly be treated to a short, untampered piece from the classical Western repertoire—favorites were the schmaltziest of the Beethoven piano sonatas ("Moonlight Sonata" or "Sonata Appassionata"). Invariably, though, these interludes would end with another burst of pop music. The effect of this concussive succession of clashing musical styles was not unlike that of being forced to listen simultaneously to several different radio stations.

Trains were one of the worst places of entrapment. Music was piped into each car and could not be turned off. On one twelve-hour ride from Qingdao to Beijing, I felt as if our train had been hijacked by a deranged disc jockey. We were forced to listen to a nonstop medley consisting in part of a John Denver song, a Strauss waltz, a love song from Taiwan, Beethoven's *Ode to Joy* (without chorus), a rock version of "The Red River Valley," the "Toreador Song" from *Carmen* played on a synthesizer, a Chinese ballad about the Yangtze River, and a Cantonese rock and roll number from Hong Kong which sounded like arguing ducks quacking in syncopation. Short of getting off the train, there was no relief.

Planes soon also became danger zones. While sitting in Beijing on one recent flight waiting for clearance to take off, I discovered that the Civil Aviation Administration of China (CAAC), the state-owned national airline, had recently installed a new airport diffusion system so that passengers now had to endure an in-cabin program of elevator music just as if they were in Atlanta or Denver. If someone had told me when I landed at Capital Airport in Beijing aboard a Russian-built plane during the Cultural Revolution that one day I would be sitting on the same runway in an American jet listening to the strains of syrupy instrumental versions of Hawaiian mood music, "Vaya con Dios," "Puff the Magic Dragon," and the theme song from the soft-porn film *Emmanuelle*, then one of the most popular pieces of music in China, played with a bouncy beat on an electronic synthesizer, I would have thought them mad. What made the experience particularly depressing was that traditional Chinese music is actually among the most soothing in the world and would have served perfectly as an alternate form of mood music.

The final sad stage of musical poverty in China was not airport background music, but what the Chinese had come to know as *di-si-ke*, or disco. When played by most Chinese bands, this obviously imported genre is as painful to listen to as fingernails scratched across a blackboard. Of course, most people never hear the live music but get their daily disco fix from the tape cassettes that have flooded the country. In fact, where once a sewing machine and a bicycle were considered the most sought-after household consumer items, now the ghetto blaster (along with the refrigerator and washing machine) has become the new rage. Small private shops, equipped with dual-drive cassette machines for dubbing, can support whole families by cranking out and selling inexpensive counterfeit copies of disco tapes. Popular music cassettes have become such an enormous and profitable industry in China that even most large state-owned bookstores have devoted large parts of their street-level floors to the sale of pop music tapes.

What distinguishes Chinese disco is its utter lack of distinctiveness. Almost every singer is backed up by an automatic and completely repetitive electronic base line pounded out on a synthesizer, a drum, and an electric guitar, with possibly a few wind instruments and strings providing the change in mood (brasses representing excitement and strings representing the love interest). Almost every group sounds alike. The singers are invariably youths whose photographs appear on the front of the cassette, and who in their high-heeled boots, loud shirts, and tight designer blue jeans are parodies of the kind of Hong Kong chic they are trying to imitate. One recent popular song was even called "Blue Jeans" (in Chinese literally "cowboy pants" [*niuzaiku*]) and included the lyrics:

> *Wa Wa blue jeans!*
> *Wa Wa blue jeans!*
> *When my guy wears blue jeans,*
> *He looks so slick and fast.*
> *When my girl wears blue jeans,*
> *She looks so slick and lively.*
> *Oh why, oh why, oh why,*
> *Do blue jeans cast such a spell on me?*

My most numbing involuntary disco experience took place in the lobby of Shanghai's Hongqiao International Airport, where I was trapped for twenty-four hours waiting for a plane held up by bad weather. When I arrived in the morning, the PA system, to my surprise, was softly playing tapes of traditional Chinese flute and pipa music. But as soon as the rush of early morning flights was over, the service attendants suddenly took over the PA system like a band of guerrillas occupying a government broadcasting facility. The traditional music stopped abruptly, and, after an ominous moment of silence, a high-volume frenzy of *di-si-ke* suddenly shattered the quiet of the airport. Unmindful of the passengers sprinkled around the waiting room trying to sleep or read, the attendants sprawled on the chairs in the lounge like an occupying army and listened to their favorite disco selections at ear-splitting volume.

This went on for hours, until I thought my head would explode. At that moment I would gladly have supported even Jiang Qing (Mao's ultra-leftist wife, who, as the pre-eminent member of the Gang of Four, now resides in jail), had she been able to project herself astrally into the room and liberate the PA system from its occupying force. I would have resolutely supported her counter-coup even if she had insisted on playing "Our Revolutionary Family Is Filled with Sunshine" or "I Want to Become a Good Warrior for Chairman Mao."

When I could stand it no longer and went to the service counter to inquire if the volume might not at least be lowered a little, a sweet young woman who was reading a magazine about movie stars looked up at me with uncomprehending blankness.

"What's the problem?" she asked.

"I'm trying to read and find the music a little loud."

"Really? You don't like disco?"

"Well . . ."

"But doesn't disco come from your country?" she asked with a look of bewilderment, which made me feel the way a black person might upon being accused of not liking rhythm and blues.

The music did not stop until the midday "rest period," at which point it ended as suddenly as it had begun since almost all the service attendants vacated the premises for what one friend in China jokingly refers to as "the big sleep."

By 1987 disco was everywhere. As the musical director of the Central Philharmonic, Li Delun, observed to a reporter from *Asiaweek*, "The floodgates have been opened and we have had an unprecedented inundation. Since World War One, 'mass culture' from the United States—from jazz to disco—has conquered the world. China is the last battleground, and we are hardly putting up any resistance."

There were disco nightclubs at the beach resort of Qingdao, nightly disco dances at most of Shanghai's old Western-built hotels, rooftop disco dance halls above Wuhan restaurants, and "taxi girl" disco night spots and gay disco dives in Canton. In fact, disco music seemed to have developed not just as a musical taste but as a full-blown cultural phenomenon that, transcending music, included fashion and life-style as well. Young people spoke of disco almost with reverence, as if this imported musical form had magical curative powers. A book even appeared for sale at private street stalls entitled *The Official Guide to Disco—A Revolutionary Step-by-Step Approach to Being a Hit on Saturday Night*. As the lyrics in one song, "Queen of Disco," said:

Oh oh oh, what a disco queen!
See how happy she is!
She is even able to forget about earthly affairs.
What worries could she have . . .
Disco makes you forget all worries and feel elated.

*What other dance is so rhythmic and able to make your whole body
  so relaxed?*

Its ultra-contemporary electronic sound, the bright high-tech flashing lights, the demonstratively fashionable way people dressed to dance it, and the very fact that the dances themselves were held at night, when most good comrades were in bed, created for it a seductive aura of exotic foreignness and modernity that even the Party and the Army sometimes found hard to resist.

One night in early 1987 while watching Central Chinese Television in Beijing, I happened to catch the broadcast of a provincial New Year's variety show, and watched in disbelief as the lights slowly came up on a small stage bejeweled with blinking lights on which stood a young woman from the People's Liberation Army (PLA). Instead of baggy khaki fatigues and a rifle, she wore a provocatively tailored uniform and high heels. Clutching an electric guitar to her gyrating pelvis, strumming and writhing, she broke into a song called "Battlefield Disco," whose lyrics turned out to be about China's war with Vietnam.

Only later did a friend and longtime resident of Beijing tell me that this song was just part of a whole new genre of music called "foxhole disco," composed by Party artists to extol the "heroes" who were fighting China's futile but ongoing war against Vietnam. In fact, during 1986, whole PLA propaganda teams had been touring schools and university campuses, holding dances, and performing foxhole disco music for students. Whatever the form, its content was a shameless appeal to nationalism, a reminder to students that while they were safe at home studying (and possibly demonstrating against the government), their heroic comrades in the army were shedding patriotic blood for the motherland in a war against foreign villainy.

Undeniably true as it was that China's youth had gone dance-crazy, watching PLA soldiers sing disco may not have been exactly what they had in mind. Rather than update or add luster to the Army's image, such efforts only lent the PLA, claimant to the tradition of the Long March and the Yan'an days of guerrilla fighting against the Japanese and Chiang Kai-shek, an aura of absurdity. Watching "Battlefield Disco," I felt the irony in Mao's own warning: "There may be some Communists who were not conquered by enemies with guns . . . but who cannot withstand sugarcoated bullets; they will be defeated by sugarcoated bullets. We must guard against such a situation."

Party and Army leaders alike must have felt desperate indeed to inflict on themselves the humiliation of having to disco-ize their appeals to the masses. There was an undeniable pathos to their clumsy efforts, especially since this kind of hybridized Party propaganda probably convinced few people of anything except that disco was no longer taboo. Such clumsy propagandistic efforts were best described by the Chinese aphorism *Niutou budui mazui,* or "A horse's mouth will never fit a cow's head."

Programs like the one on which "Battlefield Disco" appeared raised another question, which transcended the issue of the effectiveness of military or Party propaganda. One could understand how the Party might have trouble controlling spiritual pollution in the streets, but television was a different matter. Since it was a state-run monopoly, with one flick of a switch the Party could have rid China of the polluting influence of "Battlefield Disco" and its ilk. As Deng Xiaoping was to note to Stefan Korosec, a visiting Party dignitary from Yugoslavia, "The greatest advantage of the socialist system is that when the central leadership makes a decision, it is promptly implemented without interference from any other quarter. . . . We don't have to go through a lot of repetitive discussion and consultation, with one branch of government holding up another and decisions not being carried out. From this point of view our system is very efficient."

While not exactly a formula for democracy, Deng's vision of governmental efficiency would certainly have allowed the Party unilaterally to decree a higher level of cultural programming on TV. It was paradoxical, to say the least, that China, a country that claimed to fear spiritual pollution, and that had enormous powers of cultural control, proved not unable but actually unwilling to purify even the content of its own television network.

As China headed into the second half of the decade, its fascination with Western pop music seemed to know no bounds. In the early eighties individuals and groups like country-rock singer John Denver, the traditional Irish music group the Chieftains, and New Age musician Jean-Michel Jarre had come to China, and although their performances were rather sedate, their impact was profound. By 1985 China had also produced a more-or-less homegrown rock band called Beijing Underground. It was made up of overseas students who were studying in Beijing. Organized by a Frenchman, it also included singers from Zaire and the United States and performed around the capital, until, under the patronage of one of Deng Xiaoping's sons and billed as the Official Tour for the Promotion of Disco, it made a cross-country trip to Canton, Shanghai, and six other cities which ended up at the Capital Gymnasium for two concerts in front of audiences of eight thousand enthusiastic fans.

In April, 1985, the British rock group Wham arrived in China with a 105-member entourage for a concert tour. The tour reached a crescendo of sorts when, while on a Chinese jet to Canton, one of the band's backup musicians went berserk, charged into the pilots' cockpit with a knife, sent the plane into a nosedive, and then stabbed himself in the stomach. These may be the kinds of incidents from which rock legends are made in the West, but in China they cause furrowed brows, high anxiety, Party censure, and usually a search for scapegoats. Wham's ill-fated tour left little in the way of official goodwill toward rock and rollers, and caused the immediate cancellation of another upcoming tour, by the Australian band Men-At-Work.

However, in the fall of 1986 China again took a cautious step into live Western pop music culture when the director and conductor of the Shanghai Symphony Orchestra, Chen Xieyang, impressed by what he called their "healthy attitude," invited to China a virtually unknown quintet of young American women pop musicians who called themselves SheRock. Before SheRock left China, it performed sixteen concerts in Shanghai, Hangzhou, and Canton before an estimated total audience of 125,000 people, with Chinese youths lining up twenty-four hours in advance to buy tickets.

Perhaps the most celebrated American rock group to perform in China was the surf-sound duo of Jan and Dean, who arrived for concerts in Shanghai, Beijing, and Canton at the end of November, 1986, during the zenith of that year's political thaw. Their Friendship Tour 86 was sponsored by a company based in Santa Monica, California, called China Amusement and Leisure (CA&L) in conjunction with the Shanghai Cultural Bureau. The rock tour was only one part of a larger deal in which CA&L also planned to bring to the People's Republic Stars on Ice (featuring figure skaters Dorothy Hamil and Scott Hamilton), an International Arts Festival, the band Manhattan Transfer, a daughter-and-mother country music group called the Judds, Rod Stewart, Donny Osmond, and the "multiplatinum" rock act Genesis. Shanghai, for its part, had agreed to send various cultural troupes to tour the United States. In addition to this exchange of live entertainment, CA&L was also responsible for helping negotiate a deal between Lorimar-Telepictures and Shanghai Television which gave the Chinese their choice of 7,500 hours of TV programming (including rights to air series like *Falcon Crest, Knott's Landing,* and *Dallas*) in return for advertising airtime that Lorimar was entitled to sell to American and other foreign corporations.

Jan and Dean (Jan Berry and Dean Torrence) had become popular legends in the United States during the sixties with such hits as "Dead Man's Curve," "Fun, Fun, Fun," "The Little Old Lady from Pasadena," and their classic, "Surf City." The connection between Southern California surfer music, beach culture, and life in China was admittedly remote, but before Jan and Dean's tour was over, surfing songs had inadvertently become one of the catalysts for a series of momentous political events that were soon to shake China.

These touring bands brought to young Chinese their first glimpse of live foreign rock and left them more smitten than ever, not just with pop music, but with the Western youth culture it implicitly promoted. All across the country young people desperately tried to find the money to buy tape cassettes, ghetto blasters, and guitars, and they frequented a new kind of youth nightclub, such as the Karaoke in Beijing, where anyone could fulfill a dream by stepping up to a public microphone with a guitar to try his luck as a popular singer. Guitar factories simply couldn't keep up with the demand. Newly opened private music schools boomed. Talent shows were organized in almost every city as fantasies about joining the People's Liberation Army or entering the Party were rapidly replaced by the idea of becoming a pop music star.

There were endless imitators of the famous Taiwan love balladeer Deng Lijun and thousands of aspiring singers who adopted one or another of Hong Kong's rock stars as their artistic model. In Canton there was a local singer who had become a cult figure by doing imitations (in Chinese) of black soul singer Lionel Richie, and even some Chinese who had taken up the unlikely arts of rap music and break dancing.

Nonetheless, with no official patronage (most classical and traditional Chinese musicians were under the sponsorship of music academies and state-supported orchestras), without any local tradition to draw on as a source of inspiration, and without audiences experienced in hearing good music, Chinese pop musicians existed as members of a rootless, orphaned art form governed more by brazen imitation than by real artistic inspiration. It was not until 1986 that a few bands of real talent emerged with styles more or less their own. While the Party seemed unthreatened by the morass of proliferating disco bands, groups that played hard-driving rock and roll (*yaogunyue*, literally "shaking and rolling music") tended to receive a chilly reception. In fact, often they were persecuted outright. Unlike those self-taught youths smitten by disco fever, the most talented newcomers in rock and roll were apt to be from China's classical music establishment, which had itself been restored to respectability only after the Cultural Revolution. Obstructed by a chronic shortage of money, no decent place to practice, a scarcity of good, foreign-made electric guitars and amplifiers, little or no access to recording studios, and very few places to perform, these bands existed on a hand-to-mouth, more or less underground, basis. Often they did not even take on an official name, preferring to operate under different aliases so that they could regroup, if necessary, or just melt away and lie low if and when it became politically prudent to do so.

One such group, which had been playing informally around Beijing and slowly acquiring quite an underground reputation, was first introduced to me as *Dajaolü*, or the Honking Donkeys. The band was led by Cui Jian, a guitarist who normally played classical trumpet with the Beijing Song and Dance Ensemble orchestra, and included five other musicians: a Chinese saxophonist (originally a classical oboist), a female keyboard player (originally a classical pianist), a self-taught drummer, a guitar player from Madagascar, and a bass player from Hungary. Like Cui, the saxophonist and keyboard players both performed with various state-run symphony orchestras and other musical ensembles when not playing with the Donkeys.

What was surprising about this unusual collection of musicians was not only their varying backgrounds and nationalities but the seriousness with which they took their music. Their technical skill was obvious and their subtle lyrics spoke poetically if obliquely to current Chinese issues. Several of the Donkeys' songs, like the "Long March Rock," had been penned by the short story writer Ah Cheng.

Throughout 1986 the group played at various benefit concerts in Beijing, such as one celebrating the International Year of Peace and another organized to raise money for the restoration of the historic Marco Polo Bridge over which the Japanese had marched into Beijing in 1937. But without any official approval or patronage, and unable to book a concert hall to give performances for Chinese audiences, they found China a difficult place to make their way. Even though they were China's pre-eminent rock group, in the end they were forced to survive by playing at parties given by members of Beijing's foreign community.

"The authorities don't understand this kind of music," Cui told *Los Angeles Times* correspondent Jim Mann. "Our words are very respectful of the leaders and their undertakings. But when you combine them with [our] style and the music, they refuse to accept it."

In a country where almost every entertainment group has an official connection to a "unit," and where there has been no tradition of bohemian artistic life beyond Party control, existence on the margins of official society proved a difficult task. (Cui, for instance, lived with his family in a tiny room plastered with foreign rock posters.) But the fact that they could survive at all and were not simply shipped off to "reform through labor" camps was a testament to how much things had changed in China since Deng's reforms began. Just as it had recently become possible for private businessmen to exist on the fringes of the state-run economy, so path-breaking artistic groups like the Honking Donkeys had begun to pioneer a rudimentary existence outside the controlling and artistically smothering embrace of the Party. What was dangerous about their situation, however, was that their financial survival depended on the patronage of foreigners rather than Chinese. This was a situation I saw repeated again and again during this period as writers and artists as well as musicians, spurned by their own government and unable to find artistic nourishment within their own society, turned to foreigners for artistic and financial support and, more and more frequently, finally for help in leaving China. This not only helped isolate Chinese artists from their own culture and alienate them from their own people, but often literally separated them from their own culture and country by forcing them to go abroad to survive. At the very least, this sort of association with foreigners gave powerful ammunition to the Party hard-liners intent on suppressing all such cultural experimentation anyway. For by being able to sully these artists with the taint of having "sold out" to foreigners, it was that much easier to discredit them. It certainly could not have improved the Donkeys' standing with hard-liners when in early 1987 it was rumored that a foreign intermediary had arranged a deal for them with Columbia Pictures.

In February, 1987, while in Shanghai, I ran into a Chinese-American film maker, Victor Huey, who had become interested in Chinese rock groups while working on a documentary about Luciano Pavarotti's concert tour in China several months earlier. When I met him, he had just finished filming the Honking Donkeys both at Maxim's de Paris, the Beijing branch of Pierre Cardin's renowned French restaurant chain, where the Donkeys often performed for their foreign clientele, and at a TV taping that I was surprised to hear the band had just done for Shanghai Television.

"It's a great misapprehension that the Donkeys are completely Westernized," Huey told me one evening in Shanghai. "They are actually one of the rare groups whose music shows some Chinese influence and whose lyrics address what's going on here in China right now. What makes them so unique is that in spite of the fact that they play rock and roll and have two foreign members, they *are* still so Chinese. They don't just regurgitate stuff from Hong Kong and the West. Instead, they've been reinventing a new kind of Chinese popular music and are rapidly becoming a voice of their generation. It's a pity the Party can't embrace this band, because they are good and only make China look good."

When I asked him how, if the band was in such a sensitive situation, he had managed to shoot the footage he wanted and get it out of the country, he replied, "I never know what I'm going to be able to get. Every day and every place is different. Things can get pretty weird, particularly when a rock group begins to attract attention, especially among foreigners. These guys could get into trouble because there is a lot of official sensitivity to the sort of music they are playing. But on the other hand, there is really no uniformity or logic to Party policy, so a band like the Donkeys sometimes can slip through."

Huey then produced a large album full of color photos of the band that he had taken during their taping session (the airing of which I subsequently learned was cancelled for political reasons). Although by American rock band standards their costumes were tame, they were wearing an assortment of boots, trench coats, and hats that were pretty far-out for Chinese TV, where most performers now appeared in neat Western suits and ties. The stage set, presumably a creation of the television studio itself, was even stranger. It was a gaudy puce and pink construction that, at least in the photographs, gave the sensation of being inside someone's brightly lit mouth.

Although I had heard tapes of the Donkeys, I did not actually see them play until the fall of 1987, at a Maxim's party given by NBC for their crew, which was in Beijing to broadcast a week of live programming called "China in Change." Cui, a serious-looking young man with a boyish smile and close-cropped hair, performed in a pair of baggy blue trousers and a red tank top. The keyboard player, a plain-looking young woman who wore her hair in pigtails, looked more like a member of the corp of "educated youth" whom Mao sent to the countryside to "learn from the workers, peasants, and soldiers" than an incipient international rock star. The band's only slightly punky accoutrement was a pair of dark glasses worn by the saxophonist. Though not flamboyant in the way Westerners expect of their rockers and rollers, the Donkeys played up a veritable storm of music that was both sophisticated and fun to listen to. They switched from a reggae-like sound, in which the guitar player from Madagascar seemed to specialize, to slow jazzlike numbers, to ear-splitting hard-driving rock that instantly provoked the whole roomful of revelers to dance as if possessed.

It was obvious that the Donkeys were skilled musicians who just happened to enjoy rock and roll. But what was most distinctive about them was an indefinable Chinese-ness to their music. (They sang in Mandarin, and the saxophonist played the tenor sax as if it were a *suona*, or Chinese oboe.) One was reminded, despite the Belle Epoque surroundings of Maxim's, that the real mise-en-scène was the People's Republic of China. And although the music was clearly Western rock and roll, it did not radiate the kind of slavish mimicry of foreign rock music that characterized most other Chinese bands I had heard. To listen to Cui Jian and his Honking Donkeys after all the other knockoff disco bands that were drowning China in background music was equivalent to listening to Bach afer Barry Manilow.

However, the music of the Donkeys was not, evidently, part of the synthesis between East and West that the Party seemed to visualize when it spoke of its much-vaunted idea of a new "spiritual socialist civilization with Chinese characteristics." And this was a great shame. The inability of the Party to embrace such new and authentic currents of art underscored their lingering ambivalence—or worse—about relaxing controls over art and politics. The band's very existence, however marginal, suggested that China now at least had the possibility of relating to the outside cosmopolitan world of contemporary culture without slavish imitation, if the Party would only allow, and perhaps encourage, its younger people to create their own synthesis. It was also evident that such a synthesis would never come to term in any sphere of endeavor as long as the Party kept on suppressing new artistic currents with its controlling hand; as long as it ignored or scythed down those creative people who dared to move beyond the permissible, and thus pedestrian, boundaries of creative discourse.

That these verities were applicable to China's scientific and tech-nological community (as well as its political system) was also obvious.

If China was to regenerate, to reinvent itself as something more than a pale imitation of the industrialized West, the Party would have to allow those talented pioneers to arise regardless of where they might appear and what they might choose to say, sing, discover, paint, or write. The truth was that once the doors to the outside world were opened, there was no easy way to interpose a filter across the aperture. Bad disco and trashy tabloids would enter along with good rock and roll and innovative forms of literature. Undesirable values and crazes would infiltrate the culture along with much-needed foreign technology and overseas capital. If each new phenomenon, whether it was the music of the Honking Donkeys or the ideas of an outspoken political theorist, was crowded out by the Party for not being sufficiently socialist or too Western, it seemed likely that China, instead of finding a new equilibrium, would languish in an inhospitable and barren no-man's-land between East and West.

If the experience of the Donkeys was any indication, the cultural and political refoliation of China was not going to come easily. After their taped rendition of the old Yan'an-era revolutionary song "Nan-niwan" (which the band sometimes performed in a satirical fashion so that it sounded as if it were being sung by Alvin the Chipmunk) had been passed on to hard-line ex-general Wang Zhen, the Honking Donkeys were reportedly banned from making any more public appearances before Chinese audiences, their upcoming record contract was cancelled, and Cui Jian himself was let go from his job with the Beijing Song and Dance Ensemble. Such an official reaction to one of China's cultural pioneers did not bode well for those who might choose to espouse other new art forms or ideas.

PART 3

A

SECOND

KIND OF

LOYALTY

||||||||||||||||
· ——— Three ——— ·
Critics and
the Party

Throughout history Chinese intellectuals have had a uniquely close relationship to their government. Since the former Han Dynasty (206 B.C.–8 A.D.), government officials had been drawn from the country's scholar class through a system of national examinations. This system, which lasted until 1905 just before the fall of the Qing Dynasty, tested scholars on their knowledge of the Confucian classics and over the centuries established a tradition of a strong political orthodoxy which bound scholarship and government together in a single intellectual universe. Unlike the situation in the West in which intellectuals and artists frequently found themselves at odds with government—often cultivating and even treasuring the roles of critic and rebel—for a Chinese scholar there was no higher intellectual calling than to succeed in the examination system and to serve the government as an official.

While this tradition of a shared orthodoxy was often able to bring the most educated and talented men to serve the empire, and while it created history's longest, perhaps most glorious continuous civilization, it also left China relatively devoid of a tradition of cultural diversity, not to say political dissent. Unlike the West, which, since the Reformation and the Renaissance, fairly boiled with religious, intellectual, and political ferment, China remained, in the end, largely resistant to new and potentially disruptive schools of thought. Instead of seeing diversity as healthy and creative, and fashioning political institutions to contain it, Chinese governments, and the scholar-official class that served them, saw such diversity as threatening the kind of desirable Confucian harmony that lay at the foundation of Chinese metaphysics.

Until the bitter end of the last dynasty, Chinese conservatives tried to beat back those new ideas that in the nineteenth century began invading China along with Western and Japanese imperialist armies, traders, and missionaries, and that threatened to disrupt not only the cultural homogeneity of the country but also the notion of a body politic and government built on a single unifying ideology. In the end, the Qing Dynasty and the old order fell in no small measure because their ideological rigidity prevented them from being able either to incorporate dissenting thinkers or to utilize them as an engine of change.

The same may be said of Chiang Kai-shek's ill-fated Nationalist government, which foundered when it, too, because of its repressive policies and corruption, lost the support of the country's intellectuals. Once the bond between this crucial sector of the people and the state had been rent asunder, the "mandate of heaven" (the basic justification for a traditional Chinese ruler's power) was presumed to have passed from emperor, generalissimo, and Party chairman alike.

It was ironic indeed that Mao Zedong, the apostle of revolution and arch-opponent of "feudal culture," should have so completely inherited this tradition of a state orthodoxy and of intellectuals as the servants of the state. Since he had spent much of his life in opposition, one might have thought that the notion of a political system that at least had a loyal opposition might have had more appeal to Mao. He did fight against the privilege, arrogance, and disdain for the common people that had been characteristic of educated bureaucrats over the centuries. But despite his ceaseless attacks on this class of people— who had for so long monopolized learning in China—he was finally no more disposed than Ming and Qing emperors or Chiang Kai-shek to allow political pluralism of any sort. And so the presumption that intellectuals existed to serve the state continued, the only difference being that the new orthodoxy was now Marxism–Leninism–Mao Zedong Thought rather than Confucianism. As a result, for the first three decades after 1949, almost any intellectual who expressed views at odds with the Party's current orthodox line was as ruthlessly suppressed as unorthodox thinkers had been during the Ming Dynasty.

It was one thing to liberalize the economy, as Deng Xiaoping and the liberal reformers of the nineteen-eighties had done, but quite another to liberalize and democratize politics. For once the process was set in motion, as China's reform-minded leaders had cautiously done in 1986, intellectuals quite naturally began to assert their individual views, creating a specter of intellectual and political chaos that appeared every bit as menacing to the Chinese Communist Party as to the Imperial governments of old.

During the first half of the nineteen-eighties, the Party tried to endure—with some notable exceptions—the growing clamor of diverse opinions, because it was aware that if China's educated elite was to help modernize China, it also needed a modicum of freedom with which to think and act. During this time three men in particular burst onto the scene, and each in his own way challenged the Party's intellectual and political domination. Fang Lizhi, a brilliant astrophysicist, in effect challenged the Party's exclusive right to rule by calling for human rights and democracy. Liu Binyan, a muckraking journalist and professed Marxist, exposed the dark, bureaucratic side of Communist rule, so impugning China's Party leadership that it was hard to understand how he, or anyone else, could continue to lend it wholehearted support. And Wang Ruowang, an acerbic theorist and writer, fearlessly exposed injustice wherever he found it and criticized the socialist system in such harsh terms that it was difficult to imagine how he could continue to call himself a Marxist.

‖‖‖‖‖‖‖‖‖‖‖‖‖‖‖‖‖‖‖‖‖‖‖‖‖‖‖‖‖
· —— Fang Lizhi: China's ———————— ·
Andrei Sakharov

No place was the thaw of 1986 more keenly felt than on the campuses of China's universities. In the newly relaxed political climate, not only was there a renewed sense of intellectual excitement, but student organizations were allowed to book rooms, invite speakers to address them, and freely put up posters to announce events. Campuses came alive with a kind of unregimented political discussion that had been unknown for decades.

A deep wariness against speaking too freely had been scorched into many senior academics by the crackdowns that had, with a horrifying inevitability, terminated all previous interludes of liberalism in Chinese Communist history. There were, however, a few who, seemingly without regard for their futures, still dared speak out openly. The most vocal of these was a fifty-one-year-old astrophysicist named Fang Lizhi, who by 1987 had become legendary for his forthrightness and courage in publicly saying what he believed.

When I first met Fang in his Beijing apartment, what impressed me about him was his good cheer and guilelessness. He laughed easily—an infectious laugh that spiralled spontaneously into something like a whinny, carrying everything with it in a burst of unpremeditated mirthfulness. He was dressed simply, in a knit shirt, a tweed coat, and stay-pressed slacks. Nondescript tortoiseshell glasses gave him a slightly owlish look. He left an initial impression of ordinariness; until, that is, he began to talk. Then one instantly sensed one was in the presence of a man not only of keen intelligence and conviction, but of fearlessness. The longer I was with him, the more this quality struck me. For far from being a studied posture adopted consciously as a means of resisting intimidation, Fang's fearlessness appeared deeply rooted in his personality, which radiated self-confidence. And yet there was no suggestion of arrogance or even self-consciousness about him. Seldom have I met a man who, although at the center of an intense and dangerous national controversy (when we first talked in the fall of 1987 he had attained national prominence for his role in the student demonstrations of the previous winter), so utterly lacked the kind of polemical energy that often makes zealots of a lesser kind so shrill and self-justifying. Although Fang obviously cared deeply about the cause of democracy in China, he was not one to thrust his convictions upon anyone; and although he had been politically persecuted throughout his life, there was no suggestion of rancor or resentment in his politics. What he was *for* seemed so ascendant over what he was *against* that the notion of enemies was absent from his intellectual, political, and emotional vocabulary.

However, what made being with him so strangely disorienting was his complete lack of the kind of self-censorship that rendered so many other Chinese intellectuals of his generation timid and incapable of speaking their minds. Never overriding his thoughts and feelings with subtle (and often unconscious) genuflections to the official line of the moment, Fang spoke so openly about what he was thinking and what he believed that one instinctively, if ludicrously, had to suppress the urge to warn him of the dangers of such candor.

"Everything I have ever said is open," Fang told me, impervious to such warnings, which have in fact come from many quarters. "I have nothing to hide. And since I have already said everything that I believe many times in public, what is the point of trying to hide things now in private?"

To recount those many times is to tell the story of his life, which began in Beijing in 1936 when he was born into the family of a postal clerk from Hangzhou. He entered Beijing University (Beida) in 1952 as a student of theoretical and nuclear physics, and although he quickly distinguished himself as an unusually capable scientist, his interest in politics was equally passionate. His first recorded brush with political dissent occurred one February day in 1955 during the founding meeting of the university chapter of the Communist Youth League (an organization that arranges political and recreational activities for young people and that is a prerequisite for anyone who intends to become a Party member). The league branch secretary from the Physics Department had been addressing the gathering in the auditorium of Beida's administration building and had just begun discussing the role of the league in stimulating idealism among China's youth when Fang Lizhi, then a nineteen-year-old student, dashed up onto the stage, indicating his own desire to speak.

"Some of us students in the physics department thought the meeting was too dull, just a lot of formalistic speeches. So we decided to liven things up a bit," Fang remembered later on. "When it came time for our branch secretary to speak, he let me express my opinion since I had the loudest voice." Taking over the microphone from the league secretary, Fang redirected the discussion to the general subject of the Chinese educational system. "I said that this kind of meeting was completely meaningless. I asked what kind of people we were turning out when what we should have been doing was training people to think independently. Just having the Three Goods [good health, good study practices, and good work] is such a depressing concept and hardly enough to motivate anyone.

"After I spoke, the meeting fell into complete disorder. . . . The next day the Party Committee Secretary, who was the top person in charge of ideological work for students at Beijing University, spoke all day. He said that although independent thinking was, of course, a good thing, students should settle down and study."

In spite of his attraction to politics, Fang did in fact settle down to study, earning straight A's at Beida, where he also met his future wife,

Li Shuxian, who was a fellow student in the department of physics, which she ultimately joined as a faculty member. In 1956, at the age of twenty, Fang graduated from Beida and was assigned to work at the Chinese Academy of Sciences' Institute of Modern Physics Research. But a year later, when the Anti-Rightist Campaign began, Fang was severely criticized for having written a lengthy memorial on the need to reform China's educational system so that politics would not control scientific research; and for refusing to recant his alleged misdeeds, as many other intellectuals did under pressure, he was expelled from the Party.

"For a long time after the Anti-Rightist Campaign I continued to believe in communism," Fang later told me. "Even after I was expelled from the Party, I continued to have faith in Chairman Mao and believed that it must have been me who was wrong."

Wrong or not, as a promising young scientist greatly needed by China in its early efforts to industrialize, he was allowed to keep his position at the Institute of Modern Physics Research and was ultimately even sent to help organize a new department of physics at the University of Science and Technology (Kexue Jishu Daxue, or Keda for short), which was just then being set up in Beijing. During the next few years, while teaching theoretical classes in quantum mechanics and electromagnetics, Fang also conducted research on solid state and laser physics. In 1963, because of his obvious talent in his field—and in spite of his previous political troubles—Fang was promoted to the position of lecturer.

But no sooner had Fang's life begun to return to normal than the Cultural Revolution broke out, and like so many other Chinese intellectuals, Fang once more ran afoul of politics. This time he was "struggled against" as a "reactionary" and incarcerated in a *niupeng,* or cow shed, a form of solitary confinement especially devised by the Red Guards to imprison intellectuals of the "stinking ninth category." (Opponents of Mao's policies had been divided up into "nine black categories.") After a year's imprisonment, he was released and sent down to the countryside to work with the peasantry. Here, because of the paucity of scientific books available to him, he was forced to change the focus of his scholarly work and to concentrate on the study of relativity and theoretical astrophysics.

"I had only one book with me, the Soviet physicist Landau's *Theory of Fields,*" Fang told me. "For six months I did nothing but read this book over and over again. It was this curious happenstance alone that caused me to switch fields from solid state physics to cosmology.

"Around the time of the Cultural Revolution, I began to notice a lot of things and to feel that perhaps Mao was not so good for the country. But because at the time we still believed in communism, it left us with the difficult question, who should we follow? There was, of course, no one else but Mao. He was supposed to be the embodiment of all idealism.

"It was only later, although my sense of things was still quite unclear, that I began feeling that the Party was not telling the truth. Then, after the Cultural Revolution started, everything became much clearer. I realized that they had in fact been deceiving people and that I should not believe them any more. You see, a sense of duty, responsibility, and loyalty to the country had been inculcated within me as a youth, but what I saw around me now made me feel that the leaders weren't similarly concerned about the country and weren't shouldering responsibility for its people."

In 1970, when the academy decided to move the undergraduate departments of the University of Science and Technology from Beijing to the provincial capital of Hefei, in Anhui, Fang, along with several dozen other academics who had also been stigmatized with rightist labels, was exiled to the provinces. In Hefei, Fang began to study and teach astrophysics, but because of the political cloud still hanging over him, he was only able to publish the results of his research by writing under a pseudonym.

His full rehabilitation did not come about until 1978, two years after the fall of the Gang of Four. At this time he regained his Party membership and, receiving tenure at Keda, became China's youngest full professor. The next few years were perhaps his most creative, from a scientific point of view. Becoming increasingly interested in the cosmology of the early universe, he began to publish frequently on this subject, now under his own name. (By 1986 he had over 130 articles to his credit.) In 1980 his popularity at Keda led to his being elected director of the Fundamental Physics Department, with more than 90 percent of the faculty's 120 votes. However, his politically progressive views and outspokenness continued to cause the Party to distrust him. Because secret reports from a fellow professor impugned his political reliability, Fang, though three times nominated for the post of Vice-President of the University of Science and Technology, was three times rejected.

What was ultimately to have the profoundest impact on Fang were his readings in politics and his travels abroad, which became possible as a result of Deng's open door policy. In 1978 Fang left China for the first time, to attend a conference on relativistic astrophysics in Munich. Subsequent trips took him to a cosmology conference at the Vatican; to Bogotá, Colombia, for another conference; to Italy, again as a visiting professor at the University of Rome; to England, where he was a Senior Visiting Fellow at the Institute of Astronomy of Cambridge University Observatory; to Japan, where he was a Visiting Professor at Kyoto University's Fundamental Physics Research Institute; and finally to the United States, where he was in residence at the Institute for Advanced Study in Princeton from March through July 1986. These trips abroad were to deeply influence the way that Fang looked at the Chinese socialist system and the role of intellectuals within it.

In the meantime his international reputation as a physicist continued to grow. In July, 1985, he and Fumitaka Sato, from Kyoto University, were awarded the United States International Gravity Foundation's prize for their co-authored article on cosmology, "Is the Periodicity in the Distribution of the Quasar Redshifts an Evidence of the Multiple Connected Universe?" In spite of many years of political harassment and periodic near-total isolation from the world scientific community, Fang had now become one of the very few scientists from the People's Republic in nearly four decades to have received international scientific attention and acclaim. What made Fang even more unusual was his special interest in education, philosophy, and politics as well as science, interests that grew out of his conviction that in any truly creative mind, science and philosophy—of which he took politics to be an extension—were indissolubly bound together.

As early as 1979 Fang had argued against the suggestion that science and philosophy had nothing to do with each other. In *The Beijing Journal of Science and Technology*, he had written, "There is a traditional authoritarian point of view that states that since Mach and Poincaré, natural scientists have shown themselves to have no philosophical depth; that the best that could be said of them was that they managed to utilize dialectics unconsciously. . . . In fact, however, the methodology of science research itself embodies a philosophy of science. And if a scientist achieves great success in his research, how can it be said that the philosophy that guides him lacks 'depth'?"

Just as scientific research was a way of bearing witness to truths about the natural world, so Fang believed intellectual and political inquiry were ways of bearing witness to truths about the political and social world. Interviewed by the writer Dai Qing in the newspaper

Guangming Daily in the fall of 1986, Fang explained his notion of the special role that he hoped scientists as intellectuals would play in the development of a newly modern China. He noted, prophetically in his own case as it turned out, that "almost invariably, it has been the natural scientists who have been the first to become conscious of the emergence of each social crisis." Then, evidently paraphrasing Einstein, he declared, "Scientists must express their feelings about all aspects of society, especially when unreasonable, wrong, or evil things emerge. If they do otherwise, they will be considered accomplices."

When questioned by Dai Qing that December about a scientist's responsibility for social problems, Fang said, "Because science and technology have become more and more important in the world in which we are living, there are a great many social problems that only people with some background in science or culture may be able to grasp clearly. At the same time, intellectuals are becoming more aware that their function in society should not be limited to technological matters, but should also embrace a sense of responsibility for making a contribution to the progress of society as a whole."

Fang's remedy for the claustrophobic intellectual climate of most Chinese educational institutions was to scrutinize their shortcomings relentlessly and honestly. "The emergence and development of new theories necessitates creating an atmosphere of democracy and freedom in the university," he said. "In the university, there should be nothing that . . . allows no questioning of why it must be upheld. There should be no doctrine allowed to hold a leading or guiding position in an a priori way."

As Wu Guosheng, then a Beida graduate student and now a research fellow at the Institute of Philosophy, wrote about Fang in a Beida student journal called *The Beijing University Student Newspaper* (banned as soon as it came out, in 1985), Fang believes that intellectuals "should place great value upon issues that concern public welfare, take personal responsibility for matters of national importance, employ criticism as a scalpel with which to cut to the core of socially accepted irrationality, and point out the path of virtue. Because they perform these functions, intellectuals are called the 'conscience of civilization.' . . . Spinelessness and complacency not only exist in the Chinese scientific world but actually constitute the norm. Nevertheless, there are some intellectuals who are aware of their duty to society and scientific truth. Fang Lizhi is one."

In this highly admiring portrait, Wu went on to say that Fang was a man whom "no danger can compel to abdicate his intellectual responsibility to bear witness to the truth. His students love him, and he readily accedes to their invitations to speak and teach, even though there are those who are quietly working against him. Because Fang is always ready to state his opinion on crucial social questions of our day, he is often the victim of invisible persecutors. When friends advise him to soften his statements, he tells them that anything he has done wrong would have reached the ears of authorities long ago, so he may as well go ahead and say what he means."

One of the most shocking things that Fang had been saying publicly was that socialism as an ideology was passé for China. "When I first said this back in 1980, the Vice-Premier in charge of science and technology, Fang Yi, called me in and criticized me," Fang Lizhi told me one day with an impish smile. "He said, 'How could you say a thing like that?' And I replied, 'I said it because I believe it.' He said, 'Well, I might go even so far as to say that I agree with you, but one can't just come right out and say such a thing!' "

In 1984 Fang Lizhi was finally promoted to the position of Vice-President of the University of Science and Technology, and a colleague in physics, Guan Weiyan, was appointed President. Fang's star was now clearly rising. There were soon efforts among the liberal reform faction in China's central leadership to nominate Fang for high provincial office and even to confer upon him membership in the Party's Central Committee, all this despite his intolerance of hypocrisy and his refusal to help maintain Party mythology—or any other mythology, for that matter.

That same year, the Ministry of Education issued a report, "The Reform of China's Educational Structure," calling for dramatic changes in the country's university system, including the election of administrators to top positions by committees of academics rather than their appointment by the Party. Fang, Guan, and three other professors, all of whom had had difficulties during the Anti-Rightist Campaign of the late fifties and/or the Cultural Revolution in the late sixties, were appointed to a special leading administrative group, under the guidance of such power-packed organizations as the Communist Party Central Committee's Ministry of Organization, the Academy of Sciences, and the Anhui Provincial Party Committee, and they were charged with devising a program of academic reform for Keda. Fang and Guan proposed a plan that would implement a radical horizontal redistribution of power at the university. Instead of having all authority concentrated in the hands of top-level administrators, allowing them to control research funds, degree giving, and faculty promotions, these functions would be spread out among special committees and the departments themselves. As Guan later said, "Monopolization of power invariably leads to corruption. As soon as power comes into the hands of any one individual, it signifies a loss of democratic rights for the people."

A second reform involved establishing the rights of faculty and staff to audit all administrative meetings. Fang held that since the socialist system claimed to have made the people the masters of their own country, the people should have the right to know what their leaders were up to. This was an especially important concept for Fang, because he believed that one of the major defects of Chinese society was that, in the absence of any oversight provisions, problems and grievances piled up unsolved until any given situation became so explosive that there was no way to rectify it short of outright violent struggle and upheaval.

A third area of reform that concerned Fang and Guan was that of free speech. They wished to establish firmly the right of students and faculty not only to speak out on campus, but also to remain free from all subtler but not necessarily less crippling forms of ideological repression. Fang and Guan wished to create an open academic and political environment at Keda, and since in their view diversity was something to be cultivated, not suppressed, it was their conviction that anyone should be able to put up a handbill and hold an event on campus without having to seek prior approval from some higher authority.

This was indeed a bold vision of academic freedom, such as the People's Republic of China had never known. But Fang and Guan did not stop there. To foster an openness that would have a cosmopolitan dimension, they also sought to establish as much contact as possible with the outside world. By the end of 1986 more than nine hundred faculty members and students from Keda had been sent abroad to visit, lecture, and study, and over two hundred foreign scholars had visited Keda. Exchange programs had been set up with educational institutions in the United States, Japan, Britain, Italy, and France.

Fang's experience with this reform process convinced him that the most meaningful task he could undertake in China was not scientific research but pressing for even more changes in the country's educational system. "I am determined to create intellectual and academic freedom. This will be my top priority," he said with his usual directness when asked about his future plans. Although such declarations may sound commonplace in the context of a Western democracy, where such traditions as intellectual and academic freedom are taken for granted, coming from a university vice-president in a China just emerging from the Cultural Revolution, they were like casting down a gauntlet.

While Fang was helping fashion these educational reforms at Keda, he was by no means shutting himself off from the broader political issues and currents of the country at large. In fact, in 1985 and 1986 Fang seemed to turn up whenever and wherever there was open political discussion or ferment, a habit that must have caused consternation among those hard-liners in the Party hierarchy whose conception of the mass line had never included such radical educational reform, never mind spontaneous political movements for the democratization of Chinese life.

For instance, on September 18, 1985, the anniversary of the invasion of China by Japan, students at Beida organized a demonstration to protest what they called "the second occupation of China by Japan," a reference to the invasion of Japanese goods and Japan's growing commercial domination of Chinese markets. In spite of the fact that the police had thrown a cordon around the campus to contain the demonstration, students succeeded in breaking through it and marching on Tian'anmen Square, in the heart of the capital. While the major focus of student disaffection was Japan's new economic role in China ("Dear Compatriots: Should the crashing waves of our blood be chilled and frozen, what will we have gotten from all this? Just police and refrigerators!" exclaimed one wall poster), the students were also protesting in a more general way the lack of democracy in their country. ("Respect Human Rights" and "Return Democracy and Freedom to Students," their banners and placards also proclaimed.)

Not only were these student demonstrations finally suppressed by police, but the event was hardly mentioned in the Chinese press. Accounts published in the West concentrated on the anti-Japanese and anti-foreign aspects of the students' demands, almost completely overlooking their more general appeal for greater democracy. The only nonstudent voice to speak up on behalf of the demonstrators was that of Fang Lizhi. On November 4, 1985, in a stirring, free-ranging, and sometimes even humorous talk that held his Beida audience spellbound, Fang encouraged the students to hold on to their social concern and political activism, and, if none could be found in China, to look to the West for new models of intellectual commitment. Addressing himself to the larger issues of China's backwardness and his hopes for its future, Fang spoke directly to the students' concerns in a speech worth quoting at some length because it so clearly reveals Fang's great appeal to China's youth.

"As intellectuals, we are obligated to work for the improvement of society," he told them. ". . . This requires that we break the bonds of social restraint when necessary. Creativity has not been encouraged over the past three decades as being in keeping with Chinese tradition. It is a shame that, as a result, China has yet to produce work worthy of consideration for a Nobel prize. Why is this? . . .

"One reason for this situation is our social environment. Many of us who have been to foreign countries to study or work agree that we can perform much more efficiently and productively abroad than in China. . . . Foreigners are no more intelligent than we Chinese. Why, then, can't we produce first-rate work? The reasons for our inability to develop our potential lie within our social system. . . .

"Intellectuals in the West differ from us in that they not only have a great deal of specialized knowledge, but they are also concerned about their larger society. If they were not, they wouldn't even be qualified to call themselves intellectuals. But in China, with its poorly developed scientific culture, intellectuals do not exert significant influence on society. This is a sign of backwardness. . . .

"In August, I was invited to attend a convention of scientists from around the world. The subject was disarmament. I wasn't allowed to attend, of course. The involvement of scientists in a subject like disarmament makes no sense to our government. It is a subtlety beyond their comprehension. [Laughter] Not only do they fail to understand the relationship between scientists and disarmament, but they don't even want scientists thinking about issues such as this! And this is exactly the same attitude they take in regard to China's internal problems. . . .

"Lately the state has been trying to promote idealism and discipline. Its idea of idealism is that we should have a feeling of responsibility toward our society. Of course, our goal should be the improvement of society, but our goal shouldn't just be some utopian dream that can only be realized a million years down the road. [Applause] Even scientists like myself who study the universe cannot see that far into the future. What is much more important is to identify problems that exist *now*, and to try to solve them; to identify problems that will beset us in the near future and that we might be able to minimize or avoid. . . .

"What is the real reason for the lack of ideals and discipline in our society? Some say it is because we have opened up our door to the outside world. I say that this is a completely wrong analysis. It is patently false. If they are honest, all those who have been to foreign countries must admit that discipline, order, morality, culture, and civilization in those countries are superior to what they are in China. [Applause] Many people think that selfishness is very common in foreign countries. One may be able to find examples where this is true. But speaking in general terms, these countries are more civilized than we are. Some people say that Westerners are 'empty.' While there certainly are some empty people there, this cannot be said about their societies as a whole. It is simply untrue. In those societies there are intellectuals who are rich in their sense of responsibility. They, too, discuss morality and social responsibility frequently. When our Party members meet, they certainly do no better. . . .

"There is a social malaise in our country today, and the primary reason for it is the poor example set by Party members. Unethical behavior by Party leaders is especially to blame. This is a situation that clearly calls for action on the part of intellectuals. . . . Some of us dare not speak out. But if we all spoke out, there would be nothing to be afraid of. This is surely one important cause of our lack of idealism and discipline.

"Another cause is that over the years our propaganda about communism has been seriously flawed. In my view this propaganda's greatest problem has been that it has had far too narrow an interpretation—not only too narrow but too shallow. I, too, am a member of the Communist Party, but my dreams are not so narrow. They are of a more open society, where differences are allowed. Room must be made for the great variety of excellence that has found expression in human civilization. Our narrow propaganda seems to imply that nothing that came before us has any merit whatsoever. This is the most worthless and destructive form of propaganda. Propaganda can be used to praise Communist heroes, but it should not be used to tear down other heroes.

"For example, contributions of the great men of the Renaissance were no less significant than those of our modern heroes. But when they are mentioned in our propaganda, a certain sentence is always added to the effect that 'they were, unfortunately limited by their historical circumstances.' [Applause] This view is simply wrong, and it has contributed to the anemic condition of our culture. If we eliminate all accomplishments before 1949, what we are left with is very shallow indeed. And because the Great Proletarian Cultural Revolution wiped out nearly everything positive since 1949, there is just about nothing left. Now that is what I would call an absolute vacuum! [Applause]

"We Communist Party members should be open to different ways of thinking. We should be open to different cultures and willing to adopt the elements of those cultures that are clearly superior. A great diversity of thought should be allowed in colleges and universities. For if all thought is narrow and simplistic, creativity will die. At present, there are certainly some people in power who still insist on dictating to others according to their own narrow principles. They always wave the flag of Marxism when they speak. But what they are spouting is not Marxism. It is not even worthy of Duhring! [Eugene Duhring was a German turn-of-the-century liberal political philosopher who advocated the retention of capitalism, believing that a strong labor movement could ameliorate its worst abuses.] Even Duhring was a hundred years ahead of them! [Loud laughter]

"We must not be afraid to speak openly about these things. In fact, it is our duty. If we remain silent, we will fail to live up to our responsibility."

The Beida students had never heard a respected faculty member speak publicly like this before, and Fang's effect was electrifying. Moreover, it was only one of many talks that Fang would give over the next year as he travelled to other cities, quickly earning himself a reputation for being, in short, China's foremost freethinker. Fang Lizhi was a singular figure in post-Mao China. The content of his speeches made it difficult to remember that he still was a member of the Chinese Communist Party, where, as ever, the watchwords were discipline and obedience.

Meanwhile, so successful were Fang and Guan's reforms at Keda that even the *People's Daily* ran a series of five articles in October and November, 1986, describing them in the most adulatory way, which was tantamount to giving them the Party's seal of approval. In fact, the writer Lu Fang was so impressed by what he had seen at Keda that he was unable to control his enthusiasm from the very first sentence of the first article. Instead of employing a litany of facts and statistics to introduce his subject, as this genre of news feature often called for, he dove right in and began, "During my whole trip to Keda, everywhere I breathed the air of democracy." At Keda, wrote Lu, "all, regardless of their qualifications and previous experience, have the right to express their own opinions, and any member of one school of thought is free to discuss and argue with others. Those who first visit the university invariably ask why this place has become such a 'paradise' of academic freedom. Fang Lizhi, vice-president of the university, says that academic freedom springs from political democracy, which is based on a division of powers and the maintenance of checks and balances between them."

Lu went on to praise the openness and "unconstrained atmosphere" in which students and faculty worked together: "Students at Keda maintained that scientific development not only requires 'external freedom,' or freedom to speak up without fear of persecution, but also 'internal freedom,' or freedom from the oppression of ideology or social bias. If they do not dare to speak, how will they ever be able to make contributions to science and technology in our country?"

Discussing Fang's responsibility for the financial management of the university, Lu praised him for not acting the role of the "big shot 'Minister of Finance' who requires everyone buying a screwdriver to get written approval first." When queried on the sensitive subject of an intellectual's responsibilities to the Party, Lu reported Fang as having replied, "An intellectual's relationship to the Communist Party should be that of a friend who will always give frank advice."

Still mindful during those halcyon days of democratic dialogue that even the warmest political climate in China can suddenly frost over, Lu asked Fang if he was not concerned lest someday his radical experiments in educational reform be branded as wholesale Westernization.

"Perhaps someone will bring up the question," admitted Fang. "In applying a system of 'separate and balanced powers' to run a college, is there not always some danger of being suspected of imitating Western capitalism? But the methods used at Keda are in accordance with the directions of Party Central regarding the 'practical application of democratization to every aspect of social life.' They are in accordance with the Constitution, which prescribes academic freedom. It [democracy] is not something that is being 'sneaked in the back door' here. We should have no suspicion about that."

The effect of these articles in the *People's Daily*, was to transform Keda into a new, official, model university, as well as to elevate its two leaders, Guan and Fang, to the status of semi-official national heroes. The glare of the public spotlight, far from cowing Fang into silence as it might have some intellectuals ("People fear notoriety just like pigs fear becoming fat" being the traditional attitude toward such notoriety), seemed hardly to faze him.

In November, Shanghai's *World Economic Herald* ran an article headlined, "Fang Lizhi Says That China's Greatest Tragedy Is That Its Intellectuals Have Not Yet Been Recognized As a Leading Force of Social Progress." Written by Yan Xun, the article quoted Fang as lamenting that China's intellectuals "lack an independent mentality. They have not yet become an independent social force. . . . Chinese intellectuals as a social group have a very great weakness, namely a strong feudal mentality. They lack independence and a standard of value, always yield to power, and link their futures to an official career. . . . And once they become officials themselves, many intellectuals change their attitude from being absolutely obedient to higher levels to being absolutely conceited. They suppress and attack other intellectuals. These [traits] are in fact the opposite side of our 'feudal' mentality. . . ."

Fang went on to call on intellectuals to "remake" themselves and instead of being slavishly obedient to those above them, to "straighten out their bent backs." Then, as if he had already despaired of the older generation, he ended with an appeal to Chinese to "place their hopes in those younger intellectuals who are growing up during the nineteen-eighties."

"Many people in society complain that the young people of this generation lack ideals and that they think too much about themselves . . ." Fang told Yan. "But in a certain sense, it is precisely because of this that we place our hope in them; because intellectuals of the younger generation have their own independent intellects and have begun to show a strong desire to master their own fates. All this is exactly what our present era needs."

It was one thing to crusade for educational reforms, even to discuss democracy, human rights, or checks and balances in the abstract, but here was Fang Lizhi implicitly appealing to youthful intellectuals (as well as his academic peers) to straighten out their backs and form a powerful new check against Party power. This was a bold challenge indeed, for what Fang seemed to be implying was that the Party's failure to reform itself from within now justified pressure from without.

The Party's reaction to such challenges was predictable. It allowed for no notion of a loyal opposition. As Mao had said in *On the Correct Handling of Contradiction* in 1957, there are only two kinds of contradictions: those among the people (which may be resolved through discussion and dialogue) and those between the people and their enemies (which are antagonistic in nature and can only be resolved through the victory of one side over the other). What Fang was saying so clearly challenged the primacy of the Party that it fell perilously close to, if not within, the category of being an "antagonistic contradiction" in the Party's eyes.

Few other ranking figures in Chinese Communist history had carried the public dialogue on political reform as far as Fang; and in recent times, no one had so forcefully addressed this upcoming young generation of intellectuals, who, not having experienced the last great reign of political terror during the Cultural Revolution, had backs which were perhaps less bent than their elders.

A powerful chemistry now began operating between Fang and China's university students, who clearly delighted in not only his intelligence and candor but also his irreverence. Never had a leader spoken to them so unguardedly about Party pomposity, prejudice, favoritism, even corruption. Fang was even willing to name names. The Party might have tolerated his tweaking its tail over such apparent hypocrisies as a Constitution that guaranteed rights that it was not prepared to defend, but it could hardly countenance his outright attack on high-ranking officials.

In 1985, for instance, Fang publicly denounced the Vice-Mayor of Beijing, Zhang Baifa, for contriving to join a scientific delegation that had been invited to attend a conference on synchrotron radiation in New York State. Fang had learned of the case only because China's lone synchrotron was jointly operated by his own university and the Institute of High Energy Physics in Beijing. Fang's refusal to overlook this kind of junketing and featherbedding of the Party elite, and his willingness to bring such cases to the attention of student activists, made him an instant favorite of young intellectuals disgusted with such Pary favoritism.

"What is the real reason we have lost our ideals and our discipline?" he asked a group of Beida students as he got ready to take on Zhang Baifa. "The real reason is that many of our important Party leaders have failed to discipline themselves. I will give you an example. Recently there was a symposium on accelerators. Both Taiwan and mainland China were to be represented. To my mind, of course, the participants should have all been scholars and experts who were directly involved in this kind of work. . . . But many of those sent had no qualifications in physics and no familiarity with accelerators. Is this considered 'observing discipline'? Moreover, among those attending was Beijing's Vice-Mayor, Zhang Baifa. I have no idea what he was doing there. [Loud laughter] If you are talking about discipline, this is an excellent example of what it is not. [Applause] This kind of breakdown of discipline is the same thing as corruption. [Loud applause] In the future, as you learn more about our society, you will find that this sort of corruption is very commonplace. If we are really serious about discipline, we should start at the top. [Applause] There is a social malaise in our country today, and the primary reason for it is the poor example set by Party members. Unethical behavior by Party members is especially to blame. This is a situation that clearly calls for action on the part of intellectuals.

"I don't care if it's Zhang Baifa, or who it is, I will speak out. If a person in his position in a Western country behaved like this, he would be called back home and forced out of his job. We cannot ignore this sort of thing. When we see it happening, we cannot just let it pass. . . . Surely this is one important cause of our present lack of idealism and discipline."

The day after Fang criticized Zhang Baifa, he found that Gu Yu, wife of Hu Qiaomu, the hard-line Marxist theorist and Political Bureau member who was easily outraged by free-speaking intellectuals, had telephoned Guan Weiyan, president of Fang's university, to demand that he compel Fang to make an apology to the Beijing Party Committee for slurring the Vice-Mayor. When Guan refused to do so, an infuriated Hu Qiaomu was reported to have asked whom the administrators of the University of Science and Technology "reported to"—a thinly veiled threat that some higher authority could be drawn into the fracas to make life politically difficult for these reform-minded provincial mavericks. Indeed, a short while later, Bo Yibo, the powerful hard-line permanent Vice-Chairman of the Central Advisory Commission, criticized Fang's views as being not just anti-Marxist but far more radical than those of the student demonstrators who sought his counsel and encouragement. To these menacing warnings, which would have thoroughly intimidated most Chinese academics, Fang replied, "As for Zhang Baifa appropriating the conference seats that should have gone to the university, I just want to ask him what he knows about synchrotrons. Is he willing to take a test?"

As a result of his attack on the Vice-Mayor, Fang's planned January, 1986, departure for the Princeton Institute of Advanced Study was suddenly cancelled. It was not until three months later that Fang, still refusing to recant, was finally allowed to leave the country. The fact that he had not been more strenuously chastised, or even cashiered from his Party and university posts, was a sign of how permissive the political environment had become. It also suggested how wary liberal reform leaders were about any sort of crackdown against even the most outspoken intellectuals, lest this whole class of experts, upon whom reform and modernization depended, once again become so alarmed for their safety and so alienated from the Party that they withdrew their energies from the process of rebuilding China. From Fang's perspective, such victories over the system were heartening signs that China was at last becoming more tolerant of dissent, and they encouraged both his belief in the possibility of reform and his desire to press his critique further.

Fang, in fact, came to use the Zhang Baifa affair as a symbol of the kind of abuses he opposed in China's political system, where leaders remained unscrutinized by the people they theoretically represented. "Last year I made trouble after openly criticizing Zhang Baifa, the Vice-Mayor of Beijing," he told a group of students at Jiaotong University in Shanghai in the fall of 1986. "In August this year I criticized Hu Qiaomu by name at a press conference. No one did anything to me. All I can say now is that at a minimum, people should explore and make use of their rights. . . . Last year I criticized the Municipal Party Committee. This year I will criticize the Political Bureau. What I am saying is that at least I can now engage in some criticism. . . . Democracy means that I am allowed to express my views. If I criticize your opinions as being wrong, you may refute me. . . . Although it cannot be said that democracy has been realized, there are at least signs of a trend."

As appeals for political reform reached a crescendo that fall, Fang travelled to several more Chinese cities, making speeches, holding discussion groups, and giving interviews. His calls for democracy were bolder and more uncompromising than ever and his fearlessness more pronounced. In fact, during the month of November, particularly in student circles, one began to hear Fang Lizhi's name spoken more and more often. In Beijing, Hefei, Hangzhou, Ningbo, Shanghai, wherever he spoke, young people listened, recorded, and even hand-copied his talks, and sent them on to other friends and student groups all across

China, or even to colleagues studying in the United States and Europe. Chinese students, who had almost completely lost the kind of socialist idealism that had so distinguished them during earlier phases of the Chinese Communist Revolution, now seemed perched on the precipice of a whole new foreign belief system. In the ideological vacuum of the nineteen-eighties, they thirsted for someone and something to believe in. Just as this new generation of Chinese had come to worship the West for its appliances, style, culture, and technology, so they were now becoming entranced with its political ideas and isms. Nowhere was the threadbare nature of the appeal of Marxism–Leninism–Mao Zedong Thought more evident than in the way this key segment of a new generation of Chinese intellectuals found themselves drawn to the gospel of democracy as brought to them by Fang Lizhi. While there were some who found his views too extreme and disapproved of his unbridled criticisms, regarding him as being insufficiently patriotic, his frankness, courage in speaking out, independence of thought, and intellectual honesty impressed tens of thousands of students, and at the very least gave the Chinese world of political discourse a new and missing dimension.

When the Party repeatedly urged Fang to tone down his message, he refused, and even fired a salvo or two at Deng's sacred Four Cardinal Principles. When asked what he thought of them, he replied that although he realized they were "articles of faith among the political leadership," he preferred four different principles, namely "science, democracy, creativity, and independence," and then he went on to observe wryly that if his principles conflicted with those of the Party, it was only because the latter "advocated superstition instead of science, dictatorship instead of democracy, conservatism instead of creativity, and dependency rather than independence."

While Fang soon came to be China's most visible political dissident, he was not alone. There were other intellectuals, some older than Fang, who had suffered even more at the hands of the Party over the last two decades and who were just as disaffected as he.

|||||||||||||||||||||||||
Liu Binyan:
· —— A Second Kind ———————————— ·
of Loyalty

"There is a certain type of man or woman who in being honest and hardworking demonstrates one kind of loyalty to the Party and to the people. But there is another type who has his or her own individual insights, and in seeing defects in society wishes to criticize them. This type, too, demonstrates a kind of loyalty to the Party and to the people. Those of the first type are willing to give up material pleasure and even life itself. Those of the second type are not only willing to sacrifice their lives, but also to endure mental suffering. The second, I think, is the nobler kind of loyalty."

These words were written in 1985 by Liu Binyan, one of China's most revered writers, shortly after the appearance of his explosive piece of "literary reportage" "A Second Kind of Loyalty," which recounted the struggles of two loyal Chinese to remain true to their own principles in the face of Party criticism and censure. Liu's notion that there was a higher loyalty than the obedience that a member owed the Party was in direct conflict with long-articulated notions of discipline that the leadership of the Chinese Communist Party expected from its followers. In a 1938 speech to a plenary session of the Party Central Committee, Mao Zedong had clearly set forth this concept of Party loyalty: "We must affirm anew the discipline of the Party: 1) The individual is subordinate to the organization; 2) the minority is subordinate to the majority; 3) the lower level is subordinate to the higher level; and 4) the entire leadership is subordinate to the Central Committee. Whoever violates these articles of discipline disrupts Party unity."

Like Fang Lizhi, Liu Binyan had also used the relative openness of the nineteen-eighties to break ranks publicly with this strict notion of Party discipline and to speak his mind. Like his colleague, Liu was well acquainted with the rigidity of the Party, the fickleness of its ever-changing political lines, and the drastic extremes to which it could go to defend itself against enemies, both real and imagined. Liu wrote as fearlessly as Fang spoke for what he perceived to be in the best interest of China. But unlike Fang, into whose company fate was soon to cast him, Liu never took the final step of challenging either the primacy of the Party or the fitness of Marxism for China. While what he had to say was more revelatory in a concrete sense of the failures of Chinese Communism than all of Fang's analyses, Liu remained the ultimate critic from within. Although he repeatedly depicted the Party in his own writing as a mere shadow of the ideal institution he imagined it could be, Liu continued to express his allegiance to it and, in doing so, demonstrated exactly the second kind of loyalty about which he wrote.

Now in his early sixties, a tall man with broad shoulders, a silver mane of hair, a reserved manner, and a pensive smile, Liu Binyan was by 1987 probably the most widely read contemporary writer of nonfiction in China. He was born in 1925 into a middle-class family in Changchun, Manchuria, where his father worked as an interpreter for the Manchurian Railway, which was first operated by Russia and then Japan as part of the network of concessions that foreign powers had wrested from various weakened Chinese governments. As a firstborn son, Liu remembered being both pampered by his parents and forced at the early age of three to begin a rigorous course of study that was almost classical in its severity.

"I think that my father had hopes of raising me as some kind of a child prodigy, so from age three I was locked up at home to study my Chinese characters," wrote Liu in a short autobiographical portrait in 1979. "I never had a chance to laugh and play with other children in the streets. . . . First confined to our house, I later found myself circumscribed by the city in which we lived, and I grew up with very limited horizons, so that even today I am unable to recognize the most common flowers and plants."

After the Japanese invasion of Manchuria, in 1931, Liu's father lost his job with the railway and his family's fortunes rapidly declined. Like so many young Chinese of his generation, coming of age during Japan's invasion of China gave Liu a unique kind of social and political consciousness. "The broken-down condition of my country and the penurious state of my family both conspired to accelerate my awareness of the acute social contradictions around me," he wrote. "And so, a sense of nationalism developed side by side with a sense of dissatisfaction over the inequities I saw in society." In the years that followed, Liu never lost these two forms of social consciousness. In fact, they were ultimately to form the foundation of his muckraking style of reportage.

Unable to finish high school because of his family's poor financial condition, Liu sought escape in books. He read the literature of the May Fourth Movement period and some Russian works, hoping that they would help "diminish the corrupting influence of the decadent and vulgar" world around him. Longing as a teenager to read Pushkin and Tolstoy in the original, Liu started to teach himself Russian from a Russian dictionary. Then, wanting to read some of the works of Marx, which were only available to him in Japanese, he began studying that language too, and, as he casually adds, "Since my appetite for foreign languages had been aroused, I learned some English as well."

In the bitter later years of his life, during the political fire storms of the Maoist era, Liu was to savor deeply his self-taught linguistic abilities. "When all the other windows to the outside world had been closed off, only this one remained open, allowing me to peek out and get some small sense of what was happening in the world beyond," he wrote.

In 1943, sympathetic to the Communists' stress on social conscience and idealism, Liu began participating in underground Party activities and in 1944 became a member. In 1951, two years after Mao's triumph over the Nationalists, he was sent by the Party to Beijing to work as an editor and writer for the newspaper *China Youth News*.

During these years, Liu's interest in and concern over China's seemingly endless social and political problems gradually eclipsed his love of literature. "After 1951, journalism had almost completely captured my interest. Literature had become a sideline activity, and creative writing only a remote possibility in reserve for sometime in the future," he wrote. But Liu soon found that the life of a reporter for the Party-controlled press was "extremely narrow." His efforts to experiment with and expand the scope of rather prosaic newswriting, which came with a whole stultifying official language and form of its own, only ended up getting him in trouble. In 1955, because of his "small attempts to try out new things," he was accused of "anti-Party activity." Fortunately the charges were dropped several months later and Liu's name was cleared, but this affair set a pattern of antagonism between him and literary Party watchdogs that was to be repeated again and again throughout the rest of his life.

In May, 1956, Mao Zedong launched the Hundred Flowers Movement, presaging one of the freest periods of intellectual thought and one of the most prolific periods of writing in contemporary Chinese history. Still eager to break out of the confines of normal reporting, Liu responded to Mao's call by experimenting with a new style of journalism, which came to be called literary reportage, or *baogao wenxue*, an investigative form of fiction-based-on-fact writing, in certain respects similar to the New Journalism that hit the United States in the late nineteen-sixties.

As later described by Liu, literary reportage is a genre "halfway between journalism and literature . . . [which] offers much more freedom [than journalism] because its structure does not have to be so compact and well organized, and it can encompass a rather free blend of factual events, fictional images, and one's own thoughts."

Literary reportage allowed Liu not only to combine his love of literature and creative writing with journalism, but it also gave him a means of writing about corruption, hypocrisy, dehumanization, and bureaucratism in society and the Party (subjects that subsequently became his stock-in-trade). At the same time, it allowed him to avoid having to name names of specific people, and particularly Party leaders, which usually would have been sufficient cause to keep a piece of journalism out of print altogether, and would probably have ruined his life as a writer in the bargain.

The first of the three major pieces Liu published at the time in this style was a novella entitled *On the Bridge Construction Site*. It appeared in the April, 1956, issue of the prestigious national journal *People's Literature*, while Liu himself was attending a journalists' conference in Poland, and created an immediate sensation. It contrasted two emblematic figures: Zeng Gang, a young, idealistic, courageous, and hardworking engineer who represented all those ideals for which Liu believed the Chinese Communist Party should stand, and Lo Lizheng, an older work brigade leader who was self-serving, haughty to his inferiors, obsequious to his superiors—in short, an embodiment of everything that Liu held to be oppressive about China's bureaucratic mentality.

In the story Liu related a series of actual events that he had learned about while on a trip to Lanzhou, in Gansu province. When a flood hits a bridge construction site on the Yellow River, the young engineer Zeng Gang, without waiting for orders from above, boldly takes action and saves a section of the uncompleted bridge. Lo Lizheng, on the other hand, fearful of making a mistake and being criticized, does nothing on his own, thereby allowing massive destruction of another part of the project. For having taken such decisive, independent action, Zeng is criticized for not having first sought directives from the Party, found guilty of "arrogance and self-satisfaction," and demoted. For having done nothing but maintain Party discipline, Lu is allowed to remain in office uncriticized.

The less than optimistic ending of *On the Bridge Construction Site* was enough in itself to cause a sensation among readers who had otherwise been fed a steady diet of upbeat conclusions in which model proletarian heroes at one with the Party invariably triumphed over all adversity. Otherwise, Liu's work still retained many of the features of Chinese journalistic (and fictional) writing of the time. From its abundantly proletarian title, naive didacticism, and innocent but righteous indignation, to the way in which real emotions were stylized, one could still see through Liu the incipient rebel to Liu the still-faithful Communist journalist. His writing style was simple, without either literary pretension or a hint of indirection, and lacked even a touch of sarcasm, cynicism, or irony. His early works revealed a writer who, despite his attacks on the Party's bureaucratic work style, still ardently believed in the ideals of Chinese Communism and the Party system—a trait that was to become as much a hallmark of Liu's style over the next thirty years as his social conscience. Liu's heroes might struggle against shortcomings in the system, but they never struggled against the system itself.

In the June and October, 1956, issues of *People's Literature*, Liu published another novella, called *Inside Story*, a semi-autobiographical tale of an idealistic young woman reporter, Huang Jiaying, who struggles with an increasing sense of futility to get her investigative reports revealing the hardships of ordinary people accepted by her newspaper's timid editors. She is repeatedly thwarted by the inertia and caution of an editorial bureaucracy fearful of publishing anything giving even the appearance of running counter to official policy. Chastised for her emotional involvement with her subjects, Huang ends up totally alienated from her fellow workers at the paper. She views them as trapped in a propaganda mill that is endlessly turning out meaningless articles "full of slogans and orders like 'forge ahead vigorously,' 'resolutely persevere,' and 'actively respond,' while stories concerning the lives of the masses themselves, their demands, and their suggestions were so pitifully scarce."

Not even in fiction can she find an escape. "Why was it that life and characters in so many novels appeared so ordinary, drab, and simple?" she wonders. "It seemed that people had lost their feelings of pleasure, joy, sorrow, and anger after Liberation. They had all suddenly become so polite and cheerful. They all attended meetings, went to the office, and left the office with perfect punctuality. Some novels seemed no more than a chronicle of events in a factory. . . . Was this the true nature of things?"

Angry and dispirited, but hoping at least to be admitted to the Party, Huang works on until even this hope is dashed due to her alleged lack of respect for "leadership, organization, and discipline." "The most terrible thing that can befall a Communist," laments the omniscient narrator at the story's end, "is to lose one's spirit."

But just like Fang Lizhi at the time, Liu was unable to imagine China without the leadership of the Communist Party. Like so many other idealistic Chinese intellectuals, his natural inclination was to believe rather than to doubt. Indeed, in spite of the travails that were to follow in his life, he never completely lost either his faith or his desire, first seen in these early works of his, to believe in the basic goodness of the Revolution and the Party. As he wrote of this period two and a half decades later, "For a thirty-one-year-old youth, China in the nineteen-fifties was already more than confusing enough in itself, while my naïveté and yearning to believe still bordered on the childlike. Twenty-odd years later, when my own mind was much more sophisticated and the growing confusion of the realities of China had irrevocably overtaken me, I could not then help but look back and sigh regretfully at my own excessive naiveté."

It was in June, 1957, that the "confusion of the realities of China" first began to overtake Liu as Mao suddenly launched an Anti-Rightist Campaign. The year before Mao had declared war on sparrows (which he accused of eating grain meant for human consumption) by exhorting Chinese throughout the country to beat gongs and pots until the birds fell exhausted from the sky. Now, by inciting the broad masses of the people to expose and criticize as bourgeois and rightist all those who had expressed any criticism of China's "great socialist revolution," Mao turned on the very intellectuals he had just so magnanimously encouraged to speak their minds. As one who had dared speak out in his writing, Liu was quickly attacked, becoming part of what he later referred to as a "whole generation doomed to misfortune."

On July 8, 1957, when Liu was informed that he had been labelled a rightist, his whole world caved in. Like tens of thousands of fellow intellectuals, he was denounced, his salary was reduced to less than one-seventh its previous level, and he was expelled from the Party he still loved. "I lost everything," Liu told an interviewer from the *Far Eastern Economic Review* in July, 1986. "I was deprived of all rights. I became a peasant."

That summer and fall, the press savagely attacked him. "Like all rightists, Liu Binyan repudiates the achievements of our socialist construction," delcared an article in *China Youth News*. "With tinted glasses, he scrutinizes and deliberately exaggerates our defects, frequently spreading the mistaken notion that serious problems exist in our society, and that society as a whole is a morass of darkness. . . . He spares no effort in compiling evidence of 'problems' and the 'negative aspects of things.' It is his purpose to use these things as a cleaver with which to mutilate the Party and socialism."

Another article claimed that Liu had imbued the hero of *The Inside Story* with a "hideous anti-Party soul" and condemned his writing as "rubbish" and "poisonous weeds." Liu himself was vilified for having rejected socialist realism and "for propounding such notions as 'exposing the dark side of life.' " In such attacks one can discern the bitter legacy of China's humiliating past—the sensitivity to any suggestion that its new Communist society had flaws or weaknesses, even if the suggestion was made constructively by a loyal member of the Party itself.

In the late nineteen-fifties, during the period of the Great Leap Forward and the communization of agriculture, one of the most turbulent times of Chinese Communist history, Liu was humiliated to the final degree by being labelled a class enemy and was sent down to live and work in the remote countryside of Shanxi and Shandong provinces. To pass the time, he continued his language studies, even memorizing a whole English-Japanese dictionary. As he wrote of those first few years of exile, "Although I was aware that even if my rightist label were to be removed, no publication would ever dare publish articles bearing my name . . . I never gave up the dream of writing." But five years later Liu had surrendered even this dream. "The clamor for class struggle [in which those assigned bad bourgeois "class backgrounds" were "struggled against" by those with good proletarian "class backgrounds" in endless and sometimes violent public sessions organized by the Party] totally drowned out my dreams. Having given up hope for my own political future, and for the future of art and literature in China, I made up my mind to wash my hands of writing."

As painful as they were, however, these years proved seminal ones in Liu's life. "In my own personal experience," he said in a speech to the Fourth National Congress of Literary and Art Workers, held in November, 1979, "the most unforgettable years were 1958–60, when I shared a bed and sometimes even a quilt with poor peasants. The things I saw in the villages, and the grievances I heard from the peasants, were all vastly different from what was being reported by the authorities and the press.

"Whom was I to believe? I had resolved at the time to obey the Party and to remold myself from the bone marrow outward. But there was no avoiding the fact that objective material things were more powerful than subjective spiritual ones. However great my will to reform, it was no match for the continual onslaught of certain obvious incongruities. For instance, the higher authorities told us that our poor impoverished gully of a village ought to build a zoo and a fountain. Now, what were peasants who hardly ate meat all year supposed to feed to lions and tigers? With no water source (man and beast alike still drank rainwater), how were they to build a fountain?

"A struggle began to rage deep inside me: How could two diametrically opposed 'truths' co-exist in the world? The longings of the peasants were one truth, and the policies of the higher-ups and the propaganda in the newspapers were quite another. Which should I follow?" At this time Liu decided if he ever again faced a conflict between these two opposing demands, he would "follow the interests and demands of the people."

It was not until March, 1966, that Liu had his "rightist cap" removed and was rehabilitated by the Party. A mere two months later, however, largely on the basis of some entries he had made in a personal diary which had been surreptitiously copied by an informer, he was again criticized as a rightist, and when the Cultural Revolution began that summer he was once more denounced and ultimately incarcerated. Imprisoned for two years in complete isolation, he was finally exiled in 1969 to a so-called May Seventh Cadre School (one of the rural camps set up to re-educate intellectuals and Party cadres through manual labor). This time his exile in southern Henan province lasted eight years, a time that he later described as intellectually "like being in a complete vacuum."

Not only was Liu unable to write, but his family life was completely disrupted. "My wife and I were in the same camp, but we couldn't speak to each other even when we met," Liu told an interviewer in 1986. "When my children came to visit, they were not allowed to speak to me. During the day we worked in the fields, and sometimes we worked through the night as well. When the weather was bad, when the wind blew and the rain fell, the 'good' people [those who were accused of ordinary rather than political crimes] were allowed to do political study, but we had to do double work."

As he recalled in 1985 to the founding members of the Chinese journal *Selections from Legal Literature*, "The distinguishing characteristic of this ultra-leftist line was the belittling of human beings, the trampling down of human beings, and the humiliation and suspicion of human beings." Even though at times Liu claimed he "lost all hope in the future and even thought of suicide," he somehow managed to survive and, years later, even to recognize positive aspects to these trying experiences. "There were several roads in front of me in 1957, and being branded a rightist was the best way to go. Suppose I hadn't said anything at the time and hadn't been branded a rightist. Then, it is true I could have lived an easy life and gotten through those twenty to thirty years in an extremely peaceful but mediocre manner. But I would have accomplished nothing. Certainly, I would not envy such a life.

"The second possibility was that I might have said a few things too vociferously, which still would not have gotten me labelled a rightist, so that I would have been able to remain a Party member and to go on writing. When the situation moderated in 1962, I might have written some more articles of a critical nature. But then in 1966 [when the Cultural Revolution started], my old crimes and my new crimes would have been lumped together and I would have been hounded to death for sure.

"Another possibility could have been that when the Cultural Revolution broke out, I might have supported it, participated in one of the factions, and put up big-character posters. In that case, I would have fallen in with Zhang Chunqiao and ended up like Yao Wenyuan [both members of the Gang of Four who are still in prison]. So no matter how I now ponder it, I think that the best thing was to have been a rightist."

In 1979, twenty-two years after his troubles began, Liu Binyan once again had his name cleared by the Party, had his Party membership restored, and was even given the prestigious job of reporter at the *People's Daily*. But to this day he is tormented by recurrent nightmares.

"Anybody who stays in the same room with me knows that I have nightmares almost every night. Sometimes I dream I am starving and I want something to eat, but there is nothing. Then I appear on the street naked. Everyone is staring at me as if at a ghost. . . . Sometimes someone will curse a dog behind me, cursing very loudly, and I will think that they are cursing me, because that is how I was treated."

During these first few post–Gang of Four years, the whole Chinese literary world began to come alive again. By 1980 the old Maoist slogan "Literature in the service of politics" had been replaced by the softer and vaguer notion of "Literature in the service of the people and socialism." For the first time in two decades, journalists, novelists, and poets began to write, however hesitatingly, about the dark rather than just the bright side of Chinese life. Having lasted through so much suffering and persecution, Liu had decided that "there was no way back," and he himself began once again to write: "I thought it over and decided that I had to speak out. If I did not, then what was I doing in the Party? What would it mean, then, to be a Communist? What would my life mean?" Just as before, Liu was possessed by an almost messianic quality to speak out against political injustice. In November, 1979, less than a year after he had been exonerated and rehabilitated, while attending the Fourth National Congress of Literary and Art Workers in Beijing, Liu reminded delegates that "literature is a mirror. When the mirror shows us things in life that are not very pretty or fall short of our ideals, it is wrong to blame the mirror. Instead we should root out and destroy those conditions that disappoint us. Mirrors show us the true appearance of things, and literary mirrors speed the progress of society. Smashing a mirror is no way to make an ugly person beautiful, nor is it a way to make a problem evaporate."

It was during this heady time of new freedom that Liu went back to his native Manchuria to investigate the case of a notoriously corrupt Party cadre named Wang Shouxin who had risen to power during the Cultural Revolution in Heilongjiang province. The result was *People or Monsters?*, which, like Liu's earlier writings, was done in the genre of literary reportage and, like Liu's earlier works, first appeared in *People's Literature*. Published in September, 1979, his revelations of how a single Party-branch secretary came to power in Bin County and fashioned an illegal empire through influence, bribery, corruption, and graft—including the embezzlement of large amounts of money from a small fuel company—comprised the most powerful indictment against the Communist Party ever published in China. As Liu wrote in *People or Monsters?*, "Party cadres themselves gradually became transformed into parasites who devoured the people's flesh and blood and who blighted the socialist system like an infestation of canker-worms."

While readers were evidently shocked both by Liu's disclosures and by the uncompromising quality of his language, what was even more shocking was that a writer had been able to publish such a story at all. Liu's new work proved so damning and subversive not because of its exposure of a single instance of corruption within the Party—which came as no surprise to most Chinese—but because of his revelation that such activities had gone on as a matter of common practice for years and years without anyone in the Party calling attention to them, much less doing something about them.

"Why was it that even now, three and a half years after the fall of the Gang of Four, this half-human, half-monstrous behavior could continue unabated under the leadership of the Communist Party in Bin County?" asked Liu. "Leafing through the minutes of the County Party Committee meetings from 1972 onward is an intensely depressing experience. All sorts of problems are discussed: military conscription, family planning, criminal sentences, sowing plans—but hardly any mention is made of the problems of the Party itself. The Communist Party regulated everything, but it would not regulate the Communist Party."

Liu could easily have branded Wang Shouxin, who was finally executed for her crimes, as one bad apple in an otherwise sound barrel—and ended on just the sort of note of rose-tinted optimism that had characterized other Party exposés in China. Instead Liu closed his investigation as follows: "The case of Wang Shouxin's corruption has been cracked, and this was no doubt a result of the great political changes that have taken place in China since the smashing of the Gang of Four. But how many of the social conditions that gave rise to this case have really changed? Isn't it true that Wang Shouxins of all shapes and sizes, in all corners of the land, still continue to devour the substance of socialism, continue to corrupt the body of the Party, and continue to evade punishment by the dictatorship of the proletariat? People, be on guard! It is still too early to be celebrating victory."

People or Monsters? hit China like a thunderclap. Copies of the September issue of *People's Literature* in which it appeared instantly sold on the street for many times their face value. It was reprinted in newspapers and broadcast from radio stations throughout China, as well as in Taiwan. After the *Heilongjiang Daily* refused to reprint the article (because local officials, offended by all the bad publicity, accused Liu of inaccuracy), supporters at Heilongjiang University moved into the breach and printed twenty thousand copies of the report. Nonetheless, so precious did copies of Liu's article soon become that they were sometimes even clipped out of newspapers and sold in the streets or passed around from person to person until they disintegrated.

"The repercussions it evoked among the people, some of whom were high officials, were far beyond my wildest expectations," wrote Liu. "It provoked such a raging torrent of reaction among some of the local leading officials at the county, prefectural, and provincial level that the commotion did not die down until a year later."

Liu became such a popular hero that some people even began referring to him as Liu Qingtian, or Liu the Just, after the upright Song Dynasty official Bao Qingtian known for his Confucian moral rectitude and willingness to right miscarriages of justice wherever he found them. Indeed, despite his Marxist loyalties, in a certain sense Liu himself was very Confucian. Not only did he view writing as a means of imbuing society with a moral sense, but he also seemed to aspire to become an updated, if proletarianized, version of a Confucian "gentleman" (*junzi*), whose power came neither from might nor threats of force, but from the example of rectitude he set as a cultivated, moral being acting with righteousness. The publishing of *People or Monsters?* did indeed confer on Liu enormous power of moral suasion, as well as a massive quotient of national notoriety. What was paradoxical about Liu's situation was that his new power had been conferred on him not by the Party hierarchy but by his readers, out of appreciation for his truthfulness.

The most obvious emblems of this appreciation were the sackfuls of letters that began to pour into his office at the *People's Daily* and into his home. Most were paeans of praise or expressions of thanks; others detailed similar cases of corruption elsewhere in China that the supplicants desperately hoped Liu, "the good official," would help rectify with the power of his pen.

"There is the fate of one person or an important event in each envelope," Liu told an interviewer. "Often they [the letters] are about the dark side and negative things. Although now my position is good and my life is good, I have not been cut off from these common peasants, the workers, and the intellectuals. When they have been treated unjustly, they come to me."

"As long as we see your writing, we know that China has hope," wrote one admirer. "I don't know how it happened, but while I was reading your *People or Monsters?* I actually squeezed the tea cup I was holding so hard that it shattered in my hand," wrote another in a long and laudatory letter. "The pieces of broken glass cut a deep gash in my palm, but I didn't even feel pain. In fact, it brought a strange sense of euphoria. . . . In study time, after work, I read your *People or Monsters?* aloud to the fourteen workers on our shift with feelings of enormous excitement. Among them were women with children, busy young people, and older workers who were exhausted and should have been resting. But not one of them got up and left during the entire three-hour reading. In fact, they called other people to come over and join us. That is how much they wanted to listen. I am not saying this to flatter you, for that would be a waste of time. I am saying this simply because I was asked by these fellow workers to write and congratulate you. What we mean to convey is this: We hope that our comrade Liu Binyan will continue to speak the truth on our behalf. We do not wish to hear any more lies and deception. . . .

"We do not know you," the writer of this unsolicited letter concluded, "but should you ever need to find us, we will of course protect you and care for you, because you have been singing out the song that is in all of our hearts."

"The encouragement, care, and warm support I received from these friends of every age group, social class, and occupation offset by far all the threats, abuse, and attempts to interfere with my work," Liu wrote the following year. "For me the message from this experience was that what I was doing was needed by the Party and the people. Therefore, no matter how blunt my pen might be, I decided to go on writing, even if it only left a few scraps from this great era behind for history."

When he addressed the Fourth National Congress of Literary and Art Workers, Liu made an impassioned plea for literature to be reinstated as the conscience of society. His speech, typically forthright and guileless, articulated the pent-up, unspoken feelings of his generation of Chinese intellectuals. "There are only two ways in which the feudal, patriarchal style of leadership supports and extends itself: One is by coercion and command; the other is by attack and retaliation. And, because they have in contemporary political life become common ways in which a minority can subdue the masses, both of these methods warrant our closest vigilance. 'Power corrupts, and absolute power corrupts absolutely.' Without the supervision of the people, a good person will turn bad and an honest official will turn corrupt."

There was another theme to his speech as well, one reflecting an uncommon stance for an intellectual in China in 1979. Unlike many other intellectuals who, after the bitter experience of being "sent down" to the countryside during the Anti-Rightist Campaign and the Cultural Revolution, wished only to escape from politics and "from the masses," Liu reaffirmed his commitment as a writer to politics and to the people with such ardor that it sometimes appeared as if he were more of a Maoist than Mao himself. "Looking back over the last twenty years or more, I feel we [China's intellectuals] have gained certain things in spite of our losses," he told the delegates. "Fate has brought us into intimate contact with the lowest levels of the laboring masses. For a time our joys and worries became the same as theirs, and our hopes were no different. This experience allowed us to see, to hear, and to feel for ourselves the things that others have been unable to see, hear, or feel. . . .

"We must answer the people's questions. We have no right to be auditors in the courtroom of history. The people are the judges, as well as the plaintiffs. We must help supply them with scripts. But before we offer answers, we must first learn."

Remaining true to his belief that literature should "delve into life," even when it sometimes interfered with the established order, Liu went on to say, "Writers should face life squarely and listen carefully to the voice of the people. The policies of the Party must pass the test of practice and be corrected when they are wrong. When faced with two kinds of truth . . . we writers must maintain a strong sense of responsibility to the people in reaching our conclusions."

Even after his meteoric rise to the Chinese equivalent of media celebrity, Liu continued to try to "speak for the people," to resist, as he said, "that tendency in literature and art to evade the contradictions and conflicts in reality, and to cosmeticize life." His keenly felt sense of social responsibility manifested itself in almost everything he wrote. If the burden of accepting this responsibility sometimes put him at odds with the Party, it was a price he was willing to pay. In fact, more often than not since 1979, his articles were too controversial even for his own paper, the *People's Daily*, and appeared instead in publications that were not quite so directly under Party control.

In a literary commentary published in 1979 and entitled "The Call of the Age," Liu wrote, "Life has to be described as it actually is if literature is to play any part in making it better. There is no way that a writer can be safe. Anyway, during the Cultural Revolution, those who had only written about the bright side of life ended up being persecuted just as mercilessly as those writers who had been more critical."

Even in the relative openness that followed Deng's rise to power, there were limits, and Liu frequently pushed beyond them. None of his declarations of fealty to the Party could compensate for the sense of betrayal that some leaders evidently felt because of his depictions of Party cadres as undemocratic, venal, bureaucratic, and self-serving. Even though he was ultimately elected Vice-Chairman of the Chinese Writers' Association, in 1984 (the first time in the association's history that such an election had been held democratically), and even though such liberal reformist leaders as Vice-Premier Wan Li and Party General Secretary Hu Yaobang were reputed to be his supporters, it was common knowledge that many hard-liners in the Central Committee would have liked nothing better than to silence Liu.

"Some people have said that so-and-so is my protector. But I don't have any protector," Liu commented in 1986, alluding to rumors circulating in Beijing that his political survival was closely connected to Hu's patronage. "I haven't seen Comrade Hu Yaobang for at least eight years. The last time I *really* saw him was in 1958. . . . At the final banquet of the Fourth National Congress of Literary and Art Workers we went over and toasted him. I suppose that also counts as seeing him. But I've never seen him since then. I believe that my greatest protector, my most reliable protector, is simply the Chinese people!"

In 1982 Liu received permission to visit the United States, where, along with his wife, Zhu Hong, he attended the International Writing Program at the University of Iowa. Of his visit to the United States, he facetiously said, "It improved my understanding about newspaper journalism in that country quite a lot. My first impression there was that people did not consider newspapers as tools or as propaganda. In fact, the expression 'tool' in America is considered a very derogatory one. At the same time, the television stations, the radio broadcasts, and newspapers actually do fulfill the function of 'tools' or 'propaganda' very effectively. We [writers in China] are constantly talking about serving as a mouthpiece of the Party, about being a 'tool' for 'propaganda.' But the reality of the matter is that our propaganda doesn't come anywhere close to achieving the effect it ought to."

In April, 1983, Liu joined a delegation of Chinese intellectuals to Europe, and in an interview in Paris he appeared positively optimistic about the way Deng's reforms had improved the political climate for intellectuals in China. "Before, as a member of the Communist Party, you could only speak to other members of the Party. Now, you can speak with whomever you wish, even with foreigners. In fact, you can express yourself more easily in China than in the Soviet Union." In 1984 Liu was allowed to leave China again, this time for another trip back to the United States.

All the while he continued to write articles exposing official wrongdoing. But, by far, Liu's most daring work was a trilogy of literary reportage pieces: *A Second Kind of Loyalty*, *My Diary*, and *Incomplete Burial*. Publication of the first installment, *A Second Kind of Loyalty*, was initially held up because of certain official objections, but it did finally appear in March, 1985, in the first issue of the Beijing journal *Pioneer*.

The two real-life protagonists of these works were Chen Shizhong, a mechanical engineer, and Ni Yuxian, a PLA soldier, who had not only dared to question the disastrous leftist agricultural policies of the Party in the nineteen-fifties and sixties, but had also risked writing Chairman Mao letters of criticism. Ni's criticism of the Party continued into the nineteen-eighties, when he finally succeeded in getting to the United States, where he openly repudiated the Party and became active in the democracy movement among Chinese students.

Perhaps the more emblematic of Liu's two heroes in *A Second Kind of Loyalty* was Chen Shizhong, who upon returning to China in 1963 after studying mechanical engineering in the Soviet Union became so disillusioned with what he saw in his country that he decided to write directly to both Chairman Mao and Premier Nikita Khrushchev, begging them to bury their differences (the Sino-Soviet rift had erupted in 1958) and to get on with the process of nation building. When neither leader replied, Chen wrote a second statement, which he tried to hand-deliver by forcing his way into the Soviet embassy in Beijing. Not surprisingly, he was immediately arrested and imprisoned. Determined to be heard, even from his jail cell, he set about writing a thirty-thousand-character letter to Chairman Mao that he entitled "Admonishing the Party."

It was a beguiling, devastating indictment of Chinese Communism. But, like so many other letters of grievance, it never saw the light of day—that is, not until Liu Binyan, who had been sought out by Chen for help in clearing the name of a fellow detainee in a labor reform camp, heard Chen's harrowing life story and quoted from his letter to Mao in *A Second Kind of Loyalty*.

Writing as if he were chatting with a friend, Chen alternately tries to chide, beg, plead with, and flatter Mao. "It is my belief that the line of the Party Central Committee . . . while achieving great successes, has both domestically and internationally led to a whole string of serious mistakes, some of which have to do with matters of principle and direction. It goes without saying that for a ruling Party or an individual to make this or that kind of mistake during the long course of history is nothing unusual. But what is most frightening is that the Central Committee of the Chinese Communist Party hasn't yet become aware of its own serious mistakes. . . ."

What appealed to Liu was not just Chen's willingness to point up Party errors without regard to personal risk, but his concern with the integrity of the Party itself, whose leading role he was criticizing. In this sense, perhaps Liu saw Chen as being similar to himself.

The leadership's refusal to acknowledge its mistakes "worries me deeply," Chen wrote Mao. "If I kept this opinion to myself, I wouldn't be a close friend of the Party." The reasons for the mistakes of the Party were many, continued Chen, "but the primary one is the veneration accorded Chairman Mao and the personality cult that has grown up around him. Basically, the point is this: You [Mao] don't allow criticism of your shortcomings or mistakes, and in the face of more penetrating criticisms of principle, you immediately turn hostile and attack ruthlessly. If things continue this way, who will dare speak the truth? After a long period of this sort of thing, how will you ever be able to hear other viewpoints?"

Not content to stop with this prophetic indictment of Mao, Chen went on to admonish the Great Helmsman directly: "Each sentence you speak, indeed almost every word you utter, is regarded as absolute truth. You allow compliance but never opposition. . . . However, of all your errors, there is none comparable to that of believing yourself to be eternally incapable of making mistakes. The phrase 'Marxism fears no criticism' falls blithely from your lips, even while the facts point to the contrary. There is no need to look into the distant past; just from 1957 to the present, what critic of Mao Zedong Thought has come to any good end?"

As in Liu's own remonstrations with figures in authority, one sensed in Chen's eagerness to be heard the voice of a child pleading for reason and understanding from the father figure of the Party. But Chen could also preach. "Dear Chairman Mao, please repent before it is too late!" he implored. Then, lest Mao become infuriated by his entreaties and banish his supplicant from his sight before he has had a chance to finish his memorial, he begs Mao: "Please hold your anger for a moment. . . . The reason I feel that the veneration personally accorded to you is the worst kind of disaster for our Party and country is based totally on conclusions I have reached from the grimness of the objective reality that I have seen around me. . . . I have seen your inscription 'Learn from Lei Feng' [a model soldier much touted by the Party at that time for his obedience]. Everyone is studying Lei Feng. I admit that Lei Feng has many fine qualities, and of course I ought to learn from him. But I think Lei Feng is far from being a perfect model. He has serious, even fatal, defects . . . [namely] that he only knows how to follow orders from above; he does not know how to make decisions on his own that would enable him to resist the mistakes of the authorities. . . .

"I feel that this attitude is incorrect, unscientific, and replete with grave dangers that even you cannot foresee, because it presupposes that you will always be correct; that not only what you have already said or are saying is absolutely correct, and that Lei Feng should follow it to the letter, but that even those things that you have not yet said will be correct, and that Lei Feng must also follow those to the letter too. If this isn't blind obedience, what is it?

"Consider this: If every member of the Party, and even every citizen of the entire nation, were all actually to become Lei Fengs, what kind of a predicament would we find ourselves in? The social atmosphere and its mores would no doubt change entirely. But if you yourself made one mistake, if you as a representative of the Party Central Committee made a bad decision, who would there be to help you correct it? If everyone were like Lei Feng, there wouldn't be anyone around who would even dare consider making a criticism. How could there be any suggestion of uncovering mistakes and correcting them? But there you are, appealing to everyone to act like Lei Feng! Obviously, all your earlier promises that channels of communication would remain open and free of blame to all those who would address you are just empty talk!"

By way of conclusion, Chen wrote Mao, "After you have finished reading this letter, there is a possibility that, moved to fury, you will order my execution. In the forty-two-year history of the Chinese Communist Party, examples of this kind have certainly not been few."

As Liu Binyan depicted Chen to Chinese readers in 1985, he was a hero precisely because he was so willing to confront the obvious risk of sticking to his principles, even to the point of admonishing the great leader himself, at a time when Mao was treated like a deity in China. In Chen's case, the consequence of such behavior had not been execution but thirteen years of jail; in Liu's case, it was twenty-two years of exile and incarceration. It should be noted that by calling attention to the life of a person like Chen, as well as by printing his very critical letter to Mao, even at a time when the Chairman's legacy had been partially discredited, Liu was throwing down nothing short of a brazen challenge to every leader in the Party, all of whom still publicly espoused Marxism–Leninism–Mao Zedong Thought as truth. After all, Liu's report implicitly declared an open season of criticism on all Party mistakes and leaders, not just the dead Mao and his policies.

"Although Chen Shizhong has done many Lei Feng-style good deeds, he is still not, after all, a Lei Feng-type person," commented Liu admiringly. "If Chen Shizhong had limited his activities to the 'Learn from Lei Feng' arena, he would have offended no one. . . . Yet he continually overstepped this boundary and so could not help but upset his own equilibrium as well as that of those around him."

Of course, Liu risked upsetting his own equilibrium by associating himself with a "hero" such as Chen, for, as he pointed out, "The natural psychological response would be to say that Chen Shizhong is an 'oddball,' not normal. Thinking it over, one might even come to the conclusion that this guy is at least mentally ill. . . . It couldn't be that he doesn't realize the consequences he's calling down on himself by acting this way, could it?"

Liu's belief was actually quite the contrary: "There are two kinds of loyalty in this world; one exposes itself to risks while the other is safe, and Chen Shizhong and Ni Yuxian chose the former. For twenty years they travelled down their own paths, making ultimate sacrifices. Isn't this enough to prove which kind of loyalty is more precious?"

Because Liu's piece so undermined the notion of Party discipline, many Party leaders wished to move quickly to stamp out the heretical notion of two kinds of loyalty before it could spread. So the journal in which the second installment of Liu's trilogy, *My Diary*, was to appear was closed down. But the publishing situation was at that point so chaotic and decentralized that this was not quite the end of the matter. Soon, like Bo Yang's *Ugly Chinaman*, Liu's pieces began popping up elsewhere. For instance, in Xi'an, the journal *Prose Gazette* soon came out with its own edition of *A Second Kind of Loyalty*, quickly selling more than a million copies, and not incidentally making a good deal of money, before it, too, was ordered shut down. By that time newspapers in the remotest regions of China had begun to tout Liu's subversive notion of a second kind of loyalty. In October, 1986, for example, even the *Guangxi Daily*, in distant southwestern Nanning, spoke reverentially about the way Chen Shizhong's loyalty was "characterized by independent thinking, a sense of social responsibility, as well as a sense of the responsibility of the individual to society and history." It spoke of this new kind of loyalty as a "truth obtained through serious examination of the Cultural Revolution," and as a "virtue all revolutionaries should possess." It went on to counsel Chinese, "As we reform our political system, build a democratic society, and create a harmonious social atmosphere, we must not ignore . . . or abandon the concept of a 'second kind of loyalty.' "

Even Wan Li, the liberal reform-minded Vice-Premier, provided an intimation of how deeply split the Party leadership could become over the question of intellectual freedom and freedom of the press when he spoke at the National Symposium of Soft Science Research in the summer of 1986 and memorialized Liu's conception of loyalty, reportedly saying, "The reforms currently under way in China require not only the first kind of loyalty epitomized by Lei Feng, but also the 'second kind of loyalty' demonstrated by Chen Shizhong."

By the end of 1986, it must sometimes have seemed to hard-line Party leaders as if the Liu Binyan phenomenon had acquired a dangerous and uncontrollable life of its own. They were alarmed not only by Liu's writing, but by the fact that, like Fang Lizhi, as the political climate thawed, Liu, too, had started going around the country making more and more speeches in which he attacked Party malfeasance and unabashedly advocated democracy and freedom of the press. In October during one such speech, in which he sounded very much like Fang himself, he told the founding meeting of the new journal *Selections from Legal Literature*, "In European revolutionary history, the first step in the fight for the establishment of a constitution was freedom of speech. Of course, freedom of speech . . . wasn't obtained as a result of someone [from above] granting it as a favor. It wasn't just a matter of some king being particularly enlightened or some chief minister being especially generous and just announcing that from this day on people will be permitted to publish newspapers, and from this day on speech will be freely granted. It wasn't like that. Freedom of speech was created by the people themselves. It was only after it became a reality that governments were forced to recognize it." And

Party watchdogs could not have been pleased when he went on to criticize press controls in China by saying, "In West Germany, Japan, and the United States, newspapers are constantly reporting on various crises and powerful adversaries of their countries, and saying that if such and such a measure is not taken, then such and such is going to happen. . . . [But] the tradition of our Party, for who knows what reason, is that of being very fearful of letting anyone see our difficulties. . . . Our newspapers and news broadcasts put out only hypnotic lullabies: An electrical power station is completed; a factory has gone from operating at a loss to profitability. . . . I think it would not do any harm to have a little sense of crisis. . . . Let everyone take a look; let everyone get a little nervous, get a little more active, and have a little more sense of urgency . . . our soporific atmosphere is a little too stifling."

Hard-line Party leaders were also opposed to the upcoming gathering that Liu was organizing with Fang and Xu Liangying, a research professor at the Chinese Academy of Sciences' Institute of the History of Science, to commemorate the thirtieth anniversary of the Anti-Rightist Campaign. The three had already written a letter in October, 1986, inviting a wide group of Chinese intellectuals who had suffered during this campaign to attend a conference the following February, the object of which was to collect oral histories of their experiences and to begin at last a dialogue on how this political nightmare had come about. The results were to be published later in book form.

In choosing to delve into the relations between the people and the Party, which was itself supposed to be the embodiment of the people, Liu had hit on officialdom's tenderest nerve. In a way that was always implicit, his exposés challenged the notion that the Party and the people were indivisible; and, needless to say, even though he claimed to be writing in the service of the Party—to help it cast out its own demons and purify itself—many cadres felt scandalized by his revelations, not to mention the upwelling of popular support that his work produced. By 1985, the Central Discipline and Inspection Committee of the Party had even started an investigation of Liu's dissidence.

But Liu himself vigorously eschewed any suggestion that he was a "dissident," a word for which, interestingly enough, there is still no proper translation in Chinese. In fact, after Liu was elected Vice-Chairman of the Chinese Writers' Association, in 1984, he pointedly told a Hong Kong journalist, "This was not an election by young people and radicals. I hope that this fact will make some comrades understand that what I have written in recent years is not harmful but beneficial to the Chinese people. I am not a dissident."

Liu also tirelessly reiterated that he had never attacked the system or the Party per se, nor, he asserted, had his writing ever been calculated to mortally wound or even harm the Party—but only to help it see itself more clearly.

"I must ask why it is that scientists and politicians are permitted mistakes, while writers alone are forbidden theirs?" he had asked the delegates to the Fourth National Congress of Literary and Art Workers in 1979. "It is said that the mistakes of scientists are forgivable because they produce no undesirable 'social effects.' But then what about the social effects of politicians? Which are greater, the consequences of mistakes made by politicians or consequences of mistakes made by writers? . . . We should ask ourselves what the 'social effects' would have been if stories like these [he had just mentioned several suppressed stories critical of Party policies in the fifties] had been permitted to be published twenty-one years ago? Would the masses have risen in opposition to the Communist Party? Would the peasants have rebelled? History tells us they would not have. The effect of these stories would have been quite the opposite. They would have helped the Party see its mistakes while there was still time to make changes. Such changes would only have heightened the Party's prestige, strengthened the collective socialist economy, and stimulated the peasants both economically and politically. Recent experience has taught us time and time again that true harm to the prestige of the Party and to socialism is not done by literary works that describe problems, but by the problems themselves. . . ."

Even so, in his address at the founding of *Selections from Legal Literature*, Liu claimed that despite the attacks Party hard-liners continued to make against him and his works, he was still feeling increasingly "optimistic about the future," although, he hastened to add, his optimism was not "absolute." Nonetheless, he said he thought the tendency toward reform could not now "be turned around by anyone, no matter how powerful, [because] our Party's central leadership has initiated this reform with such great momentum, depth, and breadth that many of us here, myself included, are unable even to measure it."

In a way that was so characteristic of the general optimism spreading through Chinese intellectual circles in that fall of 1986, he went on to say, "If we use a very simple phrase to express the significance of the reform that is presently under way, I say we should call it human liberation. . . . The entire policy is aimed at allowing each person to use his life's energy to the utmost degree. Words like freedom, happiness, and well-being, which we dared not mention during the past decades, are now no longer empty slogans, but have become, or are beginning to become, a reality in our daily lives."

||||||||||||||||||||||||||||||||

Wang
·—— Ruowang: Political ———————— ·
Iconoclast

By the mid-eighties an expression, *Nanwang Beiliu* ("In the South there is Wang, and in the North, Liu") had become a catch phrase in Chinese literary circles. It referred to the fact that China had two great investigative writers: one, Wang Ruowang, lived in the southern city of Shanghai, while the other, Liu Binyan, lived in the northern city of Beijing. Aside from geography, their lives demonstrated a remarkable symmetry. They were both writers of the same generation and had a similar capacity for outrage at injustice; both wrote in a similar investigative style; both had been relentlessly persecuted by the Party in almost exactly the same way, but neither man had been robbed of his moral temper by the considerable suffering he had endured.

A wiry, pale-faced, gray-haired man of medium height, Wang Ruowang (né Wang Shouhua) was born in 1918 into the family of a Jiangsu province primary-school teacher. After his first year at a provincial teachers training school, he was dismissed and, at age fifteen, left home for Shanghai to work as an apprentice in a Chinese medicine shop. That same year, having become interested in politics, he joined the Communist Youth League. While working as a printer and editor for a periodical called *Professional Life*, which was sponsored by the

League of Left-Wing Writers, Wang himself became enamored of writing. By the end of 1933 he had published his first article, a sarcastic piece that criticized Chiang Kai-shek (leader of the Nationalist government) for relinquishing China's four northeastern province to the invading Japanese. For his premier journalistic effort, Wang was arrested by the Nationalist police and in 1934 sentenced to ten years in prison. He was, however, already so wedded to the craft of writing that he managed to smuggle some of his prose and poetry out of prison and have it published under a pseudonym.

Fortunately for Wang, when the war with Japan intensified he was released after serving only three years of his sentence; and in 1937, like so many other young progressive Chinese intellectuals of the time, he made his way to Mao's revolutionary mountain redoubt in Yan'an. "At that time, my whole understanding of communism as an ideology was actually quite fuzzy. . . ," he recalled many years later in a 1986 interview with Guan Yujian from the the the Hong Kong–based magazine *The Nineties*. "As a young man, the real reason I joined the Revolution was to fight evil, autocracy, and oppression." In this statement lay a clue to one of the important ways in which Wang's political disposition was to diverge from that of his confrere, Liu Binyan. For unlike Liu's keen sense of injustice, which was tempered by his struggle to understand and remain faithful to Marxist ideology, Wang's sense of outrage over injustice ultimately overpowered his Marxist convictions, leaving him a far less obedient Party member.

Initially no less dedicated than Liu to the cause of Communist Revolution, Wang joined the Party in 1937. His first major literary effort was a novel about the emancipation of the peasantry in the Yan'an border regions held by the Communists. But in a way that was also to become characteristic, Wang refused to limit himself literarily to Party venues and, during the same period of time, also continued to write under the pseudonym Wang Ruowang (literally meaning Wang Who Is Hopeful) for the *New China Daily* in the Nationalist-controlled city of Wuhan.

In 1940 Wang married Li Ming, a young and idealistic student who like himself had left Shanghai in 1937 for the Communist-held "liberated areas." In 1942, with the war against Japan raging, he was sent by the Party to do "cultural work" with local guerrilla units of the Red Army stationed in the northeastern province of Shandong. Here, still idealistic and loyal to the Party, its cause, and its leadership, he published a popular hagiographic series of stories about Chairman

Mao's life in the *Masses Daily*, a local newspaper. He also wrote many poems and drew cartoons, which soon became the cause of the first of many altercations with the Party.

In 1942, when the Party launched its first "rectification" movement (*zhengfeng*, or, literally, movement to correct unorthodox tendencies), some of Wang's poems and cartoons that had satirically criticized local cadres and their policies came under attack. After meeting for no less than twenty-two days to discuss his case, these local Party leaders finally censured Wang for having committed grave "anti-Party errors."

With Liberation in 1949, Wang moved back to Shanghai, where he was appointed to a curious variety of posts, including deputy chief of the propaganda department of the All-China Federation of Trade Unions, manager of the Shanghai Diesel Engine Factory, and then in 1955 deputy editor in chief of the Shanghai-based journal *Literary Monthly*. He also continued to write, producing poems, fiction, an opera, essays, short stories, and even a five-minute film script. As the Party entrenched itself as China's new ruling establishment, however, Wang found himself more and more regularly piqued by its behavior, and less and less able to subordinate his intellect and his writing to its dictates. Increasingly, he turned his barbed wit and sense of irony, which call to mind the great essayist and short story writer Lu Xun, against the injustices caused by the Party rather than those caused by the "old society." By the mid-fifties Wang was finding it very difficult to keep the critical, wry edge to his writing in check, particularly when it came to Party duplicity, arrogance, or oppressiveness. For instance, in his 1957 piece *A Visit to His Excellency: A Five-Minute Movie* he satirized a pompous high-ranking Party official who is mortified when his peasant father suddenly appears at his office in Shanghai for a visit. Wang was also a master at taking a seemingly trivial or absurd idea or statement and spinning a sardonic and damning critical web around it. In the early fifties, for instance, in one of the many Byzantine twists and turns of its line, the Party temporarily stopped advocating collectivized feeding of livestock and instead advocated private feeding. Wang seized on the occasion to write a piece called *Feeding Cattle, Bringing Up Apprentices, and Whatnot*, in which he compared the collectivization of livestock to that of art:

"It seems that when the trend was toward collective feeding of livestock in the cooperatives, various theatrical groups and publications in Shanghai were also in the process of being collectivized. Evidently, at the time the collectivization of everything and the mass production of everything was a powerful trend. One could hardly escape being branded a conservative if one failed to support this movement. Nonetheless, the facts have shown that when both cattle and men were collectivized, the cattle became scrawny, the arts became scrawny, the theatrical troupes became scrawny, and even the publishing houses became scrawny. This indicates that the drive toward collectivization and mass production within theatrical troupes, publishing houses, and film studios does not reveal the superiority of socialism; on the contrary, it reveals our blindness."

Wang went on to suggest that a valuable philosophical lesson could be derived from this event, namely that "after things have remained together for a long time, they must in the end undergo a process of division; a breaking up of the whole into parts . . . so that individual initiative can be brought into full play." Such a point of view was, of course, considered heresy at that time, when China was mobilizing to collectivize everything in sight.

The Hundred Flowers Movement of 1956 allowed Wang momentarily to write even more audaciously. In *Building Walls Everywhere*, for instance, he accused the Party of being riddled with "walls inside walls," of separating itself from the people by "walls beyond walls," and he condemned it for "displaying a lack of faith in intellectuals" by always trying to limit their freedom of speech. In this and numerous other essays, Wang began to stake out a position that stubbornly, though often with an artful indirection, resisted the idea of an infallible all-controlling Party.

By the time the Anti-Rightist Campaign suddenly began, in the early summer of 1957, Wang had acquired such a local reputation as an iconoclast that he was immediately criticized by no less than the Secretary of the Shanghai Municipal Party Committee, Ke Qingshi— a signal that quickly set the local media upon him like a pack of wolves. "Wang Ruowang Spits Venom When He Lectures on Literature" and "Wang Ruowang: Anti-Party Careerist" were two *Wen Hui Bao* headlines that August. "Wang Ruowang's Designs on the Party Have Been Fully Exposed" and "Wang Ruowang Resorts to His Old Tricks," trumpeted the *Liberation Daily*.

A lengthy criticism of Wang, which appeared in the *Literary Monthly* that summer, claimed that investigations of him by the Shanghai Branch of the Chinese Writers' Association had "thoroughly revealed the ugly nature of his rebellion against the Party and socialism." It attacked him for being "systematic in his reactionary arguments," and for being a person who "perpetually confused right and wrong through an outpouring of honeyed words. . . . The poison he spread among the masses is therefore all the more pernicious. This is especially the case among literary youth, so much so that it becomes necessary for us to lash out at him from all sides." And that was just what the article continued to do with a vengeance. It accused him of opposing "the transformation of industrial and commercial enterprises owned by capitalists"—that is, the confiscation of factories—"thought reform of intellectuals," and "the collectivist road" taken to reorganize agriculture. It also attacked his notion of "breaking up the whole into parts" as a form of apostasy "tantamount to a rejection of the Party's leadership [because] it advocates individual farming methods contrary to the principles of socialism and disapproves of the administration by fellow members of such artistic and cultural enterprises as printing offices, publishing houses, magazines, and theatrical groups." What turned out to be ironic, yet typical of this particular attack against Wang, was that he was being criticized for a stand the Party itself had previously taken in the fifties (and, of course, that it would espouse once more in the nineteen-eighties).

Reviled in the press, soon after expelled from the Party, and finally sent down to work with the peasantry, Wang was devastated. "By the time I was sent to the countryside to do manual labor, neither the political pressure nor the social discrimination (for I was hardly treated as a human being) could wound my will or spirit any more," he wrote in a *Sketch Autobiography*, which was published in 1981. "To tell you the truth, they had already lost any capacity they might originally have had to awe me into submission, for my nerves were already numb and my senses dulled."

Far worse for Wang than the ruin of his own life was the humiliation, fear, and mental agony that his fall caused his children and his wife, Li Ming. For it was common practice at the time, as soon as any individual was declared a rightist, to stigmatize all family members with the same label. Because of Wang's position as a publicly repudiated writer, his wife was soon mercilessly hounded and bullied by the Party too. Finally asked to choose between retaining her coveted Party membership or her husband, she chose her husband. But the stress, anguish, and humiliation that the persecution wrought drove her beyond the brink.

"My wife, Comrade Li Ming, was truly unable to comprehend the enormity and ruthlessness of this political struggle," wrote Wang remorsefully in a preface to his book *Unsuppressible Streaks of Light*, published in 1981 after his most recent rehabilitation by the Party. "The only thing she could imagine doing was to stand by me emotionally, and because of this she had to suffer through endless, ruthless struggle sessions in her own unit."

In the end, she lost not only her post on the Shanghai Municipal Communist Party Committee and her other official positions but her sanity as well. "From that day on, her spirit and her faith in life crumpled, and she began to manifest signs of strange behavior," wrote Wang. "At one moment she would hold me and cry aloud; at the next she would rebuke me, 'Why did you have to go and oppose the Party?' And then she would sometimes use her head to butt me, or even slap me and kick me. At the time, I accepted her blows with docility. It never occurred to me to resist her. . . . If only I could have somehow lessened the pain inside her, I would have gladly walked through fire or water. Throughout the ordeal, I deeply blamed myself for having provoked this terrible calamity through my writing, which so harmed her that she was driven to the edge of schizophrenia. . . . But somehow I had to take care of myself, too. . . . I had to maintain my sanity so that I could repay her by looking after and comforting her."

After being "sent down," Wang was no longer able to help his troubled wife, who he feared might at any time have another serious mental breakdown or even try to take her own life. "The moment I allowed myself to imagine such tragic scenes, I would break out in a cold sweat, my breathing would become strained, and, once, unable to stop myself, I even began to run off westward down the road. But after running a few steps, I found myself suddenly exhausted. My legs ached. I was panting and unable to catch my breath. Only when I had stopped did I realize that these tragedies that seemed so real to me were actually just things I had imagined, palpitations from my heart that I could never reveal to anyone. . . . 'Take it easy, Wang Ruowang,' I said. 'What is most important is that you don't allow yourself to lose your mind. You must keep going for Li Ming and the children. . . .' And then I remembered that I was there in the countryside to do 'penal labor under the surveillance of the masses' and that leaving without permission could only call forth new persecutions. So, dragging my weary feet, I slowly walked back."

Wang did not have his "rightist hat" removed and was not rehabilitated until 1960. Then he was at last allowed to return home to Shanghai. Although he was neither reinstated in the Party nor reimbursed for lost wages, being given a job with the Shanghai branch of the Chinese Writers' Association and being reunited with his family were reward enough. Even better, with Wang no longer under attack, Li Ming's mental health improved and she was soon able to go back to work.

Although Wang swore to himself never again to become involved in the "dangerous avocation" of writing, in 1962, when Premier Zhou Enlai proclaimed a new, more relaxed Party policy toward intellectuals and writers, encouraging them to "dare to think" and "dare to write," Wang reconsidered. "I believed the Party's new policy, and besides I was itching to write again," he wrote. Yearning to prove to his wife that the Party no longer considered him an enemy, he once again set pen to paper. The result was a novella called *The History of One Big Pot*, in which Wang described the absurdities of the backyard steel furnaces Mao had called on the Chinese people to build in 1958 during the Great Leap Forward. This proved a desperate attempt by the Party to show that the "redness" and political commitment of the masses rather than the "expertness" and technological know-how of China's educated elite could raise steel production. Into these crude furnaces went everything from scrap iron to the cooking pots of the peasants who ran them. Although the Great Leap Forward, as Wang's story suggested, was a disaster that left starvation in its wake, the following period for Wang was one of euphoria. As his relationship with his wife repaired itself, he wrote, "Having passed through such traumas, our love rose to a higher level. . . . Even a steam engine could not now have pulled us apart."

Being able to write again also seemed to him an unalloyed joy. "My pride and happiness at seeing myself back in print by far exceeded the joy I experienced the first time as a youth. It swept away every trace of the sad grayness that had settled over our household, so that it seemed almost as if we were embarking on the beginning of a wonderful new, festive era. With laughter and happiness restored, our observant children all congratulated me on my new life . . . and the pressure that had been weighing so heavily on my heart vanished like a mist." But the Wang family's euphoria soon ended when, in October, 1962, at a meeting of all ranking Party officials in Shanghai, Ke Qingshi once again denounced Wang by name. "Shanghai's rightists have begun to writhe once more," he warned. "Even though he has just had his rightist hat removed, just as soon as the winds stir the grass, Wang Ruowang sticks his tail up in the air again and writes something like *The History of One Big Pot*. . . . Just go and have a look at it yourselves and you'll be able to see how clever but poisonous his attack is. . . . When the proletariat relaxes, then the bourgeoisie attacks. If we were to relax class struggle, one can well imagine what a state of affairs would follow!"

"That story of mine had touched a nerve," wrote Wang. "The Boss of Shanghai [as Wang called Ke] . . . seized on some kind of new trend or other favoring class struggle, and, with drums beating and flags waving, he let loose his denunciation. And to drop someone's name at such a city-wide meeting of cadres was the same as pronouncing a death sentence."

While such a direct public criticism by the ranking Party official in Shanghai spelled doom for anyone, what made the attack doubly tragic for Wang was that his wife, as Party Committee Secretary for the factory where she now worked, happened to be attending the very meeting at which he had been denounced. Caught completely off guard and half crazed by this new public humiliation, Li Ming stumbled out of the hall alone under the censuring eyes of the other cadres. "For Li Ming this new attack was like a clap of thunder on a clear day, a dagger thrust deep into her heart," recalled Wang. "Her spirit could not stand up to such mortification. As if running from raging flood-waters, she hurried from that infernal place filled with dread, confusion, and resentment. . . . Her soul had already left her, and bereft of her wits, all she wanted to do was to hide her eyes from the world . . . and find her way home. But by that time she was already showing signs of schizophrenia."

Wang bitterly blamed himself for visiting this new torment on his wife. "Why couldn't I have written something safe that would not have given them such a pretext for an attack? Why had I gone and torn off scabs already well hidden beneath their dressings? Wasn't I just impatient; like a moth drawn toward a flame or someone knowingly throwing himself into a trap? . . . I became utterly helpless. I was unable to do anything but to try and rally from my misery and despair to accept this calamity from heaven. I had nothing more to succor me than Li Ming's delirious rantings interspersed with weeping. . . . Even now, whenever I recall her voice crying out as mechanically as a recorded message, 'It is finished!' as she entered our house . . . I recognize it as a cry of helpless indignation, the cry of someone wrestling with the madness induced by persecution, the cry of someone who welcomes death."

In one lucid moment during her ensuing mental illness, Li Ming begged her husband, "For the sake of our children, listen to me just this once: Do not ever take pen in hand again." Then, after slowly wasting away until she looked like nothing more than a "piece of kindling," in August, 1964, she died, leaving her husband not only desolate but racked with guilt. Wang Ruowang did not write again for almost two decades.

In 1966, when the Cultural Revolution broke out, Wang was publicly denounced once more, this time by Yao Wenyuan, then a young journalist and member of the propaganda section of the Shanghai Municipal Communist Party Committee, who was soon to become one of the Gang of Four along with Mao's wife, Jiang Qing. In the years that followed, Wang was criticized, "struggled against," and finally thrown in jail. "I've tasted fascist brutality and cruelty at first hand," Wang told Guan Yujian of those four bitter years in prison. "Several of my cell mates were so old and weak that they were finally unable to endure the persecution and died, one of them in my arms. It nearly broke my heart. It was then that I swore in the name of those who had died that if I ever got out alive, I would struggle for the rest of my life against such injustices, inhumanity, and fake Marxism-Leninism."

It was not until 1979 that Wang was once more rehabilitated, had his Party membership restored, and was appointed vice-chairman of the editorial board of the journal *Shanghai Literature*. Despite his wife's plea, seventeen years after *The History of One Big Pot* had caused him to be denounced as a rightist Wang began writing again. Explaining how he now justified overriding his wife's fervent appeal, he wrote, "Li Ming, forever gone! Your life was given in sacrifice for my scribblings. My dying a hundred times over could never atone for the sense of regret I bear now in my winter years. Unable to comply with your plea . . . I have taken up my pen again for the sake of the children, hoping that perhaps they will be able to create a more ideal world for the next generation, a land of gladness and peace of spirit. Perhaps this pen of mine with its meager powers can make a contribution yet."

In July of 1979, as the Chinese literary world was just beginning to thaw out from the long freeze of the Cultural Revolution, Wang published an article entitled "A Gust of Cold Wind in Spring" in the *Guangming Daily*, which subsequently was reprinted in papers throughout China. True to his prison pledge, it was an impassioned plea against the kind of "cold winds" that had repeatedly chilled China's intellectual climate. It was also a call to action for all those intellectuals who were still fearful of the consequences of speaking out against the "dark side" of Chinese life.

From 1979 on, Wang grew increasingly outspoken and unrepentant. For instance, when the Fourth National Congress of Literary and Art Workers convened in Beijing in the fall of that year, Wang gave an address in which he did something no Chinese intellectual in memory had dared to do: He publicly criticized a high-ranking Party official by name. The man was Chen Yi, Director of the Shanghai Municipal Party Propaganda Department and a member of the powerful Shanghai Party Central Committee. Although Chen himself had been labelled a rightist in 1957, after his rehabilitation he had taken to harassing intellectuals, exhibiting, in Wang's words, the same kinds of "extreme leftist tendencies" as the Gang of Four. Chen, who was a candidate for a seat on the Administrative Council of the Chinese Writers' Association board, was defeated, whereas Wang was elected.

By the mid-eighties Wang had remarried. He had also begun to infuriate many high-ranking Party leaders with his writing. For instance, he mockingly applied the ancient Taoist sage Laozi's formula "*wu wei er zhi*"—which implied that the best government is government by noninterference—to the contemporary scene, averring that the most helpful thing the Chinese Communist Party could do was to "retire from active duty." He compounded the insult by arguing that "since Party secretaries know how to do nothing but frame people, they, too, should stop meddling."

While Fang spoke openly of China's need for Western-style democracy, and Liu exposed abuses within the Party system while calling for a return to what he took to be essential Marxism, Wang began attacking not just the system and its abuses but the very ideology that underlay it. For instance, on one occasion he declared that "the capitalist mode of production is precisely what China badly needs." On another occasion he defiantly proclaimed, "If I am not given freedom, I will fight for it." And he ridiculed the notion that Communist poverty was any better than capitalist poverty. Of course, the Party took note, collecting his utterances and writings, which they put into his dossier; it would be there ready should the time come to once again strike down Wang Ruowang.

But Wang was not easily silenced by dossier collectors or even warnings of Party displeasure. Like Liu Binyan, he believed that it was the moral obligation of a journalist to involve himself in society and to use writing as a weapon against injustice. "Writers and journalists who mix in political and legal affairs should not be criticized for meddling in matters that do not concern them," he told Guan Yujian. "If political and legal organizations carry out the law justly, then they should welcome writers and journalists who try to ascertain the truth of certain cases. Besides, the Constitution has stipulated that every citizen has the right to oversee law-enforcement personnel."

Wang insisted on speaking his mind as if he were free and actually living in a democracy, even though he knew he was not. For example, in November, 1986, when he wrote an article called "My Views on Polarization: A Discussion with Comrade Deng Xiaoping" for the *Special Zone Workers' Daily*, a newspaper published in the liberal Shenzhen Special Economic Zone just across the border from Hong Kong, Wang seemed to be exhibiting exactly this trait. He took for his text a statement that Deng Xiaoping had just made in a CBS interview with Mike Wallace for the American television show *60 Minutes*. "Our policy is to let some people improve [their financial condition] before the others," Deng had told Wallace. "[But] our policy must not lead to the rich getting richer and the poor getting poorer. In other words, we do not want to develop a new capitalist class. In our social system it is very hard for anyone to become a millionaire."

Wang began by modestly admitting that he wished to express a "heterodox view." That done, he charged irreverently into a jousting match with China's supreme leader. First he pointed out what was obvious to most Chinese: As a result of Deng's economic reforms, a significant amount of new class polarization had already occurred. "As far as economic returns go," Wang added, "the phenomenon of the rich getting richer and the poor getting poorer must occur. The development of the two extremes is unavoidable."

This was a sensitive issue in post-Mao China. That the country might be regenerating a new class system à la capitalist society as a result of the much-vaunted economic reforms was an unacceptable concept, given the mythology of Deng and the Party. It would be putting the matter mildly to say that Deng preferred to maintain the fiction that one person getting wealthy while another remained poor (or grew even poorer, as seemed to be happening in at least some areas of China) had nothing to do with inequality. But as Wang was infuriatingly quick to insist, if you adopt a system, as China had, of "rewarding the superior and penalizing the inferior, it creates a difference between richer and poorer. Comrade Xiaoping's remark that 'some will improve' implies that others will deteriorate. Those whose conditions improve will get richer, and those whose conditions deteriorate will get poorer and poorer. It is an inescapable situation and the logical result of free competition."

Did this mean that Wang was nostalgic for the days of Maoist egalitarianism and that he was about to blame Deng for taking the capitalist road? Not at all. Wang just wanted to go on record acknowledging that social polarization was in fact taking place and, what was even more heretical, that he believed it was a good thing for China: "If we do not allow 'differences' to develop, if there are no 'two extremes,' the only alternative is the implementation of egalitarianism, levelling off and trying to distribute everything equally. This method is the one we have been following for the last thirty years, and everyone has lived in Communist poverty.

"As far as the present economic administration is concerned," Wang continued, pursuing Deng's logic like a hound after a fox, "the two extremes have not been sufficiently developed. Relics and traces of egalitarianism are to be found everywhere, and because of this, production cannot be positively stimulated."

Criticizing those who have "a morbid fear of capitalism," and who "mistake the ideals of communism for a practical policy," Wang warned, "If we go on emphasizing that we don't want inequalities to develop, we may as well attack the economic reforms and turn everything back to the egalitarians. Let them carry on their highly authoritarian management. Let them decisively and fearlessly cut down to size those who were so bold as to get rich sooner than others."

Then, so that it was impossible to tell whether he was being facetious or not, Wang launched into a discussion of millionaires, a notion every bit as unsavory to a Marxist as a crucifix reputedly is to a vampire: "Let us now consider the concrete implications of [Deng's] remark, 'In our society it is still very hard for anyone to become a millionaire.' " Deng's manifest wish to inhibit the rise of millionaires in China, Wang claimed, amounted to "imposing a certain limited quota on those who can 'get rich sooner.' In such a large country as China, when the day comes and the economic reforms have been smoothly accomplished, if there are as many as three thousand, or even five thousand people who are millionaires, in my opinion that should not be considered too many. And if a few are multimillionaires, that should be an entirely welcome phenomenon."

Why should such a capitalist phenomenon be welcomed in China? Because, said Wang, "If we started setting up a limited quota of people who could make it . . . as soon as the wealth [of those who succeeded in getting richer sooner] came close to a million, they would throw up their hands and quit. . . . This would make it impossible to achieve what Comrade Xiaoping himself declares to be his goal." Then, as if to parody the way the Party resurrected old Deng speeches for every new permutation in line, Wang quoted Deng himself from another context: "The main mission of socialism is to develop productive capacity, in order to improve the lives of the people day by day and to continually increase the material wealth of society."

This particular line of argument displayed two aspects of Wang that did not sit well with the Party leadership: The first was his willingness to subject the Party's own words to close scrutiny and reveal in them glaring contradictions and gross illogic; the second was the extreme, uncompromising quality of his position, both in his apparent rejection of so much of what the Party was saying and also in his evident embracing of not just democracy in a Western sense but the economic system of capitalism to which it was tied. This put Wang about as far beyond the Party line as it was conceivable for an intellectual to get and still be in China, even during this period of political thaw. It was hardly surprising, then, that because of Wang's broadside against Deng's rather puerile notions of egalitarian enrichment, the *Special Zone Workers' Daily* was ultimately closed down, providing yet another reminder, if in fact one was needed, that after periods of thaw, chill winds inevitably blow, particularly when writers dare attack supreme leaders in less than oblique ways.

While Liu Binyan was steadfast in his criticisms of wrongdoing in the Communist system, and while Fang Lizhi continued to call for new infusions of democracy into China's political structure, Wang Ruowang, the one-man truth squad, often seemed to be calling for an outright restoration of capitalism. "Over the past few decades we have had one political mass movement after another," he told the *Special Zone Workers' Daily* in 1986. "The goal of these movements was always to criticize capitalism. We have run capitalist theory right into the ground. We have criticized it until it was putrid, always having to reiterate over and over again how ugly and rotten capitalism was. It had rich and poor, after all; the rich got richer and the poor got poorer. Then, of course, there was the cruelty and the greed of the 'big fish swallowing the little fish' phenomenon. As a matter of fact, though, perhaps just because the capitalist world had such difficulties as a result of the development of these extremes of wealth and poverty, and because of the antagonism between capital and labor, in the last several decades it took measures to readjust and reform itself . . . and the absolute poverty of the working classes described by Marx was considerably alleviated, or even eliminated. . . . Although there is still a contrast between the rich and the poor, it is not as stark a contrast as it was in the days when we ran capitalism down into the ground. . . ."

What must have irritated Party leaders almost as much as Wang's theoretical unorthodoxy was the way he investigated, and with his writing championed, the cases of common people he believed to have been falsely accused of wrongdoing. For instance, in 1984 he published two pieces reminiscent of Liu Binyan's investigative works. "Hero or Criminal" told the story of a young woman factory worker erroneously sentenced to prison and not released for three years, and "The Astonishing Six-Eight Case" recounted the travails of a manager who had set up several factories and had been unjustly sentenced to eight years in prison for having allegedly accepted bribes.

As an added irritant to the Party, Wang was an unbelievably prolific writer. In the seven years between 1979 and 1986 he claimed to have written well over two hundred novellas, articles, and essays. Forthcoming projects included a dictionary on the political jargon of the Cultural Revolution, a collection of his essays, and a long autobiographical work entitled *Good Feelings About Myself*. Moreover, as the political climate began warming up in 1985, Wang, like Fang and Liu, took to travelling around China, giving an increasing number of talks and interviews, and thereby providing yet another outlet for his uncompromising iconoclasm. What he had to say was, by Chinese standards, often as blunt as it was extreme.

"So far the vital point has not been touched upon," he told a Shanghai audience in 1986. "The most crucial issue will arise over the reform of the Party. . . . What will the situation be like after such reform? Please permit me to propose something openly and freely: We must begin to practice multi-Party politics."

"Just to import science and technology [from the West] without also introducing [new] ideology will amount to nothing," he declared in Hangzhou that same fall. "It would be like importing computer hardware without any software."

"If someone wants to put the 'hat of bourgeois liberalization' on my head, all that it will prove is that bourgeois liberalization is not anything bad," he said in his 1986 interview with Guan Yujian. "I am duty-bound not to turn back, but, quite the contrary, will vigorously uphold my ideas and beliefs while at the same time washing myself clean of all 'leftist' pollution."

Like Fang and Liu, Wang was, of course, greatly encouraged by his ability to say such things so freely in 1985 and 1986, without, amazingly enough, even being stripped of his newly reinstated Party membership. But he was also well aware that, as he put it, he had repeatedly "violated many previously forbidden areas." In fact, after he had given a series of talks at university campuses in the spring of 1985, certain nameless leaders, already stung by Wang's writings, criticized him for being like the electrical buses of Shanghai, which, unlike trolley cars, are not limited to running on tracks. They also began lobbying behind the scenes to silence him.

Alerted to the growing opposition to him in the Party, Wang remarked facetiously, "I don't think it's such a bad thing to be one of those electrical buses. After all, trolley cars that have to run on tracks often just end up creating traffic jams, whereas electrical buses can avoid them." Then, instead of dropping the issue, he went on to counter-attack, saying, "There are some leaders who are not only the beneficiaries of privilege, but because their children are corrupt as well, are very scared of any writer who threatens to reveal their 'dark sides' and the ways in which they form cliques to pursue their selfish interests. Therefore, they look upon freedom of creation as a kind of nightmare and are as afraid of it as they are of death itself. . . ."

At sixty-eight years of age, with his children grown up, and with a lifetime of experience in combat with the Party behind him, Wang could no longer be intimidated or silenced by threats from Party leaders. He was far beyond that. As he summed it up to Guan Yujian, "During my life, I have never surrendered or bowed my head to anyone, whether it was in a Nationalist prison or a Gang of Four jail. My operational principle is to never be superstitious about people of authority, high rank, or fame, and instead to keep obeying and speaking out on what I believe to be true, just, and in the interests of the people and the country. If something or someone is autocratic or deceitful or unjust, then, without even inquiring how high a person's position is or how famous he is, I begin to boil uncontrollably with rage, and either end up having a face-to-face confrontation with him or criticizing him in my writing, caring nothing about my own personal safety. This is just the way I think, and the way I act. Toward such negative things and people, I am willing enough to have hard bones. Because to submit to humiliation, to bow my head or bend my back, is just not part of my moral character."

||||||||||||||||||||||
· —— Communist ——————————— ·
Traditionalism

Against this array of new critical thinking, exemplified by Fang, Wang, and Liu, the Communist Party maintained a bulwark of ideological defenses of its own. These ran the gamut from the neo-Maoism of hard-liners, whose whole lives had been politics and who were still nostalgic for the arduous struggle of the Long March and the simplicity of life at Yan'an, to younger, technocratic Party reformers, many of whom had been abroad and who bore their Communist ideology, or for that matter any other intellectual framework besides pragmatism, lightly. In many ways, though, to me the most convincing group of spokesmen for Chinese Communism and the continued leadership of the Party were those few veteran cadres who, having been imbued with a sense of traditional Chinese culture as youths, had later in life grafted on the ideals of Maoism and, later still, a receptivity to reform, to form a new if complex ideological synthesis.

One night over dinner at a friend's house, I had a long and interesting conversation with a man, an uncle of a close friend, who exemplified just this kind of blend. What interested me about Mr. Wu, as we shall call him, was the way in which he had been able to combine a classical education and a deep appreciation of Chinese history and literature with a devotion to the ideals of Communism, all the while keeping his mind open to the need for reform. In fact, he struck me as exactly the sort of Party member who might have justified Liu Binyan's continuing faith in the viability of the Party. What distinguished Mr. Wu most was that his devotion to Marxism, his traditionalism, and his interest in the West all managed to co-exist symbiotically within him in a way that did not appear to leave him riddled with contradictions. He seemed to have come to terms philosophically with these three currents that had collided in his intellectual life, as they had in the lives of all Chinese intellectuals during this century—including Mao himself—and that had given him strength rather than dividing and weakening him, as they had so often divided and weakened China itself since 1949. I was curious to know what this man was like, and what his limits as a good Communist were when it came to questions of reform and democracy.

Mr. Wu came from a well-known, highly educated provincial family in southwest China. At age seventeen he interrupted his studies to join Communist guerrillas in their struggle against Chiang Kai-shek's Nationalist forces. He had been a supporter of the Revolution ever since and was presently the director of one of the country's twenty-two Provincial Cultural Departments.

Mr. Wu is a tall, slender, and modest man, who, on the night we met, wore a necktie fastened around a shirt collar that was several sizes too large. The awkwardness with which he wore this piece of foreign haberdashery suggested that even though he was well versed in Western culture, he was not the sort of person who easily affected Western habits. In this sense, his vein of cosmopolitanism was in no way to be confused with wholesale Westernization.

In fact, the first thing I noticed about Mr. Wu was his traditional manner. From the time we met he evinced that kind of decorous Confucian reserve that mixes politeness and restraint with affability. It was obvious that he was a member of that older generation of Chinese whose balance came not so much from political convictions, which he also had, but from a deeper cultural understanding about who he was and what was important to him. It was his early immersion in traditional Chinese culture, he told me, that had given him his love and respect for Chinese poetry, literature, calligraphy, and art. It had also given him a deep love of country, as well as endowing him with a sense of cultural confidence, a confidence that China as a whole now so often appeared to lack.

As I was to learn, however, Mr. Wu, who had somehow managed to retain his appreciation of traditional Chinese culture, had paid dearly for his love of things "feudal" with seven years of imprisonment during the Cultural Revolution. But, ironically, it was this very appreciation of feudal things that sustained him during his long ordeal. As he told me, the only thing that had helped him maintain his sanity in jail was his joy in reading and writing.

I knew that as director of a Provincial Cultural Department, Mr. Wu had been involved in dealing at a high level with the clamor for democracy that had swept his province, like many others, in 1986. When I asked him whether he thought democracy was realistic or might soon be realized in his country, he sighed, put down his chopsticks, and replied, "One of the things that makes China seem so inexplicable to foreigners is that we Chinese have always seen the social role and function of a human being so differently from you in the West. Whether Communist or traditionalist, our notion of a human being emphasizes responsibilities rather than rights. Chinese have always defined themselves in terms of their obligations to society, not in terms of what society and government owe them. I guess you could say it is a clash between Confucius and Rousseau." He laughed heartily at the analogy. "Yes. That's it! Independence versus dependence. But I don't mean this in a purely theoretical way. What I am trying to describe is more like an innate sensibility that lies at the heart of people in these two very different political cultures. Chinese simply have never been imbued with the sense so characteristic of you in the West that rights are due them.

"It's not that Chinese do not *want* to be free or endowed with human rights," he continued, "but that with the exception of a small stratum of Westernized intellectuals, most Chinese have an inbred sense that to take advantage of individual rights is to do something selfish. It is our cultural inheritance to feel that the mere act of taking these rights somehow taints us with a suggestion of self-indulgence, of putting our own desires ahead of the interests of the group or society as a whole. This is both very traditional, in the sense that Confucius always emphasized controlling selfish feelings with proper forms of selfless behavior, and it is also very Marxist, in the sense that both Marx and Mao always viewed things from the standpoint of the good of society as a whole rather than that of the individual. And so, while some may talk about such things as rights and democracy, these are not things that have come to us as fundamental aspects of our inbred culture, as they have in the West."

"What about the recent appeals of some intellectuals and even some Party officials for more democracy?" I asked. "Do you mean that democracy, at least as its advocates have recently been defining it, is irrelevant for China?"

Mr. Wu paused for a moment to take a few hasty mouthfuls of food, then smiled and said, "Well, you must remember that the Chinese intellectuals are a very small segment of China, and it is only in the past few years that most of the younger generation have begun to have any contact with the outside world. Those things that the more extreme advocates of democracy have been asking for may sound very familiar and reasonable to you as Westerners, but they are not representative of what most Chinese are thinking about.

"Unlike you Westerners, who love not only to talk about but to exhibit your desires and needs, we Chinese tend to suppress ours. We are far more comfortable talking about our responsibilities and obligations, what we should do and ought to do." Here Mr. Wu laughed, as if he had just revealed a slightly embarrassing secret.

"Anyway, what I mean to say is that this attitude creates a very different foundation for an idea like democracy. Let me give you an example. If I, for instance, were a young man coming to Beijing from the provinces to meet a girlfriend whom I very much wanted to see, I would never dare say that I was coming all this way just to meet her. I'd very naturally tell everyone that I had come for some other reason, perhaps for my work, or to see my parents or relatives if they happened to live here. I would say this even if it were not true. Moreover, I would not feel that I was lying. You see, in order to come at all, I'd need an unselfish, filial reason for making the trip. If I didn't have any parents or relatives, and no plausible work, I'd have to make up another respectable excuse that emphasized my obligations rather than my own selfish cravings."

"Doesn't this create a great deal of indirectness and dishonesty about people's motives?"

"Yes. But it also puts controls on manifestations of rapacious self-interest. For instance, our classical literature is full of stories that exhort people to be obedient and to put proper social obligations ahead of individual needs and wants. Take the classic Chinese tale about the minister who, when he received a valuable present from the Emperor, turned around and gave it to his favorite concubine. When the Emperor heard what he had done, he immediately ordered his minister to be executed. Why? Not because he thought that it was wrong to give a gift to a concubine, but because his minister had not first fulfilled his filial obligations and given the gift to his father or mother.

"In Chinese culture there are all these relationships that demand loyalty and obedience, and that one must attend to before one attends to oneself. Perhaps this is why Chinese have been so accepting of and loyal to the Party. We simply have not had the tradition of individual rights upon which the whole Western notion of independence and the right of rebellion is based."

"You think, then, that these factors militate against democratic reform?"

"What I think most Westerners don't understand about China is that the Party's reluctance to grant more democracy has not always just been a question of its unwillingness to give up power, but is also born of its recognition that if China is to change and become more democratic, it first needs to have a more fundamental shift; to gain some deeper appreciation of what rights really are and what obligations they entail, lest people think that democracy is just the opposite of responsibility, a chance to enjoy the total absence of restraint."

"In this regard, what have your feelings been about such critics of Party centralism as Fang Lizhi, Liu Binyan, and Wang Ruowang?"

"The problem with people like them is that they see democracy primarily as a theoretical problem, not as a cultural problem which, if it is going to succeed, must first be embraced by some very different part of a human being than his mind." Searching for words, Mr. Wu suddenly clapped the palm of his left hand over his chest and, holding it there to emphasize what he meant, continued, "China needs a change of heart, at the level of those deep cultural values that lie underneath everything. Fang, Liu, and Wang deal with the problem of democracy on the surface without addressing themselves to the question of these other kinds of more fundamental changes that China needs first."

"Fang has said that people cannot learn democracy unless they can practice democracy. Would you agree?"

"Yes. But it must come gradually. We Chinese have a very deep conservative streak in us. It is both our weakness and our strength. *Yi li bi you yi bi*. 'For every asset there is a liability.' "

Perhaps noticing a look of skepticism on my face, he added, "Too much freedom in China can only lead to chaos. And if there is anything we Chinese have learned to fear, it is chaos. We feared it a thousand years ago, and we fear it even more now, particularly after the Cultural Revolution. Many students and young intellectuals do not remember this period. Stability to them just seems God-given. Now they claim to want democracy and freedom. But, you know, when I asked some students at home to tell me about democracy and freedom, they couldn't really explain what they were. Basically, what I think most Chinese really yearn for is peace: a family, a good job, and a chance to develop their talents."

After a pensive moment of silence, Mr. Wu continued, "You must realize that we have never even had a tradition of law in China. During the Cultural Revolution there were no courts, no lawyers, and no laws. I hope we can develop such things now. But the idea of laws and courts as a means of settling disputes is still far from being inculcated into the hearts and souls of the Chinese people."

As if he feared our discussion had become too polemical, he paused again and then in a hushed voice continued, "You might say that we

Chinese are of a certain cultural breed. Even though we may be fascinated with the West, we are not Western. Human rights, never mind how laudable the concept is, have simply not been part of our tradition. And if we get rid of what we are, then what? This is neither easily done nor necessarily advisable."

"But what is China now? Hasn't the Chinese Communist Party in its campaigns against feudal culture largely erased any sense most people had of being part of a special ongoing cultural breed?"

A troubled look passed over Mr. Wu's face. "Yes. We are all contradictions when it comes to our past. We want it and need it but still feel ambivalent about it. Lu Xun [one of China's foremost writers, who died in 1936] is a perfect example of the contradiction. He hated traditional Chinese culture for its conservatism and deadness, but still at heart he *was* a traditional Chinese who relied very much on the old language when he wrote. The enduring problem is how much to let go and how much to keep. We all agree that we should accept only what is good from the West. But just as it is so hard to know what to hold on to in our own culture, so it is difficult to know what to borrow; how to find a balance. Moreover, it has been so hard for us Chinese to accept criticism. For, particularly when it comes from the outside, it feels like an attack."

By this point Mr. Wu had become so involved in our conversation that he had stopped eating entirely. Unlike at the beginning of the meal, when he had seemed quite cheerful and relaxed, now there was a suggestion of anxiety in his delivery, as if he were exercised by the way some crucial point, some way of putting things, was eluding him.

"The truth is, we Chinese have always had such a hard time dealing with ambiguity. Perhaps for too long everything was too clear. There was always an orthodox way of thinking, Confucianism, that ill prepared us for all the different currents of thought that began to enter the country toward the end of the Qing Dynasty. In the past, we have either felt superior or inferior; we want to defend everything Chinese or throw it all away. We are such extremists."

When I asked Mr. Wu what he thought of the recurrent campaigns against such things as spiritual pollution and bourgeois liberalization, a skeptical smile crossed his face.

"Finally I don't think any such campaign will now be able to change much because things have already moved so far. The momentum is too strong, particularly in the countryside, where, as a result of the economic reforms, peasants are so well off that they will never consent to turning back the clock.

"You know, on Chinese New Year I went to the countryside in my province and asked the peasants what they wanted most. They said that all they wanted was for the present policies to continue. They didn't care who was in power as long as things did not change."

I came away from my conversation with Mr. Wu refreshed by his thoughtfulness but reminded of how close traditional and Communist attitudes in China were when it came to the question of democracy. Both attitudes, converging as they did with such symmetry in the mind of Mr. Wu, tended to view democracy as a form of government for which China was at least unready, and at most inherently unsuited. While sympathetic to certain aspects of democratization, Mr. Wu saw the process as something that might at best be dispensed from the top by the government leadership when it deemed the populace at the bottom was ready for it, rather than as something that might be demanded or even taken by the populace as an inalienable right. As I left that night, the vast gulf that still remained between Mr. Wu's conception of democracy—one that was shared by the vast majority of China's liberal reformist Party leaders, not to speak of their hard-line adversaries—and that of Fang Lizhi and younger Westernized Chinese intellectuals was painfully obvious to me. And it seemed inevitable that sooner or later these two very different conceptions of democracy would clash.

||||||||||||||||||
A Unity
of
Opposites

Certainly it was a relief to find a dedicated Party leader who had as enlightened, not to say interesting, views on the issue of democracy and human rights as Mr. Wu. For, behind the facade of unity that the Party tried to maintain, there was great factional dissension over how far and in what manner (if at all) to press China's policies of economic and political reform and its opening to the outside world; how far and in what manner to allow critics and dissidents to speak, and to what degree to allow the Chinese people themselves to engage in an increasingly consumer-oriented society and privatized economy no longer directly under the iron grip of Party bureaucrats. Factional struggles over such issues existed from the lowest levels of the Party up to the deeply divided Political Bureau of the Central Committee, and were greatly exacerbated by even deeper personal animosities, often barely held in check, between individual members of various factions and even within the factions themselves. Nonetheless, just as there was profound divisiveness behind the Party's public show of unity, so, too, there was an even deeper unity that lay behind this divisiveness. In their hearts most Party leaders shared one strong common assumption, namely, the primacy of the Party in Chinese political life. Whatever leaders might control it, and whatever they might stand for, all agreed that the Party should remain unchallenged as China's guiding political force. It was this basic assumption, implicit in everything Mr. Wu had said to me, but so much a given that it hardly needed to be mentioned, that in the end made it very difficult to imagine how any attempts at truly democratic reform could succeed in present-day China. Even though the Party might grudgingly call for democratization to "arouse the spirit of the people," as Deng Xiaoping put it, and to keep intellectuals and technocrats from becoming alienated from China's modernization process, any real challenge to Party power appeared doomed to meet with predictable results.

Unity on this one basic issue was what had made the Party invulnerable to meaningful change for so long despite the intense and, in the past, even murderous maneuvering of its internal factions, which, by the end of 1986, could be broken down into three main groupings.

The first consisted of those Maoist hard-liners—often septuage-narian and octogenarian veterans of the Long March and the Yan'an era—who had spent their lives fighting for Maoist principles and who looked askance at many of the changes brought about by the reform program that their old comrade-in-arms Deng Xiaoping had initiated in December, 1978. Although these hard-liners were in many respects throwbacks to the past, their continuing affinity for many Maoist precepts gave them a power base among those Chinese who were not benefitting from reform; who, through inflation, elitism, or exactly the kind of class polarization Wang Ruowang had spoken of, were being left out of the new reformist dream of "getting rich." This first tier of leadership included eighty-four-year-old Peng Zhen, Political Bureau member and Chairman of the National People's Congress; eighty-one-year-old Chen Yun, an advocate of Soviet-style central planning and now Political Bureau Standing Committee member; seventy-eight-year-old Wang Zhen, former general and Vice-Chairman of the Central Advisory Commission; seventy-eight-year-old Bo Yibo, former Political Bureau member and now Vice-Chairman of the Central Advisory Commission; seventy-three-year-old Yu Qiuli, former director of the PLA's General Political Department and now Political Bureau member; seventy-four-year-old Hu Qiaomu, Political Bureau member and cultural czar; seventy-one-year-old Deng Liqun, former head of the Propaganda Department and member of the Central Committee Secretariat; and eighty-two-year-old Song Renqiong, former head of the Organization Department of the Party and now Vice-Chairman of the Central Advisory Commission.

The second faction of leaders consisted of generally younger men whom we may call the conservatives. Although they tended to be more cosmopolitan in their world views than the hard-liners and generally supportive of Deng's reform movement, they still believed in a stronger measure of Party economic control and central planning than Deng himself seemed to want, were circumspect about unleashing too large and too rapid a dose of economic liberalization, were wary of the foreign influences and values they saw entering China through its wide-open doors, and had a finite tolerance for democratization. They derived much of their support from middle-aged Party members, some of whom were educated in the Soviet Union, and who were in many ways transitional figures caught between China's Maoist past and the new world of radical reform. Leaders of this second faction included eighty-one-year-old Li Xiannian, a former Political Bureau member and now China's President; fifty-eight-year-old Li Peng, trained as an electrical engineer in the Soviet Union during the nineteen-fifties, godson of former Premier Zhou Enlai, Vice-Premier, and Political Bureau member; sixty-three-year-old Qiao Shi, Vice-Premier and a member of the Political Bureau, known for favoring traditional Marxist economic approaches to China's problems; and sixty-nine-year-old Yao Yilin, formerly in charge of the State Planning Commission and now Vice-Premier and Political Bureau member.

The third and the last of these main political factions was composed of committed liberals who had determinedly pushed China forward into reform by decentralizing the economy, by enlivening intellectual life with new and unprecedented freedoms, and, to a more limited extent by democratizing political life itself. This faction derived much of its support from reform-minded students and intellectuals, many of whom had been abroad to study, and from China's growing new class of young professionals and technocrats who viewed production rather than politics as the focal point of Chinese life. In spite of their relatively radical views on the need for reform in China, most of them shared, as already mentioned, a common commitment with both the hard-liners and the conservatives. They, too, were committed to a one-party system and the supremacy of the Chinese Communist Party.

Leaders of this faction included the peppery seventy-two-year-old Secretary General of the Communist Party, Hu Yaobang, who had been on the Long March, was a Political Bureau Standing Committee member, and was the protégé and handpicked successor of Deng Xiaoping; sixty-seven-year-old Zhao Ziyang, another Deng protégé who was Premier, a Standing Committee member, and a key architect of a more liberalized and decentralized economy; fifty-seven-year-old Hu Qili, the dapper protégé of Hu Yaobang and member of the Central Committee's Secretariat and Political Bureau; seventy-year-old Wan Li, a Vice-Premier and Political Bureau member; fifty-five-year-old Zhu Houze, chief of the Central Propaganda Department; and fifty-seven-year-old Tian Jiyun, a Vice-Premier, a Political Bureau member, and protégé of Zhao Ziyang.

Then, of course, there was eighty-two-year old Deng Xiaoping, China's paramount but uncrowned leader, who served as Chairman of the powerful Central Advisory Commission and Central Military Commission, where his influence in keeping the hard-line and potentially restive People's Liberation Army in line was the key to the success of the reforms. He skillfully presided over this mosaic of contentious Party leaders by force of his seniority, his political acumen, and a complex web of old relationships, keeping this faction-ridden coalition from falling completely out of alignment or from moving too precipitously in one direction or another.

||||||||||||||||||||
· ——— Wondering ————————— ·
About the
Thaw

When I first came to Beijing in 1975, Mao was still alive and the idea of a China without him was unthinkable. At that time, I entered China from Hong Kong, crossing the frontier by foot on the Lowu Bridge, at Shenzhen. In those few steps I passed from one discrete universe to another. Once on the other side of this territorial divide I found myself in a world so starkly unlike the glittering commercial frenzy of Hong Kong that the transition felt like a form of reincarnation.

What set China off from the outside world was not just the obvious visual differences in the people, but the way in which they acted, how they thought, and what they spoke about. So steeped were they in politics that it often seemed as though the thoughts of Chairman Mao were more important than food and life itself. Class struggle, sacrifice, Spartan living, collectivization, egalitarianism, and self-reliance were the stern watchwords of the hour; and, of course, Mao's iconography was everywhere, as if immortality could be achieved by the transference of an image to material objects. Pictures of him hung in every meeting room. His bust could be found in people's houses, his face was on postage stamps, his quotations were highlighted in every publication, and his calligraphy was emblazoned on posters, dishes, postcards, notebooks, cigarette lighters, limousines, and almost every other imaginable surface. His ubiquitous statues littered the landscape like oversize chess pieces.

So seamless was the web of Maoist thought, symbols, and politics that had anyone tried to tell me that the seeds of an anti-Maoist reaction had already been planted and would soon grow into a full-fledged reversal of his revolutionary line, I would not have believed it. Many times since, I have asked Chinese friends, acquaintances, and interviewees whether during those years they had had any intimation of the changes to come. While many said that as of the early seventies they had already started to be disillusioned, none of them said they would have imagined that Maoism in China would be anything but eternal.

But with Mao's death and the rise of Deng Xiaoping, the unimaginable did begin to happen. From 1978 on, reform followed reform, presaging changes perhaps unequalled during this century in any country not at war. Far from fearing the dissolution of their old world of revolutionary purity, hundreds of millions of Chinese—particularly those intellectuals who had suffered so grievously—heaved a tremendous sigh of relief and embraced the reforms with enthusiasm. What made it even more tempting to believe in the durability of the changes was that so many Chinese who had in the past remained defensively cynical and pessimistic were now expressing optimism about the Chinese Communist Party's eagerness to reform itself. A nationwide poll (such surveys having become something of a fad in China at that time) seemed to confirm their assessment. Conducted by the All-China Federation of Trade Unions, one poll claimed that 93 percent of the 640,000 people questioned supported Deng's open door policies and 82 percent agreed that the Party's call for more self-government was necessary.

One day in that fall of 1986, I stayed up with a Chinese friend until dawn discussing all that we saw going on around us, wondering with a certain unbanishable bewilderment both where it had come from and where it would lead. Like so many others in China, we, too, wished to believe that the country was at last on the verge of transcending those circular and self-defeating patterns that had stymied fundamental reform for more than a century. But the country's current success left us wondering what had happened to those impediments that had always tripped up Chinese reform movements in the past and that finally led to Mao Zedong's revolutionary extremism. What, for instance, had become of China's long-standing cultural arrogance, which, when coupled with its humiliating defeats at the hands of powerful foreign invaders in the nineteenth and twentieth centuries, frequently prefigured episodes of extreme anti-foreignism? Was it possible that this could have miraculously vanished with the elixir of Deng's open door policy and the orgy of foreign joint ventures, loans, technology transfers, and cultural exchanges that followed? Had the country's long-standing predisposition to strong, unifying orthodoxies been transformed into a sudden yearning for democracy by the wondrous alchemy of Deng's reforms? And if the Party was now actually willing to decentralize power, what had happened to China's age-old propensity for authoritarianism? Had these tendencies, too, just passed like a cloudy day?

Only when my friend asked, with the sort of finely tuned sarcasm that characterized certain cynical young Chinese intellectuals, whether we could possibly be witnessing a tandem historical first—the first Communist Party in world history to democratize itself and the first to commit piecemeal self-extinction—did the hard reality of China's political situation hit home. Although temporarily out of sight, a powerful hard-line Maoist faction continued to resist the thrust of Deng's reforms, not to mention the reform proposals being put forth by younger, more liberal Party leaders and outspoken intellectuals. It was hard to imagine how those older revolutionaries, who had given their lives and fought so aggressively to build a society shaped in the image of Chairman Mao's thought, would now wish to or even be able to reconcile themselves to the role of passive spectators, watching as their lifelong work was dismantled before their eyes.

For years Deng had been trying to force older cadres resistant to change into retirement. But while he had had some success at the lower levels of the forty-four-million-member Party apparatus, conservatives in China's ranking elite had proved far more refractory and difficult to remove. It was anyone's guess how these hard-line Maoists still entrenched at all levels of the Party structure would next choose to manifest their perseverance and strength. Frequently over the last decade they had appeared to vanish. But like whales that when they dive leave no sign of their presence until they suddenly spout at their next breach, so these hard-liners had a tendency to drop from sight only to reappear when least expected.

Although it was tempting to believe that China might sail effortlessly forward from the fall of 1986 on this zephyr of reform and democratization, even before the first light of day it appeared dubious to my friend and me that a national identity could be as easily discarded as a suit of clothes. China might be able to trade in its Mao jackets for Western suits and ties, but it seemed unlikely that its political personality would prove quite so exchangeable.

PART

4

THE

STUDENTS

MARCH

|||||||||||||||||||||
Liang Qichao: China's First Democrat

It was a cold February day, and the bare branches of the fruit trees in the orchards surrounding the Sleeping Buddha Temple in the Fragrant Hills were dark and lifeless. The pale winter sun cast a flat, shadowless light through an overhead haze. In the distance I could hear a train hooting as it chugged through the outskirts of Beijing. A rooster crowed nearby. From the hillside, the brittle dead leaves on the poplar trees made a sound like rushing water as they rustled in the wind.

I had driven out to Liang Qichao's grave that winter day in much the same spirit as I had gone to Beijing University a week earlier—searching for some tangible sense of the roots of Chinese democracy, which had been enjoying its most recent revival that fall. What with the nationwide debate over the need for political reform, I had imagined that Liang's tomb would naturally have become an important shrine for this country's most recent generation of reformers. After all, hadn't Liang been China's earliest prominent advocate of democracy, as well as a significant force for reform, an avid reader and translator of Western political philosophy, and an opponent of China's last dynasty?

I could still vividly recall his bold writing advocating reform, which I had read in the first course I ever took on China, as an undergraduate at Harvard College. It had been written in 1896, at a time when the Qing Dynasty court, like Deng Xiaoping's Central Committee, had been dangerously divided between conservative and reformist factions on the issue of how to deal with the West. "Why is it necessary to reform?" Liang had asked. "In general there is nothing in the universe that does not change. . . . Throughout the span of one thousand years there was not a single time without change, and not a single thing without change. . . . Those who insist that there is no need for reform still say, 'Let us follow the ancients, follow the ancients.' They coldly sit and watch everything being laid waste by following tradition, and there is no concern in their hearts. . . . [But] the *Book of Changes* says, 'When there is exhaustion, there should be change; after change, there is cohesion; when there is cohesion, things will be long-lasting.' Yi Yin says, 'Make use of the new, dispose of the old, then illness will not stay.' "

As I walked toward Liang's grave site, I kept thinking about the similarity between Liang's intellectual dilemma and the one Party reformers now faced almost a century later, namely how to introduce new ideas to a resistant bureaucracy and change a political system paralyzed by tradition without alienating powerful conservative forces deeply entrenched in that very system. Full of such thoughts, I passed through a gate set in a tumbled-down wall and by several large holes in the frozen earth, half filled with refuse. Ahead of me lay two stately rows of cypress trees leading up to a series of steps, atop which was a stone-tiled area that, strangely, resembled a suburban patio, although it was overgrown with thorn bushes and weeds. In the middle of this space stood a large granite tombstone, whose spare, Art Deco lines completed this curiously foreign-looking mise-en-scène. Without the Chinese characters engraved on the tombstone, and the two huge white limestone tortoises topped by stone stelae, one might have mistaken this for the burial site of some long-forgotten Westerner. To my surprise there was not another pilgrim in sight.

Later that day one of Liang's grandchildren told me that Deng's economic reforms had, in fact, affected Liang's grave, though hardly in the way I had imagined. Many years ago, the acre-large site had been endowed by the family and left in the care of a peasant. In recent years, far from minding the tomb, he had availed himself of the vacant land inside its walls, and, like peasants elsewhere who had set up private farms on pieces of land leased from the abolished People's Communes as part of Deng's responsibility system, he had constructed a new house and, animals and all, moved in as if it were his. Although the tomb had theoretically been declared a historical shrine by the city of Beijing, and although Liang's own grandchildren had written the municipal government to remind it of its acknowledged responsibility, little had been done by way of upkeep. In truth, so ambivalent have the Communists been about China's long history that during the perilous political times of the last several decades, few historical landmarks had fared better than Liang's tomb, and many had been destroyed. So much of the rest of China's historical heritage (including the intellectual legacy of Liang Qichao) had been so battered by ideological warfare that by the time of Mao's death, in 1976, almost nothing of historical importance remained for Chinese to discuss, much less celebrate, except a select list of peasant rebellions and constantly retouched versions of the Chinese Communist Revolution itself. Save for small sanitized patches of official history and culture that somehow had escaped the vicissitudes of a decades-long cultural extermination, China had been left a historical wasteland. Perhaps the grave of Liang Qichao (whom Mao labelled a "bourgeois democrat" and an advocate of a "bankrupt" ideology) was fortunate simply to have been more or less ignored. Nonetheless, I felt a certain sadness that winter day to see how neglected the final resting place of this towering figure in Chinese intellectual history had become, and I wondered if the Party, fearful that Liang's ideas might once again find resonance among youthful Chinese intellectuals who were so rapidly losing their faith in Marxism–Leninism–Mao Zedong Thought, was not purposefully avoiding this shrine.

Having had a chance to return home and reread some of Liang's writings, as well as certain historical works on his life and thought, I returned to China in the spring of 1987 and once again visited his tomb. This time I was not surprised to discover that in the intervening months someone had pulled up the weeds, cut down the thorn bushes, and begun to water the cypress trees, for my recent reading had reminded me of how similar Liang's ideas on reform and democracy were, not to those of China's emerging dissident intellectuals and rebellious students, but to those of Deng Xiaoping and the Party leadership.

Liang Qichao, who was born in 1873 in a small southern village, not far from the Portuguese colony of Macau, died in 1929 after an intellectually tumultuous life. He wrestled continuously with the problem of how to reform China without destroying what he took to be its cultural essence and without humiliating its people with cultural annihilation. Among Liang's formative political experiences was his participation in China's first student demonstration, in 1895. The Imperial government had just signed a humiliating peace treaty with Japan following China's defeat in the Sino-Japanese War; in response, eight thousand young Chinese scholars, who had come to Beijing to take the national civil service exams, signed a petition expressing their opposition to the treaty. They then formed a line one-third of a mile long in front of Duchayuan, the Censorate of the Qing government, in protest. Their public demonstration proclaimed for the first time that Chinese citizens had the right, indeed the obligation, to regulate those by whom they were governed. Confucius's disciple Mencius had written, "He who restrains his prince, loves his prince." But Liang belonged to the first generation of scholars who, instead of going into voluntary exile when their entreaties were rebuffed by the Imperial government, dared to organize a constituency outside of the government to apply political pressure.

In 1898, a conservative counter-attack ended the Hundred Days' Reform, which had been spearheaded by Liang's mentor, the renowned "self-strengthener" Kang Youwei. Kang had called for a radical restructuring of the Imperial government, including a national assembly, a constitution, and even local "bureaus of people's affairs." The progressive young Guangxu Emperor was deposed, and Liang was forced into exile in Japan, where he began his long, celebrated career as an essayist and journalist. As Andrew Nathan in his informative book *Chinese Democracy* put it, "For Chinese in the first years of this century, Liang's writings were the window on all that was modern and foreign and might be used to save China. He introduced new ways of thinking about literature, history, international relations, science, religion, language, the races of mankind, and the meaning of life. . . . For political thinkers, his work defined the tradition within which later Chinese debates over democracy took place."

Like other forward-thinking Confucian scholars, Liang came to see "wealth and power" as the only salvation for a beleaguered China living under the threat of national extinction at the hands of Japan and the technologically advanced, rapacious Western powers. Just as intellectuals in the nineteen-eighties were debating the causes of China's backwardness and searching for ways to remedy it through "modernization," so too had Liang and his generation of reform-minded scholars sought to understand the origins of China's dynastic weakness and to suggest remedies.

A brilliant Confucian scholar, Liang came to believe that the source of Western wealth and power lay in democracy. He held that the energy generated by popular participation in the political process was what drove any dynamic society forward. But while he valued the dynamism that free, competing individuals might contribute to the building of a nation, he was vague indeed about how these Promethean, alien forces he wished to see released in China might be reconciled with the interests of the Chinese state. In fact, in optimistically Confucian fashion, he avoided entirely the problem of possible conflict by assuming that the natural order of things was harmony between rulers and the ruled. Whereas Western thinkers such as Hobbes and Rousseau (who recognized how particular interests easily come into conflict with the "general will") had immediately identified this obvious point of discord in any democratic social contract, Liang missed it completely. In holding his new convictions that individuals should and did have "rights" (*quan*), he never imagined that a state might become tyrannical or that its people might become rebellious.

"This faith in the innate potential harmony of human beings in the social order was a tenet of the Confucianism in which Liang was trained," remarks Nathan. "During centuries when Western philosophers labored over the question of how humanity's selfish nature could be reconciled with life in society, Confucian thinkers instead discussed ways of educating people to follow their instincts for social cooperation. When Western thinkers were trying to design political systems as vessels to contain irrepressible conflict, Chinese philosphers designed systems where no such conflict would be engendered."

Liang's thought proved a weak foundation on which to anchor any durable notions of democratic rights. For if no inherent conflict was envisioned between the individual and the state, and if no institutions were constructed to protect the separate rights of each, then what was to stop a tyrant from ignoring the rights of his people when it suited his purposes to do so?

In fact, after a trip to the United States, Liang did become discouraged with the possibility of liberating Chinese dynamism through democracy. In 1905 he wrote, "For years I have been intoxicated with the idea of a republic. Now . . . my beliefs have lost their ground overnight. Freedom, constitutionalism, republicanism: these are but the general terms that describe majority rule. [But] if we were now to resort to rule by this majority, it would be the same as committing national suicide. Freedom, constitutionalism, republicanism—this would be like wearing summer garb in winter or furs in summer: beautiful to be sure, but unsuitable. No more am I dizzy with vain imaginings; no longer will I tell a tale of pretty dreams. In a word, the people for now must accept authoritarian rule; they cannot enjoy freedom. . . . Those born in the thundering tempest of today, forged and molded by iron and fire—they will be my citizens twenty, thirty, nay, fifty years hence. Then we will give them Rousseau to read and speak to them of Washington."

Although Liang would later regain a taste for at least constitutional monarchy, China, alas, never gained a taste at all for Rousseau. There was something too fundamentally alien to Confucian culture about the Western notion of natural rights, which liberal Western political philosophers held all citizens to possess by the fact of birth. In Liang's more Confucian scheme of democracy, rights were not considered "natural," but rather something a leader might manufacture and grant to his people if it served his purposes. It was this legacy of individual rights as a device, and democracy as a utilitarian means of energizing the nation so that it might become wealthy and powerful, that Liang codified and passed on to future generations of Chinese. In so doing, Liang, as the founding father of Chinese democracy, left a legacy in which, if rights did not serve to "save the nation" (*jiuguo*), or even to "build the nation" (*jianguo*), they were dispensable.

There was one other legacy that Liang passed on to his successors. Although he was envious of the West, and believed that China needed to borrow science, technology, and even political philosophy and aspects of governmental systems from the West, he was also sensitive, like every proud Chinese, to any imputation that such borrowing meant China had nothing worthwhile of its own to offer. Although he overlooked the dangerous friction that was likely to develop between the interests of the individual and the interests of the collective state, he was all too aware of the potential conflict between what was Chinese and what was foreign. He was equally aware of the painful damage that could be done to China's sense of identity and self-esteem by devaluing its cultural currency with too massive an infusion of borrowing from the outside. Advocating a cautious selectivity, Liang revealed a fierce pride that was to be the hallmark of almost all later Chinese efforts to borrow from the West, and that left the process of learning from the outside world fraught with enormous potential strife and political peril.

"If there is no moral culture in the schools, no teaching of patriotism, students will, as a result, only become infected with the evil ways of the lower order of Westerners and will no longer know that they have their own country," wrote Liang. "The virtuous man, then, will become the employee of the foreigners in order to seek his livelihood; the degenerate man will become, further, a traitorous

Chinese in order to subvert the foundations of his country"—a statement that, with only a few touches of stylistic modernization, could have come from a Party ideologue writing in the nineteen-eighties on the dangers of "wholesale Westernization."

Liang may have been a modernizer, but he was also steeped in the myth of Chinese cultural superiority, and deeply sensitive to even the faintest suggestion that the Central Kingdom might end up a debtor to the materialistic, albeit more powerful, West. Unwilling to engage in the kind of arrogant, self-defeating isolationism advocated by conservative Qing Dynasty officials who wanted somehow to continue shutting China off from the Western threat (a policy that Mao and his followers would pursue more successfully seventy-five years later), Liang supported learning from the West. But for him, the act of borrowing—whether it was technology or democracy—necessitated a nonstop effort in intellectual gymnastics to assure that China would at least give the appearance of being an equal in the exchange, lest it lose face not only in the eyes of the world but, worse, in the eyes of its own people.

Liang was attempting to walk a fine line between a new conception of reformism and the old hard-line Confucian conservatism that wanted to maintain the status quo. "Our so-called new people," he wrote, "must not be like that class of men infatuated with Western ways who, in their zeal to equal Westerners, throw away the morality, the learning, and the customs of some thousands of years. Nor should we be like the class of empty conservatives who say that they cherish only the morality, learning, and customs of these thousands of years, and that consequently it is sufficient to have their feet planted on the ground."

Liang hoped to have it both ways at once: to acknowledge China's weakness and rectify it, while continuing to proclaim China's cultural and political health. In this respect, Liang's heirs were not Fang Lizhi, Liu Binyan, Wang Ruowang, or the radical students eager to establish some notion of real democracy and inalienable human rights in China, but rather Sun Yatsen, Mao Zedong, and Deng Xiaoping, all of whom shared his wariness of cultural and political annihilation as well as his very practical and limited view of democratization. For unlike Fang or Wang, these men saw democracy only as a means to an end, a tool to be used or cast away depending on the needs of the moment. In Sun, Mao, and Deng, Confucianism merged with Leninism to form a system in which political participation was sometimes esteemed but inevitably sacrificed in the end for unity and stability. After all, single-party tutelage was all too easy to justify in a world where the survival of the state was so often endangered by foreign predation or domestic chaos.

"With domination, society will survive; without it, it will disappear. From the viewpoint of society, it is not too much to say, 'Domination is sacred,'" wrote a disillusioned Liang in 1905 in his treatise *On Enlightened Despotism.* It is hard to imagine any of China's recent Communist Party leaders disagreeing with this sentiment.

In many ways, it was Liang Qichao who set the pattern for Chinese democracy, even socialist democracy, for the rest of the century. Even though Mao and Liang never met, in his youth Mao was an avid reader of Liang's writings. And although the idea of Marxist class struggle never appealed to Liang the Confucian, who had ever been in search of the *datong*, or "great harmony," the idea that the social interests of the collective should always be placed above the private interests of the individual survived unscathed, to reappear in the Marxist-Maoist notion of democratic centralism, which decreed that once one's leaders had reached a decision, the rights of individual dissent ceased.

As Mao said, "There can be no public interests without private interests. Likewise, there can be no private interests without public. [But] public interests come first and private interests come second."

"Without Stability and Unity, We Will Get Nowhere," a February, 1987, article written in the wake of the student uprisings that winter by conservative Party Secretariat member Deng Liqun in the *Guangming Daily*, echoed Mao almost word for word and spoke of the need for students to study hard rather than talk about democracy and "self-design." "We [the Party] must enable young people to understand that the interests of the state should be put first," explained Deng. "The future of individuals is possible only when the state has developed. We should link the destiny of individuals with that of the state. Moreover, when personal interests contradict the interests of the state, they should be subordinated to those of the state."

Like Liang and Mao, Deng Liqun and other contemporary Party leaders ultimately saw the interests of the collective nation as being pre-eminent not because they believed individuals had no rights or interests, but rather because they viewed the Party as the best representative of those rights and did not envision any great contradiction between them. As a commentator in the *Liberation Daily* put it in March, 1987, "The individual and the collective have a relation of supplementing each other. Just as a drop of water will be dried up if it fails to get into the sea, likewise it is very difficult for an individual to survive independently without merging himself with the collective.

Stubbornly laying conspicuous emphasis on the 'stressing of the individual' and playing down or negating the 'sense of the collective' run counter to dialectical materialism. In building ethics, we do not generally oppose the development of the individual; however, such development must be linked with the interests of the Party, the state, and the people. The individual can accomplish perfect development only through his infinite service to the people. Developing the individual at the cost of the interests of the Party, state, and the people will inevitably lead to extreme individualism and anarchism."

In this sense, Fang Lizhi was a proponent of "extreme individualism," a "drop of water" that did not yearn to merge with the sea. As such, he, along with Liu Binyan and Wang Ruowang, was outside the historical mainstream of Chinese democratic thought. By stepping beyond those boundaries circumscribed by Liang at the beginning of the century, Fang and Wang both stepped off into a new, very un-Chinese world. Not only did Fang, in particular, view rights as natural and inalienable entities that could neither be granted nor taken away by any government or leader, but he also did not fear borrowing from the West the concepts that lay behind such rights, even if their adoption might seem to some Chinese like the severest form of cultural capitulation, self-annihilation, and humiliation. It was a bold step and raised philosophical and political issues that had not been publicly heard in China for almost a decade.

The Democracy Wall Movement

In 1977, just after Mao's death, the fall of the Gang of Four, and the return of Deng Xiaoping to power, China's newspapers began to proclaim publicly the need for democracy. The *People's Daily*, reborn with a completely new voice, declared that if China's socialist bureaucracy remained unchecked by elections and other democratic institutions, it might again run amok and degenerate into "feudal fascism." That June, in an important speech at an Army political conference, Deng told incredulous delegates that it would no longer do for China just to "copy straight from Marx, Lenin, and Chairman Mao"; henceforth criteria for truth should be sought in facts rather than in politics.

By February, 1978, a new constitution had been adopted, whose Article 45 guaranteed "freedom of speech, correspondence, the press, demonstrations, and the freedom to strike," as well as what the Chinese came to refer to as the Four Big Freedoms, namely the right of people to "speak out freely, air their views fully, hold great debates, and write big-character posters."

Hu Yaobang, Deng's protégé and the new chief of the Party's Organization Department (he became Party General Secretary in 1980), launched a far-reaching program to rehabilitate the tens of millions of Chinese who had been slandered, persecuted, and imprisoned for being landlords, rich peasants, rightists, counter-revolutionaries, bad elements, antisocial elements, and capitalist roaders. Tens of thousands of people were released from jail as, that fall, commentators in the press began exhorting Chinese to "break through all spiritual shackles" and "emanicipate their minds" in order to carry out Deng Xiaoping's new slogan, "Practice is the sole criterion of truth."

At a Central Work Conference held that November, Deng stated, "Some people say that we must do what Chairman Mao said. But actually there are many things that the Chairman did not say. Engels never rode in a plane. Stalin never wore Dacron. Practice is developing. We must study the new situation and solve new problems."

Not surprisingly, 1978 was a time of enormous ferment and excitement as Deng went about the task of repudiating the Cultural Revolution. After ten years of political suppression and terror, the new sense of freedom and excitement in the air was palpable. Chinese intellectuals who had lived in a state of almost perpetual fear once again became emboldened to speak out. "Literature of the wounded," a new genre of writing that recounted the horrors of the Cultural Revolution, began to be published. Before long, this new sense of freedom began to translate itself into political sentiment, producing a crop of wall posters expressing a variety of long-pent-up ideas and complaints.

The epicenter of this cultural and political tremor was an unprepossessing stretch of brick wall in front of a streetcar yard, located near the intersection of the Avenue of Eternal Peace and Xidan, one of the capital's main shopping streets. There, for several months during the winter of 1978–79, behind a scruffy hedge and under a row of leafless sycamore trees, Democracy Wall flourished. There, people spent hours at a time reading, talking, and listening with an openness never before seen in the People's Republic. What brought them were *dazibao*, "big-character posters," a form of public expression to which Chinese have long turned when denied access to government-controlled media. During the fall of 1978 *dazibao* suddenly began to appear on Democracy Wall, their content becoming bolder and bolder as the weeks passed, so that by the middle of November young activists had covered and re-covered the wall with savage attacks on the Cultural Revolution, the Gang of Four, and sometimes even Mao himself. Before long, they even began bringing up the taboo subject of democracy, proclaiming:

> "It is incredible that in a People's Republic there should still be among the officials to whom the people have entrusted national sovereignty, executioners and murderers, whose hands are stained with the blood of the people. . . . In China . . . a country of proletarian dictatorship armed with the Great Thought of the Era, we certainly do not measure up to the people of ancient times or to foreign countries. . . ."

> "If Chairman Mao had not agreed, would the Gang of Four have been able to achieve their aim . . . of striking down Deng Xiaoping? . . . If we do not permit the masses to express their own opinions of Chairman Mao, then freedom of speech and democracy are only empty words."

> "Citizens of China do not want just a paper constitution. We don't want hunger. We don't want to suffer any more. We want human rights and democracy."

"However great and wise a leader might be, he certainly cannot be immune from making mistakes. Several thousand years of feudal history and over a hundred years of the people's dauntless struggles have taught us one truth: We must place our hope in a healthy, effective, scientific, and democratic system, so that both the common people and the public servants they elect are bound by this system and strive for the well-being of the people. . . .

"To make people think that democracy and human rights are only slogans of the Western bourgeoisie and that the Eastern proletariat needs only dictatorship . . . is something that cannot be tolerated any more."

"The Chinese people want to learn more than just technology from the West. They also want to learn more about Western democracy and culture. We demand the opening of the gates that have been locked against us for so long, and to let true liberty blow across the land."

As the movement progressed, some Democracy Wall activists even began shouting their messages through hand-held bullhorns:

"We must uphold the Party! But we must also supervise the Party and make it the public servant of the people!"

"We have no particular ambitions. We are common people. . . . But we want to be common people who are free and happy!"

"We demand democracy! We demand freedom!"

By the end of December, 1978, when the Third Plenum of the Eleventh Party Central Committee published its path-breaking communiqué on reform, Democracy Wall had been in existence for five weeks. Thousands of people flocked to it each day to see what had been written the night before and to join throngs of activists in heated discussion groups or to listen to spontaneous speech-making. This unruly liberated zone of free expression was not closed down by the authorities because the activists initially supported Deng Xiaoping. Still consolidating his position against his opposition, Deng found his interests well served by having a cadre of such activists in the streets ready to protest against his opponents at a moment's notice.

"Putting heaven and earth in harmony, opening doors, establishing order, discipline, and great democracy, Vice-Premier Deng is open-minded, humble, and honored by the entire world," wrote one Democracy Wall scribe, extolling Deng as a classically benevolent Chinese ruler. "His greatness, beauty, and success in seizing the seat of government are hailed in the north and the south. . . . [Under him] the nation will be rich and strong, and the economy will be pushed ahead."

To encourage the protesters, on November 26, 1978, Deng told the visiting Chairman of Japan's Democratic Socialist Party that wall posters were "a normal phenomenon, a manifestation of a stable situation in our country . . . [which] is permitted by our constitution. . . . The masses should be allowed to vent their grievances. . . . We should not check the demands of the masses to speak."

A short time later he bluntly told the American reporter Robert Novak, "Democracy Wall is good." Echoing these sentiments, the *People's Daily* proclaimed, "Let the people say what they wish, the heavens will not fall. A range of opinions from people is good for a revolutionary party leading the government. If people become unwilling to say anything, that would be bad. When people are free to speak, it means the Party and the government have strength and confidence. . . . If a person is to be punished for saying wrong things, no one will say what he thinks. . . . The suffocation of democracy produces bad results."

Predictably, these Democracy Wall activists grew more and more outspoken and soon began to criticize the whole Chinese political system rather than just the Gang of Four and the Cultural Revolution. But at the point where they began to blatantly level their fire at Mao himself, they had outlived their usefulness for Deng. Perhaps fearing that he would be their next target, Deng was reported to have said, "The masses have their doubts on some questions, [but] some utterances are not in the interest of stability and unity."

"Vice-Premier Deng, you are wrong, completely wrong!" wrote one displeased protester. "There is no doubt that a long time ago the Chinese people took note of Chairman Mao's mistakes. Those who hate the Gang of Four cannot fail to have grievances against Chairman Mao."

As the focus of the posters began to switch from criticisms of the Cultural Revolution to broadsides against Mao and increasingly strident calls for democracy, the marriage of convenience between Deng and the Wall activists chilled rapidly. Soon plainclothesmen began disrupting activities at the Wall, and rumors circulated that Party leaders had branded the democracy movement as "underground." Then, on January 18, the first arrest was made. The honeymoon had been short-lived. Paranoia and disillusionment quickly replaced the earlier optimism and ebullience of the protesters. Rumors were soon rampant that a struggle between reformers and hard-liners over both Democracy Wall and the new Party line was raging within the leadership.

As *Explorations*, one of the democracy movement's most outspoken underground journals, put it, "Some bigwigs in the Beijing Municipal Party Committee are afraid that the people might be able to enjoy true democracy." The editor of *Explorations*, Wei Jingsheng, a young ex-soldier who worked as an electrician at the Beijing Zoo and whose family had suffered grievously during the Cultural Revolution, was one of the most radical and eloquent advocates of democracy during these hectic months. His now famous wall poster, "Democracy: The Fifth Modernization," had first appeared on the Wall and was later published in *Explorations*. It not only called for basic reforms in China's system of government but expressed a bitingly cynical attitude toward Deng's Four Modernizations (of agriculture, industry, science, and defense). Like other reformers before him, Wei set out to ascertain why Chinese society was so backward and weak, and like Liang Qichao, he concluded that the cause of that weakness lay in the country's lack of democracy.

"We have not heard so much about 'class struggle' on television, radio, or in our newspapers and magazines recently," he wrote. "This is because people are thoroughly sick of hearing about it. But as the old passes away, it is replaced by the new. So now they [the Party] have dreamed up a new promise called the Four Modernizations. There is an old saying, *huabing chongji*, 'To paint a picture of a cake in order to satisfy one's hunger.' This shows that the ordinary people of ancient times humorously saw through this fallacy. But there are some people who still believe it.

"For several decades the Chinese people followed the 'Communist ideals' of the 'Great Helmsman' . . . always marching onward. Thirty years passed like a day and taught us this lesson: The people are like the monkey who tried to grasp the reflection of the moon in a pond. Don't they realize there is nothing there? . . . So when Deng Xiaoping raised the slogan of 'getting down to business,' the people cried out over and over again for him to be restored to power. . . .

"Do the people enjoy democracy nowadays? No! Is it that the people do not want to be their own masters? Of course they do. This was the very reason the Communist Party defeated the Nationalist Party. After its victory, did it do what it promised it would? The slogan of 'people's democracy' was replaced by the 'dictatorship of the proletariat,' making a very small percentage of the hundreds of millions of people the leaders. But even this was cancelled, and the despotism of the Great Helmsman took over. Then came another promise. Because our Great Leader was just so great, we arrived at the superstitious belief that a great leader could bring the people far more happiness than democracy could. Up until now, the people have been forced time and time again, against their will, to accept 'promises.' But are they happy? Are they prosperous? We cannot hide the fact that we are more restricted, more unhappy, and the society is more backward than ever. . . .

"If the Chinese people wish to modernize, they must first establish democracy and they must first modernize China's social system. Democracy is not a mere consequence, a certain stage in the development of society. It is the condition on which the survival of productive forces depends. . . . Without democracy, society would sink into stagnation, and economic growth would encounter insuperable obstacles."

Although a passionate and devoted advocate of democracy, like Liang Qichao, Wei, too, tended to justify democracy as "the condition on which survival of productive forces depends." This traditionally utilitarian Chinese cast to Wei's argument for democracy did nothing, however, to mitigate the reaction of China's Party leaders to his criticisms. The leadership had already been increasingly unsettled by what was being written on the big-character posters by upstart democrats like Wei, not to mention what had begun to appear in the more than fifty underground journals now being published in Beijing.

In February, 1979, Deng Xiaoping made his historic trip to the United States to celebrate the establishment of diplomatic relations with Washington. Once back home, with his own leadership position secure, Deng made his move. On March 16 he claimed that protesters had used the issue of democracy to fan old resentments from the Cultural Revolution, that they had formed secret cabals with agents from Taiwan, and that they had had unauthorized relationships with foreigners. In short, Deng cast his lot with those hard-liners who had long agitated for an end to the Wall and at the same time delineated his Four Cardinal Principles (to uphold socialism, the dictatorship of the proletariat, the leadership of the Communist Party of China, and Marxism–Leninism–Mao Zedong Thought), which henceforth became the new ideological standard of the Party.

On March 25, hearing through the grapevine that a crackdown was imminent, Wei and his colleagues rushed out a special edition of *Explorations* entitled "Do We Want Democracy or a New Dictatorship?" in which they savagely attacked Deng's statement of March 16 and accused him of having "metamorphosed into a dictator." On March 29 new regulations were issued by the government forbidding "slogans, posters, books, magazines, photographs, and other materials that oppose socialism, the dictatorship of the proletariat, the leadership of the Communist Party, Marxism–Leninism–Mao Zedong Thought" from being publicly displayed. Almost instantaneously, Party propaganda organs began churning out diatribes against "extreme democracy" (*daminzhu*) and in favor of socialist democracy and the Four Cardinal Principles.

On the same day, Wei was arrested on charges of publishing counter-revolutionary materials. According to the soon-to-be-minted Chinese criminal code, counter-revolution was defined as any act undertaken "for the purpose of overthrowing the political power of the dictatorship of the proletariat and the socialist system and jeopardizing the People's Republic of China."

"For the past four months Wei has been active in the spontaneous democracy movement," wrote the other editors of *Exploration* by way of an epitaph. "He has fiercely criticized all backward factions that he thought prevented China's modernization, including the obstructive role that he thought was played by Marxism and the Thought of Mao Zedong. Because of that, the Chinese government arrested him for the crime of counter-revolution.

"Where is freedom of speech in China? . . . All criticism is fiercely suppressed as being contrary to socialism and to the dictatorship of the proletariat. So much for democratic freedom under the Chinese government! What brutal hypocrisy!"

"Some people have the audacity to say that there is no democracy in the whole of Beijing, or even the entire country," rejoined the *Beijing Daily*. "These words not only show ignorance, they are out-and-out slanders and distortions. . . . If we allow [people like Wei] to promote their so-called democracy, we will do harm to the democratic rights of the masses of people."

Why had Wei persisted against such futile odds? "Because I know that democracy is the future of China, and if I speak out now there is a possibility that I can hasten the day when the Chinese people will enjoy democracy," he had optimistically told British diplomat and author Roger Garside before his arrest. "Two years ago it would have been pointless for us to speak or write as we do now, for we would have been arrested as soon as the words were out of our mouths. Now, through our posters and journals we can make our voices heard."

By April, 1979, some thirty other Democracy Wall activists were rounded up. That October, Wei Jingsheng was brought to trial and accused of "supplying military intelligence [on China's war with Vietnam] to a foreigner and of openly agitating for the overthrow of the government of the dictatorship of the proletariat and the socialist system in China."

At his trial, Wei declined to be represented by a government lawyer and instead spoke in his own defense. Answering the government's indictment that he had "put forth the banner of so-called freedom of speech and the demand for democracy and human rights to agitate for the overthrow of the dictatorship of the proletariat," Wei eloquently replied, "I must point out that freedom of speech is not a wild demand, but something that is guaranteed in black and white in the Constitution. The tone in which the prosecutor talks about this right not only shows that he is prejudiced in his thinking but that he has forgotten his responsibility to protect the democratic rights of citizens." Instead of trying to defend himself against his indictment by claiming that his acts were not counter-revolutionary, Wei attacked the very notion of a "counter-revolutionary crime":

"Some people have the following view: that it is revolutionary if we act in accordance with the will of the leaders in power and that it is counter-revolutionary to oppose it. I cannot agree with this debasement of the concept of revolution. . . . Revolution is the struggle between the new and the old. . . . To label the will of the people in power as forever revolutionary, to wipe out all divergent views and theories, and to think of power as truth—this was precisely one of the most effective tools of the Gang of Four in the past twenty years. . . .

"The current historical tide is a democratic tide, one that opposes feudal fascist dictatorship. The central theme in my articles, such as 'Democracy: The Fifth Modernization,' is that without democracy there can be no Four Modernizations. . . . How can such a central theme be counter-revolutionary?"

Wei concluded his impassioned defense with an unrepentant re-statement of his belief that the Constitution guaranteed him the right to criticize the government. "Criticism cannot possibly be nice and appealing to the ear, or even always correct. To require criticism to be entirely correct, and to inflict punishment if it is not, is the same as prohibiting criticism and reform. It is tantamount to elevating leaders to the position of being deities."

For his outspoken views, Wei was given fifteen years in jail.

In December, 1979, by belatedly banning further displays of posters on Democracy Wall, the Party authorities formally ended Beijing Spring, just twelve months after it had begun. When later asked for his views on the whole movement, Deng replied, in his characteristically terse way, "As to the so-called Democracy Wall, the demonstrations and the sit-ins cannot represent the genuine feelings of our people."

On September 10, 1980, at the direction of Deng Xiaoping, the Third Session of the Fifth National People's Congress rescinded the Four Big Freedoms, which had been written into Article 45 of the 1978 constitution. The vote was unanimous except for one defaced ballot, which, Andrew Nathan has noted, "was unusual enough to merit front-page comment in the *People's Daily*, which welcomed the anonymous delegate's courage as a sign of the new vigor of democracy in China." As Deng Xiaoping observed after the sentencing of Wei, China could never develop if "so-called democrats and dissidents such as Wei Jingsheng and his ilk," who are openly opposed to the socialist system and to Party leadership, obstruct the "unity and stability" of the country.

In November, 1987, Amnesty International reported that reliable sources within China claimed that Wei Jingsheng had died of kidney and heart problems in a "labor reform" camp in the remote north-western desert province of Qinghai. According to the Amnesty report, "His condition was said to have resulted from his conditions of incarceration in Beijing during his first years of imprisonment and the lack of medical care afterward." Shortly thereafter, Acting Premier Li Peng denied Amnesty's report, saying that Wei was still alive.

|||||||||||||||||||||||||

The Student
Demonstrations
Begin

In the fall of 1986 demonstrations demanding democracy once again broke out in China, but unlike the activists of the Democracy Wall Movement, these new demonstrators took to the streets spontaneously, unmotivated by any notion of restoring a benevolent ruler to power. As Fang Lizhi had pointed out, in the absence of a democratic tradition the Chinese had almost always "placed their hopes in upright officials" and consequently ended up with "too many heroes." What animated this new generation of students was both a deep sense of malaise and an ill-defined but nonetheless powerful feeling that something was very wrong with Chinese society as a whole—something that could only be corrected by fundamental changes in the system itself. In this sense, the new generation of protesters was far more alienated from that system than its predecessors.

Although it was extremely difficult to gain admission to China's universities, many of those fortunate enough to be accepted found even the most elite schools to be archaic, authoritarian, and boring. In a survey of university students in the city of Wuhan, published in the *Guangming Daily*, 43 percent said they found life on campus "dull and uninteresting," while 88 percent said they found extracurricular activities organized by the Party and Youth League "full of formalism, dull in content, and incapable of helping to solve problems." Over one-quarter of them found Party cadres "stiff, orthodox, and difficult to approach."

A November, 1986, issue of *Fortnightly Talks*, a New China News Agency publication aimed at lower-level cadres, explained the students' malaise this way, "Young people . . . do not like being taught in a dictatorial manner and are happier with democratic consultation and free discussion. . . . They are characterized by independent thinking and the desire to decide for themselves. . . . They have no superstition about authority and yearn to have their own democratic rights protected."

Although often incompletely understood, new ideas of democracy and freedom, articulated so forcefully even in the official press that summer and fall, had created a strong sense of expectation among China's university students. Unlike their parents, this new generation was far removed from the utopianism of Mao's early Revolution and relatively unblighted by the fear of political oppression. They had come of age during the Three Beliefs Crisis (lack of belief in the Party, lack of confidence in socialism, and lack of trust of cadres). No longer could most young people be animated by vacuous notions like "socialist spiritual civilization" with which youth was supposed to be imbued by campaigns such as the Five Stresses, the Four Beauties, and the Three Ardent Loves. Compared to what was now known of the West (mainly its freedom, consumer goods, and glittering pop culture), China as a "people's republic" had simply lost its allure.

Within their spiritual and political vacuum it was all too natural for educated youth to fantasize about the West as the promised land and to idealize the political concepts and systems that had brought it such evident wealth and power. In any case, if Chinese students were unsure of what they did believe, most were ever more certain of what they did not believe. They no longer believed naively in socialism, and a decreasing number had become unwilling to blindly follow the Communist Party.

What had stirred up student interest in democracy in the first place was the Party's own call for political reform that summer and fall. This was particularly ironic since, in actuality, no Chinese Communist Party leaders could have been anything but wary about arousing such unfulfillable expectations among the country's students and intellectuals. For the historical record amply showed that, however small a percentage of China's population they might be, when students were dissatisfied and rebellious, they could shake the foundations of a regime. In the May Fourth Movement, for instance, disillusioned students, protesting against the inequities of turning over German concessions in China to the Japanese after World War I at the Paris Peace Conference, not only forced a Chinese cabinet to resign but also sparked a prolonged nationwide movement opposing imperialism and traditional Confucian culture while favoring Western science, individualism, and democracy. In 1935–36, students again brought a government to bay: Their December Ninth Movement protesting Chiang Kai-shek's appeasement policy toward Japanese aggression in North China helped force him into a united front with Mao's Communist guerrillas. Far more ominously, in 1966, responding to Mao's call to "bombard the headquarters" of the Party, student Red Guards took to the streets, bringing all of China to the brink of chaos; and again in 1976, students turned out in force to mourn the death of Premier Zhou Enlai in the Tian'anmen Square Incident. Whether as anti-imperialists, young democrats, or the spiritual children of Mao, once a critical point of disaffection was reached, students (as few Party leaders in China could have been unaware) had the potential to become catalysts for large-scale disruptive political change.

Nonetheless, liberal reformers within the Party seemed to have convinced themselves that intellectuals and students alike would understand that they had everything to gain from the Party's new reformist direction, and that, fearful of the alternatives, they would see their own self-interest tied to patiently supporting the new status quo. But perhaps liberal reform-minded Party leaders were too accustomed to a docile intelligentsia and therefore erred in this judgment. As one twenty-year-old student from Qinghua University in Beijing later said when asked why he and his friends had taken to the streets, "We were responding to the call last July by Deng Xiaoping for political reform. We are impatient that in spite of all the newspaper articles advocating mass participation, nothing concrete has yet been done to allow us a say in government affairs."

So when on December 9, 1986, the anniversary of the anti-Japanese demonstrations that had swept the country in 1936, student protests began in the provincial city of Hefei, the capital of Anhui province, the Party was caught off guard. It quite literally had no idea how to respond when students from the University of Science and Technology (Keda), protesting the way candidates for the December elections to the county-level People's Congress (China's legislative branch of government) had all been designated by the Party, began to put up big-character posters.

"No democratization, no modernization!"

"Give Me Liberty or Give Me Death!"

> "Almost every day the newspapers talk about
> democracy. But where can we actually find any?"

> "Government of the people, by the people, and
> for the people."

One of the main supporters of the student movement was, of course, the university's Vice-President, Fang Lizhi. Already lionized for his free thinking, he had, on December 4, given a speech that encouraged disgruntled students to stand up for their democratic rights, telling them, "Democracy is not a favor bestowed from above; it should be won through people's own efforts."

But as Fang told me when I talked with him some months later, "Actually, when the students first wanted to demonstrate, I tried to persuade them not to. I let them know that I agreed with their political points, but that demonstrating was very risky; that when they walked off the Keda campus, one never knew what might happen; that even though I was Vice-President of the university, I would then no longer be able to protect them."

On December 9, with their grievances unredressed, Keda's students, three thousand strong, marched on the offices of the government and demanded that outside candidates be allowed to run for office. News reports of these first provincial demonstrations were sketchy, to say the least, but what news did get out travelled fast and caused intellectuals all over the country to take notice. In addition, to the delight of the students, the initial demonstrations were successful in getting local officials to postpone the elections and to allow the submission of the names of non-Party candidates.

"Because the Hefei students had been successful in overturning the candidates' list on their very first meeting with officials, they became extremely optimistic," recalled Fang. "But it was very easy for us at Keda, because we as leaders of the university were also against the election and supported the students. However, I kept warning them that they should not be deceived, because in reality things were not the same in the outside world as on campus."

Nonetheless, carried away by their initial success, and spurred on by their belief that no such electoral concession could have been granted without the approval of the highest authorities, many students even came to wonder if Deng Xiaoping himself was not behind the concessions.

"Actually, at that time the students themselves thought of Deng Xiaoping as a liberal and really believed he would support them," Fang told me. "There was even a big-character poster put up which promised that Deng would visit Keda after the New Year. Whether it was a rumor or not, I don't know. But at least everyone wanted very much for him to come. You see, the students trusted Deng. They felt that he had been running the country similarly to the way in which we had been running Keda."

Some students even imagined that Deng and Fang were in league, working together to push the democratization of China forward over the protests of the hard-line Maoists. Such assumptions, however, proved only to be the optimistic fantasies of anxious students and intellectuals still yearning to retain a belief in the viability of the notion of a "benevolent ruler." When Wen Yuankai, a noted liberal professor of chemistry and a colleague of Fang's at Keda, arrived in Hong Kong for a symposium that December, he made it clear that no Deng-Fang axis existed by describing the Hefei demonstrations as a spontaneous uprising. But Wen (who, though more moderate than Fang, was still an ardent reformer and supporter of democratization in China) felt called upon to issue a warning: "It is of paramount importance that the ongoing reforms be carried out under a stable society. The cost we paid for the tumultuous past has been too much. Democracy needs time to grow and can only be built upon other developments in the economy—on politics, education, and culture, which are all backward in our country. A full democracy is impossible now."

Already it was evident that even among the most reform-minded Chinese something of a split was developing over the question of the student protest. This split between Party reformers and the more liberal wing of China's academic community initially focused on the issue of how to run the universities, which were seen by the Party as the forges on which a new modernizing elite for China would be tempered. That no pan-reformer alliance existed became even clearer when Vice-Premier Wan Li arrived in Hefei to try and dampen student unrest.

"Actually, Wan Li had been following me," Fang told me with a twinkle of amusement in his eye. "When I was in Shanghai, he was in Shanghai. When I went to Ningbo, he went to Ningbo. Then he followed me to Nanchang and back to Hefei. What his other motives might have been, I can't say. But I do know that he wanted to get tapes of all my speeches. For instance, in Ningbo, where the president of the university, a friend, had asked me to speak, Wan Li requested a tape right after my talk. My friend said he wasn't in charge of such things and didn't know where it was. However, Wan was insistent and told him that he would wait until they found the tape. So, finally, they had to give in."

When I asked Fang why a Vice-Premier, a liberal one at that, would be chasing down tapes of his speeches, Fang explained, "Wan Li is himself a reformer, and I have to say that I feel he is not bad. He is, in fact, one of the rational members of his generation of leaders. He wants to do right by the people; to be a good official. That means he would like to do good things for the Chinese, give them enough to eat and so on. What he doesn't want is the people answering back all the time.

"What I think he was trying to do by following me was to protect the reform wing of the Party against the hard-liners by finding an opportunity to criticize me. He wanted to put up a good front by reproaching me in public, as if to say to people, 'You see! We don't agree with Fang either.' "

Wan later met with administrators and professors from local universities in Hefei, where he had once served as head of the Party's Anhui Provincial Party Committee. While agreeing that both the Party and universities needed further democratization, Wan reminded the assembled university officials and scholars that they had an obligation to "earnestly implement the political principles and line of the Party" in a way that combined democracy with discipline.

"If one goes only for democracy and does not want any centralism, if one always wants freedom but not discipline, this will not correspond with the directives of 'central' on spiritual socialist civilization," he was reported to have said.

But Wan, who had been pursuing Fang like a hound, still found his prey elusive. "I gathered that Wan's whole purpose in coming to Hefei was to criticize me," Fang said. "But I really didn't want to debate him. Why should I? However, at the meeting, which was attended by at least a hundred other people, Wan finally called out, 'Fang Lizhi! Come up here and report to me!' He insisted on bringing me up on stage with him. Although he was obviously addressing me, I still didn't want to say anything and had spoken no more than a few sentences when he started to recite verbatim parts of my talks evidently taken from the tapes he had gotten."

At this point a full-scale debate did develop between Wan and Fang and reached a crescendo over the question of where democracy comes from. It was, in fact, one of the few times in the last three and a half decades of Chinese Communist history when someone publicly challenged a high-ranking Party leader on the question of democracy.

"One of the issues I had been discussing in my speeches was my belief that democracy cannot be handed down by a leader to someone else," remembered Fang. "I had criticized this notion in Ningbo and Shanghai, and feel it is a misguided concept. Loosening someone's bonds is not democracy. But Wan insisted that democracy is something that can only be handed down. This is a very fundamental point of difference, and I told him that it was one on which I would never surrender."

Actually, Wan's intention did not appear to have been to crush Keda's democracy movement but to temper it and bring it back under the umbrella of Party leadership. For the paramount desire of Party reformers was certainly not to alienate this future modernizing core of scientists and intellectuals. Instead, Wan and other reform-minded leaders wanted to mobilize them behind Deng's ambitious program of economic reform. Wan simply hoped to remind the Hefei student movement's leaders not to carry their protest forward too fast or too far, and especially not to forget the unchallengeable primacy of the Party, which would be the ultimate dispenser of any democracy in China.

Wan found Fang particularly intractable on the subjects of academic freedom and university independence from Party control. When Fang condemned the government's interventions in academic affairs, Wan disagreed, maintaining that a university could not view itself as separate from society and that extreme views and support for demonstrating students would only jeopardize the whole reform movement. After Fang quoted the Constitution (Article 35 states: "Citizens of the People's Republic of China enjoy freedom of speech, of the press, of assembly, of association, of procession, and of demonstration") to make the point that the Keda students had done nothing illegal by demonstrating, the two men reportedly departed at loggerheads.

As it turned out, the Hefei protest ended peacefully and to good effect. After the elections were postponed and provisions made for students to propose candidates of their own, people like Fang could have won a seat when the election for the local People's Congress took place. Hefei Party officials had been badly ruffled by the experience of being at the epicenter of these student tremors that immediately sent shocks waves pulsing throughout the rest of the country. Hardly able to comprehend what had taken place, a commentator in the *Anhui Daily* wrote, "Recently some young people, mainly college students, raised the slogans 'Strive for Democracy! Strive for Freedom!' and 'We Want Democracy, We Want Freedom!' But against whom were they 'striving for freedom,' and from whom were they 'demanding democracy and freedom'? From the state? It is illogical for the masters of the country to demand this from their own country. . . ."

|||||||||||||||||||||||||||||||||||||

·— Fang Lizhi Addresses ————————·
the Students of
Shanghai

Earlier that fall, having just returned from an academic trip abroad, Fang Lizhi gave several speeches in Shanghai. On November 18 he appeared on the campus of Tongji University, where he addressed a crowd of students on the subjects of democracy, reform, and modernization, rousing them to repeated rounds of applause. It is worth reprinting substantial excerpts of this speech, not only because it helped galvanize those university students to action, but because it was representative of the kinds of provocative and influential addresses Fang had been giving on campuses in other Chinese cities.

"We now have a strong sense of urgency about achieving modernization in China," he began. "Chinese intellectual life, material civilization, moral fiber, and government are in dire straits. . . . The truth is, every aspect of the Chinese world needs to be modernized. . . . As for myself, I think all-around openness is the only way to modernize. I believe in such a thorough and comprehensive liberalization because Chinese culture is not just backward in a particular respect but primitive in an overall sense. . . . We are still far behind the rest of the world.

And frankly, I feel we lag behind because the decades of socialist experimentation since Liberation have been—well, a failure! [Long applause] This is not just my opinion; it is clear for all to see. Socialism is at a low ebb. There is no getting around the fact that no socialist state in the post–World War II era has been successful, nor has our own thirty-odd-year-long socialist experiment. . . . I am here to tell you that the socialist movement from Marx and Lenin to Stalin and Mao Zedong has been a failure. . . .

"Clearing our minds of all Marxist dogma is the first step. . . . We must remold our society by absorbing influences from all cultures. What we must not do is isolate ourselves and allow our conceit to convince us that we alone are correct. . . .

"We are hobbled by many old ideas that we have grown to accept as natural. But going abroad leads one to realize that those old habits of thought are flawed, that there are many reasons for China's failure to keep up with the rest of the world. . . .

"The critical component of the democratic agenda is human rights. Human rights are fundamental privileges that people have from birth, such as the right to think and be educated, the right to marry, and so on. But we Chinese consider these rights dangerous. Although human rights are universal and concrete, we Chinese lump freedom, equality, and brotherhood together with capitalism and criticize them all in the same terms. If we are the democratic country we say we are, these rights should be stronger here than elsewhere, but at present they are nothing more than an abstract idea. [Enthusiastic applause]

"I feel that the first step toward democratization should be the recognition of human rights. . . . But [in China] democratization has come to mean something performed by superiors on inferiors—a serious misunderstanding of democracy. [Loud applause] Our government cannot give us democracy by loosening our bonds a bit. This gives us only enough freedom to writhe a little. [Enthusiastic applause] Freedom by decree is not fit to be called democracy, because it fails to provide the most basic human rights.

"Our newspapers often report the inspection tours of the 'people's representatives.' Can 'representatives of the people' make inspections? Think about it. Does such a thing take place in a democracy? Representatives are selected *by* the people. They should represent their constituency, not inspect it. [Applause] An institution that 'inspects' the people is not democratic.

"Early this year I spent several months at a research institute in

New Jersey [the Institute for Advanced Study in Princeton]. One day I received in the mail some information from a state congressman describing what he had recently accomplished in the state legislature, his voting record, what issues were being discussed—in short, giving an account of his political activities. . . . He even cared about the views of a Chinese man who had been accustomed to calling American society a false democracy! On the other hand, in our 'genuine democracy,' I have never received a report of my representative's activities or his voting record! [Applause] My representative is only too happy to cast my vote for me without having the vaguest idea what I think. That is why our genuine democracy will never be a match for their false democracy.

"In a democratic nation, democracy flows from the individual, and the government has responsibilities toward him. . . . The citizens of a democratic society expect their taxes to be returned as government services and to be used to protect their individual rights. The situation in China is quite different: We praise our government whenever it finally gets around to doing something for us, when in fact by doing so, the government does nothing more than fulfill its obligations to us. . . . We must make our government realize that it is economically dependent on its citizens, because such is the basis of democracy. But feudal traditions are still strong in China; social relations are initiated by superiors and accepted by inferiors. . . .

"People of other societies believe that criminal accusations arising from casual suspicion harm human dignity and privacy. In China, on the other hand, it is not only normal for me to inform on you but considered a positive virtue. I would be praised for my alertness and contribution to class struggle in spite of my disrespect for democracy and human rights. . . .

"In many Western nations universities are independent of the government. Indeed, the management of a university system, its educational content, academic standards, and goals should be determined by academic, not political leadership. [Applause] Money, of course, is still a necessity, and for this a university needs the government's helping hand, but the government's responsibility should end there. . . .

"My point is that higher education can become an important democratizing force. To liberate oneself from the slavery of governmental and other nonintellectual authorities, one need only view knowledge as an independent organism. But this is not so in China.

What our universities produce are tools, not educated men. [Applause] Our graduates cannot think for themselves. They are quite happy to be the docile instruments of someone else's purposes. China's intelligentsia has still not cleansed itself of this tendency. . . . Knowledge should be independent of power. It must never submit, for knowledge loses its value as soon as it bows to power. . . .

"Science should be allowed to develop according to its own principles, free of any ideological straitjacket. Marxist critiques of academic methods since Liberation have been utterly erroneous. . . . I have heard grumbling about my political ideas, and that is fine. But I simply will not accept any interference in my scientific research. . . . Democracy will have no protection until the entire scientific community is filled with this spirit. The products of scientific knowledge should be appraised by scientific standards. We should not be swayed by the winds of power. Only then can we modernize, and only then will we have real democracy."

Fang's speeches, verbalizing what many of his colleagues thought but dared not utter in public, were like detonations set off beneath the whole edifice of Party thought control. Here at last, after thirty-five years of suppression of almost all alternative or oppositional thoughts, was a man who when he spoke made no effort to censor the forbidden or divide his thoughts between the private and the public. For many in his audiences his speeches were almost like dreaming. In refusing to abide by the unspoken strictures as to what was acceptable to the Party, Fang himself manifested a whole new range of individual freedoms hitherto unimaginable to most Chinese. His speeches not only planted new ideas in the minds of his listeners but were living evidence of what a political intellect that refuses to be fettered and intimidated is like at work. Because Fang and a small number of other dissidents had begun to speak out publicly—suggesting alternative ways of looking at the Party, China, and even the world—political discourse in China acquired a new depth of field, a three-dimensionality in which Party orthodoxy at least momentarily lost its monopoly.

Although Fang himself could sometimes sound cynical, he was in fact not a cynic. Quite the contrary, he was in the deepest sense an idealist, and it was his infectious idealism about democracy that made him not only a compelling speaker but apparently such a threat to the Party. In talking with Fang myself, I was often struck by the utter lack of alarm or anxiety he expressed in the face of the chaotic world of Chinese politics that swirled so menacingly around him. His strong convictions and deep beliefs seemed to render him invulnerable not only to threats of retaliation but to exactly the kind of defensiveness and intellectual disorientation that characterized so much of the rest of the Chinese political dialogue.

Although Fang had had more personal experience in combatting the Party than most people, because of his unfailing equanimity I sometimes wondered whether he really did fully grasp its unyielding nature and propensity for lashing out when confronted with heterodox ideas or challenges to its supremacy. For he always seemed unrattled, even cheerful, often exhibiting a disarming strain of insouciant optimism, accompanied by a buoyant sense of indestructibility that was uncommon among most other Chinese intellectuals. In the end it seemed to me that his powerful aura of self-confidence was somehow connected not only to his unusual personality but to his being in the sciences, a member of that tiny crucial elite that Deng's reforms could not do without. As perhaps China's most renowned scientist, Fang seemed to sense that, in some measure at least, he was armor-clad in a way that most other intellectuals were not; and very consciously he seemed to have decided to trade on the unique protection that science afforded him in order to leap into the parlous arena of Chinese politics.

What was so paradoxical about the situation in which Fang found himself was that, by December, 1986, the expanding openness of the very system he so relentlessly criticized had begun to give him cause for some real optimism. It was a paradox of which Fang himself was well aware, that he appreciated fully, and that, with his usual magnanimity, he was willing to acknowledge, even in public. As he admitted to students at Tongji University that November, "Lately China has come a long way. . . . Speaking of the present situation, we are better off this year than last, and last year was better than the year before. Although I would certainly not have dared say these words a year ago, now they can be expressed."

IIIIIIIIIIIIIIIIIIIIIIIII
The
·—— Students March ————————————·
on Shanghai

At the end of November, 1986, the American surf-rock band Jan and Dean arrived in Shanghai for a series of concerts in the city's 18,000-seat Shanghai Stadium. As the first well-known American rock group to tour China, they were given a rapturous reception. During the last of their six concerts, some members of the audience, carried away by the music and urged on by band members, climbed over the barricades that separated the seats from the stage and began to dance. This was a kind of spontaneous audience participation with which Chinese authorities, already uneasy about this unusual form of pop-cultural exchange, were unfamiliar.

"During the last two concerts things did begin to get pretty wild," recalled Shanghai-born Tiffany Chu, president of the Santa Monica–based company called China Amusement and Leisure, which organized the band's Friendship Tour 86. "People began to get up out of the audience and started dancing in the aisles. Then a few of them got pretty excited and jumped onto the stage and began dancing there, too. I think that some of the dancers were from Tongji and Jiaotong universities and that one or two of them were even American students. I guess the whole thing just made the security people real nervous. They certainly weren't used to that sort of concert. And, I must admit, if all eighteen thousand fans had started dancing, there would have been chaos."

Although there are varying versions of what happened next, it appears that the concert itself ended without major incident. Afterward, however, stadium security guards reportedly tried to arrest one of the dancers, a student from Jiaotong University. When he protested his innocence and resisted arrest, he was beaten. Angered by the behavior of the security guards, a group of fellow Jiaotong University students formed to demand that authorities punish the offending guards, or at least put them on notice that what the students called such "special privileges of certain cadres who are above the law" would no longer be tolerated. When their demands were ignored, the agitated students reportedly appealed directly to the mayor of Shanghai, Jiang Zemin, who happened to be a university alumnus.

At approximately the same time, word of the student demonstrations in Hefei reached Shanghai. During the second week of December big-character posters suddenly began to appear at Fudan, Tongji, and Jiaotong universities. These criticized the slowness of political reform, university living standards, boring curricula, inflation (which had hit students on fixed stipends particularly hard that year), and the stultifying bureaucracy of the Party, which operated more on the basis of *guanxi*, or "connections," and corruption than on merit.

On December 18, Jiang Zemin went to Jiaotong University to have a "dialogue" with the students in hopes of calming them down, but in front of an overflow crowd of three thousand at the university auditorium Jiang was less than convincing in answering student complaints. He even denied that there had been brutality at the Jan and Dean concert; nor did he make the situation any better for himself when he demanded that students stop putting up wall posters and cease other activities that he viewed as "unfavorable to the political stability and unity" of the country. Instead of speaking to student concerns, he simply lectured his audience on how Shanghai's economic development could be carried forward only if "citizens, especially students, refrain from divisive political activities." In the end, he was unceremoniously hooted out of the hall.

That afternoon, thousands of students broke through the locked gates of Jiaotong University and marched off the campus, located in the city's suburbs, and to Shanghai's People's Square—the old parade ground at the heart of the city where Maoist political extravaganzas were once held. They carried banners declaring: "Give Us Back Our Human Rights," "Long Live the Power of the People," "Long Live Democracy," and even "To Hell with Marxism–Leninism–Mao Zedong Thought!" Playing on the words *sui* ("years") and *shui* ("taxes"), one banner used the term *wanshui* ("ten thousand taxes") rather than *wansui* ("ten thousand years"), a traditional phrase once used to wish the Emperor longevity, proclaiming *"Deng Xiaoping Wanshui!"* ("Deng Xiaoping, Ten Thousand Taxes!" rather than "May Deng Xiaoping Live Ten Thousand Years!")

Wall posters also proliferated:

"Jiang Zemin, who elected you to office?"

"If you want to know what freedom is, just go and ask Wei Jingsheng."

"I have a dream, a dream of freedom. I have a dream of democracy. I have a dream of life endowed with human rights. May the day come when all these are more than dreams."

"When will the people be in charge?"

The next day, December 19, thousands of students from Jiaotong, Fudan, and Tongji universities flooded into downtown Shanghai, marching through the streets in what a New China News Agency dispatch called "utter disorder." After a mass meeting in People's Square, they surged off to the buildings of the Shanghai Municipal People's Congress Standing Committee (site of the city's legislative body). There, after breaking into the courtyard, they began milling around this nerve center of municipal government, causing a monumental traffic jam on the Bund, the downtown roadway and esplanade that runs along the embankment of the Huangpu River. Although Vice-Mayor Ye Gongyi made an appearance and talked with the demonstrators, student representatives would not be placated until they saw the mayor himself.

"Jiang Zemin! Come out and answer our questions!" they shouted up at the mayor's office.

Several orders to disperse issued by police from the city's Public Security Bureau, which by now had several thousand men on duty in the area, were ignored. Although a few scuffles between police and students broke out, the police acted with notable reserve, which suggested that they were under orders from top echelons in the Party leadership to take great pains not to incite the students further. In fact, after claiming students had beaten thirty-one of their men, the Public Security Bureau suddenly retracted the charge, as if it wished to do nothing more to inflame an already explosive situation.

Not until midnight did the mayor appear and consent to talk with student representatives. Although he said that their demands for an acceleration of socialist democracy were "understandable," he faulted them for disrupting "public order and social stability," and for inconveniencing thousands of workers who had been unable to get to their jobs through the downtown congestion caused by their protest. He also pointed out that the Constitution had been amended so that it was no longer legal to put up big-character posters.

Unsatisfied with this response, student leaders continued to press a list of their demands, asking that no reprisals be taken against demonstrators, that the government acknowledge the legality and constitutionality of the marches, that students be granted access to the media to air their views, and that political reform in both Shanghai and the rest of the country be speeded up. According to some reports, Jiang finally promised to accept the first and second of their demands, but warned them that if they wished to demonstrate further, they would have to apply for police permits.

"I cannot but point out that a tiny number of people are attempting to disrupt stability and unity, to derange production and social order by taking advantage of the patriotic zeal of the students and their longing for freedom and democracy" was Jiang's commentary on the matter. In another appeal to the students, he said he hoped that "students with a sense of patriotism would never do anything that would harm the interests of the state and the people."

As it turned out, such appeals to patriotism fell on deaf ears. On December 20, an estimated 30,000 students from almost all of Shanghai's major institutions of higher learning poured into the streets shouting such slogans as "Jiang Zemin Is a Coward." Together with thousands of middle-school students, curious onlookers, and workers (some of whom were themselves angered by inflation and rising food prices), the crowd spilled onto Nanjing Road, Shanghai's main shopping area, bringing traffic to a dead stop.

Having repeatedly called for greater democracy and the right of free expression, the Chinese government was now in the awkward position of being hoisted on its own petard by the very class of people it most urgently needed marching behind its own banner of modernization; the group on which it pinned its greatest hopes of turning China into an economically advanced country. On Sunday, December 22, in spite of police attempts to section off "rebel centers" by guarding the gates at Tongji and Jiaotong universities, no fewer than 15,000 students managed to slip out and march to the center of Shanghai, where they once more snarled traffic and this time even overturned and burned several cars. One manifesto handed out on three-by-five-inch mimeographed slips of paper was addressed "To our countrymen" and said: "Our guiding principle is to propagate democratic ideas among the people. Our slogan is to oppose bureaucracy and authoritarianism, and to strive for democracy and freedom. The time has come to awaken those democratic ideas that have long been suppressed."

Another handout, an "Open Letter to All Fellow Citizens," said: "Between the past and the future, there is only the present. We cannot rewrite history, but we can change the present and create the future. In the face of the reality of poverty and autocracy, we can endure. However, we cannot just allow our children to grow up abnormally in shackles and in the absence of freedom, democracy, and human rights. We cannot just allow them to feel poor and abused when standing together with foreign children. Fellow citizens, please understand! Bureaucracy, obscurantism, and the lack of democracy and human rights are the roots of backwardness."

This time, still showing restraint, the police were successful in herding the mob into People's Park in downtown Shanghai, where for the rest of the day students listened to speeches, including one by a twenty-two-year-old student from the Huadong College of Political Science and Law who told the crowd, "So long as there is one-party domination and no rule of law, the enterprise of liberation is not finished." He concluded by emotionally proclaiming that he was willing to shed his blood "for the early achievement of real democracy in China."

Some pedestrians and bystanders, more concerned with issues like inflation and Party corruption than democracy, demonstrated sympathy for the boldness of the protesters and made small contributions of food and money to the hungry, cold students. But many others just stood around watching curiously, swelling the crowds, so that it became more and more difficult to tell who was an actual protester and who was just an onlooker.

As in Hefei, official reaction in Shanghai was tentative at first. Both the local and national Party leaders seemed confused and uncertain about how to respond to this bizarre, unexpected series of events. Symptomatically, a person described as "a leading official of the higher education department of the State Education Commission" told the New China News Agency on December 20, "It is true some college students . . . have recently held demonstrations. But according to our Constitution, Chinese citizens have the right to demonstrate. . . . According to the resolution of the Sixth Plenary Session of the Twelfth Party Central Committee, one of the important planks of the restructuring of the political system is to expand socialist democracy. It is understandable that college students should be concerned about the restructuring of the political system and hope to express their views on these issues."

On December 21 the *Guangming Daily* even published a commentary that seemed to support the marchers; it said that in the future China should place even greater emphasis on "consciousness of democracy, freedom, rights, and political participation of the people." A representative from the Shanghai Municipal Foreign Affairs Office offered this not atypical, if noticeably fuzzy, comment: "If people want to give their suggestions or express their opinion, that is normal." Such local statements still seemed to reflect accurately the Party line coming down from "Central" in Beijing, where leaders appeared to continue to hope that the demonstrations would remain isolated in Shanghai and finally peter out on their own.

When Western reporters contacted Fang Lizhi by phone in Hefei, he, too, spoke as if there had not yet been any big rupture between the students and the Party. "Many people's attitudes have changed as a result of discussions on democracy," he said, not without a hint of pride. "In the government, attitudes have changed too."

The government press was naturally not in a rush to report the events in Hefei and Shanghai to the rest of China. In fact, the Propaganda Department of the Shanghai Municipal Communist Party Committee had explicitly forbidden even local papers to carry accounts of the unrest. However, editors of one local paper did succeed in evading the eye of the censors and included one small article on the demonstrations at the very bottom of a page. It was only after 300,000 copies of the paper had been printed that the offending piece was discovered by officialdom, necessitating the destruction of the whole press run.

But what the authorities had not counted on were those extraterritorial communications networks—the British Broadcasting Corporation and the Voice of America—that the Party could not silence. Nor could they control the formidable Chinese *xiaodao xiaoxi*, or "grapevine," which Shanghai students aided and abetted by making long-distance phone calls and sending thousands of letters to friends in other cities. Some students even went directly to train stations, where they persuaded sympathizers to carry messages, letters, and leaflets explaining what was happening in Shanghai directly to friends at schools in other cities, thus spreading the news of the Shanghai demonstrations across China with virtually no help from the Chinese media.

With the demonstrations bringing downtown Shanghai to a virtual halt for four days and no end of them in sight, on December 22 the Shanghai Municipal Public Security Bureau issued a notice prohibiting demonstrators from "harming the interests of the state, society, or collectives and the legitimate freedom and rights of other citizens." The notice decreed that public order in the city must be maintained at all times and that demonstrations and rallies could be held only after permission was granted. With typical Party obsessiveness about detail, the order meticulously catalogued the acts that would be considered offenses: "Citizens are prohibited from disrupting or attacking government offices, radio and television stations, newspaper offices, and the offices of foreigners in Shanghai, as well as from obstructing state functionaries from performing their official duties. It is prohibited to encircle, sneer at, insult, abuse, or beat state functionaries such as cadres and members of the people's police. It is prohibited to infringe on the legitimate rights of the masses, to start rumors creating trouble, or to confuse and poison the people's minds. It is strictly prohibited for anyone to invent a story that in any way slanders or insults others. . . ."

At the same time, the authorities saturated the city with posters that warned that bad elements had infiltrated the student movement. The gates to Mayor Jiang's office were chained shut and barricaded with heavy timbers. A statement read from the Municipal Public Security Bureau over Shanghai Radio called on citizens to "expose trouble-making, disruptive activities by a small number of people and criminals with ulterior motives in order to maintain public order."

When reporters interviewed Deng Xiaoping's daughter, Deng Lin, who had arrived in Hong Kong a few days earlier to exhibit her plum blossom paintings in a show of Chinese art, she said in a voice that few assumed to be her own that while she could "understand the students . . . want democracy," it was her view that democracy was "already on the way. . . . Our society is becoming more and more liberal, and all kinds of reforms are going on. . . . It is perfectly all right to air grievances and make suggestions. Knowing the way things are managed in China, their demands for improvement are probably justified. . . . But I find their demands for democracy rather one-sided. I also disagree with the way they express their dissatisfaction, if violence has indeed been reported. . . . We have to take things step by step because stability is essential for the reforms to succeed. . . . What the leadership wants is that the reforms be accepted by the public and continue in a stable environment so that everyone can get rich soon. . . ."

Taking a similar if more strident approach, Shanghai officials now began a full-fledged propaganda campaign against the students. Calling out old revolutionaries to make the requisite testimonials for socialism, peace, and quiet, and drafting sundry officials to equate demonstrating students with the mob rule and the chaos caused by the Cultural Revolution, the municipal government began to paint a most unflattering picture of the student rebels and the "so-called" democracy which they had advocated. "People of our age know from personal experience what so-called Western democracy is all about," Zhao Chaogou, director of the Shanghai-based paper *Xinmin Evening News*, was provoked to declare. "Western democracy is, in essence, rich people's democracy, not poor people's democracy. This has been verified by numerous facts."

"Now some people believe that opening to the outside world should mean 'wholesale Westernization,' " said Gu Chaohao, Vice-President of the Chinese Mathematical Society and former President of Fudan University. "But, as a matter of fact, many things in capitalist society are unacceptable to us. Take the democratic system, for example. People in Western nations are unable to enjoy genuine democracy. All that we can learn from foreign countries is their advanced science, technology, and management."

Although authorities had every right to congratulate themselves for the aplomb with which they had handled this very delicate matter—avoiding force, mass arrests, and severe punishments, which might easily have escalated the conflict—these weary rebuttals indicated that Party tolerance was hardly infinite. Fortunately, just as officials were promulgating strict new regulations that specifically prohibited street marches without permits, the student demonstrations in Shanghai began to fade. Although there were still calls on various Shanghai campuses for a student boycott of classes, because they lacked leadership and there was no specific *casus belli*, they went largely unobserved.

For now, the moment seemed to have passed. One disappointed student at Jiaotong University wrote an open letter in wall-poster form that ended with the couplets: "The masses have yet to awake. We walk forward alone, like orphans into a den of wolves. When we die, there will be no burial place for us."

But the student need not have been quite so despairing. The official reaction and counter-attack may have succeeded in dampening the protest movement in Shanghai, but, to use Mao's words, it had already become "the spark that lit the prairie fire." Unbeknownst to the Shanghai rebels, student demonstrations began breaking out all across China and would ultimately sweep through at least eighteen other large Chinese cities.

||||||||||||||||||||||||||||||

The
·——— Students March ———————————·
on Beijing

No sooner had the student protests quieted down in Shanghai than they erupted in Beijing. On the evening of December 23, 1986, the day after students in Shanghai had begun to return to their classes, thousands of student protesters in the capital shocked Party officials when they massed on the campus of Qinghua University to demand a debate with school officials on the question of democratization. When their demand was not met, they took to the streets and marched toward People's University, chanting such slogans as "Maintain Solidarity with Our Fellow Students from Shanghai," "Long Live Freedom and Human Rights," and "Recognize Freedom of the Press and Freedom of Publication." A smaller group of bolder students broke off from the main body and tried to march on Tian'anmen Square in front of the Forbidden City and the Great Hall of the People at the heart of the capital, but at one in the morning they were intercepted by police and turned back.

Even with the example of the Shanghai demonstrations before them, the government's initial response was a hesitant one. An editorial in the *People's Daily* did nothing more than admonish students not to jeopardize the achievements of Deng's eight years of leadership by "excessive action." An article on December 25 in the *China Youth News*, a publication controlled by the liberal reform-minded Hu Yaobang faction of the Party, still pleaded with the students to understand the dangers of what they were doing. "One of the most fundamental and important conditions for achievements in the various fields over the past eight years has been stability and unity," it said. "Hence, every youth must be duty bound to defend and develop the current good situation in a highly responsible manner while at the same time being inspired to plunge into the motherland's cause of reform. Our reform is the self-perfection and development of socialism. Its nature determines that the reforms in China must not take the form of a tempestuous political movement. . . . The Great Proletarian Revolution has taught us the lesson that turmoil must not be permitted to wreak havoc but must instead be repulsed."

The next day, *China Youth News* used a similar tone of imploring exasperation to convince the students to drop their demonstrations: "Reform cannot be accomplished in one day. Difficulties and contradictions are unavoidable in the process of reform, and smooth progress is usually interwoven with frustration. . . . Ideas, opinions, and demands of youth should be offered through reasonable, regular democratic channels and must not be expressed in simple or emotional ways. This will only make reform more difficult, increase its complexity, and impede progress. . . . The masses should understand the difficulties of their leaders and support their work. Even when it comes to leaders who may have made mistakes in their work, the masses should help them with zeal or truthfully report their mistakes to higher authorities. Experience has proven that the extreme democracy prevailing during the period of the Cultural Revolution brought us nothing but damage."

While one might have thought that any Communist government would have reacted with more resolution when rebellious students from its most prestigious universities took to the streets criticizing it in such harsh terms, at first the Party seemed to avert its collective gaze and tread water in hopes that the whole problem would simply disappear. Liberal reformers within the leadership in particular were fearful of giving Maoist hard-liners a pretext for portraying their reform program as a recipe for certain social and political chaos.

Trying to placate student demands, city officials even announced that they would allow more candidates than there were slots available for the upcoming election for delegates to the local district People's Congresses. However, by December 26, with students still marching in Beijing and the demonstrations having spread to at least eleven other cities, a special meeting of the now thoroughly alarmed Party leadership convened in the capital. Appearing to resolve their differences for the moment, Party leaders decided to crack down. Key to this decision was Deng Xiaoping, who had evidently come to believe that firmness was now in order before further unravelling affected the delicate balance in leadership circles on which his reform program was based. A notice released by the General Office of the Party Central Committee to local Party committees reflected the leadership's new position: "A handful of vicious elements have collected instances of defective government leadership and, exaggerating and expanding them, have used and abetted students, leading them on the road against the Communist Party and socialism in a bid to topple the Party leadership."

It was no secret that the military and conservatives within the Party leadership viewed the student unrest with extreme consternation and as the bitter consequence of the reformers having loosed too many infectious, polluting, and uncontrollable Western ideas on China. Now the moment for their long-awaited counter-attack appeared to have arrived—with Deng Xiaoping firmly in their camp. The Standing Committee of the Beijing Municipal People's Congress immediately joined other Chinese cities in issuing new regulations. While these did not officially suspend the constitutionally guaranteed right to demonstrate, they did require students wishing to march to apply for a permit five days in advance, stating their names and the purpose of their demonstration. The new regulations also placed the Great Hall of the People, Communist Party headquarters, the airport, and the gates to Zhongnanhai (the compound in which the Communist Party leadership worked and lived) out of bounds.

When Shanghai students had made an application based on similar regulations, issued several days earlier, they had immediately been turned down. Lest there be any confusion about the intent of the new Beijing regulations, Mayor Chen Xitong, who had been infuriated by the student protests, clarified the situation by saying, "Demonstrations are useless. Workers do not support them. Peasants do not support them." And, he went on to add, he did not support them either.

With demonstrations effectively banned, and wall posters long since outlawed, the students were left with virtually no legal means to express their dissenting views. Should students have had any lingering doubts about the permissibility of wall posters in China, an editorial in the

People's Daily on December 29 reminded them that "big-character posters, which wrought such havoc during the 'Great Proletarian Revolution,' are loathed and opposed by the overwhelming majority of Chinese. Not a single dignified government in the world allows big-character posters to run amok in its country. During the Ten Years of Chaos, however, big-character posters were even written into our constitution [and they] ran rampant all over China, bringing untold suffering to our people . . . and plunging our socialist motherland into darkness. They were abused by one person after another as tools to spread all kinds of rumors, slander, abuses, threats, blackmail, demagoguery, and instigation. They were used to sow discord, stir up trouble, and practice intrigues and conspiracy. . . . The catastrophe brought our national economy and culture to the brink of collapse."

But as one wall poster at Beida tried to point out, "We write big-character posters because it is the only way we can express our opinions. There is no crime in the posters, but even so, some people want to close off our only breathing hole, letting us quietly suffocate under layers of mud and dirt just so we can regain 'social stability' and 'unity.' "

However, the *Beijing Daily*, a hard-line paper run by the city of Beijing, was insistent in its opposition, warning its readers, "No citizen should ever again use big-character posters, which are illegal instruments, to express his ideas, and any citizen has the right to remove them on sight." Almost immediately Party cadres appeared on Beijing university campuses and began tearing down the offending posters, while, following the lead of the Beijing press, newspapers across the country launched attacks on the wall posters and the demonstrations. Some papers cited Article 102 of the Criminal Law of China (passed in 1980), which stipulated that those "who through counter-revolutionary slogans, leaflets, or other means propagandize for or incite the overthrow of the political power of the dictatorship of the proletariat and the socialist system [will be] sentenced to not more than five years of fixed-term imprisonment, criminal detention, control, or deprivation of political rights." They also menaced the students with Article 145, which stipulated, "Whoever, by violence or other methods, including the use of big-character posters and small-character posters, publicly insults another person, or trumps up facts to defame another person, when the circumstances are serious, is to be sentenced to not more than three years of fixed-term imprisonment."

Most ominous for ordinary Chinese, particularly for intellectuals, was the way in which the language of official attacks on the students had begun to include the term "counter-revolutionary." Although counter-revolutionaries were defined by the Chinese government as any "individuals who incite others to resist arrest or to violate the law and statutes of the state," people recalled all too vividly the kind of state terror that the Party had been capable of perpetrating under the simple and often indiscriminate label of "counter-revolutionary activity." Common as it once was, the whole concept of designating people as belonging to such anti-Party categories had largely been dropped since Deng's reforms began. Still, few older people, at least, had forgotten the past, and the mere official mention of such words as "counter-revolutionary," "rightist," "capitalist roader," or "anti-Party element" was enough to instantly chill most Chinese to the bone. Not only was such rhetoric now being revived, but another category of heresy was also coming back to life: The student movement suddenly started being accused of having been infiltrated by agents from Taiwan, a charge that in the past had spelled instant doom to anyone tainted by it.

To make matters worse, on December 27, a "tea party" was held in the Zhongnanhai leadership compound next to the old Imperial City, ostensibly to honor a storyteller named Yuan Kuocheng. The tea party, however, was attended by Wang Zhen, Bo Yibo, Song Renqiong, Hu Qiaomu, and Deng Liqun, a veritable rogues' gallery of China's most hard-line Maoist Party leaders. Each of them, after making the briefest genuflection to China's glorious storytelling tradition, promptly eulogized the Party and Maoist revolutionary values in a series of only thinly disguised attacks on the policies of the reformers.

"The Chinese Communist Party is a great, glorious, and politically correct party that has always retained its revolutionary vigor," proclaimed the seventy-eight-year old Wang Zhen. "The leadership of the Communist Party is not granted by heaven, but by the countless revolutionary martyrs who, wave after wave, shed blood and sacrificed themselves for half a century. . . . Chinese possess a rich and precious cultural heritage. But some people who advocate national nihilism debase and negate China by calling for a wholesale Westernization of China. This is bourgeois liberalism, to which the people and the masses are opposed."

Seventy-four-year-old Hu Qiaomu, dispensing with the idea of storytelling in the blink of an eye, said, "Serving the people is the starting point and purpose of all our work. The idea of putting money above everything else is not good. . . . We need to introduce foreign things that are useful to us . . . [but it is] wrong to think everything we have is bad. To influence others, especially youth and juveniles, with such national nihilism is the most inappropriate thing to do." Bo Yibo, in turn, lambasted those who "advocate 'bourgeois liberalism' and 'wholesale Westernization,'" calling this "tantamount to negating the socialist system and favoring the capitalist system."

Before dawn on a bitterly cold morning two days later, on December 29, the students made their next move. Ignoring the ban on demonstrations and the new stridency of Party leaders, students from Beijing Teachers' University (Shida) took to the streets again. The immediate cause of this demonstration was a dispute with university authorities, whom students had caught ripping down wall posters and banners. Brandishing burning brooms as torches, carrying cotton banners covered with slogans, and shouting "We want freedom!" they surged off campus and marched toward People's University (Renda) and Beijing University (Beida). There they broke open the locked gates, poured inside, beating drums and washbasins, and exhorted the other students to join them. One demonstrator from Guizhou was reported to have been arrested after he climbed on top of the Beida university wall and loudly proclaimed the four demands of the students: an end to the new rules banning demonstrations, the right to distribute the magazine *Chinese Intellectual* (edited in New York by the expatriate Chinese writer Liang Heng), the right to establish an association to promote democracy, and an end to one-party dictatorship in China.

The demonstration wound up at Beida that morning without further incident. But the following night, when again several thousand students from Shida tried to leave their campus, they found their own gates locked and barred by police. The next day a new flurry of wall posters appeared around the capital:

> "When we began our struggle for freedom and democracy, you panicked and now consider us terrible animals. This shows that your democracy is fake."

> "Dictatorship by one party has monopolized the entire legislative, judicial, executive, foreign policy, military, and propaganda machinery of the country. . . . The wantonly distorting propaganda has unceas-

ingly cheated the people. This is our political system: little better than feudal despotism and even more ruthless, dictatorial, and terroristic. In every respect it is identical to the most tyrannical feudal despotisms we've had."

"Beijing University comrades: The circumstances for democracy are ripe. Raise your hands in an iron fist. What we must now do is act like heroes."

"It is astonishing that the government has so rapidly taken off its mask and is so scared. The one billion Chinese are but a toy in the hands of the rulers. . . ."

". . . In the United States there is the false freedom to support or not to support the Communist Party. In our country we have the genuine freedom of having to support the Communist Party. In the United States there is the false freedom of the press. In our country we have the genuine freedom of no freedom of the press."

On December 31, on the occasion of the Central Committee Party School's sponsorship of a meeting to "greet the new year," Wang Zhen gave another speech, which was, after a fashion, the Party's response to the students, and it was ominously hard-line:

"Recently some people have stopped paying attention to adhering to the socialist road, the dictatorship of the proletariat, the leadership of the Communist Party, and Marxism–Leninism–Mao Zedong Thought. They advocate bourgeois liberalism and say that democracy means that 'no one is afraid of anybody.' They are completely wrong. We must wage resolute struggle against these people and these things that openly negate the Four Cardinal Principles." Wang's point of reference was a rather optimistic statement Fang Lizhi had made to Jiaotong University students just the month before. "Democracy does not mean that I will impose my views on you. Democracy means that I am allowed to express my views. If I criticize your opinion as being wrong, you may refute me. That is why I said that in today's China, no one is afraid of anybody." Was Wang implying that under socialism, everyone should be afraid of everyone else? It seemed to be an unavoidable conclusion. Certainly Wang's statement accurately reflected the historical experience of socialism for China's intellectuals.

On the same day the *Beijing Daily*'s front page carried a "New Year's message" from Mayor Chen Xitong, in which he warned portentously, if vaguely, of "elements hostile to socialism," of "evil winds," and of "class enemies." The specter of arrests for crimes of a class nature, however, was raised in its starkest form when Beijing Television announced on that final day of 1986 that the Public Security Bureau had arrested an unemployed worker, Xue Deyun, for "impersonating a student and making trouble" during one of the recent demonstrations in Beijing, and then that the Shanghai Public Security Bureau had arrested Shi Guanfu, the "ringleader" of a "counter-revolutionary organization." He was accused of allegedly plotting to set up a "so-called Chinese People's Party for the Defense of the People," of "instigating" students, publishing incitive literature (in which he reportedly wrote that "the Chinese, chained day and night in jail, want freedom"), and of vowing "to topple" the Chinese Communist Party itself.

On January 1, in subfreezing weather, several thousand students, refusing to be intimidated, began a march on the spiritual seat of political power in China, Tian'anmen Square. This vast square, enlarged under Chairman Mao's direction into the most spacious socialist parade ground in the world so that it could host the mass rallies of which he was once so enamored, lies at the heart of Beijing, in front of both the Imperial City and the Great Hall of the People. Traditionally, the mere act of reaching the square had a legitimizing effect on any protest movement in Beijing. It was in Tian'anmen Square that China's first mass student demonstrations touched off the May Fourth Movement in 1919. Students returned again in 1935 to launch the nationwide protest against Chiang Kai-shek's policy of non-resistance to Japan. In 1949 Mao stood atop the Gate of Heavenly Peace looking out across this square and proclaimed that the Chinese people had "stood up." During the Cultural Revolution millions of Red Guards massed here to adore their Chairman and commit themselves body and soul to his cause. And in 1976 students had braved police and the Gang of Four to flood into the square in memory of Premier Zhou Enlai, who had recently passed away.

When the students reached the square this New Year's morning, however, they found it surrounded by thousands of police, organized into a human chain to block their way. They discovered, moreover, that during the night the square had been sprayed with water, leaving the concrete covered with a treacherous film of ice, presumably to make either advance or escape doubly difficult. Leaderless and uncertain about what to do, the demonstrators milled about, chanted slogans ("Long Live Freedom!" "Give Us Freedom of the Press!" "Long Live Democracy"), and soon attracted a much larger crowd of curious onlookers. Roving plainclothes police with video cameras combed the crowds compiling a running photographic documentary of the faces of those students who had "dared to rebel."

By late morning several hundred students had finally managed to break through the police cordon and to enter the square. In the process, the police had arrested and hustled away a group of twenty-four demonstrators. Having attained their goal, the remaining students gradually dispersed without further incident.

The New China News Agency, trying to play down the event, gave this almost bucolic description of the demonstration: "Tian'anmen Square, in the center of Beijing, resumed normal order at around 1 P.M. today. At 12:50 several hundred college students had staged a short demonstration on a road east of the square. Snow began falling at about three o'clock, blanketing the square, creating a beautiful landscape for picture taking."

In reality, the students had taunted the police with, "You are the people's police and should be on our side!" and scuffles had broken out. Moreover, as word of the twenty-four arrests began to spread around college campuses, students at Beijing University took the news in a less than bucolic spirit, reassembling to demand the release of the detained demonstrators. "Return our comrades! Return our comrades!" they chanted in front of the house of university President Ding Shisun. When President Ding finally appeared, he was presented with a list of demands, which included release and amnesty for the arrested students, a guarantee that no reprisals would be taken against other demonstrators, and a promise that access to the media would be given to student representatives so that the viewpoint of the demonstrators could be explained to the Chinese people. Student representatives claimed that a boycott of classes would be carried out if the demands were not met. President Ding, claiming that he was in touch with Beijing Mayor Chen Xitong, promised to consider the requests.

It was almost midnight when he returned and announced to cheers that the detained Beida students would be released. He added, "If you don't believe me, get a new president." But when it was learned that the promised release did not pertain to non-Beida students who had been arrested, a crowd once again assembled to march on Tian'anmen Square. In the early morning hours, Beida Vice-President Sha Jianxun, obviously fearful that if student demands were not met the protests would grow in both size and intensity, went out into the streets himself to announce to the students that the government had agreed to release all of those arrested. What was so curious about this denouement—and other events during this spate of nationwide demonstrations—was that despite the obvious anger of the leadership and the bluster about "counter-revolutionary" activity and "evil winds," the Party proved so cautious in its actions. As awesomely powerful as it was, when it came to dealing with the disaffection of its students and intellectuals, again and again the Party, at both the local and national levels, refused to take strong punitive action. Its restraint was a tacit admission of how reliant on the goodwill of its "experts" the reformers, at least, felt themselves to be.

Although the January 1 protests marked the end of street demonstrations, occasional flourishes of wall posters continued. Students, still furious at the way they had been portrayed in the media, indulged in one last bit of political theater and revenge. It was little wonder that they chose as their target the *Beijing Daily*, which had taken such an obdurate line against them, portraying their demands in as unflattering a manner as possible. In a typical article, Mayor Chen Xitong, who controlled the paper, had called the demonstrators "a little group of socialist enemy elements, stirring up trouble and vainly attempting to rouse the masses and to cause chaos in the capital."

Gathering at Beida under a banner that said, "*Beijing Daily* Go to Hell!," the students, in a clearly intended slap at the Party's desire to foster an image of modernity abroad, burned copies of the hated newspaper in front of foreign reporters, who promptly relayed photos of the incident around the world. So it was hardly surprising that the paper lashed back at the students, claiming that their actions "had helped the enemy" and that the "ideological root of the disturbances has been the poisonous ideological trend of bourgeois liberalism."

In support of its municipal comrade-in-arms, the *People's Daily* dove into the rhetorical fray with an editorial praising the *Beijing Daily* for "hitting those who are against the socialist system where it hurts," and it went on to denigrate the protests of the students. "There are some people who remain muddleheaded at all times. They continue to do things that sadden our own people and gladden our enemies. . . . We believe that when these young people cool down, they will blush at their naive acts and draw beneficial lessons."

Providentially for the government, nationwide examinations were about to begin, after which students were to take their month-long winter vacations over the Chinese New Year. In the highly competitive academic environment of China, few students could afford to ignore their schoolwork any longer. With a suddenness that was eerie, their protests died away, so that when I arrived on the Beida campus that February, the only sign of these momentous events were a few shreds of big-character posters fluttering here and there on walls in the chilly winter wind.

||||||||||||||||
The
Aftermath

The student demonstrations that engulfed more than a hundred fifty university campuses in at least twenty cities across China represented the largest mass movement in the country since the Cultural Revolution. But as shocked, angered, and even panicked as the government must have been at the sight of tens of thousands of its finest students marching through the streets of its cities, it dealt with the situation with remarkable coolness. What kinds of struggles went on within an obviously divided central leadership, we can only imagine. All one can say is that whatever the strident rhetoric of enraged hard-liners, cooler heads prevailed, thus averting what would have been for both the students and the Party an otherwise devastating collision.

Notable about this uprising was not only the levelheaded way in which it was finally put to rest by the authorities, but also its curiously spontaneous and ad hoc quality. It sprang up more from a general spirit of impatience and irreverence than from any coherent body of thought. There was a vagueness about the students' understanding of democracy that gave the movement a curious air of insubstantiality, even at the height of the crisis. The movement had little structure, published no underground newspapers or journals, indulged in little serious political or philosophical dialogue, and, to the end, remained virtually leaderless. In addition, with the exception of Fang Lizhi's speeches, this momentous upheaval left surprisingly little in the way of a corpus of ideas. It left no martyrs, not even a rallying cry for an imprisoned dissident like Wei Jingsheng. Unlike the participants in the Democracy Wall Movement, which included many older, more sophisticated protesters who had cut their political teeth on the ideological struggles of the Cultural Revolution, the students of 1986 were younger, less formed intellectually, and surprisingly naive about both the intricacies of Chinese Party politics and the complexities of constitutional democracy and human rights theory.

Given all this, by Chinese standards the students paid a surprisingly light price for their actions (although one would not want to have been one of the unfortunates photographed or videotaped by police during one of the marches). The movement had burst onto the horizon with a momentary brilliance, and even though it could hardly be said to have been defeated, it had quickly sunk out of sight, leaving the country in the gathering throes of a hard-line crackdown.

In its aftermath, even those students who had participated in the demonstrations seemed bewildered by what to make of it all. When James Schiffman, correspondent for the *Asian Wall Street Journal*, tried to get a sounding from some of those who had demonstrated, what came back was a curiously incoherent set of responses.

"Every person has a different idea about what democracy is," explained one young man. "For students and other people, demonstrating is a device. We use this device to stimulate change because we can't express our ideas freely. Newspapers don't emphasize what is in the people's minds. They emphasize what is in the mind of the Party."

"Some students think that we should eliminate the Four Cardinal Socialist Principles," offered another student cynically. "I don't know whether I'd go that far. Maybe we could keep one or two around for the sake of appearances."

When Schiffman asked a third student what kind of democracy was appropriate for China, he replied, "I think your question is off the subject. . . . Before, we could not speak about anything. Now it's enough just to raise slogans. We are exploring ideas. A lot of debate is going on. We don't know if capitalism is best or socialism is best."

In their way, the demonstrations of 1986 were indeed a great exploration. It is true that the students neither accomplished much in a practical sense nor greatly clarified which ism or ideology (or combination thereof) would ultimately be suitable for China; and it is also true that by antagonizing Party hard-liners, they had in the short run even retarded—or at least provided an excuse for retarding—the process of political reform. But the tumultuous events of December had most emphatically reminded students of the power their relatively small numbers had traditionally been able to wield in China, and revealed both to themselves and the Party leadership how unconvincing Marxism–Leninism–Mao Zedong Thought had become as a belief system. As one Tongji University student told me that February, "What is the alternative to democracy for China? Communism is finished. It has bankrupted itself. Power struggles have robbed the top leadership of idealism. For us students there is no alternative to democracy except to leave the country."

At the very least, in those few weeks the next generation of Chinese intellectuals absorbed not only the idea of demonstrating as a means of redressing grievances, but also the idea that democracy was something that might be fought for. By acting on their ideals, however vague and incompletely understood, the students put themselves, at least momentarily, beyond the Party and all it had represented.

Ironically, the very crisis of belief that had left such a vacuum in the lives of this upcoming generation of intellectuals ended up being their greatest asset in their quest for a new political direction. For unlike their fathers and mothers, or even men like Fang, Liu, and Wang, this new generation had no burdensome legacy of socialist doctrine to shake off and no catalogue of regrets to rationalize. Being the post-Mao generation, the children of the open door policy, these students had come of age at a time when Marxism and Maoism were in retreat. They had never waved the Little Red Book and wept for the Chairman, nor had they been sent to the countryside as "educated youth" to "learn from the workers, peasants, and soldiers." At their center was a political and spiritual void waiting to be filled. In this respect, they were, as Mao had once enthusiastically described the Chinese peasantry, "blank." "On a blank sheet of paper free from any mark," Mao had written, "the freshest and most beautiful characters can be written, the freshest and most beautiful pictures can be painted."

Mao was, of course, speaking of writing on his "masses" with a

Marxist brush, but what these demonstrations underscored was that Marxism's time as an animating belief system was passing and that young Chinese were beginning to be written upon with a new brush, the idealism of democracy. But even if the seeds of a new kind of idealism had been planted, in January, 1987, it certainly was too early to proclaim the death of Marxism in China, not with the orthodox wing of the Party thundering back onto the political stage. The symptoms of its further weakening, however, were everywhere apparent. For clearly the Party had been dislodged as a credible source of moral leadership, not so much by the critiques of the students and intellectuals as by the attacks that Party leaders had long been directing against each other, attacks that in the following months would only intensify into another disruptive battle for Party control.

PART 5

EMULATE

LEI

FENG

The New
Political
Climate

It is impossible to be in China any length of time without becoming aware of what the Chinese refer to as the *zhengzhi kongqi*, or political climate. It is a reality as palpable as any seasonal climate, and every bit as changeable. Although there are no scientific means for predicting shifts in this unique climatic condition, there are few Chinese, particularly intellectuals, who can afford to lose touch with its fluctuations for very long.

It is not out of simple curiosity or a sense of civic duty that Chinese maintain their vigilance over the political climate, but out of a sense of self-preservation. Their futures, sometimes their very lives, have often in the past depended on their ability to sense early signs of change that signal larger political storms to come. At the very least, a person must at all times know as precisely as possible where the unspoken but ever changing boundaries of permissible political discourse and behavior lie. Otherwise it is possible to be caught off base and to end up being accused of some thoughts, statements, or acts that, because of the changing Party line, have suddenly become unpardonable crimes. Like Marcel Marceau miming a man groping for the dimensions of an invisible room around him, Chinese have learned through bitter experience how to feel out the shifting, unseeable boundaries of Party tolerance.

What put vigilance at such a premium in recent years was the awareness that as the situation in China changed, if one were to be caught too far out of these acceptable boundaries the penalty might be ruin, exile, or prison. What made the business of staying within these margins such a parlous one was not only the erratic way in which leaders came and went but the rapidity with which the Party's correct line could itself be transformed—and often was—into its opposite. Not only did such sudden reversals leave unwary Chinese high and dry, but those changes in political line were also applied retroactively. This meant that one had to consider one's immediate actions in relation to the present correct line *and* in relation to any number of possible future correct lines. And since personnel offices kept lifelong *dangan*, or dossiers, filled with various reports, evaluations, and accusations on every Chinese, it was impossible to escape from one's past. Although the subject of a dossier was never allowed to look into it, it followed him or her until death, ready to be opened at any time to reveal an incident, a comment, a friendship, a trip abroad, or a piece of writing that at one historical moment had been inconsequential but at the next might become grounds for political disenfranchisement or imprisonment.

The situation in China could be compared to life on certain coral reefs where there are two distinct colonies of marine organisms: One hides by day and comes out at night; the other hides by night and comes out during the day. Each has adapted to survive and flourish on its own shift but comes into great danger if inadvertently caught out of hiding as the changeover time approaches. It is during these short periods of overlap that a predatory slaughter takes place, in which those unfortunates who failed to gain cover perish.

Instead of being controlled by the ebb and flow of the tides or the rising and setting of the sun, China's political climate over the past thirty-seven years has been dictated by the waxing and waning of the warring sides of its political personality as manifested in an ongoing, titanic struggle in the Party leadership itself. Unlike the natural environment, which changes with a certain predictability, China's political mood has moved with capricious irregularity between its two opposing poles. Just as suddenly as a period of openness has arisen, it will abruptly end, leaving all those who have spoken out exposed to being tagged with the devastating labels of class enemy, rightist, or counter-revolutionary.

It is no wonder, then, that Chinese follow these expansions and contractions of Party tolerance (one could hardly call it freedom) with as much attention as a prisoner listening to the irregular breathing of his slumbering captor. People automatically read between the lines of the official press to detect slight shifts in nuance that might suggest the advent of a new political line. They look for minute changes in the ritualistic wording of official statements. They follow key government and Party appointments for clues to which factions are ascending and which declining. They check official photos and lists of leaders to see who has failed to appear at otherwise unmemorable banquets and may consequently be headed for disgrace. Above all, they keep tuned to the grapevine, the informal communications network that spreads unofficial information like wildfire. Particularly in the capital, where information may come directly from Party sources or from family members of high-ranking officials in the know, such news proves uncannily reliable in warning of political movements and campaigns to come.

When I arrived in Beijing in February, 1987, in the wake of the student demonstrations and only four months after my previous visit, the political climate had already undergone a chilling change not unlike that between spring and fall, though it is worth noting that it was still by no means like the frozen, frightening days before the death of Mao. There was, however, in the attitudes of people I met, even those Chinese I knew well, a somber fearfulness and a sense of depression and uncertainty that had been almost completely absent a few months earlier.

Friends lowered their voices to talk about politics, an old habit that had largely been abandoned over the past few years. Some people expressed renewed concern that their phones might be bugged. A good friend, who was a Party member, feared she might be accused of having "incorrect relations with foreigners" and thought it best that I not drop off a package of books at her office. And when Agence France Presse English-language correspondent Lawrence MacDonald (whose coverage of the student demonstrations had been the most extensive and informative of any member of the Western press) was expelled from China at the end of January and a young student contact of his was arrested in Tianjin for "secret collusion" with foreigners, journalists in Beijing began to fear that their association with Chinese friends might also cause trouble.

In fact, a noticeable chill in relations between Chinese and foreigners was generally evident as Party hard-liners moved to consolidate their newly won power. "The Maoist holdovers are lunging for the big kill," said Wang Ruowang. "Throughout the country, reform-minded people are scurrying for cover. The very fate and direction of reform is at stake."

||||||||||
The
Party
Reacts

The spectacle of students pouring through the streets of urban China denouncing the revolution with impunity had tapped into that vast underground water table of conservative values that had been inculcated into the collective unconsciousness of China for centuries, and that now reappeared in virulent form in the persons of older hardline Party revolutionaries. These hard-liners, who had previously been like political superegos hovering over the reform movement, had suddenly re-emerged on the public political stage, giving the appearance, at least, of once again being the main force in Party life.

The demonstrations had not only taken Party leaders by surprise but had also divided them, throwing even those who had been wholeheartedly in favor of reform off balance. What seemed to upset reformers, hard-liners, and Deng Xiaoping alike was not so much the full-scale abandonment of China's old revolution but the impossibility of filtering out the distasteful, or "spiritually polluting," part of what was coming in from the West. If modernizing was to depend on an "open door," then pop music, consumer culture, Cadillacs, bodybuilding, as well as notions of individualism, human rights, and democracy would inevitably infiltrate China along with foreign technology, management, and capital. It was this unwelcome recognition of the indivisibility of the whole Western package—of which, paradoxically, Party hard-liners were already painfully aware—that the students had forced upon the reformers and Deng Xiaoping.

To call for limited democratic reform to enliven the country's economic life was one thing, but to implement it was quite another. Democracy did not lend itself well to partial application, because it had a predictable way of raising expectations, particularly among Chinese students and intellectuals, that the Party was still far from willing to satisfy. Even the most starry-eyed optimists of 1986 had found it difficult to believe that the Party was about to relinquish its monopoly on political power—something few other totalitarian governments have been disposed to do—in favor of democratic political participation. As the hard-line reaction that followed the demonstrations showed, the Chinese Communist Party was to be no exception.

In spite of his reputation as China's pre-eminent reformer, Deng Xiaoping was especially unwilling to see Party authority challenged. Although he was far from being an outright Maoist hard-liner (his whole reformist plan, after all, was in essence an attempt to take economic but not political control out of the hands of the Party bureaucracy), there were real limitations to his reformist flexibility. Chairman Mao was said to have once likened him to "a ball of cotton with a pin inside," indicating that beneath his soft liberal exterior lay a sharp, rigid essence. This rigidity was manifested in Deng's tenacious commitment to his Four Cardinal Principles and his antipathy to what was known in Party circles as bourgeois liberalization and wholesale Westernization.

In January, 1980, Deng had given a speech in which he said, "I should point out that some infiltration of bourgeois ideology is inevitable because of the non-socialist ideas that already exist in our Party and country, the ten-year rampage of Lin Biao and the Gang of Four, and the fact that we are maintaining diplomatic and trade relations with capitalist countries. . . . That is why it is necessary to stress repeatedly that our cadres must keep to the socialist road. . . . When we study the technology and management experience of capitalist societies, we must never allow ourselves to worship capitalist countries, to succumb to corrosive capitalist influences, or to lose the national pride and self-confidence of socialist China. We must eradicate resolutely the trend toward anarchism that was introduced by the Gang of Four, as well as the trend toward bourgeois liberalization that is emerging within the Party."

In January, 1987, this speech, reprinted over and over in the official press, became one of the new canonical texts for China's re-emerging Party conservatism. To be progressive when it came to the economy and even to open the door to the outside world were permissible, but to allow heterodox foreign ideas to take too firm a root and challenge the primacy of the Party and the ideological supremacy of Marxism–Leninism–Mao Zedong Thought was not.

Deng had waited out the month of December, neither speaking

publicly nor acting while the students filled China's streets. Only when the demonstrations rocked Beijing itself did he reach the limits of his tolerance. A special meeting of the Party's leadership (which included Premier Zhao Ziyang, Vice-Premier Wan Li, Party Secretariat member Hu Qili, Party Secretary General Hu Yaobang, and Deng himself) was convened on December 30 to discuss the student unrest. Deng was fearful that the protests would further undermine Party prestige. Doubtless he was also piqued at having been personally attacked by the demonstrating students, some of whom carried banners proclaiming such messages as "Down with Deng Xiaoping!" and "Better the Gang of Four than the Gang of Three" (an allusion to the four earlier Maoist leaders, who had been arrested in 1976, and Deng and his two new protégés, Premier Zhao Ziyang and Party General Secretary Hu Yaobang). When the student demonstrations showed no sign of letting up, Deng finally decided to make use of the hard-liners in a crackdown meant to leave no questions in anybody's mind about one issue: the unchallengeable primacy of the Party. Later on, the standard of reform might be taken up again.

Central Directive No. 1 (directives are internal documents sequentially numbered each year and ordinarily used only to lay down major new policies) contained unedited excerpts of Deng's remarks at the meeting and included his instructions to the police: "When necessary, we must deal severely with those who defy orders. We can afford to shed some blood. Just try as much as possible not to kill anyone." According to the directive, the Party was also to undertake a mass education project during the next year to remind the Chinese people of the "superiority of socialism and the inferiority of bourgeois liberalism."

In discussing the dissident movement, Deng said, "These few years we have been too lax in curbing the tides of bourgeois liberalism. . . . Allowing some rightist influence is essential and correct, but we have gone overboard. . . . We cannot continue to make concessions in the face of current student troubles. We must remember the lesson [of the current demonstrations] and increase our vigilance." Considering the question of how the outside world would view the suppression of the new Chinese student movement, Deng spoke of Wei Jingsheng, who, as he reminded his comrades in the Party leadership, was arrested for "counter-revolutionary propaganda." "We arrested Wei Jingsheng and put him behind bars and the democracy movement died. Even though we haven't released him, it didn't tarnish our image abroad."

There was another telling, very Chinese aspect to Deng's response to the events of that winter. Deng chose to view the student upheaval from a distinctly conspiratorial perspective. If the students had caused trouble, he seemed to reason, someone must have provoked them. In Deng's view these provocateurs were none other than certain "big shot" intellectuals, who had ignored Party discipline and filled the minds of the students with unsuitable dreams of bourgeois democracy. In the meeting on December 30, Deng named Fang Lizhi, Wang Ruowang, and Liu Binyan as the main intellectual instigators of the student movement. "Why are these men still in the Party?" he was reported to have asked incredulously. He then criticized Hu Yaobang, whom he himself had had chosen General Secretary of the Chinese Communist Party, for not having taken adequate measures to control these errant intellectuals and to stop the student demonstrations before they had swept the country.

Just as he had joined the hard-liners and turned against the Democracy Wall activists when they threatened his concept of public stability and no longer served his political purposes, so Deng once again took his stand. But this time he was in many ways the embodiment of the very problem he saw bedeviling China. If bourgeois liberalization was, as he seemed to believe, a serious affliction, Deng really had no one to blame but himself. In spite of his claim that China's economic system would never "go capitalist" as long as the "means of production were state owned," it was his economic reforms and open door policy that were in fact largely responsible for generating the capitalist and nascently democratic ethic that now offended him and that he considered a "threat" to stability.

On January 6 the *People's Daily* ran an editorial entitled "Take a Clear-Cut Stand to Oppose Bourgeois Liberalism." It was a public expression of the exasperation that Deng himself had evinced at the leadership meeting on December 30. Stressing the need for stability, the editorial blamed the demonstrations not on the students but on the influence of bourgeois liberalism, which it spoke of as having run "rampant" for several years and as having "poisoned our youths, jeopardized society's stability and unity, hindered our reforms and opening up, and arrested the progress of modernization." Just as Deng had done, the editorial blamed the malady on "specific comrades in the Party who not only refuse to admit the danger of the trend of 'bourgeois liberalism,' but even to a degree supported it directly or indirectly. . . . Some comrades have turned a blind eye to all this, but now it is time for them to wake up."

Like a conductor cuing an orchestra with a single sweep of the baton, the *People's Daily* editorial sounded the first notes of a veritable symphony of like-minded editorial comment in newspapers, on the radio, and on television around the country. The thaw of 1986, which had started in April, on the thirtieth anniversary of the Hundred Flowers Movement (when Hu Qili had urged intellectuals to "truly speak their minds"), seemed to be ending as rapidly as its precursor had in 1957.

On January 12, the *Beijing Daily* let rip with a tirade against China's new enemies. "In the past few years, some comrades have not taken a clear-cut stand against 'bourgeois liberalization.' They have shown weakness and have not sufficiently resisted its appeal. Those leading figures spreading erroneous ideas have been seen making speeches and publishing articles everywhere, and they have had a good market for their views. Comrades who have criticized their erroneous ideas have even been ridiculed. . . . What they really want to do is to make China totally capitalistic. . . . They have called the Party leadership a 'black' leadership, charged that the Party leadership is a bureaucratic, privileged class, saying that it is dictatorial and authoritarian. They have said that the Party leadership should be sidelined or, at best, given a symbolic role. They have even called on people poisoned by 'bourgeois liberalism' to join the Communist Party so as to reform it and 'change its color.' They want to abolish Marxism as the guiding principle of China. Some media outlets have even rejected publishing Marxist views. Clearly what they want to do is to negate the leadership of the Party."

Then, manifesting that quality of rhetorical excess that is often the hallmark of uncertainty and self-doubt, this impassioned article went on to discredit those who advocate "the illusion of bourgeois democracy," saying that they "try to confuse people's minds and incite anarchism. They distort reality and spread rumors, instigating students to make the Party and the government the objects of their struggle and urging them toward violent struggle to obtain democracy. They say the east wind is blowing, the war drums are beating, so who is afraid of whom? These people have created an atmosphere of turmoil; they have egged on young students to show their strength and to get ready to rush against and to stab at the Communist Party. Is this not inciting troublemaking?"

Red Flag now assaulted those who "adopt a loose and slovenly attitude toward the partisans of liberalization, as a result of which good men fail to get support and bad men become more wanton. Some

Communist Party members engage in 'bourgeois liberalization' and refuse to change. Such people disqualify themselves as Communist Party members by their own actions and therefore will have to leave the Party. . . . We should use the forceful weapons of the people's democratic dictatorship to crack down on this small minority of people who break the law. Those who put up big- and small-character posters, who print and distribute leaflets, who make speeches against the Four Cardinal Principles, who offend against criminal law, and who organize processions and demonstrations against the Constitution and other laws should be dealt with. Those people who form illegal associations and organize counter-revolutionary groups should be punished seriously, according to law. Only by doing this can we really protect the people's democracy and surely win people's support."

There was a bewildering aspect to this blizzard of articles and editorials now spewing from all the media. In trying to justify the crackdown by summarizing the alleged crimes of the "bourgeois liberalizers" against the Party, these propaganda organs only succeeded in providing far more publicity for the ideas of their adversaries than they themselves could ever have generated on their own. In a completely unintended way, the Party was not only absurdly attacking people and ideas it had largely supported a few weeks earlier, but now inadvertently served as their public relations agent as well.

In an effort to stanch the hemorrhaging of its credibility, the Party began leaning on well-known figures not already identified as Party factotums to deliver short socialist testimonials, which invariably came out sounding like paid commercials. The New China News Agency, for instance, quoted members of a panel of legal "experts," including Zhu Qiwu, a professor from the Chinese University of Political Science and Law, and Li Peichuan, Deputy Director of the State Council's Legislative Bureau, as dismissing Western democracy for the sham that it was and as hailing "socialist democracy" as the "most extensive democracy for the people in the history of mankind. . . . By demanding 'democracy' and 'freedom' in their street demonstrations, the students failed to grasp the real basis of these concepts," said the socialist legal experts. "They regard Western democracy, which protects bourgeois interests, as a flower, while failing to treasure socialism, which has been won by the Chinese people through bloody sacrifice. . . ."

Numerous other celebrities not identified with the hard-line faction were also called upon for product endorsements. Rong Yiren, the Party's resident capitalist and head of the China International Trade and Investment Corporation; Wang Meng, noted author and liberal Minister of Culture; and Fei Xiaotong, world-renowned sociologist and anthropologist, were among those goaded into making public obeisances to the Party and its new line.

Fearful that the protests might spread from intellectuals to the workers, who had become increasingly restive about the government's inability to control inflation, the *People's Daily* started running testimonials from "ordinary" people. One such effort was an "open letter" to the Shanghai Public Security Bureau from the parents of one Cheng Keqin, a twenty-three-year-old worker who had been arrested during the student demonstrations in Nanjing. Entitled "Cheng Keqin, Worker at the Nanjing Quilt Plant Arrested for Sneaking into University Demonstrations to Make Trouble," this cautionary tale was clearly aimed at workers who might have had incipient sympathies for the student cause.

"Ten years ago the total income of our family was only about 100 yuan a month, while at present it is nearly 500," Cheng's parents wrote to him in jail. "You have worked for only seven years, and yet your monthly income has already reached 100 yuan. Our family is now rich enough to afford a fancy tape cassette recorder, an eighteen-inch color TV, a washing machine, a refrigerator—in fact, a complete set of all the high-quality things we need in daily life. Moreover, you have savings in the bank. Do we not owe all these things to the Party's correct leadership since the Third Plenum of the Eleventh Party Central Committee in 1978?"

After this eulogy to consumerism, Cheng's parents proceeded to flagellate themselves for having failed to raise their son correctly. "Our child violated criminal law and was punished according to law. He is eating his own bitter fruit. . . . We will draw lessons from this and give a better education to his younger brother and sister." Their parting words to their new anti-model-worker son were that he had better "turn over a new leaf . . . strictly abide by the law, and treasure the greatly favorable situation of stability and unity" that he would now have plenty of opportunity to contemplate from prison.

Deng's prescription for those who, like Cheng Keqin, had been seduced by bourgeois liberalism and wholesale Westernization was a strong dose of the Four Cardinal Principles. In conceiving them, Deng must have hoped that they would serve as a kind of sustained baseline, which, like a pedal point in an organ work, would give harmonic stability to the freer, often more dissonant voice lines above. His bold economic reform program had indeed long cried out for some such ideological center of gravity, lest the centrifugal force of change spin Chinese society into pieces.

In search of at least an illusion of coherence and continuity, Deng used the Four Cardinal Principles as a substitute for a more comprehensive political framework, a sort of ersatz ideological containment vessel meant to control dissidence in the country and warring factions in the Party. Sometimes he used them rather roughly, as if they were a club with which to beat his opposition; at other times he used them rather gently, like soothing incantations that, if repeated often enough, might mesmerize doubters and critics into subservience. Party officials employed them both as an ideological litmus test of loyalty and orthodoxy and as a weapon with which to menace ideological backsliders into line. The Chinese people themselves, sick of a quarter of a century of "politics in command," treated them as annoyances whose only virtue was their convenience as ideological masks that could be donned expediently at a moment's notice. Deng had, in effect, reduced the collected works of Chairman Mao to four cheerless principles. Conceptually vacuous as they were, however, the Four Cardinal Principles were all that lent Deng's mutant form of Chinese communism an aura of meaning and unity. For most Chinese, who were in any event busy trying to get rich, that was quite enough politics.

In the past, when I had asked Chinese friends to locate a certain phrase in Chairman Mao's collected works (now up to six volumes), often they were so well versed in his writings that they had been able not only to recite the full quotation but also, like game show contestants, to cite its chapter and verse as well. However, when I asked Party members, or even in one case a ranking official, simply to list Deng's Four Cardinal Principles, I often found them at a loss. They would come up with two or three principles before foundering in an orgy of embarrassed demurrals. Even those few who could recall all four usually got bogged down in meaningless platitudes when asked what each principle meant and how a good Marxist might translate them into correct political practice. It was no accident that the Four Cardinal Principles had been in a state of remission during the period of openness preceding the student demonstrations. They were hardly the stuff on which creative minds fed.

In January, 1987, however, they came into their own, as, in anticipation of worse to come, people all across China ducked for safe political cover. One could feel the suddenness of the ideological realignment, like a bulky cargo shifting in the hold of a ship that is rolling precipitously to one side in heavy seas. Rich peasants kept their money at home rather than incurring reputations as big spenders by buying ostentatious products or, for that matter, stocks and bonds; writers stopped submitting questionable manuscripts for publication; students hurried to get passports and exit visas; and officials occupied themselves with the endless task of checking on the direction of the switching political winds before making decisions.

||||||||||||

Fang Lizhi Is Purged

Early that January the *Anhui Daily* (published in Hefei, home of Keda) ran an article that, like advance artillery fire softening up an enemy target, seemed to be preparing its readers for a larger political campaign to follow. Taking a surprisingly soft line on the recent demonstrations, the article allowed that student "enthusiasm and concern about the fate of our nation and the future of reforms are understandable." The real blame for the recent upheavals, it suggested, lay elsewhere, namely in the hands of that "very small number of people who had spurred on the trend of 'bourgeois liberalism,' propagated opinions against the Four Cardinal Principles, and taken advantage of the students' enthusiasm and lack of experience in society to achieve their political aims."

Darkly suggesting that there had been a hand within the glove, the article declared that this "small number of people" had "publicized the view that both the socialist movement as a whole and the socialist construction of our country are failures. They claimed that Chinese-type socialism is just a term and even ranted that principles for building the Party should be reappraised. Moreover, they even expressed the view that no positive success has ever been achieved by using Marxism as the Party's guiding theory and ideology. . . ."

No names were mentioned. But the paper did hint that "among those making such remarks and doing such things were Communist Party members." Then it went on to ask incredulously, "Are these people really Communists? Do they really have any Marxist qualities? . . . If we allow such words and deeds to spread freely without restriction, will not the Constitution of our country be fundamentally undermined? Will not our country suffer another setback and will not the Party lose its capacity to fight on?"

The *Guangming Daily*, which just the previous year had jubilantly proclaimed, "Our socialist system not only does not fear people speaking out, but encourages them to do so," now lashed out menacingly against overly Westernized notions of democracy. On January 11 it ran a commentary entitled "The Essence of Political 'Wholesale Westernization' Means Discarding Socialism," which claimed that the students had been manipulated into demonstrating by a certain unnamed "Vice-President comrade of a university." "We would like to ask him, if we totally copy 'the political structure and system of ownership' of the Western bourgeoisie, what would the difference then be between a socialist country and theirs? How could we tell that ours is a socialist country with Chinese characteristics? Well, there is certainly a reason why these advocates of 'wholesale Westernization' raise this slogan. It is because they hold that capitalism is better than socialism, that socialism is 'fake,' and that 'fake' things must be thrown away. In a nutshell, what they are in fact preaching is 'wholesale Westernization.' They want to discard Chinese socialism and bring the capitalist system to China intact in order to lead China down the capitalist road."

On January 12, Zhou Guangzhao, a member of the Central Committee of the Chinese Communist Party and Vice-President of the Chinese Academy of Sciences, summoned a special meeting of the Keda faculty in Hefei. In the very center of the front row of the large meeting hall, like riderless saddles in a funeral procession for fallen warriors, were two conspicuously empty seats. When the room fell silent, Zhou announced that the Party Central Committee and the State Council had decided that Guan Weiyan, President of the University, and Fang Lizhi, Vice-President, had been removed from office and reassigned respectively to the Institute of Physics and the Beijing Observatory. He told the somber gathering of scientists that Teng

Teng, an engineering chemist who was then Deputy Head of the Propaganda Department, had already been appointed their new President. Paradoxically, Teng's last post had been under the Party's liberal propaganda chief Zhu Houze, who was soon to lose his own job. Zhou informed the faculty that because Guan and Fang had been unable to "ensure Party and state leadership over this university," a new Party committee had been formed to oversee all Keda activities, and that Peng Peiyun, Vice-Minister of the State Education Commission, had already been appointed Party Secretary. For an institution of higher learning that had so recently prided itself on democratically choosing its leaders, this was indeed a bitter coup d'état from the top.

Zhou Guangzhao accused Fang of having "disseminated many erroneous statements reflecting 'bourgeois liberalization,' " and of having departed from the Four Cardinal Principles. He continued his attack by saying that Fang's "ideas of running the school by attempting to shake off the Party leadership and departing from the socialist road had resulted in extremely nasty consequences for Keda. These erroneous ideas were fully revealed in the recent disturbance created by students of this university." Zhou accused Guan of being "responsible for a bad influence on the whole country," and of having "seriously neglected his duties, with the result that the ideological and political work in the school were weakened."

The assessment of the Secretary of the Anhui Provincial Party Committee, Li Guixian, was even more extreme. He claimed that Fang had "defamed the Party's leadership and Party cadres, negated the cause of our Party over the past few decades, slandered and distorted the socialist system, and sown discord in the relations between the Party and intellectuals, especially among young intellectuals." He went on to say that what Fang had done ran "counter to the fundamental interests of the Party and the masses of people, as well as counter to the trends of the development of history, and is in no way permissible."

Then, in that Maoist way so recognizable to all Chinese, Li began to speak directly to Fang's former colleagues in the audience, seeming to offer understanding while actually delivering a threat. "It should be noted that most cadres and teachers at Keda disapprove of, and many comrades resolutely reject, Fang Lizhi's erroneous words and deeds. Some comrades may have made some erroneous remarks under Fang Lizhi's influence, but it is a good thing that today they have realized their mistakes and corrected themselves. Those few comrades who up to now have failed to do so are allowed to take some time to realize their mistakes, but they must observe discipline."

The *Anhui Daily* chimed in like an echo, saying: "Although leading comrades of the provincial Party Committee had solemnly criticized him again and again, he [Fang] feigned compliance but, acting like a double-dealer, refused to mend his ways. His conduct was against the Party Constitution, the Party's program, the fundamental interests of the Party and the people, as well as the trends of historical development. . . . Fang instigated students to cause disturbances, openly opposed the guidance of Marxist philosophy and many other things, making it quite apparent that the tip of his spear was directed at the Four Cardinal Principles."

The paper went on to note: "The political regulations of the Party stipulate that . . . even if a Party member has a differing viewpoint . . . he may not act according to his own judgment and openly disseminate ideas that are at variance with its lines, measures, and policies. It is even more impermissible for him to take actions that are in violation of decisions and resolutions of Party Central."

Then, half pleading with its readers to understand and sympathize with the Party's difficult decision to purge Fang, it said: "If we do not strictly enforce this political regulation, what kind of centralized Party control will remain? What concentrated force, what power to struggle will we have left? . . . Fang Lizhi is a middle-aged intellectual whom the Party has taken by the hand and raised to his present eminence. Once upon a time the Party placed great hopes in him, appointed him to high position; but he has turned his back on the Party; he has turned his back on the people. . . . If, however, he shows by his conduct that he has truly reformed, he will be welcomed back by the Party and the people."

Other articles in the official press were less conciliatory, perhaps recognizing the depth of the conflict between Fang and the Party. They railed against Fang for proclaiming that Marxism was out of date, quoting him as having said, "As a science, Marxism has completed its historical mission, and now we must seek some new truth." They criticized him for "negating the socialist system." They accused him of having advocated the "wholesale Westernization" of China, by calling for the "Westernization of China's political system and means of production." They vilified him for "inciting" people to change the Party, quoting him as having said, "I am for the idea that everybody should join the Party in order to change its true color."

These attacks against Fang were so relentless, repetitive, and overblown that it sometimes seemed as if the Party doubted whether the sheer force and volume of its own rhetoric could convince even its members, not to mention other intellectuals, of the righteousness of its actions. Any lingering doubts about whether the orders for Fang's ouster had come from the very top of the Party were dispelled when, a day after his dismissal, Deng Xiaoping denounced Fang Lizhi, Liu Binyan, and Wang Ruowang by name during a meeting with Noboru Takeshita, Secretary General of the Japanese Liberal-Democratic Party.

Fang's ouster set off an immediate reaction at Keda. Students organized a petition drive to protest his dismissal and put up banners, one of which said, "It Is China's Shame That It Cannot Embrace Such a Scholar As Fang Lizhi," and "Mr. Guan and Mr. Fang, You Have Already Made Your Sacrifices. We Will Miss You and Hope We Will See You Again." Authorities tore down the banners and quashed the petition drive.

A week and a half later, on January 19, as if Fang's dismissal from his position at Keda had not sufficiently purged him from China's system, Xu Leyi, Deputy Party Secretary of Anhui province, appeared on evening television and for seven minutes of the half-hour news broadcast read a statement from the Anhui Provincial Party Committee announcing that Fang Lizhi had not only lost his job but had also been expelled from the Chinese Communist Party. "Over the last few years, Fang Lizhi has made a series of extremely erroneous speeches both inside and outside the country advocating bourgeois liberalization. Especially during the past two years, he constantly went to institutions of higher learning in various localities to make speeches aimed at instilling the idea of bourgeois liberalism into the minds of young students, sowing discord between the Party and intellectuals, and inciting dissatisfaction with socialism and the Party."

In the communiqué that followed, the Party enumerated the now familiar litany of Fang's "extremely serious" mistakes, each one backed up by a list of offending quotations, presumably from the talks that Wan Li had so ignominiously been sent to record. But the Party did not even stop here. Like surgeons who, after successfully removing a primary tumor, go on to excise the surrounding tissue for fear of further metastasis, on January 22 the Party also dismissed Lu Jiaxi, a structural chemist, and Yan Dongsheng, a ceramic chemist, who were respectively the President and Vice-President of the Chinese Academy of Sciences, the parent organization of Fang and Guan's university. Although no immediate reasons for Lu and Yan's dismissal were given, many assumed that their crime had been their appointment of Fang and Guan in 1984 and their subsequent support of them. What made their summary dismissals so ironic was the fact that, like Guan and Fang, they, too, had gained their positions through an election, in 1982, which had been officially praised as a stellar example of democracy in China. The newly appointed academy president was none other than Zhou Guangzhao, who had gone to Keda to announce Guan and Fang's dismissal.

The Fang Lizhi affair quickly became a political cause célèbre in China. Within days of his dismissal, members of the foreign press and the diplomatic community in Beijing were referring to Fang as China's Sakharov. Chinese intellectuals, even those who did not completely agree with Fang's uncompromising vision of democracy, applauded him for his unwavering boldness. The Party, desperate to stem this hagiographic treatment of Fang, kept up its relentless media campaign against him. Even the *People's Daily*, which only two months earlier had lionized Fang and Guan for having created a new model university at Keda, now ridiculed them, claiming that in "waving the banner of running universities in a democratic way," they were "passing fish eyes off as pearls" and letting "vulcanized copper masquerade as gold."

This was certainly not the first time that a Chinese publication had been forced to reverse itself to keep its political position parallel to a wildly careening Party line. And surely there are few worse kinds of intellectual debasement than when a writer or an editor is forced to repudiate passionately held, publicly expressed beliefs. But what made this particular capitulation both sad and comical was that the editorial staff of the *People's Daily* was manifesting exactly the kind of slavish acquiescence to higher authority that Fang had criticized when he said that many older Chinese intellectuals had been too "strongly influenced by the doctrine of obedience."

The revised *People's Daily* appraisal of Fang appeared on January 17 and savaged Fang's notion that universities should be independent of the Party. "According to his ideology for running a university," said the paper, "our universities would become independent kingdoms of 'bourgeois liberalization' that would get funds from the state and the people but that would not be controlled by the state and the people. Oh, how outrageous!"

When I later asked Fang if he had been astonished by the way the Party struck back at him, he replied, "Yes, I was somewhat surprised. Although I had, of course, known all along that to give such speeches was very dangerous, I had hoped that China had at last outgrown this kind of reaction against divergent opinion."

Still unable to leave Fang alone, on January 20 the *People's Daily* attacked him again, this time in an article by two writers from Jiaotong University itself. They called him "wildly arrogant" and "inordinately proud of his abilities," accusing him of believing that he was the "saviour" of the student movement. They also reminded him that he himself was "the biggest beneficiary of the Party's policy toward intellectuals," conveniently forgetting the many ways in which the Party had obstructed Fang's life and work during the twenty-year period dating from the Anti-Rightist Campaign to the end of the Cultural Revolution. "Those in science, technology, and educational circles who are familiar with Fang's experience know how it was after things were set to rights, that the Party and the people gave him a very high title and elevated him to a very high position. . . . Thus Fang Lizhi suddenly went from being a scientific and technological worker unknown to the public to being a widely known figure, and gained superior conditions for carrying out research and social activities. However, today, it is precisely by exploiting this fame and position, as well as the power entrusted to him by the Party and people, that he has managed to be so antagonistic and to assert his independence from the Party."

The idea that he owed everything to the Party must have struck Fang, a veteran of many previous political struggles—even an earlier expulsion from the Party—as exceedingly droll. One was only left to wonder how many more times this bizarre ritual might be re-enacted in his lifetime.

Fang's outspoken espousal of democracy and human rights put the Party in a difficult bind and made it appear grossly inconsistent. Having vigorously tried to cultivate intellectuals at various times during the previous years with ever wider calls for ever greater freedom and democracy, it now seemed bent on persecuting them again in a way that could not but remind members of the Chinese intelligentsia of the Anti-Rightist Campaign, which had followed Mao's call for the Hundred Flowers Movement in the mid-fifties. Sometimes it appeared as if the Party, unable to find the "golden mean" (*zhongyong*)—the middle way revered by classical Chinese political philosophers—had hoped at least to be able to create an optical illusion of moderation by oscillating back and forth rapidly between one extreme and another, alternately coddling and punishing its intellectuals. When some months later I asked Fang if he believed democratization could ever take place in China under such conditions, he replied, "In China, the concept of democratization has often been nothing more than a poker chip in what is really a game of power. Maybe there are still a few idealistic leaders, but on the whole most are preoccupied with the struggle for power, and they use such concepts as democracy as just another means of defeating their opponents. One side will say, 'I stand for reform and you don't, so you shouldn't be here!' The other will say, 'No! Reform is wrong, so you shouldn't be here!' In the end, it is the Chinese people who suffer, because they get used as playthings. And yet even under such conditions, we still must hope for reform and the success of those who call themselves reformers. We cannot say reform is absolutely impossible, and since there are no democratic channels, we can only be resourceful and hope that this group will somehow succeed in bringing some real political reform to our country."

Behind the Party's wildly fluctuating treatment of Fang lay the contradiction embedded within its whole modernization program as well as within its past. If China was to modernize, it desperately needed to rally to its cause those students, intellectuals, and technocrats who had been alienated from the Party for so much of the Revolution. A key element of this mobilization process was not only to grant them more freedom but to open China's doors to the outside world. The dilemma that the Party found itself confronting was that along with foreign languages, technology, science, capital, and management techniques came foreign political ideas and values that by their nature challenged the hegemony of one-party rule and led to the kind of hard-line leftist reaction to which Fang, like so many intellectuals before him in Chinese Communist history, had fallen prey. "Over the past thirty years, China has consistently engaged in anti-rightist movements," Fang, with his usual straightforwardness, told an interviewer from the overseas Chinese paper *Queens Daily*, published in Queens, New York, some months after his fall. "The present movement against bourgeois liberalization is just the most recent example. One could say that the hard-line left is the major reason for China's backwardness. Deng Xiaoping once said that China has been stagnant for twenty years. In my view, the reason for this stagnation has been nothing but these leftist tendencies."

What was the Party to do—allow such subversive heresies as democracy, freedom, and human rights to spread unchecked, or allow the hard-liners to crush the students and intellectuals, thus losing their creative energies for the paramount task of developing China?

Neither alternative seemed acceptable. Needing to find some compromise position, the Party did the only thing it could do: It acted inconsistently. By slapping down Fang Lizhi—that is, firing him from his job and expelling him from the Party—it sent out a signal that while intellectuals were being granted unprecedented new freedoms, public political discourse was not to be among them. However, by limiting its punitive actions to what, by historical Party standards, were relatively mild forms of chastisement, it hoped at the same time to reassure intellectuals that China was not returning to the political dark ages. In effect, the message was: "As long as you are willing to leave the supremacy of the Communist Party unchallenged, we will grant you considerable freedom. If you challenge the Party, and socialism as its official canon, you will be punished—but not as harshly as before." The Party in this way was teetering on the ever so fine line between the imperatives of modernization and control. And that January, when it was rocked by renewed factional struggle, no one was quite sure what the results would be.

|||||||||||||||||||||||||||||||
Wang Ruowang
Is Expelled
from the Party

On January 14, just a day after Fang Lizhi had been fired from his job as Vice-President of Keda, the Shanghai Municipal Communist Party Committee held a meeting of "responsible cadres." Not surprisingly, the Municipal Party Secretary, Rui Xingwen, announced that because of his "serious mistakes" the Shanghai Discipline and Inspection Commission had decided, "in accordance with the provisions of the Party Constitution," to expel Wang Ruowang from the Party—an ironic anniversary present for a man who had become a Party member just fifty years earlier.

"The decision is completely correct and very necessary for purifying the Party organization, enforcing Party discipline, and maintaining a high level of political and ideological unity within the Party," Rui told the gathering of cadres. He then accused Wang of a whole string of anti-Party crimes: of having "wantonly opposed the Communist Party's leadership, vilified the socialist system, done his utmost to advocate 'bourgeois liberalization' and called for the taking of the capitalist road"; of having "fabricated things to confuse and poison the minds of people"; of having "opposed and distorted the Party's current policies"; and of having "had an extremely bad political influence on the people."

Like an exasperated parent, Rui related the way in which Party organizations had "patiently criticized and tried to educate Wang again and again," and he emphasized how they had "repeatedly pointed out to him the seriousness of his mistakes." But it was all to no avail. Not only did Wang "ignore the Party's extremely kind admonitions and refuse to mend his ways," but he continued to "openly satirize and smear the leading comrades who tried to help educate him," asserting "that he would fight to the end and become even worse in spreading fallacies against the Four Cardinal Principles and in favor of 'bourgeois liberalization.'" If a person like Wang were allowed to remain a member, Rui added, he would "seriously contaminate the body of the Party, mar its image, and greatly jeopardize its cause."

With two purgings now completed, articles against dissident intellectuals began to appear all over China. An editorial in *Red Flag*, the Party theoretical journal controlled by Deng Liqun, raged against the "erroneous and even reactionary remarks by a few people who have played a role in instigating some college students to cause unrest." This piece, widely reprinted on the front pages of other Chinese papers, was clearly aimed at Fang and Wang. It went on to say, "We must use the powerful weapon of the people's democratic dictatorship to crack down on these few lawbreakers." As a nationwide media campaign against the two went into high gear, Wang was accused elsewhere in the press of having "defamed the socialist system," of having "advocated capitalism," of having described Chinese Communism as an "illusion" and "feudal," and of having maintained that the capitalist mode of production was "badly needed." He was attacked for having said that taxes levied on private business in China were a form of "extortion" and that recent anti-crime campaigns, in which thousands of people were arrested and often detained without charges, were a "political movement" in everything but name.

The Shanghai-based *Liberation Daily* claimed that Wang's many reports, speeches, and articles showed "two clear characteristics": They maligned the objectives of the Party as a "socialist illusion" and denigrated the Party itself by "vilifying and attacking" it. "What Wang Ruowang wants is not only the capitalist mode of production, but all of capitalism's ideas, including its pollution. In short [Wang believes] China must transplant to its home ground everything that belongs to the Western capitalist countries, or, in other words, to go in for 'wholesale Westernization.' "

However, perhaps Wang's most unforgivable transgression, from the point of view of the Party press, was the mocking tone with which he treated the latest campaign against bourgeois liberalization, even to the point of proudly announcing that he was the "forefather of bourgeois liberalization" in China and that he felt "honored to be so called and would never feel ashamed" of such a title.

Also surfacing from the rancorous depths of the Party's injured self-esteem was the question of the essay Wang had written tweaking Deng over his notion that allowing "some people to get rich first" would not lead to class polarization. An article appearing on January 24 in the *Workers' Daily*, published by the All-China Federation of Trade Unions and the State Economic Commission, lambasted Wang for having "wantonly attacked the policy of achieving common prosperity set by the central leadership." This policy it described as "encouraging some people to get rich first," in order to "let . . . [them] help those who have not yet become rich to achieve prosperity in common. . . . That some people get rich first does not mean polarization. Under socialist conditions, the reasonable difference [in wealth] . . . only means the difference between getting rich first and getting rich later. . . . Under socialist conditions, 'polarization' will never appear and is not allowed to appear. The current phenomenon of increased gaps in people's incomes only indicates that people have taken different steps toward getting rich. It is in no way equivalent to Wang Ruowang's notion of 'polarization,' which means 'the rich becoming richer' and 'the poor becoming poorer.' "

Accustomed as it was to winning at least superficial signs of acquiescence from its intellectuals, the Party found Wang's frontal attacks too much to endure. Although the hard-liners clearly would have liked to see Wang lose his official positions as well as his Party membership, there was resistance from liberal reformers. As Wang himself had said the previous year in an interview with the Hong

Kong–based magazine *The Nineties*, "When the Party begins one of its periods of tightening up, it always starts with a couple of examples. This fills all writers and intellectuals with trepidation and fear that another big disaster is coming down on their heads." Aware of the effects this fearful mind-set might have on other intellectuals, the liberal reformers refused to let Wang be stripped of his membership in the Shanghai branch of the Chinese Writers' Association.

||||||||||||||||||||||||
· —— Hu Yaobang —————————— ·
Is Dismissed
from Office

On December 29, with the students still demonstrating, Hu Yaobang, General Secretary of the Chinese Communist Party, appeared to be his normal ebullient self as he met with Beijing visitor Lionel Jospin, the Secretary of the French Socialist Party. The next day, however, at a secretly held special meeting of the Political Bureau, Hu found himself under direct attack by Deng Xiaoping for having failed to control dissident intellectuals and having been unable to prevent the student demonstrations. On January 16 all of China was shocked by the announcement that Hu had "resigned."

As the evening TV news came on, it was not difficult to tell that something unusual was afoot. The set for the newscast was adorned with a special backdrop saying, "An Announcement from an Enlarged Meeting of the Political Bureau." The anchorman, who usually appeared in a natty Western suit and tie, wore a somber blue-gray Mao suit. His report was brief but electrifying. The General Secretary of the Chinese Communist Party, Hu Yaobang, had stepped down, and Premier Zhao Ziyang, Deng's other protégé, would temporarily assume his duties.

How had it happened that Hu Yaobang, who had joined the Red Army as an eleven-year-old boy, endured the Long March, served under Deng as a political commissar at Yan'an in the late thirties, been purged with Deng during the Cultural Revolution, become his hand-picked successor and General Secretary of the Party in February, 1980, and had been the key figure under his mentor in overseeing almost a decade of China's opening to the world, could now have been so unceremoniously dismissed?

For days before the announcement on January 16 Beijing had been rife with rumors about the precarious state of Hu's political health. Certainly, it had been a less than well kept secret that leaders in the military, who tended toward the position of the hard-liners, were cool at best to the idea of Hu taking over the top position in the country on Deng's retirement or death. In recent months, however, Deng, too, had evidently had second thoughts about Hu. Even prior to the student demonstrations and the December 30 meeting of the Political Bureau, Deng had reportedly been angered by Hu's behavior. At a meeting of the Party's Central Military Commission in November, 1986, Hu, undoubtedly hoping to tighten his grip on his position as heir apparent, had deigned to suggest that Deng retire immediately. The actual process of succession, he seemed to have suggested, would be smoother if it could take place while Deng was still alive, a proposal that reportedly left Deng less than enthusiastic. Hu's imprudent display of impatience with his benefactor's continuing tenure doubtless had something to do with a desire not to see China subjected to another succession struggle of the kind that followed Mao's death. And doubtless, on his part, Deng actually felt that Hu was responsible for a certain laxness in controlling the reform process. This, coupled with Hu's lack of support among military and Party hard-liners seems to have led Deng to view him as the perfect fall guy to take the blame for the student unrest.

Whatever the explanation, the confrontation alienated Hu's main patron and left Hu isolated and exposed to competitors and enemies within the Party leadership. But rumors of a split between the two men did not actually surface until the second week of January, when Hu failed to show up to greet the Secretary General of Japan's ruling Liberal-Democratic Party, Noboru Takeshita, and, a few days later, the head of the Finnish Communist Party, Arvo Aalto. Asked by puzzled Western reporters about Hu's absence, Party spokesmen dismissed speculation about his downfall by saying, "Comrade Hu has not been in good health recently, and so has not been able to meet with guests."

When the communiqué from the enlarged session of the Political Bureau confirming Hu's ouster was released on January 16, it sang a very different tune. It alleged that he had made unspecified "mistakes on major issues of political principle in violation of the Party's principle of collective leadership," suggesting, in the minds of some, that Hu's errors went even deeper than his contretemps with Deng and his failure to curb the protests of intellectuals and the student demonstrations.

Hu's official epitaph was written by one of his arch-opponents, Bo Yibo, the hard-line permanent Vice-Chairman of the Central Advisory Commission, who presented his findings to the enlarged session of the Political Bureau. His statement charged that by not struggling vigorously enough against bourgeois liberalization, Hu had hampered the Party's effort against spiritual pollution, which, Bo said, was "one and the same thing" as bourgeois liberalization. He accused Hu of having supported "pro-freedom tendencies," thereby encouraging thousands of students to take to the streets, of being too hasty to expand the economy and to encourage "consumerism," of hampering the activities of the National People's Congress (controlled by the hard-line octogenarian Peng Zhen), of being out of step with China's policies toward foreign countries, and of making public remarks without first consulting other leaders.

Although forced to make a "self-criticism"—a humiliating Maoist exercise requiring that the accused confess his crimes and acknowledge his guilt—Hu, like Fang, was spared severe punishment of the sort meted out in the past to purged or fallen Party leaders. He was even spared the supreme embarrassment of having his self-criticism published. Although participants at the Political Bureau meeting where his fate was sealed were reported to have given "Comrade Hu Yaobang serious and comradely criticism," at the same time they were said by the official press to have also "acknowledged his achievements in work, such as they were." Reports also noted that Hu would be allowed to retain his membership in the Political Bureau and its Standing Committee, which suggested that Deng and other leaders were once again sending out a very specific message to China's reformers, namely that intellectuals and Party members might be punished for their errors, but they would not suffer old-style purges, in which cashiered leaders had just disappeared into jail cells or were put under ignominious house arrest, where they often died alone and unattended.

As the Communist Party–controlled Hong Kong newspaper *Ta Kung Pao* was careful to point out on January 18 (lest overseas Chinese presume that a full-scale Maoist purge was in the works and withdraw their investments from China), "The situation is by no means comparable to the Cultural Revolution, when disputes were arbitrarily classified as struggles between two classes and between two lines, and people who held different opinions were persecuted mercilessly."

This was, indeed, a curious kind of "reformist" purge, in which the Party evinced a new reluctance to make a former leader just disappear, while his crimes, from the point of view of most ordinary people, were left rather vaguely defined. The nature of this new purge technique simply added to the suspicions of many Chinese and Westerners alike that Hu was simply being made a scapegoat for the upheavals of the past month. "As long as a disturbance can be blamed on some responsible individual," an American diplomat told me, "it takes the heat off the Party's actual policies and the system, which in this case, after all, was what has really been under attack."

Although a scapegoat undoubtedly needed to be found, Hu's "mistakes" did, in fact, transcend the events of the previous month. Probably his most serious shortcoming was that hard-liners and Deng Xiaoping alike had come to view him as too prejudicial, flamboyant, and outspoken a figure to be able to maintain the delicate balance between the political factions upon which the survival of the reform movement was predicated. On the other hand, Premier Zhao Ziyang, who was known for his cool, discreet, and levelheaded approach to politically sensitive issues and contentious factional feuds, might still be able to placate the offended old guard while continuing to shepherd Deng's economic reform agenda forward.

In spite of the rumors in January about Hu's shaky status, most Chinese were utterly unprepared for and bewildered by his fall, for whatever he may have done behind the scenes, few Chinese thought of Hu as excessively liberal or out of step with the Party's own line. Indeed, as General Secretary, he regularly gave speeches extolling the "radiance" of Marxism and the "glorious traditions" of the Party. But as one Chinese insider later admitted to me, "While Hu spoke a good Party line in public, he often did things unilaterally in private that really galled other leaders, particularly hard-line political opponents who believed in a more rigorously disciplined notion of the Party."

Hu had, in fact, stood for the "dispersal of Party control" in just about every area of Chinese life. He was for allowing more freedom and independence in cultural life, for democratizing the political system, and for granting more decision-making power to managers of factories and enterprises by restricting local Party committee authority to purely political matters. Hu's vision of the role of the Party in Chinese life, although never spelled out systematically, was very different in practice from that of the hard-liners, and, as it turned out, even from that of Deng himself.

For instance, in 1981, Hu was reported to have defended the writer Bai Hua against allegations that his much criticized film script *Bitter Love* was "seditious," and, despite Liu Binyan's denials, many Chinese claimed that he had only survived as long as he had because Hu had been his silent protector.

Again in 1984, Hu demonstrated a remarkable tolerance toward intellectuals and independence of mind when he reportedly overturned a Party decision to force a pre-selected list of candidates on the National Writers' Association for their election of officers. As a result, Liu Binyan and several other blunt, outspoken writers were elected by secret ballot to head the prestigious organization. As it turned out, Hu also had long had a tendency to side quietly with intellectuals when other controversies had broken out, a posture that did not sit well with many Party leaders, who still viewed China's intelligentsia with the same suspicion as had Mao. (Mao had called them "subjective and individualistic, impractical in their thinking and irresolute in action . . . [prone to] drop out of the revolutionary ranks at critical moments and become passive, while a few may even become enemies. . . .")

Unlike other Party leaders, Hu unfortunately had a less than tactful way of expressing himself in public, a quality that many of the Party's more secretive, disciplined leaders found offensive. For instance, in 1984, Hu stunned true believers when in an off-the-cuff manner he publicly declared that "Marxism-Leninism can no longer solve China's problems." Such a brouhaha arose over this particular statement that it subsequently had to be officially "amended" by the Party. Hu's "corrected" remark later appeared in the *People's Daily*; it read, "We cannot expect Marxism-Leninism to solve all the problems of today."

Hu's stature as a protector of the sanctity of socialist dogma was not further enhanced when, on a visit to Italy in June, 1986, he spoke out again. This time he told a group of Italian Communist Party officials, "Marxism is not an immutable, rigid dogma, and it must be enriched and developed in the course of practice." On yet another occasion, he underscored his quirky individualism by maintaining that capitalism "has many positive effects on the state of the economy and on the quality of life. We will not be able to do without it for a considerable period of time."

While such statements did indeed have a certain refreshing candor about them, they certainly did not reflect the kind of orthodoxy one might have expected from a supreme Communist Party leader. In their eagerness to maintain at least a semblance of infallibility, Party leaders in China, when they did differ at all in public, tended to express themselves obliquely or through Aesopian language, a skill as well as a mind-set at which Hu Yaobang did not appear to excel.

On the non-ideological front, Hu also had a way of putting his foot in his mouth. For instance, while on a 1984 inspection tour of Inner Mongolia, to the shock of other leaders, Hu recommended that Chinese try forks, knives, and individual place settings instead of using chopsticks and serving themselves from common dishes at the center of the table, as was the long-standing custom. "We should make more knives and forks, buy more plates, and sit around the table and eat Chinese food in Western style, each from his own plate," he had counselled the nation. "That way we can avoid contagious diseases."

A Chinese Communist Party head impugning chopsticks as unsanitary was about as politic as an American President casting aspersions on hamburgers and fries for their high fat content. Compounding this culinary gaffe, on another occasion Hu also recommended that peasants shake off their "feudalistic miserliness" and give up their traditional "diet of rough staples" for a diet of "wine and meat."

Besides delivering himself of these odd public utterances, Hu became involved in a number of other affairs that added to his reputation as an impulsive man inclined to shoot from the hip. In April, 1985, for instance, he told reporters that he was unable to remember what the impediments were to bettering Sino-Soviet relations, a remark that caused many Western diplomats to assume erroneously that China was changing its position on the Soviet occupation of Afghanistan. Then, in 1986, Hu travelled to Japan just when the two countries were involved in a heated dispute over how new, official Japanese history texts were sanitizing their portrayal of the "rape of Nanking" during World War II. Moreover, while there he unilaterally invited three thousand Japanese youths to come to China on all-expenses-paid trips, a gesture that was as tactless as it may have been good-hearted.

"He was frequently doing inappropriate things that gave him an air of being impulsive and just a little bit odd," a diplomat who had met him told me. "It was hard to put your finger on it, but there was something slightly undignified about his presence; something informal, almost unsovereign about his manner that made you wonder how he would be able effectively to rule a country like China, where outward demeanor is always so important."

Moreover, adversaries, and even some supporters, were alternately put off or enraged by the cliquish way Hu filled vacant Party positions with appointments from his own liberal Communist Youth League network rather than by spreading the patronage around. His opponents became not only threatened by the idea of such a powerful, personally controlled fiefdom within the Party but also peeved at the way Hu steadfastly refused to provide routine nepotistic appointments to friends and sons of ranking Party leaders—a leadership perk that had come to be accepted as common Party practice. His refusal was undoubtedly a perfectly reasonable response to the corruption being perpetrated by the so-called "young prince faction" in the more relaxed atmosphere of the reforms. (For instance, Hu Shiying, the son of the hard-line Political Bureau member Hu Qiaomu, was reported to have embezzled a large sum of money and raped several women.) But however reasonable Hu Yaobang's drive against such corruption may have appeared to an outsider, it certainly did not endear him to his Party colleagues, especially those with grown children.

What really irritated hard-liners, however, was the way Hu blocked the appointment of their sympathizers to Party offices, or, in several cases, even had some of those already in office fired. In fact, Hu had made one of his most important appointments at the expense of the conservative faction leader Deng Liqun. In 1984, after the abortive campaign against spiritual pollution had ended, Hu, admittedly with the evident agreement of Deng Xiaoping, had had Deng Liqun fired as head of the propaganda department and replaced him with his own appointee, Zhu Houze. Zhu was a fifty-three-year-old former Secretary of the Guizhou Provincial Party Committee who was so liberal that he often sounded more like Fang Lizhi (even calling for "democratic pluralism") than Deng Xiaoping.

In the end, however, all of Hu's alleged mistakes appeared to be something of a smoke screen for a simpler truth, namely that Deng had had no choice but to offer up Hu as a sacrificial lamb to the hard-liners in order to save his existing economic reforms and his open door policy from a fatal attack after the student demonstrations.

||||||||||||||||||||||||||||||||
· —— The Campaign ————————— ·
Against Wholesale
Westernization

The notion of wholesale Westernization was anathema to the aging hard-line members of the Party leadership because it represented such a powerful symbolic rejection of everything for which China's Communist Revolution had struggled since the nineteen-twenties, as well as a repudiation of everything in traditional Chinese culture. Even though it had once attacked its own culture with great hostility and awesome thoroughness, in recent years the Party, hoping to reinspire loyalty by evoking nationalism, had again begun touting China's "glorious past." As a result, hard-liners seemed particularly offended when their inchoate notion of China as a culture and their fantasy of creating a new "spiritual socialist civilization with Chinese characteristics" could be brushed aside so easily and replaced with what appeared to them as nothing more than the ephemeral material products and the misguided values of the West.

What gave the Party's campaign against wholesale Westernization in the new year its particular edge of hysteria was that just beneath the surface of arrogant Party rhetoric was a profound lack of self-confidence in the worth of either Chinese Communism or traditional Chinese culture. This was revealed over and over again during the winter of 1987 in the polemics of Party essayists as they tried to pump up their country's sense of self-esteem by praising what was Chinese while railing against things Western. "To think that in China during the second half of the nineteen-eighties, when the Chinese people under the Chinese Communist Party's leadership have achieved success in building a modern socialist country—a success that has attracted worldwide attention—that some people have the impudence to raise the old slogan of 'wholesale Westernization!' " trumpeted an indignant commentator in the *People's Daily* that winter. "What does 'wholesale Westernization' mean? To use the words of its advocates, it means that everything in the West, including its science, technology, culture, politics, ideology, and ethics . . . are fair game. . . . [It] means a total repudiation of the socialist system and total implementation of the capitalist system in China. . . . No Chinese with pride, confidence, and respect for history and fact will ever endorse this idea of 'wholesale Westernization.' "

What was at issue here was not just the integrity of socialism, with which the Chinese leadership itself had been rather recklessly tampering, but the question of how China could modernize by borrowing from the capitalist West without shamelessly committing cultural and ideological suicide, thereby humiliating itself. Since official ideology had itself been rendered murky by all the reforms, it was difficult for any Chinese to know what they could or should believe in or be proud of by way of national symbols. With such rapid and chaotic change, China had become an identity vacuum in which the propagandistic voices of aging leaders rang out with increasing hollowness.

"We must have strong national self-esteem and self-confidence," Bo Yibo told the Chinese people after the student demonstrations. "We should not improperly belittle ourselves and think that all things foreign are better than things Chinese; that the 'moon is rounder in foreign countries than in China.' Such people are ignorant of the history of their own country."

"For some time in the past a trend of 'bourgeois liberalization' has prevailed," Wang Zhen told a group of teachers in the middle of February. "One of its major aspects is the denial of our nation's great history and record. Some people have claimed that nothing was any good in China and have tried to import everything from abroad. . . . But the Chinese people have their own self-respect and sense of national pride. They regard their aspiration to love the motherland and their complete dedication to it as a tremendous source of glory, and any action that harms the interest, dignity, and honor of the socialist motherland is a disgusting shame."

"Youths must be encouraged to explore, to advance, and to blaze new trails," wrote a commentator in the *Liberation Daily* in February. "However, modern ideas and new concepts do not necessarily mean Western bourgeois ideology. We should not regard ideology prevalent in Western capitalist societies as a symbol of modernization. To be modern does not mean that one has to dress oneself up in Western styles, let alone revive antique Western ideas, regarding them as new concepts to which modern Chinese people must pay homage."

These strident attempts at buoying self-confidence, which filled the

Party press and flooded the airwaves during the first few months of 1987, had something of a whistling-past-the-graveyard-in-the-dark effect. One could detect an almost haunting wistfulness for that reassuring time, now long gone, when China had been pre-eminent among nations; when surrounding countries had all borrowed their culture from the Middle Kingdom rather than vice versa. Now the very measure of China's success or failure was no longer even home-grown Maoism but the materialism of the industrialized West and Japan, precisely those countries that it had once reviled as decadent and doomed to self-destruction. The recognition that China was just another backward country struggling to develop by borrowing from the West may have been a realistic appraisal but hardly a palatable one.

In March, 1987, as part of the new campaign to oppose wholesale Westernization, the *Guangming Daily* ran an editorial entitled "Chinese Are Capable of Catching Up with and Surpassing the Advanced World," which told of advances made by several Chinese scientists in the field of superconductivity. The editorial heartily congratulated these scientists, not simply for their research but for the way in which their work reflected on China's enduring greatness. "Their sense of national self-esteem and self-confidence, their high aspirations and abilities, and their spirit of dedication, innovation, seeking for truth, and cooperation should certainly be admired and respected by the people," the editorial continued.

Then, with a defensiveness long characteristic of Chinese historical polemics, the editorial went on to acclaim China's "time-honored civilization" as being "known worldwide," as if to remind people of crucial evidence they might have forgotten. Even during the European Dark Ages, the editorial noted with complete accuracy but total irrelevancy, China had "held high the banner of civilization for humanity and made brilliant contributions to the development of the world's sciences and technology." The editorial then veered off into an even more defensive discussion of the question of loving one's country, as if scientific research were primarily an act of patriotism: "Some people advocate patriotism by quoting the saying, 'A son must not look down upon his mother's ugliness.' But, in fact, this saying is not relevant, because China is not ugly at all. She has vast territory, rich resources, a time-honored civilization, a huge number of industrious, brave, and intelligent people, and a splendid scientific and cultural tradition. The Chinese nation is an outstanding nation in the world rather than the 'sick man' of Eastern Asia."

Like a defense counsel refuting a litany of anticipated allegations against his client, the editorial continued, "We are determined to catch up with advanced world levels, to change our backward conditions, and to rise again as a powerful nation in the Eastern part of the world. All Chinese people who have high aspirations and courage should cherish such a strong sense of national self-esteem. . . . The attitude of belittling our own strength, our sense of inferiority, all the talk about the deeply rooted bad habits of the Chinese people, and other totally negative assessments of our nation will only cause people to become disappointed, pessimistic, and despairing."

One could feel in such statements the wounded psychological state underlying China's conflicted feelings about borrowing from the West, particularly since across a narrow body of water lay Japan, another Asian country, which, starting at the same place as China when the nineteenth century first brought both countries into contact with the outside world, had succeeded in Westernizing and accomplishing the very wonders of modernization that now left China so envious.

The understandable fear of appearing weak, and of damaging the nation's pride, was part of what made the Party lash out against Fang, Liu, and Wang. It was bad enough to be humiliated by foreigners, but when Chinese themselves began to criticize China and the Party, and to declare the Chinese system to be unequal to those of the West, this was ignominy of an even worse kind.

By Party logic, it was the obligation of all Chinese to rally into one huge support group and minister to the country's damaged ego. Leaders, workers, scientists, even writers were to throw themselves into the cause of building "our national pride and confidence," as the magazine *Outlook* put it in March. "It is the responsibility of our literature and art to help people restore and strengthen this pride and confidence; to give them support and encouragement, rather than to engage in national nihilism, pessimism, and skepticism by destroying, attacking, and hurting this national pride and confidence, not to say vilifying, insulting, and undermining it."

China had, in fact, impaled itself on the horns of a seemingly insoluble theoretical dilemma. It wished to believe in itself and the glories of its past; yet, at the same time, it was forced to recognize that its past had failed, and that to survive it must turn to outside models of development, suffering all the attendant humiliation of seeming to kowtow to foreigners. Deng Xiaoping himself was the perfect personification of this contradiction. Whatever might happen in practice, he could never quite bring himself to acknowledge the theoretical consequences of what he had set in motion with his reforms. It was a problem that would have seemed hauntingly familiar to Liang Qichao and his Qing Dynasty compatriots, who also puzzled unsuccessfully over the dilemma of how to modernize China without further wounding its pride and destroying its "national essence" (*guocui*).

One way to help alleviate the painfulness of this predicament was to explain China's backwardness as being purely the fault of history. In a long *People's Daily* commentary entitled "Uphold the Four Cardinal Principles in the Course of Reform and Opening Up to the Outside World," disseminated by the New China News Agency in mid-January and published all over China that winter, Chen Junsheng, a protégé of Zhao Ziyang and Secretary General of the State Council, wrote: "Currently, a handful of people in society at large are saying that socialism is inferior to capitalism and that China needs to be completely Westernized. . . . But socialism has enabled the Chinese people to stand up. Gone forever is the period in which China was bullied and trampled upon. This is an achievement that makes all patriotic Chinese feel proud. . . . Nevertheless, because of our poor economic foundation, China is still a developing nation. . . . Comparisons [with other countries] must be made on the basis of similar social and historic conditions. The more one makes comparisons without taking the starting point of each country into consideration, and the more one contrasts one's own motherland, whose poverty and backwardness are caused by history, against the most developed capitalist countries, the more one will feel that we are no good. And in the end, we will lose all pride, confidence, and the resolve to fight to rejuvenate the Chinese nation."

How, then, to explain China's state of being historically disadvantaged without slurring either China's "glorious past" or socialism? As Hu Sheng, President of the Chinese Academy of Social Sciences, wrote in a lengthy March, 1987, historical review of China's unsuccessful relations with the West, "The main reasons modern China was poor and backward and was unable to develop from feudalism to capitalism [and hence on to socialism] were the aggression and oppression of [Western and Japanese] imperialism." Far from masking China's deep-seated sensitivity to being compared to the West and found wanting, such analyses, however accurate they were, only highlighted the Chinese tendency to find the cause for their backwardness outside of their own country, a tendency that in the past had often led to periods of anti-foreignism and even extreme xenophobia.

A poem called "Aria to the Moon" was published by the *People's Daily* in February, complete with a cartoon of a man in a Western suit, tie, and hat, on whose long nose were inscribed the English words "Made in USA." The poem attempted to make light of those who too slavishly worshipped the West, but in doing so only revealed how sensitive the question of wholesale Westernization still was, particularly for older Chinese:

> *There are too many defects in China's moon;*
> *It's not round, it's not bright, it's no good;*
> *There is no nightclub in the Moon Palace,*
> *And Wu Gang [guardian god of the moon] does not know about*
>   *drinking cola.*
> *The maiden there is really too uncouth,*
> *Her name now is Chang-e, not Mary;*
> *In old times people thought of their hometowns while gazing at the moon,*
> *But now traditional concepts are intolerable.*
> *If we want to feel happy in the moonlight,*
> *Then we will have to import a new moon to shine on China.*

As "Aria to the Moon" suggested, the dilemma of China's relative backwardness continued to be a troubling one for China's leaders. Much "theoretical work" was expended simply on trying to explain, justify, and rationalize how China's "superior system of socialism" could have been so outflanked by the "doomed system" of capitalism. But no matter how tattered China's socialist system and ideology looked, Party leaders refused to countenance any overt references to its bankruptcy. At the same time, they continued to promote even more economic changes, which only made the gap between the fiction of Maoist socialism and present-day realities even wider.

In this sense, the Maoist hard-liners' implacable opposition to wholesale Westernization and bourgeois liberalization had a certain internal consistency that the stance of liberal reformers and Deng lacked; the hard-liners were not pretending that China could have it both ways at once. And in the winter of 1987, while the Party was still alarmed over the sudden student uprisings and they had the ear of Deng Xiaoping, the hard-liners moved with dispatch to purge the country of intellectuals like Fang Lizhi, as well as the kind of "spiritually polluting" Western ideas and influences that they advocated.

|||||||||||||||||||||||
The Dismissal of Liu Binyan

On January 23, because Liu Binyan remained true to his notion of a second kind of loyalty, even when "relevant Party organizations . . . criticized him time and time again for his serious mistakes [of] trumpeting bourgeois liberalism" and "negating the socialist system in favor of the capitalist system," he was expelled from the Chinese Communist Party. It was no secret that, just as in the case of Fang Lizhi, the order had come directly from Deng Xiaoping. Like the hard-liners, Deng had long been disturbed by the writer's independent-minded reporting and his unsavory revelations of social and political ills within the Party and Chinese society.

What made Liu's disenfranchisement distinctive was that when the order came down to purge him, his superiors at the *People's Daily* all refused to act, forcing Party higher-ups to find some other relevant unit to perform the literary execution. Such resistance in China's intellectual community had until recently been rare. The task finally fell to the paper's Discipline and Inspection Committee, a branch of the nationwide organization that handles cases of corruption and incorrect political behavior among Party members. Liu was, of course, stripped of his office. But as in the cases of Hu Yaobang, Fang Lizhi, and Wang Ruowang, the actual punishment was once again circumscribed by the leadership's fear of further panicking the intellectual community, and Liu was allowed to keep his prestigious job as Vice-Chairman of the Chinese Writers' Association. However, as with his other purged colleagues, the tone of the Party's rhetoric quickly turned shrill, and Liu was accused of a host of political crimes: of having "made speeches and written articles on many occasions which violated the Party Constitution," of having "negated the Four Cardinal Principles," and of having "trumpeted bourgeois liberalism." As with his cohorts, exhaustive quotations from his writings and speeches were circulated by the Party and promptly began appearing in the Chinese press to back up charges against him—quotes that paradoxically gave Chinese readers everywhere a comprehensive sense of exactly those ideas that the Party was trying to suppress by defrocking Liu.

The very fact that Liu had so insistently written his exposés from inside the Party, focusing as he did on the relationship of the Party to the people, only served to heighten the Party's fear of Liu and to exacerbate its angry sense of betrayal at his insubordinate attitude. The evident outrage of the attacks against him betrayed emotions far more heartfelt than those that could be detected in the critiques of Fang and Wang, who had made no recent pretensions to being good Communists or obedient Party members.

The day after Liu's expulsion, for instance, a New China News Agency dispatch accused him of having attacked the Four Cardinal Principles as being "outdated, rigid, dogmatic concepts and worn-out phrases that have led China to calamity on several occasions." It alleged that he had slandered the Party for "having degenerated," and that he had impugned the notion of model workers and heroes as nothing more than attempts by the Party to "turn people into servile tools." It went on to lambast him for refusing "to accept Party leadership" as "lowly and degrading."

Liu had many supporters at his old paper; nevertheless the *People's Daily*, like every other Party publication in China, soon also joined the attack. From being heralded as its most exalted writer, Liu, at least officially, now suddenly became an outcast and an object of contempt. An unsigned diatribe bitterly complained, "It is apparent that Liu Binyan, although a Communist Party member organizationally, has long ago ideologically and politically ostracized himself from the Party and set himself against it. If we continue to tolerate such wanton acts of vilifying and slandering the Party, then will our Party continue to have any principles or fighting capability left to speak of?"

It was a good question. Since 1979, when Liu had once again begun writing his pieces exposing Party corruption, he had created many new enemies in high places who feared exactly this eventuality. So it was hardly surprising that his dismissal now gave every Party committee across China permission to begin a counter-attack against anyone who had ever levelled charges of corruption, bureaucratism, or authoritarianism against them. The Heilongjiang Province Party Committee, still smarting from Liu's exposé in *People or Monsters?* was one of the first to counter-attack. In the wake of Liu's expulsion, the provincial radio service suddenly erupted, indignantly excoriating Liu: "To put it bluntly, his work on so-called real people and events was nothing but a collection of random materials that he used only to exaggerate things and to make oblique accusations. His purpose was simply to uglify Party organizations and party cadres, vilify our socialist system, and dampen the people's spirit of advancing bravely to accomplish the Four Modernizations. . . . Throughout his work he turned things upside down, started rumors, slandered people, confused local citizens, and caused serious mental harm to those involved. All this created many difficulties and troubles for local party organizations and governments, which were forced to devote a great deal of effort to dealing with their aftermath."

In the weeks that followed, self-serving broadsides from the provinces, as if awaiting the official word of Liu's ouster for release, appeared to rebut his earlier exposés of Party corruption in such cities as Xi'an, Shanghai, and Xining. This chorus accused Liu of "creating chaos wherever he poked his nose," "showing no respect or consideration for the proper opinions of local Party organizations," and writing pieces that "resemble the big-character posters of the Cultural Revolution."

As Liu's English translator, Perry Link, an American scholar in contemporary Chinese literature, told me wistfully just after Liu's fall, "The real tragedy of Liu's expulsion is that it was he, more than anyone else, who represented hope to youth that the Party could be pushed toward a more democratic style of operation in China. It was Liu who represented the vision that democracy could evolve peacefully within the Party rather than violently outside it. With Liu's expulsion, this hope has dimmed."

By damaging this fragile myth of reform from within—a myth laboriously reconstructed from the ashes of the Cultural Revolution by the Party's liberal reformers—the Party wounded itself at an inopportune time. Although it was the Party that was rejecting Liu, Liu ironically needed the Party less than the Party needed him. By expelling him the Party helped create yet another opponent of mythic proportions, and Liu was all the more difficult to slur not only because he was much better known and more revered than Fang and Wang, but because as he exposed the hidden underbelly of Party life, he simultaneously swore undying allegiance to Marxism and the Chinese Revolution. How, after all, could the Party effectively attack a man whose writing had never been calculated to mortally wound it, only to help it see itself more clearly? Moreover, what was the Party to do when Liu, instead of lashing back at his dismissal, protested his innocence in a single, discreet letter and then, without trying to justify himself, refused to grant any interviews to members of either the Chinese or the foreign press? He had declared in 1979, "I have awakened to a hard fact. In today's China, if one speaks or writes and does not incur somebody's opposition, one might as well not have spoken or written at all. . . . The only alternative is to cower in a corner and fall silent. But if we do that, why live?" Yet when his expulsion order came down, he went quietly into self-imposed isolation, claiming that he wished only to catch up on his reading.

At a certain level, the Party soon seemed to grasp the self-defeating nature of its attack on Liu, and it was not long after his expulsion that the vituperative rhetoric began to die away. After the first few weeks, there were nowhere near the number of accusatory articles against Liu as there were against Fang. But if the Party miscalculated in purging Liu from its ranks, Liu, too, seemed to have made a miscalculation of sorts by so readily retiring into obscurity. Although he did write a letter justifying his actions to the Party, his refusal to fight back, as Fang did, by continuing to meet with foreigners and to give interviews to the foreign press when he could, suggested that Liu operated on many of the old expectations about the Party—namely, that it was still inclined to crush its intellectuals like insects and that the best tactic to employ when attacked was some form of outward compliance. Considering Liu's long, bitter experience of abuse at the hands of the Party, it was perhaps understandable at this moment of his second defrocking that he did not fully appreciate the bind the Party was in concerning dissident intellectuals. It was also, one imagines, far from clear in Liu's mind whether the purge in which he now found himself caught up was not just a prelude to a complete regression to the destructive campaigns against intellectuals of the fifties and sixties.

Liu Binyan's tragedy was that no matter how fervently he rejected dissident status, the Party kept thrusting it upon him. No matter how hard he tried to justify himself as a member of a loyal opposition, all the Party could see was that his writing made "the masses" love the system less rather than more. But what was, in fact, finally most enigmatic about Liu was the steadfastness of his own belief in the Party and Marxism, which he maintained long after the Party had abandoned him and most of his readers had abandoned themselves to skepticism. His own investigations piled up such overwhelming evidence of the system's tyranny, corruption, and inhumanity that the reader is left utterly bewildered to know how Liu could still have cherished the name "Comrade Liu Binyan." One looks for a certain evolution in his position after all his suffering and rejection, for some statement suggesting doubt about Communism as China's future salvation; but during the months that immediately followed his third fall from official grace and his second expulsion from the Party there was no sign of it. As with so many older Chinese whose idealism and patriotism had long ago become bound up with the idea of the Chinese Revolution and the Party, this step into outright dissidence, which Fang and Wang seemed more inclined to accept, was for Liu hardly imaginable. And so, even as the Party officially disgraced him in the winter of 1987, he remained true to his notion of a second kind of loyalty.

Emulate Lei Feng

By February, all signs indicated that if the political storms swirling around the country had not yet reached hurricane strength, a good gale at least was in the offing. Liu Binyan was not the only one to head for cover in the gathering tempest. Notwithstanding sotto voce protestations that Deng's economic reforms and the open door policy would not be repudiated (less than totally convincing, given the Party's other actions), the Maoist hard-liners appeared to be very much in the saddle. Moreover, it looked as if for Party committees throughout the country, the campaign against bourgeois liberalization and wholesale Westernization was going to offer a perfect opportunity to get rid of other people who had been irritatingly critical of Party abuses at the local level, not to speak of intellectuals who had become too bold in their statements and writing. Although most of the arrested student demonstrators had been promptly released; those who had been expelled from the Party had been neither jailed, subjected to the public humiliation of self-criticism, nor imprisoned; and for now the boom-town atmosphere of economic reform continued largely unchecked, everything in the last three decades of Chinese Communist history indicated that once a movement like this began, things were more likely than not to get worse before they got better. How was anyone to know that history in this case would prove no guide, that in only eight months the most severe of the Party hard-liners would have been unceremoniously "retired" from active leadership and the reformist technocrats would be triumphant and promising even more Western reforms? Certainly, as ominous signs of a crackdown proliferated in those early months of 1987, such a future was hard to imagine.

On January 11, Yang Wei, a young student from Fudan University in Shanghai who had recently returned to China after receiving his master's degree in microbiology at the University of Arizona, was arrested in his home, without a warrant, for supporting the China Spring pro-democracy movement while in the United States, and for his involvement with student demonstrations in Shanghai the previous month. It was what police referred to as a detention check, and it was a warning to the increasing number of Chinese who had truly been Westernized by going abroad to live and study that their homecoming might be fraught with perils. In fact, Yang remained in prison, without being either publicly charged or tried, until December, 1987, when he was sentenced to two years in prison for "counter-revolutionary" activity, "attacking the Communist Party, slandering the socialist system, and advocating that China take the capitalist road."

On February 5, *China Legal News*, a daily newspaper that covers the field of law, reported that in Mianyang, Sichuan province, Liu De, a youth who worked for a local literary magazine, had been arrested and sentenced to seven years' imprisonment for having advocated bourgeois liberalization, having "sunk in the mire of total Westernization," and for having committed unnamed "counter-revolutionary crimes." The paper quoted Liu as saying, "It is not I that the Communist Party has defeated; it is the Communist Party that is breaking itself down. . . . In fifteen or twenty years, thanks to a common struggle, I hope there will be a new Party that will replace the Communist Party."

On March 18, the New China News Agency reported from Qing-dao that a young worker, Yu Chunyan, who was employed by the

Qingdao Water Works, had been arrested "for stirring up trouble," "writing counter-revolutionary letters," and trying to form a "counter-revolutionary organization" called the New National Democratic Party. On March 22, the New China News Agency filed another dispatch about two workers who had been among the fourteen or so people arrested during the demonstrations in Shanghai: They had been given long prison sentences for inciting crowds to riot. And on March 31, Jiangsu Television announced that three "troublemakers" who had "disrupted the social order" during the student demonstrations in December had "admitted their crimes," been found guilty of "sabotage activities," and been sentenced to from four to six years in jail.

Even more ominous for those Chinese who followed the political scene was the way that, in February and March, Chinese leaders simultaneously began making ideological shifts in their public statements to conform to the changed Party line. Readjusting their political tone, deleting certain key buzzwords, and then refoliating their speeches with the appropriate new tone, themes, slogans, and vocabulary, Party leaders appeared to have been reborn into a universe of language and values that had largely been in eclipse since the end of the Cultural Revolution.

On January 27, for instance, hard-liner Peng Zhen, Chairman of the National People's Congress, met with fifty "veteran literary and art fighters" of the Yan'an era. As if the post–Cultural Revolution decade of increasing literary freedom had never intervened, he said that Mao's "Talks at the Yan'an Forum on Art and Literature" had "enriched the Marxist-Leninist literary and art treasure house," and that "some people have forgotten the historical mission of the Party's literary and art workers," which was to "serve the broadest masses and, first of all, the workers, peasants, and soldiers."

It was, of course, mind-bending for Chinese to see the same newspapers that had only two months before championed academic, scientific, and intellectual freedom now warning intellectuals that "literary and art workers should review [Mao's Yan'an talks] and make an earnest effort to understand them."

President Li Xiannian, while on an inspection tour of Shanghai, called on the Chinese people to revive the tradition of "hard work, plain living, and building China thriftily," principles that, although they might sound bland and reasonable to an outsider, were being explicitly raised now because of their currency during the Maoist era. Even the speeches of Premier Zhao Ziyang, apostle of economic reform and modernization, began to bloom with references to the "spirit of arduous struggle" and other familiar if long-lost phrases of the Maoist period.

Gone were articles extolling competition, bankruptcy laws, and stock markets. Such slogans as "To get rich is glorious" were hardly heard. Party-sponsored campaigns to encourage 10,000- or 100,000 yuan households (model peasant families who were to grow prosperous through private enterprise) were downplayed, and instead Party propagandists suddenly began dusting off the old Maoist virtues of "altruism and self-abnegation," "bitter struggle through hardships," and "self-reliance."

China Youth News, once a media bastion of Hu Yaobang's liberal reform faction, published an article headlined "Let Diligence and Frugality Become Common Practice," which advocated a return to "industry and thrift" as the "traditional virtues of the Chinese nation."

In Canton, the *Nanfang Daily*, which in recent years had often published racy articles about film stars, crime, fashion, and new wealth, appeared one day with a piece declaring that it was time to revive "The Foolish Old Man Who Moved the Mountain," an ancient morality tale favored by Mao that extols an old man who, rather than surrendering to the fatalism of nay-sayers, set about leveling some land by moving a mountain shovelful by shovelful. "Comrade Mao Zedong referred to the fable of the foolish old man to urge that everyone carry forward the Chinese nation's fine tradition of arduous struggle," said the paper. "In negating the idea of the 'foolish old man' today, certain people apparently would like to depict arduous struggle as an outmoded concept and totally to negate it. So now more than ever it seems essential to 'rehabilitate' the 'foolish old man.' "

The *Liberation Army Daily* carried a piece entitled "Continue to Carry Forward the Spirit of Selflessness," which claimed that "selflessness is a glorious tradition that has passed down from one generation to another in our People's Army." The article denigrated the view that "only personal desire can be the motivating force for social development," calling it "confusing and wrong" because it "plays down and throws mud at numerous heroes, models, and advanced personalities who dedicated their lives to the Revolution."

One such hero who had had a good deal of mud thrown at him since Deng Xiaoping came to power was Lei Feng, an ordinary soldier who in the nineteen-sixties, because of his purported selflessness, dedication to the Revolution, and obedience to the Party, had been canonized by Chairman Mao as a model proletarian. Born into a poor rural household in 1940, Lei joined the People's Liberation Army (PLA), only to be killed ingloriously, not by a capitalist bullet, but by a falling telephone pole. However, Lei conveniently left behind him a diary describing his abiding passion for serving the people. After Mao eulogized Lei with the stark admonition, "Learn from Lei Feng," his diary and the exploits of his short life became an instant legend.

In more recent years, however, the hortatory Lei Feng legend had shown signs of wear and tear. Just as PLA propaganda teams were having a hard time competing with disco, so Party propaganda cadres were having a difficult time selling the correct line (whatever it might be at any given time) with such simpleminded role models as Lei Feng. The problem was that Lei no longer spoke to Chinese youth. His selflessness and dedication had in post–Cultural Revolution China begun to appear almost comical, even camp (although the Chinese had as yet no word or phrase for this elusive Western concept). But one friend of mine had begun to collect Lei Feng memorabilia in the same spirit that Americans might collect Calvin Coolidge plates or "Harold Stassen for President" buttons. Whenever I succeeded in working an allusion to Lei Feng into a conversation with a taxi driver or a store clerk, invariably the mere mention of this model revolutionary's name was enough to trigger quizzical looks and sometimes even gales of laughter, as if the idea of Lei was now too preposterous for words. In truth, few Chinese still thought or said such things as, "I have only one desire in my heart. I want to be wholeheartedly dedicated to the Party, socialism, and Communism," or, "Whatever Chairman Mao says, I will do." In fact, since people like Liu Binyan and Fang Lizhi had argued against, even ridiculed, this "whatever-ist" notion, many Chinese now found it at best naive, at worst embarrassing, to be associated with the likes of Lei Feng.

So the fact that Lei Feng had been dredged up again was a measure of the desperate situation hard-line Maoists found themselves in as soon as they were pushed to come up with models of their own to highlight their revolutionary ethics against the much trendier reformist models. It was also certainly a measure of just how out of touch they were with the current reality of China that they could even conceive of dragging the weary image of Lei Feng back out again in 1987.

On February 6 the *Liberation Army Daily* enthusiastically took up the cause of Lei's revival with an article entitled "Lei Feng's 'Spirit of a Screw' Forever Glitters." The reference came from one of the many primitive metaphors Lei himself had allegedly used to demonstrate his self-abnegating spirit of loyalty to the cause of the Revolution. He had reputedly proclaimed, "I will be a screw that never rusts and will glitter anywhere I am placed." It was a spirit that the commentator in *Liberation Army Daily* believed had "taken deep root in the hearts of the millions upon millions of people, cadres, and fighters in the Army . . . encouraging people to make selfless contributions to our socialist construction. . . . Not long ago some people belittled Lei Feng's 'spirit of a screw' and preached the notions that materially 'one should enjoy comforts as much as possible, and that spiritually one should express one's individuality,' saying things like, 'I am myself.' These people maintained that this attitude should be fully propagated as the image of a modern person. But actually, such a philosophy of life, which is characterized by taking 'oneself' as the center of everything and by putting pleasure-seeking before all else, is nothing but an outworn concept of fostering out-and-out egoism in capitalist soil. A long time ago practice showed that as far as our socialist construction was concerned, this was a negative factor. How can modern Chinese youths, who are acting wholeheartedly on behalf of the Four Modernizations, ever regard this as their ideal image?"

On March 5, the twenty-fourth anniversary of Lei's death, the Party held a commemorative Learn from Lei Feng-Spirit Forum at Huairen Hall in the Party leadership compound at Zhongnanhai. It was as if Lei's memory were a heart that had only momentarily stopped beating and could be magically revived by proximity to this inner sanctum of the Chinese government. Attending were such noted hard-liners as Wang Zhen, Hu Qiaomu, and Song Renqiong, as well as liberal Political Bureau member Hu Qili, who was perhaps trying to ingratiate himself after narrowly avoiding being purged himself along with his mentor, Hu Yaobang, three weeks earlier. Never noted as an ardent fan of Lei Feng, Hu nonetheless now dutifully intoned, "Lei Feng is always an example the broad masses of young people should learn from, and Lei Feng always inspired them to go forward. In this new situation, it is necessary to carry out effective Learn from Lei Feng activities and, in a down-to-earth way, make the Lei Feng spirit strike deeper roots in the people's hearts."

The keynote speaker was Yu Qiuli, hard-line member of the Political Bureau and Director of the PLA General Political Department, who delivered an address so bombastic that it put Hu's to shame. After surveying the "advanced individuals" in the crowd, he proclaimed with synthetic confidence, "From these comrades, we can see that the Lei Feng spirit is being carried forward, that new Lei Fengs are continuing to grow up, and that our next generation is full of promise." Then, as if China were still back in the early sixties, Yu launched into a Homeric recitation of the old Lei Feng myth. "The Lei Feng spirit is the Communist spirit, the spirit of serving the people wholeheartedly, and the spirit of warmly loving the Party wholeheartedly, and the spirit of warmly loving the motherland and socialism, of studying painstakingly, of waging arduous struggle, of being selfless, and of taking pleasure in helping others," he gushed to the assembled delegates. "The Lei Feng spirit, as we call it today, has a deeper and wider meaning. It is representative of the advanced ideology of the young generation and has become a vital part of the great spirit of our times."

Yu cautioned that in the world of reform where China was "opening itself to the outside world and invigorating its economy, we should make an all-out effort to carry forward this spirit, and to resist corruption by decadent capitalist and feudalistic ideas such as selfishness, self-interest, putting money before all else, and the wholehearted quest for profit. . . . We should self-consciously subordinate our personal interest to the overall revolutionary interest and, if necessary, not hesitate to sacrifice all we have for the sake and interests of the Party and people."

Ever sensitive to the attacks that had been made on Lei's legacy by the likes of Fang Lizhi, Liu Binyan, and Wang Ruowang, Yu added, "The allegation that Lei Feng's spirit is outdated is wrong. As an embodiment of socialist and Communist ideology and ethics, the Lei Feng spirit still has great vitality. It is not obsolete today, nor will it become obsolete in the future."

Just as no sermon is ever given without a text from scripture, so no speech in China is ever considered complete if it has not included a quotation from the current leader. Only too eager to show that the spirit of Lei Feng had even touched the heart of Deng Xiaoping, Yu quoted China's paramount leader as saying, "Whoever wishes to become a genuine Communist should emulate Comrade Lei Feng's good moral character and work style."

This commemorative gathering, held right next to the Forbidden City itself, had the effect of an imperial edict. The whole government and all its constituent propaganda organs responded instantaneously. Articles commemorating the spirit of Lei Feng and proclaiming his spirit as "an important part of building socialist spiritual civilization" appeared simultaneously in papers throughout China—a timely reminder of how fully the Party still controlled the media, even if it had lost its former ability to attract fervent followers.

It is difficult to believe that in 1987 the hard-liners did not realize the hopelessness of getting any real ideological mileage out of Lei Feng. In fact, in the all-too-mechanical way they rolled Lei Feng back out into the public arena, it sometimes seemed that they saw him not as a reborn model citizen whose example might rally youth to march into a new and pure socialist future but as just another brick to throw up on China's Great Wall of cultural isolation.

The problem was, however, that this wall had long since been breached by all manner of "spiritually polluting" Western influences, and more and more Chinese youths now wished to adopt the very Western values against which Lei was supposed to be the bulwark. No ideological wall building could easily remedy this momentous change. How modern Chinese youth weaned on Deng's economic reforms and open door policy could ever again be expected to accept a proletarian hero as a reasonable role model for their lives was nowhere addressed by the leaders of this surreal revival of latter-day Lei Fengism.

The Emulate Lei Feng Campaign raised another question crucial to the outcome of the factional and ideological struggle that had erupted. If Lei Feng was out of date, what sort of Maoist role model in a Deng-ist age was imaginable? If hard-liners could not even come up with a role model, how would they manage to find a credible leader or a credible domestic and foreign policy (never mind a whole new alternative cultural universe) to counterpose against those of the reformers? Sometimes it seemed that the only effective tactic available to the old guard at this late date was foot dragging and obstructionism. It was all very well for commentators in the *Liberation Army Daily* to declare that China needed "tens of millions of ordinary 'screws,' " because "just as Comrade Lei Feng pointed out, it is only by putting together numerous screws that a machine can become a working entity." The practical problem was that fewer and fewer Chinese wanted to be screws, much less parts of a machine. Hard-line propagandists might be nostalgic for Lei Feng's "spirit of the screw" which "never rusts" and "never gives a thought to personal gains or losses," but clearly the next generation of Chinese, having had a glimpse into the dazzling supermarket of fast cars, television, Freud, capitalism, bodybuilding, consumer goods, stocks and bonds, golf, cosmetic surgery, fashionable clothing, capitalism, and democracy, were not.

China Youth News, the country's pre-eminent publication for young people, wrestled in its own way with this dilemma on the anniversary of Lei's death: " 'Self-realization' is not and should not be the ultimate purpose of life. Even if one's ability could develop perfectly, it would finally die with the end of one's life. In fact, there is no such thing as an everlasting value that has absolutely nothing to do with society and that is utterly of a personal nature. Only when a value belongs to mankind can it be everlasting. Lei Feng devoted his limited life to unlimited service to the people and merged his personal pursuits into the progress of mankind. This is the only correct way to realize personal value.

"If individualism becomes the model of morality, and serving the people becomes outdated, then selfishness will be allowed to spread unchecked, the attitude of 'putting money before all else' will become the norm, and extreme egoism will become the standard of morality. Not only will it be impossible to realize socialism, but such a situation may give rise to great danger. The 'cave dwellers' described by the French thinker Montesquieu in his *Persian Letters*," the *China Youth News* commentary continued, with a reference that would have had meaning only for those Chinese already Westernized in the most "wholesale" fashion, "all died because everyone in the cave was selfish. But the majority of our youth hope that the general mood of society will turn for the better, that unhealthy practices in the Party and bureaucratism in state organs will soon be eliminated, that production departments will produce good-quality products, that service and commercial units will improve their service. . . . [But] how can all this come about if publicity is given to 'self-realization' rather than to 'serving the people'?"

Whatever fragments of truth might have been embedded in such commentaries, fewer and fewer Chinese had any stomach, never mind enthusiasm, for emulation campaigns of the Lei Feng variety, or any other kind of Party-sponsored campaigns for that matter. Intellectuals, in particular, were fed up with being told what to think and how to think by Party bureaucrats, whom they now referred to derogatorily as "professional political campaigners."

Visiting with three Chinese friends after the Emulate Lei Feng Campaign had ingloriously fizzled out, I was truly shocked by the depth of outright contempt they showed for the Party and its "ideological work among the masses." All three were middle-aged professional people who had been abroad, two were actually Party members, and each of them gave scathing assessments of the hard-liners and the ways in which they had been trying to bully the country back into ideological submission with their refurbished political campaigns.

"Those old men care about nothing but their own power," said one, who was in training at a research institute sponsored by the Public Security Bureau. "Do you think Peng Zhen ever emulated Lei Feng? The thought's too laughable for words."

"They all know that socialism has been a failure, but they won't admit it, because that would be a confession that their leadership is bankrupt," said another, a middle-ranking official from a large state-run enterprise.

"When I hear those old sons of bitches like Peng Zhen, Hu Qiaomu, Yiu Qiuli and Wang Zhen sounding off, it enrages me," said the final one, a brilliant historian, unable to control his anger. "They claim to have saved China. But it's they who have destroyed China by destroying our traditional culture. When they speak," he concluded, calling on a classical Chinese saying, *chiren shuomeng*, "it's like listening to fools tell their dreams."

||||||||||||||||||||||||||||||||
· —— Chinese Students ———————————— ·
Abroad Write a
Letter Home

Of all the Chinese in danger of having the label of wholesale Westernization pinned on them now or in the future, none were in more jeopardy than the tens of thousands of students who had gone abroad (to Western Europe, Japan, Canada, and the United States) to study in the nineteen-eighties. There were few among these students who were unaware of the fate of that last generation of Chinese intellectuals—many of whom were their fathers and mothers—who had gone abroad to study in the thirties and forties, and paid dearly for their foreign educations when they returned home to participate in "national reconstruction" after 1949. Far from viewing them as patriots, the Party ended up vilifying them as class enemies and agents of the bourgeoisie who had been indelibly contaminated by foreign culture and values.

Nonetheless, after diplomatic relations with the United States were restored in 1979, a few students once again began leaving China for the West. As more and more cultural exchange programs were established, and as the post-Mao leadership became increasingly aware of its dire need for a well-trained corps of experts to head up its new, ambitious modernization program, the government began loosening up restrictions for passports and exit visas, paving the way for a surge of students to go abroad to study. By 1987, this had become a torrent, with from 20,000 to 25,000 students estimated to be in the United States alone. (As of the beginning of 1988, there were, by comparison, no more than forty students in the United States from that other Communist giant, the Soviet Union.)

What made it difficult to calculate accurately the exact number of Chinese studying in the United States was the differing nature of two distinct groups. Those who went at "public expense" (*gongfei*), namely students with scholarships who came abroad as part of one of the numerous official educational exchange programs, were relatively easy to keep track of. But many more had gone at "private expense" (*zifei*), receiving scholarships from U.S. schools or being helped by overseas relatives and friends, and thus lacked any official connections to their homeland. In fact, frequently they came on tourist or temporary visitors' visas (often supporting themselves by working illegally in Chinese restaurants), only later succeeding in getting into an educational institution. This mass exodus raised an obvious question in everyone's mind: Would these students ever return home?

The Chinese government was, of course, concerned about this hemorrhaging flow abroad of some of its best and brightest students. But just as it was caught in a contradiction at home between expanding and contracting the freedom granted intellectuals, so the Party found itself confronting a similar issue in regard to study abroad. The leadership, and particularly the liberal reformers, recognized that if China was to modernize, it needed the kind of training and expertise that could only come from abroad. And so the Party, taking the calculated gamble that enough students would return home out of patriotism or a sense of obligation to justify its experiment, adopted a relatively relaxed, although frequently fluctuating, policy toward overseas study.

Even though the difficulties of passing language requirements, securing official permission from work units, obtaining scholarships or letters from overseas financial guarantors, getting passports, and qualifying for foreign visas were daunting, thousands of students soon found themselves abroad, and it was not long before courses of study were completed and the question of returning home arose. For many, it had been so difficult to get out of China, and once abroad, they had become so accustomed to the easier life-style, that the idea of returning home seemed unthinkable to them. It was unthinkable not only because China's standard of living was so much lower and its intellectual climate so much more oppressive than abroad, but because who knew, once they were back, when or if they might ever get out again. These fears were compounded by students' awareness of how quickly and unpredictably political lines could change. The last generation of Chinese students to study abroad had learned the hard way—after it was too late to reconsider and leave China again.

The newest generation of students abroad were hardly encouraged about prospects for returning home by the events that winter. Nor were they reassured that spring when Vice-Premier Li Peng, head of the State Education Commission, told a trade union meeting that rather than training outstanding individual scholars, the "most fundamental task" of a school was to produce "talent useful to the cause of socialism," and that new regulations had been promulgated decreeing that "special attention" would henceforth be paid to the ideological, moral, and political qualifications of all university candidates. Before admission, adequate commitment to such socialist imperatives as the Five Loves (love of socialism, the Party, labor, science and technology, and the motherland) would have to be demonstrated. And they certainly did not take much heart from reports that Deng Liqun had declared that "the struggle against bourgeois liberalization over the past year has not been successful. The basic orientation of the student's thought is still rightist. The election of Li Shuxian [Fang Lizhi's wife, elected to a local Beijing district People's Congress] is significant in this respect. If the situation on the campuses continues to remain unstable, we must unleash a major anti-rightist movement in the second half of this year." Nor could these students have been thrilled when even reputedly liberal leaders like Hu Qili called for a new regimen of "social investigation" and "physical labor"—a mandatory program to send students into factories and to the countryside to study "the actual process of socialist construction." To many overseas students, such a program sounded ominously like the *xiafang* campaigns of the Maoist era in which students and intellectuals were "sent down" to work with the peasantry in the countryside, where they were often marooned for years, sometimes for the rest of their lives.

As a result of fears that China might suddenly revert to its old ways, large numbers of Chinese students had quietly been deciding to stay on in the United States and elsewhere after their terms of study ended and their visas expired. This was particularly true of "private expense" students. Younger and less likely to be married than their "public expense" colleagues, they had less binding ties to China. Some succeeded in qualifying for immigration to the United States; some got married legitimately; some arranged or paid for marriages of convenience, automatically ensuring them landed-immigrant status and a treasured "green card"; while some just disappeared underground as illegal aliens.

For the older "public expense" students, who had come on state scholarships and had left important positions, not to mention spouses and children behind, there was usually little choice but to return. For them, having the opportunity to study abroad was both a liberation and a burden. They were well aware that their tenure abroad would "gold-plate" *(dujin)* them with a certain prestige, but they were keenly aware of all the problems that could arise once they returned home. They knew that it was often difficult to readjust to crowded living quarters and lower salaries, and that older bureaucrats, jealous of their foreign training, which they viewed as a threat to their own positions, often did everything in their power to block the way and frustrate the careers of the returnees. Consequently there was nothing that caused more concern among the Chinese students abroad than these fluctuations in Party policy.

So while they were abroad, these worried students followed the oscillations of government policy and regulations with all the fascination and care of financiers following an erratic stock market. When China was experiencing a period of relative political relaxation, they, too, relaxed and were filled with a sense of well-being and optimism. But whenever a political campaign blew up on the horizon, reading rooms at the various centers for Asian and Chinese studies at large United States universities filled not with American students researching seminar papers and Ph.D. dissertations but with Chinese students reading newspapers from their homeland and Hong Kong, trying to decipher the political trends emanating from Beijing. Having accomplished the elusive dream of leaving China, they were now preoccupied, sometimes even obsessed, with the question of return.

Despite this, from 1985 until the end of 1986, Chinese students abroad appeared relatively free of anxiety about the future. They scanned the Chinese press and talked among themselves, but the increasingly liberal atmosphere that prevailed back home and the government's apparent willingness not to foreclose the possibility of future foreign travel allayed their most immediate fears. For Soviet citizens who succeeded in getting abroad the choice was still the stark one between defection or return. However, the Chinese government, by generally being more open, appeared to be learning to live with a significantly wider range of options. As a result, China had begun to give rise to a new, cosmopolitan elite that increasingly expected a certain license to go abroad more than once. So, during this time, Chinese students and scholars found themselves less pressured to make the kind of precipitous, all-or-nothing decisions that had once rendered the issue of returning home such a monumental one.

Thus it was with a real sense of shock and sudden foreboding that Chinese students abroad heard of the fall of Hu Yaobang and the expulsions of Fang and Wang from the Party. What they feared most was that these purges signalled a return to Maoist policies toward intellectuals. And so, on January 20, three days before Liu was also expelled, more than a thousand Chinese students studying in the United States took the unprecedented step of endorsing an open letter to the leaders of their country expressing concern over recent events. "A deep sense of mission for the future of our motherland has prompted us to write this letter openly to express our views to the Party's Central Committee and the State Council. We feel that the ultra-leftist practice of labelling people arbitrarily and finding fault with others has redominated the area of communications. We are concerned about the prospect of economic and political reforms in China. We fear the recurrence of the political situation of the Cultural Revolution, in which 'ruthless struggle' and 'merciless criticism' were rampant." After expressing their fears that "the historic tragedy is being repeated in which intellectuals are attacked and liberal ideas suppressed," the letter went on to say that its supporters hoped that recent events in China would not "destroy the confidence of the people, injure the reputation of the Party and the government in the minds of the people, and interrupt the stability and consistency of China's policies"; that, in short, it would not "tarnish the image of China in the world."

Praising Hu Yaobang's contributions to China, the letter said, "We are shocked and deeply upset by his departure, which will gravely harm the people's confidence in reform and the Four Modernizations. . . . We sincerely hope that the Party and the government will persist in reforms, oppose retrogression, persevere in the principle of the rule of law, and avoid punishing people for voicing their opinions."

What was even more surprising than the sentiments in the letter itself was the fact that of the 1,000 students from more than fifty-one United States colleges and universities who "endorsed" it, 480 of them allowed their names to be used. This was the first occasion in recent times that so many Chinese nationals had publicly affixed their names to anything that substantively criticized the actions of their own government.

"If loyalty were more important than freedom, we would not have written the letter," said one member of a five-person committee of Chinese students deputized by the letter's organizers to be interviewed by members of the American press.

"I put my name on the letter because I wanted to capture an opportunity to find a constructive and independent relationship between the government and intellectuals," said Yang Xiaokai, a graduate student in economics at Princeton University and one of the signatories, to a *New York Times* reporter. "Usually Chinese students in the United States must obey all orders from the government. That is the only alternative or you become an enemy. But I want to find a third way, another relationship between intellectuals and the government."

"I am very much worried about what the government is doing now," said Li Sanyuan, a graduate student in political science at the University of Chicago. "The future of China, of socialist democracy, of modernization, all the hopes of the people [could] be gone. I think it is very bad. . . . What the government is doing isn't rational."

Later that fall, Cong Dachang, a Ph.D. candidate in anthropology at Yale University, wrote a courageous and telling letter of his own to the *New York Times*, one that was in many ways reminiscent of the admonishing epistles that Chen Shizhong and Ni Yuxian had written to Chairman Mao. "I do not deny that he [Deng Xiaoping] is much more open-minded than Mao Zedong and that he has achieved a great deal in the last ten years," wrote Cong. "However, to Mr. Deng the Four Cardinal Principles (the leadership of the Communist Party, the socialist road, the dictatorship of the proletariat, Marxism–Leninism–Mao Zedong Thought) are more important than the Four Modernizations (industry, agriculture, science, and national defense), and democracy in the Western sense is totally out of the question. Probably Mr. Deng should correct his own 'ossified' thinking before he can begin any true political reform."

Having made his critique of Deng, Cong then raised the issue of China's students studying abroad. Not only, he said, would all the purges discourage them from returning home, but "if the Chinese Communist Party had not initiated so many purges in the last thirty-eight years, China would have already achieved modernization. To the best of my knowledge, almost all of the Chinese students who returned to China from the West in the nineteen-forties and fifties were persecuted in the Cultural Revolution, or even before. Yang Wei, who studied in Arizona, was arrested in Shanghai last January for his participation in the pro-democracy student movement. Yang is still in jail without having been charged or tried. Many Chinese students studying abroad have every reason to be apprehensive about these 'arbitrary political attacks.' "

What Cong's letter made explicit was that if the Party pushed too hard to reassert control over intellectuals at home, it would not only cause another generation to withdraw its creative energies from China's modernization program but might also lead to a massive brain drain as China's finest minds sought refuge and freedom of thought overseas.

||||||||||||||||||||||||||
· ——— Fang Lizhi's ————————— ·
Speeches Are
"Published"

About a month after Fang Lizhi was dismissed from his job, expelled
from the Party, and ordered back to the capital to take up the post of
researcher at the Beijing Observatory, I happened to stop by the house
of a friend and longtime Party member who is an up-and-coming
official in a state-run enterprise. He, his sister (also a Party member),
and I had been eating dried persimmons and watermelon seeds,
chatting, and halfheartedly watching a television program about new
strains of purebred swine that were being introduced into Chinese
herds, when my friend suddenly disappeared into his bedroom.
Moments later he reappeared and, with a conspiratorial smile on his
face, handed me a thick sheaf of Xeroxed papers. To my surprise I
saw that it consisted of ninety-one pages of speeches and interviews
with Fang Lizhi, printed in bold, oversize characters that even the
sight-impaired could have read in a dim light, and all arranged in
chronological order from March, 1985, through December, 1986,
complete with a table of contents. What was more, clipped to the back
of this curious compendium of heresy was a copy of the letter that
Fang Lizhi, Liu Binyan, and Xu Liangying had sent out announcing
the upcoming conference they had planned commemorating the
thirtieth anniversary of the Anti-Rightist Campaign of 1957.

Since the Party was at present ill disposed not only toward Fang
but toward all illegal publishing ventures, I expressed no small amount
of surprise upon seeing Fang's very controversial speeches printed up
in what looked like published form. I asked if my friend had found
the collection at some outdoor bookstall, thinking it might have been
put out surreptitiously by an underground network of dissidents, as
were the journals that had circulated during the Democracy Wall
period.

"Not at all. I got these from the Party itself," replied my friend, clearly enjoying my surprise. "The collection is an 'internal document' [that is, not to be shown outside restricted Party circles] that all of us in the Party are being required to study and criticize."

Smirking, his sister slapped the sheath of paper and told me that the Party had sent every government unit copies of Fang's selected works so all Party members might hold study meetings to "criticize his erroneous bourgeois liberal line."

"And did you hold such meetings?" I asked.

"You know," my friend's sister replied, her smirk breaking into a full smile, "before the Party handed down this document, no one in our unit really knew much about Fang Lizhi except that he had been Vice-President at Keda and that he had run into some trouble with the Party over the student demonstrations. Few people had paid much attention to him, and we didn't have much of an idea what he really stood for. However, after the Party compiled these speeches, disseminated them to every Party branch, and actually required members to read them, we certainly had a better sense, and an awful lot of people started saying, 'Hmmm. This guy Fang isn't bad! In fact, he makes a lot of sense!' Before I knew what was happening, many people in my unit not only became quite interested in what Fang had to say but quite sympathetic toward him as well."

"So how did the discussion sessions actually work out?"

They both laughed. "Unfortunately it was my responsibility to organize the study meeting to criticize Fang at my unit," said my friend, rolling his eyes upward. "What could I do? As a result of reading the document, so many people had ended up agreeing with Fang, the very person they were supposed to get together to criticize, that it became next to impossible for us to hold a meeting."

"So what did you do?"

"It was ridiculous! I finally just said, 'Forget it!,' wrote a report, and sent it on up to my superiors saying that we had all read the required documents and had learned much from each other's criticisms."

"Did any units you know of actually hold criticism meetings?"

"Probably. But I imagine this kind of charade went on elsewhere in the Party too."

"What's the attitude of your co-workers now toward these kinds of study meetings?" I asked.

"Well, of course, we don't have them as often as we used to,"

304 — *Discos and Democracy*

replied my friend with a suggestion of embarrassment. "But when documents do come down from Central, we have to get together to act out the ritual. Usually there's a lot of joking around, because our attitude is that if the leaders want to fight among themselves about ideology, that's their business, but that they shouldn't drag the rest of us into these struggles with a lot of propaganda and study meetings. We're tired of it and resent it."

"But aren't people now a little warier than they used to be because of the political crackdown?"

"Even though things loosened up over the past few years, people have become fearful again about stepping too obviously over official boundaries," replied my friend's sister. "Before the student demonstrations people were much more careless. Now, at least in public, most people have started to act obediently to the Party, even though they no longer believe in it. Although the situation is still nowhere near as bad as it was during the Cultural Revolution, everyone knows that a wrong move could still affect their whole life. After all, who doesn't remember the past? Several people in our office had parents and friends who committed suicide during the Cultural Revolution after they were accused of being rightists and capitalist roaders."

Just a few weeks before this conversation, the New China News Agency reported on a meeting Teng Teng, Keda's newly appointed President, had held with a group of students at the university. He, too, had encouraged them to read Fang Lizhi's speeches, which the "relevant departments" of the Party had printed up and distributed in Hefei, just as in Beijing. "Many students of this university do not understand the erroneous words and deeds of Fang Lizhi," he said. "[But] those who have read the original texts of Fang's speeches will [be able to] make a fair judgment about whether or not they are free of biased views."

The naiveté of such old-fashioned propagandizing was sublime. Rather than winning adherents, Party propaganda organs had become more like giant (if unintentional) engines of alienation. Rather than winning adherents, their efforts tended to create an automatic rejection syndrome as more and more young Chinese reacted against anything the Party supported. Far from aspiring to, or being proud of Party membership, a growing number of young Chinese now wished to distance themselves as much as possible from the Party. It was true that many ambitious young people worked for and maintained Party membership, but often simply because it was impossible to advance in the ranks of government without it, and because it did frequently provide valuable perks such as the use of cars, better housing, and opportunities for travel. But particularly among China's new, foreign-educated elite, there was a growing sense that what mattered was the outside world, with which they felt increasingly identified.

By systematically expunging from their midst people like Fang Lizhi, Liu Binyan, and Wang Ruowang, the older leaders of the Party may have enjoyed a temporary illusion of purification, but in actuality they were just isolating themselves further from the very sources of credibility and support they so desperately needed in order to remain believable. In fact, when it came to questions of trust—the most fundamental bond between a government and its people—it was rare to find anyone, particularly in intellectual circles, who still put much faith in the justness or fairness of the Party. The Chinese Communist Party of 1987 was indeed a far cry from that of the days when Lei Feng was the idol of hundreds of millions, when Party membership conferred on an ordinary Chinese the highest social status imaginable, and when the Party's leadership was looked up to with blind reverence.

The Party, though still awesomely powerful, had been cut down in stature both because of its recent history and because Chinese now had alternatives to it as an avenue of advancement. For instance, one could go into private business and strike it rich, go abroad to study and live, or sink into a more or less individualistic life of self-indulgence, if not "self-fulfillment." In short, the Party no longer had a total monopoly on all aspects of life or on all pathways to success. One of the reasons Fang, like Wang and Liu, made the political establishment so nervous was exactly because he was contributing to the creation of this new dimension of life, outside the Party's aegis. He was helping to create an ethos in which dissent was not only thinkable but laudable. So it must have been infuriating for Party hard-liners to learn that, just as Liu Binyan had received thousands of letters from ordinary people after each of his exposés of Party corruption, so after his expulsion, Fang, too, began receiving an avalanche of sympathetic mail.

"It was very heartwarming to get so many expressions of support," Fang told me appreciatively. "Some addressed their notes simply to 'Fang Lizhi, Beijing,' and still they got to me! But my wife and I were particularly touched by those people who sent postcards on which they not only expressed their outrage about the loss of my job and my ouster from the Party, but on which they openly signed their names and wrote their return addresses, as if to defy the censors and show them that they refused to be cowed into silence."

Then, with a bemused but satisfied smile, Fang added, "There was a great flood of these letters in late January and February, right after my expulsion. Then after slowly tapering off, a curious thing happened. Suddenly a whole new wave began to arrive. And this time what people wrote was much more complex. Their letters did not simply express sympathy or outrage at my expulsion, but contained longer comments on what I had been saying about democracy. At first I couldn't figure out what was going on. Then it dawned on me. They were triggered by the Party's circulation of my speeches for criticism." Fang gave one of his guileless laughs.

When I asked Fang if he would consider joining the Party a third time, he sat for a while without speaking, as if he were pondering a riddle. Finally he said, "Well, should that moment ever arrive, I would first want to see what the situation was like at the time. But basically I feel the same way as Tiziano Terzani [an Italian journalist friend of Fang's who was *Der Spiegel*'s Beijing bureau chief for five years before being kicked out in 1984]. He said he would only come back to China if it changed. My reply is just about the same. I certainly don't feel that it is up to me to reform myself. But if the Party changes, well, then I might consider rejoining it."

||||||||||||||||||||||||||||

·—— An Intellectual's ———·
View of
the Party

Life for the Chinese has long been filled with humiliations both real and imagined. One of the worst for Chinese intellectuals has been their inability to speak their minds for fear of reprisal. When Chinese dealt with each other, they at least understood the unwritten rules of this unique game of humiliation. But when Chinese confronted foreigners, this sense of humiliation was compounded by the fact that, after meeting them, their counterparts often tended to assume that the reserve manifested in any ensuing relationship was caused by dislike. In the past, Chinese intellectuals were not only unable spontaneously to invite foreigners out for a meal or to their houses to talk, but were usually unable to accept invitations, creating a confusing illusion of lack of interest, or worse.

The best that a Chinese intellectual could do in such awkward situations was to try as subtly as possible to let the foreigner know that, because he feared reprisals from the Party, he could not act or speak openly. Even this minimal degree of openness had its dangers, however, for it involved verbalizing a forbidden recognition, namely that the Party had terrorized a whole segment of its people into silence and isolation.

The Communist Party has always spoken with bombastic pride about China in terms of its "glorious" traditions, Revolution, and future. Of course, intellectuals, too, have had a fierce pride; and yet their fear of speaking out robbed them of that pride and made them ashamed not only of their own timidity but of their country, which was so lacking in confidence that it did not dare let its thinkers speak out freely, lest they say something unflattering or "incorrect."

Paradoxically, in the period after 1949, just when China was striving to throw off the yoke of foreign oppression and be treated as an equal by other nations, the Party began oppressing its own intellectuals and reducing them to such a state of servitude that they could not possibly have met with intellectuals from the rest of the world on an equal footing; nor could their controlled and strangled literature, art, or scholarship compare favorably with that of other countries. For an intellectual, what greater humiliation could there be than to be unable to share thoughts in a free exchange with others, particularly when others felt so much less ideological constraint?

Before arriving back in China in February, 1987, I had deeply feared that I would suddenly find myself plunged back into this sort of oppressive intellectual climate, and that those friends of mine who had just emerged from their long isolation would have been frightened back into silence. Indeed, when, on arrival, I discussed the changed political climate with several resident foreign correspondents, who are often more influenced by the political documents they read than by the people they meet, each independently said that he or she felt that the chilling effect of the events of the last two months had been profound. They lamented that after the student demonstrations and the crackdowns against Hu, Fang, Wang, and Liu, they had found it virtually impossible to interview either intellectuals or students.

It was true that many Chinese, particularly Party officials and members of the security apparatus, looked upon members of the Western press as little more than glorified spies, just as they tended to view Chinese with dissenting political views as enemies. In fact, only several weeks earlier, one of the ablest members of the Beijing-based foreign press corps, Lawrence MacDonald, had been expelled from China for engaging in unspecified activities that were "incompatible" with his status as a journalist. In addition, a young student from Tianjin University, Lin Jie, had been arrested for "secret collusion and providing intelligence" to MacDonald, the third correspondent to be expelled from China in recent years. (Tiziano Terzani of *Der Spiegel* had been expelled in 1984, John Burns of the *New York Times* in 1986, and Shuitsu Henmi of the Japanese news agency Kyodo in May, 1987.)

So when I began to meet with friends of my own and found that most were almost as voluble and outspoken as I last remembered them, I was not a little perplexed. Their boldness—at least in private— suggested two things: First, that the campaign against bourgeois liberalization and wholesale Westernization lacked much of the power of such campaigns in the past, and, second, that after years of humiliation, intellectuals in China were at last "straightening out their bent backs" a bit, to use Fang Lizhi's words.

Since I was not a reporter for a daily paper, my position was, of course, quite different from that of other Beijing-based correspondents. In addition, I had a tacit understanding with my friends, some of whom I had known for years, that should I decide to write about any of our conversations, I would carefully disguise their identities, some- thing that newspaper reporters could not so readily do.

Still, there were, of course, ways that the Party could make connections, if it wished. There were telephone calls that could be bugged, neighbors and informants who might report on our meetings, and exchanges of letters that could be read surreptitiously. Far from worrying about these points of vulnerability, however, my friends displayed an almost universal, weary disgust, even contempt, toward such Party threats and the clouds of Party propaganda that had recently begun to scud about the country again like so much airborne refuse.

It used to be that no one could truly afford to trust anyone in China, not even one's closest friends, because of the ubiquity of political informing. But now a renaissance of personal trust, friendship, and private intellectual exchange seemed well under way. While these were not exactly the kinds of allegiances to which Liu Binyan had been referring in "A Second Kind of Loyalty," his work had helped Chinese rethink the proposition that loyalty to the Party was the be-all and end-all of existence, and had helped release people from the exterior world of politics into the interior world of personal and intellectual relations. The emergence of some sense of compartmentalization in Chinese life was every bit as significant as the appearance of private enterprise, bodybuilding competitions, underground publications, or stock markets. For these new, private preserves offered a possible sanctuary from the vicissitudes of such a relentlessly public life. What these changes suggested was that without a supreme effort, which it now seemed unwilling or unable to undertake, the Party could no longer automatically enter into every crevice of a person's private life. As one publisher and friend told me, "Recently, we have quietly been able to draw a few lines and erect a few barriers, even if rather insubstantial ones, between the world of politics and our private lives."

Implicit in this distinction between public and private was the notion, taken for granted in the West, that one is entitled to a private life that is inviolable to outside pressure and interference. One of the greatest of Deng's reforms, whether he intended it or not, was the recolonization of Chinese life by the concept of the private—a notion without which, it might be added, a Western-style consumer economy would be inconceivable. What made these Party concessions to the private side of life so bold, even when they were motivated by economic rather than intellectual or political imperatives, was that exactly from this kind of interior life was the very seditious habit of thinking freely born, a habit that quickly led to a kind of domino effect. Soon after people begin to think freely, they begin to share their thoughts with others, ultimately want to write about and publish them, and then, finally, even to act on them.

It was precisely this dynamic aspect of individualism that Liang Qichao and his generation of reformers had been drawn to in the West at the turn of the century. Sharing Liang's belief that China could not develop and "enliven" its economy unless the imagination of its intellectuals and technocrats was released and brought to bear on the process of modernization, the Party tentatively, and somewhat spasmodically, gave this long-persecuted class of people more and more freedom. But such a trend threatened to leave the Party not only without a positive function—except, perhaps, to provide stability—but irrelevant to intellectual life. It still had the power, of course, to get people fired from their official jobs. It could still cast a pall over the intellectual climate so that writers might cease submitting certain kinds of revelatory or critical stories and articles for publication; so that maverick artists might find themselves unable to exhibit their works; so that avant-garde filmmakers might be forced to hold back scripts. But what seemed so different now was that intellectuals no longer granted the Party the prerogative to invade the privacy of their lives, to meddle with their ideas and opinions, or to ruin their reputations in the name of Party unity. In fact, in 1987 criticism and expulsion from the Party had something of a boomerang effect. Being censored or banned became a sign that a writer had something important to say, expulsion became a hallmark of integrity, and official disgrace became a badge of honor. One was reminded of the Richard Nixon "enemies list," which created consternation among those political opponents of his who felt that, by being omitted, they had had their political credentials somehow devalued.

Like a frost that freezes foliage without damaging the roots, the politically chilling power of the Party in the nineteen-eighties reached neither so deeply nor so devastatingly into intellectual circles as before. Just as a trip around the ubiquitous, freewheeling private markets of Chinese cities and towns gave one a sense that the genie of private enterprise had irrevocably escaped from its old collectivist bottle, so even during the crackdown of 1987 one got the sense in speaking with Chinese intellectuals that something fundamental had changed as to their presumptions about the freedom to think and speak, at least in private.

Mr. Song, as we shall call him, was a man who, particularly when he was among his friends, no longer felt cowed by the Party. It was a pleasure to be with him, because he did not censor either his thoughts or his language. He was in this sense perhaps typical of many Chinese intellectuals, who, while they still maintained a certain reflexive defensiveness in their public lives, had found their world of private relationships transformed by the new tolerance and freedom Deng's reforms had ushered into Chinese life. Born into a prominent Beijing intellectual family whose members had been active in politics, Song is a middle-aged man who combines a deep love of Chinese art and history with a keen interest in and appreciation of things modern and

Western. Talking with him both amazed and saddened me. I was amazed by the openness and honesty with which he now felt able to speak, but saddened by the pessimism with which the last few months had filled him.

When I asked him how he felt about events since the end of the student demonstrations, he smiled sardonically, shook his head, and replied, "One of the greatest resources China has is the patriotism and loyalty of its intellectuals, who have a love of country unequalled, I think, by any other people in the world. And what does the Party do with this love? It kicks it in the teeth, not once or twice, but repeatedly! And still China's intellectuals can't shake off their patriotism and yearning to serve. They keep coming back, again and again, to help their country, and again and again they are abused by the Party. It is indeed a bizarre situation.

"We wanted to help our country so much. So many loyal Chinese came back after Liberation to participate in national reconstruction. Why didn't they use us? Why does our country always end up just throwing us away? How can we keep on loving this country, which does not love us?" he asked somberly, paraphrasing the now famous line from Bai Hua's banned film *Bitter Love*.

"Did you ever believe in the Party?"

"Oh yes," he replied, an expression of wistful sweetness appearing on his face. "I used to believe in Marx and Mao, and wanted to build our country and the Revolution, like everyone else. But now, after thirty years of trying, we must admit we have failed. We have failed on the economic front, failed in politics, and failed in culture. Although this is plain for all to see, and although even our leaders themselves are now searching frantically for answers elsewhere, still the Party will not really criticize itself and take responsibility for its failures."

"What about Deng's recent reforms?" I asked, wondering if this subject, at least, might not elicit a more hopeful response.

"China has had a long historical tradition of reform, but we also have had a long tradition of failed reform." Song let out a long, exasperated sigh before beginning to catalogue for my sake all the major reform efforts of the last century, starting with the Hundred Days' Reform during the latter years of the Qing Dynasty and ending with those of Deng Xiaoping. "This country is so conservative that perhaps it will be impossible to change it without more upheaval and chaos. It's not a pretty thought, and even as I say this, I must tell you that although I am pessimistic on the surface, underneath I am an incurable optimist. Perhaps it would be better to say that I yearn for optimism and that this yearning has sometimes made me too much of an optimist." He laughed in a self-deprecating way. "This optimism is another great weakness of China's intellectuals. We keep believing that things will get better and then feel betrayed when they don't.

"Anyway, I must confess that last fall I fell prey to another great bout of optimism. With all the discussion of democracy, I, too, began wondering if it wasn't just possible this time that the reforms would succeed in breaking out of our old cycle of failure. They seemed to be proceeding so robustly, without any major reversals, and things had been opening up so much that I was actually beginning to conquer some of my pessimism. I began to think to myself, 'Well, maybe reform will be possible for China after all. Maybe at last we have entered a period where the old leadership struggles and ways of reacting to new ideas and the outside world will not drag us back.' "

Song fell silent for a moment, removed his glasses, and rubbed his eyes. "Then came this winter, and I could see that nothing had really changed. Now I can't say that I believe in change through reform any longer. Perhaps today's leaders are no better able to tap the reformist energy of our intellectuals than were all those leaders of the past."

"Are you referring to people like Fang Lizhi, Wang Ruowang, and Liu Binyan when you speak of reformist energy?"

"Yes, of course," replied my friend with a sudden flash of anger. "Very few people believe in anything now except taking care of themselves. Liu was one of those rare people who still cared about what happened to Chinese society, who still believed in Marxism. He was in his way the conscience of the Party. And what did the Party do? They kicked him out. What kind of a Party is it that expels its own conscience?"

"What about Fang Lizhi? Some Chinese have told me that they think his position is a little extreme for China at this point in its history."

"Ah, Fang Lizhi," replied Song, as if at last we had come to the heart of the matter. "Let me tell you something. Fang never said anything more extreme than what the rest of us intellectuals have been thinking all along in private. The only difference was that Fang said his piece in public. And what was Fang asking for? He wanted to know what was so fearful about Westernizing. If you have good things of your own, people will naturally want to keep them. But if what you have is not good and does not work, then why not exchange it for something new, even if it is Western? What is this fear of things foreign, this inferiority complex we Chinese have that prevents us from taking foreign things that might help us?"

"Isn't it just pride, the fear of possibly being overwhelmed culturally?"

"Yes, exactly. Precisely because this country now has so little notion of what it is, it fears being overwhelmed. What is pitiful is that we have made ourselves such easy prey for such feelings. The cultural level of our country is so low that no one quite knows what China is or what it means to be Chinese. We no longer know what we stand for, what is beautiful, what is right. We have weakened ourselves by destroying our own culture, and it is the Party that has led us against ourselves by calling everything from our past feudal. Now, when it is all gone and there is nothing but a vacuum into which everything Western is rushing, they attack wholesale Westernization as if it were the people's weakness, when they should be attacking themselves."

By now, Song had lost his normal reserve and become quite animated, even upset. "Mao had a sense of traditional culture. Look at his poetry! It was quite good, very traditional. No question about it. But he would never let anyone else write that way. He denied everyone but himself access to China's traditional culture. It was the ultimate form of privilege. I think Mao always felt inadequate around intellectuals. He never had any university education, never went abroad. I think this gave him a sense of lacking something when it came to intellectual matters. So even though a large part of him was in fact intellectual, another part of him felt threatened and menaced by other intellectuals. Perhaps he felt they might reveal his incompleteness if they were not put down. Basically, I think that he just didn't want competition, so he refused to grant other intellectuals the same prerogatives he granted himself. He was just like China—proud, easily humiliated, and all too ready to react out of a sense of weakness rather than strength."

Song fell silent again, and when he started to speak once more, a certain quiet control had returned to his voice. "Sometimes I get so frustrated and upset with this country. I want China to be better, but so often it seems not to know how to go about the process of making itself better. It keeps harming itself. The Party has destroyed the past, and now they are madly chopping away at those few shoots of really indigenous culture that have begun trying to grow back. Look who they expel from the Party. Our finest. And so we are left with emptiness at our center. No wonder we are filled with fears of being overcome by wholesale Westernization."

Again he paused for a moment, as if debating whether or not to articulate some new thought. "When I came home from abroad a few years ago and landed at the Beijing airport I felt so frustrated and upset to see how ugly, dishevelled, and run-down everything was compared to what I had seen abroad. Although our airport was new, the workmanship had been so shoddy, and worse, there was so little sense of Chinese style or grace about it, that it looked old even before it opened. I wondered to myself, where had all of China's sense of grace and style gone? What had happened to our sense of culture, our sense of what was fine and worthwhile? It has all vanished, and with it, our pride. Now, few of our leaders have any sense of culture. All that they know is politics, and look at the results! Even the city of Beijing, which used to be a unique place, so full of its special culture and characteristics, is a wasteland. And what does the Party speak about—trying to build 'socialism with Chinese characteristics'?"

Wanting somehow to console him, I finally said, "Surely there must be someplace left in Beijing that you find beautiful, somewhere you can go to for relief?"

"No," he said without hesitation. "There is nothing left. What I loved is all gone."

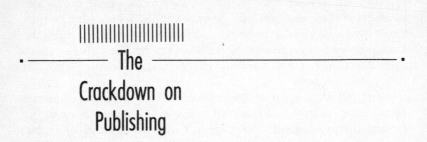

The Crackdown on Publishing

"For quite a while at some academic symposia within theoretical circles, those holding Marxist viewpoints and using a Marxist methodology to explain practical problems have often been given the cold shoulder, while those who publicly or surreptitiously peddled Western bourgeois philosophies and political theories enjoyed great popularity," complained a commentary in the *Guangming Daily* on January 8, 1987. "It even became difficult to publish articles promoting Marxism, while intentionally unorthodox or bizarre arguments that contravened Marxism were readily put out. We can only say that this was a very abnormal situation."

This "abnormal" situation was soon to change.

As the student demonstrations came to an end, a crackdown on China's freewheeling publishing industry began. Deng Liqun, former Party propaganda chief and now Secretary of the Party Secretariat, was reported to have been behind the creation of a new ministry-level department called the General Office for Media and Publications. Set up under the State Council, its duties included drawing up principles and policies to manage the press and publishing, as well as conducting press censorship by cracking down on "unhealthy and illegal" publications that had "contaminated the minds" of the Chinese people.

As the January issue of *Red Flag* put it, "Newspapers, state radio and television, and other publications are mouthpieces of the Party and the people. . . . It is necessary to close down newspapers and magazines that have the wrong political orientation and poor quality, and, according to law, ban all illegal publications."

On January 15, in the Shenzhen Special Economic Zone, the *Shenzhen Youth Herald* and the *Special Lone Workers' Daily*, which in November had published Wang Ruowang's combative reply to Deng Xiaoping on the question of getting rich and class polarization, were closed for "reorganization." Senior officials criticized both papers not only for having given "the green light to bourgeois liberal views" that polluted the reforms and the atmosphere of opening up to the outside world, and hindered economic construction in the Special Economic Zone, but for having become "bases for Fang Lizhi, Wang Ruowang, and others to preach their views of liberalization."

Five other publications, including the liberal Shanghai-based *World Economic Herald* and an amazingly outspoken four-page weekly from Canton called *Modern Being*, were similarly disciplined. Only a year old, *Modern Being* had already built a circulation of 150,000 by carrying interviews with maverick entrepreneurs, disgruntled factory managers, and overseas Chinese millionaires, as well as articles critical of domestic and foreign policy. This approach had quickly earned its corps of young editors and writers a reputation for running a paper "by the people and for the people." What made *Modern Being* such an odd entity in the Chinese media world was that as a private cooperative enterprise, it was not only financially independent of the state but also did not have to report directly to any government agency for political approval.

Like so many other new private and private-collective enterprises, *Modern Being* existed in that rapidly expanding margin of Chinese economic and intellectual life that lay outside the formal structure of government and Party. Such enterprises had taken advantage not only of the new financial latitude the responsibility system afforded them, but also of the increasingly confused state of Party ideology and control. Was Freud still "unhealthy" when even mental health professionals had once again begun to turn to him for insight? How about Nietzsche and Sartre, who were being published by state-run publishing houses? Were the Chinese classics still considered feudal now that the Party itself seemed to be back in the business of promoting traditional culture? Was Jesus, now worshipped in hundreds of newly restored and opened churches all across China, unhealthy?

Since Mao's dictum that the role of all art and literature was to serve politics as a "revolutionary weapon" had quietly slipped from sight, it was not easy for writers, editors, and publishers—even those who wanted to follow Party dictates—to be sure where the boundary lines lay. And many were just as relieved not to know, for the ideological ambiguity allowed them an unprecedented amount of freedom to experiment with exciting new literary and political trends. Editors and writers at *Modern Being* had exploited this ambiguity to the hilt, and in doing so had created a successful and profitable new publication. If this ambiguity allowed for an occasional magazine like *Modern Being* to arise, it also allowed other publications featuring everything from cheesecake photos to science fiction to flourish, which may not have done much to promote socialism but did help the Chinese publishing industry clear more than 300 million yuan in 1986. Of course, in the eyes of hard-liners, both trends were equally unacceptable—although one had the sense that these watchdogs of socialist purity preferred unhealthy popular tabloids to new kinds of legitimate experimental literature or exposé journalism of the type Liu and Wang wrote, because in the former there was at least no obvious suggestion of dissidence or rebellion.

In March an article in the *China Daily* reported (complete with the kinds of detailed statistics that the Party press had once reserved for grain harvests and steel production) that more than seven million copies of a thousand different books had been pirated and reprinted by some two hundred illegal underground publishing houses throughout China. Units responsible for the sale and distribution of paper, for banking, and for shipping were all accused of conspiring to help these illegal businesses. To give an example of this sort of operation, the paper recounted the story of two Beijing residents, Liu Yijing, who was unemployed, and Zhang Xiaosheng, who worked for a publisher in Henan province. The two had forged the name of a publishing house on *Wind and Clouds over the Misty River*, a work described as an "unwholesome three-part novel from overseas," printed 150,000 copies, shipped them all across China, and earned just under one million yuan. The article ended with a didactic note: "China's publishing houses are not encouraged to make profits, but to help educate the people and foster scientific, technological, and cultural development."

Such statements were hardly realistic in the hurly-burly of China's new marketplace. Even the *Liberation Daily*, after criticizing the way pinup girls had taken over the covers of so many magazines, admitted that "the real problem is how to make a magazine good and profitable." As was to be expected, of course, the paper had no answer to this critical question of how to combine "health" with profitability. Instead, all it could do was to pointlessly admonish editors to make the contents of their publications "readable and entertaining without pandering to some readers' low tastes."

Horrified by the way the streets of China were being flooded with these diverse books and periodicals—many of them admittedly of no redeeming social importance or value—the hard-liners used the occasion of the student uprisings as an opportunity to launch a counterattack on the publishing industry as a whole. The Party's Propaganda Department, which serves as China's overall censorate, assumed "direct control" over the Federation of Literary and Art Circles, a semi-independent professional organization for writers and artists that had been operating under the aegis of the Ministry of Culture, then headed by the well-known liberal author Wang Meng. In fact, at the time, many people suspected that Wang, too, might become a target of the hard-liners. Party Propaganda Department Deputy Director He Jingzhi (the co-author of the Cultural Revolutionary model opera *The White-Haired Girl*, much touted by Mao's wife and Gang of Four member Jiang Qing) was put in charge of the co-opted federation. He immediately sent a directive to all Chinese publications instructing them not to print any articles or stories that had to do with "the Cultural Revolution, the Anti-Rightist Campaign, sex, or the dark side of society." Deng Liqun and his hard-line cohorts evidently still dreamed that by establishing the General Office for Media and Publications and by taking over the Federation of Literary and Art Circles they could bring China's unruly world of publishing back into a more orthodox fold.

These moves came on the heels of a series of harsh critiques of the two-part novella *Show Your Tongue Coating, Or Nothingness*, by the young writer Ma Jian, which had just been published in the prestigious journal affiliated with the Chinese Writers' Association, *People's Literature*. In this portrait of life in Tibet as seen from the vantage point of a young Han Chinese, Ma touched on such unusual traditional Tibetan customs as sky burial (the bodies of deceased Tibetans are carried to special sites on mountaintops and flayed of their flesh, which is then left for hawks and eagles to devour) and wife sharing, and on tantric aspects of Tibetan Buddhism.

Shocked hard-liners not only criticized Ma's story for "sullying the image of our Tibetan compatriots" and for "wallowing in sexual desire," but also attacked the well-known writer and newly appointed liberal editor of *People's Literature*, Liu Xinwu, for publishing the piece. Since Liu had just assumed his editorial duties and claimed not to have even been responsible for the decision to run the piece, the attack on him suggested that hard-liners were using the Ma novella as a pretext to rid China's literary world of more than a single heretical work of literature. On February 20 Liu Xinwu was "temporarily relieved" of his new editorial position and told to make a "self-criticism."

Manifesting a sudden, uncharacteristic concern for Tibetans (relations between China and Tibet have been strained since the Chinese Army overran and occupied this "autonomous region" in the nineteen-fifties), the deputy editor in chief of *People's Literature*, Zhou Ming, pleaded *mea culpa* for the "abominable nature" of the novella and for having "gravely hurt the feelings of our Tibetan compatriots.

"Using a first-person account and looking through the eyes of a vagabond and liar, this short story hunts for so-called strange and bizarre events in Tibet," said the editorial. "Nowhere does it depict the struggle in the Tibetan people's new lives for the construction of socialism. Instead, it uses a sensationalistic, vulgar, and degrading writing style to . . . shamelessly announce the despicable psychology of the leading character's indulgent longings for the flesh and pursuit of money. This is a so-called exploratory work of ridiculous content and degrading style."

In fact, this attack seemed to aim higher than Ma Jian, Liu Xinwu, or even Wang Meng. It was a warning shot fired across the bow of all contemporary Chinese writing, a clear signal that China's fiction writers should not assume they now had unlimited license to create according to the dictates of their own consciences and imaginations, and that editors should not assume that artistic merit was the sole or even the main criterion for publishing a work.

Claiming that this "vile creation" had "tarnished the blooming garden of socialist literature," the editorial went on to assert: "The reasons for this huge error lie . . . in the ideological trend of bourgeois liberalization, which has brought much severe confusion into our editorial department."

"I don't really know what the Party had in mind," Liu Xinwu, a plainspoken forty-five-year-old man with a clear sense of irony and an obvious penchant for doing as he pleased, told me some months later. "At the time, their treatment of me seemed like a very grave matter. Newspapers all over China printed huge headlines about my suspension without even using the customary prefix 'Comrade' before my name. They even interrupted the evening television newscast to make an announcement about my literary demise, so at the time it seemed like quite a serious event. In fact, at that moment nothing seemed beyond the realm of possibility, and I really wondered if my suspension was not the beginning of a much bigger affair. But finally there was nothing left to do except to go home and wait. I was prepared for anything. But then the days slowly passed while I just sat there reading and waiting. And much to my surprise, in the end nothing happened."

I asked Liu how he would have felt if he had, like Fang, Wang, and Liu, been stripped of his Party membership (which he had only gained in 1983). "Well, as long as I can agree with the policies of the Party, membership is fine," he said matter-of-factly. "But if the Party's policy is going to change, then there's no purpose staying in it. I have no interest in holding on to the abstraction of Party membership. So I'm not worried about being kicked out. The problem for me is not a personal one. What concerns me is whether Party policy changes. It would be very bad for China and the Chinese people if the new reform policies do not continue. Finally, the Party must even be able to accept members with attitudes like mine, otherwise it will become lifeless and die."

Almost wherever one looked that winter, one saw manifestations of the Party's old tendency to try to control what could be written. One area where the strong arm of Party orthodoxy came clearly to the fore was in efforts to suppress any and all references to sexuality in literature. For several years unnerved hard-liners had looked on with distaste, not to say horror, as Chinese writers slowly inched toward this once taboo subject. The trend in Chinese literature away from purely social and political themes and toward ones that emphasized the individual, and even the psychological and sexual, seemed to hard-liners almost as menacing as outright student rebellions. For this subtle but fundamental shift of attention inward might, in the end, prove even more uncontrollable than students running wild in the streets. Sexuality, which is, after all, such an obvious expression of individualism, was only one of many new symbols of a larger movement that was taking Chinese society away from collectivity and toward privatism. It was hardly surprising, then, that in the winter of 1987 there was a sudden flurry of official censure in the press of sexuality as a legitimate literary concern.

The day after Liu's suspension, the *Guangming Daily* published an article entitled "National Pride and Worshipping and Fawning on Things Foreign." While admitting that "Freud's subconscious was an original idea of academic value," the article went on to decry the way in which this idea "has been introduced into China recently," making some people "particularly interested in [Freud's] 'sex psychology,' which has become a topic of literary creation and is spreading unchecked."

"Some people say that the nineteen-eighties are an era of 'fads,' " wrote Zhao Zhongfan in a *Liberation Army Daily* article entitled "Faced with a Vogue of 'Sex Literature.' " "Among stylish youths the 'fad for jeans,' the 'fad for sunglasses,' and the 'fad for discos' have been all the rage. In the literary area trends have included a 'fad for stream of consciousness,' a 'fad for obscure poetry,' a 'fad for black humor,' and so forth. Over the past few years, descriptions of sexual thoughts and acts have also become a 'fad.' "

Having reduced the desire for sensuality and sexuality to the status of a fad, and having decried too much sex in literature, Zhao went on to work a little prurience of his own into his article. "One author writes of kissing while another writes of breasts. One author writes of extramarital love while another writes of incest; one author writes of adultery while another writes of the love affairs of virginal middle-school students, and even describes one such naive student as a veteran in love affairs; one author exaggerates the delights of the bed while another portrays the pleasure of illicit copulation. While not all work dealing with sex should be criticized, it is nonetheless true that many of these works have had a bad influence on, and are harmful to, youths.

"Many of the works dealing with sex have emerged under the pretexts of 'breaking through a restricted zone' and 'exploring a new path.' However, breaking through a 'restricted zone' does not mean that the restricted zone itself should become a new continent for literary creation, or that there is a need for everyone to go headlong into it, as if they were in a gold rush. At most, sexual life is only one part of daily life. But when an author gives lengthy and tedious descriptions of sexual thoughts and acts, then the reader cannot but ask: 'Is there not something wrong with his aesthetic values?' . . . One of the principles of socialist literary creation is to let the readers enjoy beauty and to help them purify their innermost being. In this sense, such a principle rejects the naturalistic description of sexual scenes aimed only at sensory excitement."

Then, in the only published comparison between the ideas of Marx and Freud that I, at least, have encountered in the People's Republic of China, Zhao got down to the fundamental conflict the question of sex in literature raised for him, and presumably for other hard-liners in the Party: "The emergence of large numbers of works dealing with sex is closely related to our unanalytical importation and acceptance of Sigmund Freud's theories of the 'unconsciousness' and 'sexual psychology.' We do not deny that man has unconscious sexual desire. Freud's analysis of the mind is valuable. However, in literary creation, the mechanical use of Freud's theories to describe man's unconscious and his sexual desires as the ultimate imperative of human nature is unacceptable. . . . Marx's scientific thesis that man is the sum total of all social relations expanded the relationship of dialectical unity between a natural man and a social man. If things closer to the animal instincts [are thought to] reflect man's profound consciousness better, and are therefore described at great length, then literature and the humanities will degenerate into 'sexology' and 'zoology.' This is absurd. . . . [Instead, writers] should look at the broad field of social life, take part in the great Four Modernizations, and draw inspiration from our long and glorious history."

The reintroduction of sexual themes into literature was equivalent to introducing private enterprise into the economy or democracy into the political system. In their own way all were consummate expressions of individualism. If the hard-liners had hoped to stifle China's literary reawakening to sexuality, they would have done better to suggest cold showers than doses of the Four Modernizations and reflection on the country's "long and glorious history." And yet all that winter such propaganda gushed forth.

"As 'engineers of the human soul,' writers must engage in socialist literature and art work with a strong sense of responsibility," the writer Zhou Zhonghou declared that March in a *People's Daily* article entitled "Strengthen Writers' Sense of Social Responsibility." "Writers who are Party members must particularly adhere to the orientation of literature and art as serving the people and socialism, and must create literary and art works in the interests of the Party and the people. . . . Writers who are Party members and those other writers and artists who are determined to fight for Communism must be supported, provided that their literary art works are positive, healthy, and beneficial to the readers, and provided that they can help people to upgrade their ideologies, feelings, and aesthetic standards to a higher level. But their words and deeds must have Party spirit and a lofty sense of social responsibility. As soldiers fighting for a Communist cause, these writers and artists must have Party spirit, and must themselves strengthen Party spirit."

Among the new generation of writers I had recently met in China, I could not think of a single one who saw himself or herself as a "soldier fighting for communism." Nor had I met any who shared Zhou's vision of literature as a kind of medicine to be administered to the people as part of an official effort to bolster ideological health. Instead, China's most exciting new writers—Liu Xinwu, Gu Hua, Liu Zaifu, Shen Rong, Ah Cheng, Bei Dao, Dai Qing, and others—had come to view their writing more and more as a mode of self-expression rather than as a "revolutionary tool."

"At present, some writers ignore the ideological content of their works," continued Zhou, alluding in a negative way to this new literary state of mind. "They . . . give vent to narrow individual feelings in their works, but refuse to depict the social practices of the masses. They lack a deep understanding of the Party's relevant policies and need for discipline, and instead fabricate vulgar, sloppy stories out of mercenary interest."

When I read the likes of Zhou Zhonghou that winter, I could hardly believe that only recently the young writer Jin He had stood before the Fourth National Congress of the Chinese Writers' Association and said, "Not one of the world's masterpieces was written according to a set formula. But during the past decades anyone who mentioned 'freedom of the creative process' was regarded as an advocate of bourgeois liberalization, as if writers were a kind of noxious bourgeois gas that had to be sealed up in cans, lest they spread their poison or even explode. . . . One cannot dance with handcuffs on. The purpose of getting rid of the handcuffs is to dance beautifully."

By the spring of 1987 the hard-liners and their allies in the literary bureaucracy pressed their attack with equal fervor against objectionable forms of legitimate literature and trashy tabloids. By the beginning of April some thirty-nine publications in the province of Guangxi alone had been closed for what authorities called "straightening out and reregistration." Elsewhere the works of Western authors like Jean-Paul Sartre, Nietzsche, and D. H. Lawrence, whose novel *Lady Chatterley's Lover* had become an underground favorite, came under fire. Several films, including *Furong Town* (directed by the Shanghai filmmaker Xie Jin and based on novelist Gu Hua's story about ultra-leftism in the Cultural Revolution) and *Acting Mayor* (the story of a reform-minded official's troubles in Canton, directed by Yang Zaibao), were also accused of revealing China's "dark side."

In April, Central Directive No. 10 was issued. It required all periodicals and newspapers to apply for reregistration through the General Office for Media and Publications, and set forth strict regulations and penalties for violators—a move that at last gave Deng Liqun and his hard-liners a chance to try to rid China's "blooming garden of socialist literature" of all "poisonous weeds."

However, in late May, an article in the *China Daily* admitted that illegal publications were "still flooding the Chinese capital despite the municipality's call for their prohibition," and that even with the new regulations the situation had actually worsened. According to the article, a survey of the book market had turned up more than 150 "illegal publications that contain feudalistic and superstitious ideas, pornography, violence, and other similar subjects." A spokesman from the city's Cultural Bureau was quoted as saying, "Last year we discovered twenty-two printing houses, all run by rural collectives that printed illegal publications merely for the purpose of making money."

In June, as an effort to cut back the circulation of journals and periodicals considered less than "healthy" intensified, police began to raid not only illegal publishing operations but also private bookstalls such as those on Wusi Avenue in Beijing. The *People's Daily* reported that of the almost one thousand booksellers investigated, half of them had been caught with illegal or pornographic books. At the same time, in a move calculated to snuff out circulation of unsavory magazines through the mails, the government raised postage rates for all but Party-sponsored publications.

By the end of June, Song Muwen, the Vice-Director of the new General Office for Media and Publications, admitted that although "much progress" had been made, the number of illegal publications was still growing. *China Publication News*, put out by the Publications Administration Bureau, reported that over ten million copies of more than a thousand illegal titles had recently been confiscated, and that two hundred unlicensed publishing houses and forty state-run printing offices had been found to be using forged registration numbers to print contraband titles. By the following month cadres from the General Office for Media and Publications had opened an Exhibition of Illegal Publications, which was composed of over a hundred displays, including sections on "pornography," "materials propagating violent crime," and "superstition," as well as one featuring the "unhealthy" works of writers such as Bo Yang and Liu Binyan.

||||||||||||||||||||||||

· —— Limiting the ————— ·
Hard-line
Counter-attack

As the hard-line Maoist and the liberal reformist wings of the Chinese leadership clashed in their latest struggle over the future of China, only Deng Xiaoping remained as a tenuous link between the two factions. He alone had the seniority, the experience, the connections, and commanded the loyalty to keep the rupture from becoming absolute. His power was in no small measure derived from the ambiguity in which he seemed so carefully to shroud himself—and from the fact that, at heart, he felt allegiance to both sides. Although Deng was perfectly capable of political opportunism and was certainly skilled at playing factions off against each other— throwing his weight first to one side, then the other, and so always keeping both sides slightly off balance—his identification with different aspects of both the reformers and the hard-liners was genuine. Like the ancient, interlocking Chinese symbol representing the forces of yin and yang, Deng's political personality, too, contained a curious meld of contending forces.

Perhaps trying to delineate the borders of these two contending parts of his own intellect, Deng told a group of foreign visitors in the spring of 1987, "Some look upon me as a 'reformer' and others as a 'conservative' [hard-liner]. I am a reformer, that's true, but if one who advocates upholding the Four Cardinal Principles is a conservative, then I am a conservative. So, under the circumstances, I'm neither a reformer nor a conservative. To be more exact, I am an advocate of seeking truth from facts."

While strenuously denying the existence of any struggle between reformers and hard-liners, an April *Beijing Review* editorial stressed that it was Deng the "reformer" who had launched the movement against bourgeois liberalization. "If this were an attack launched by the 'conservatives' [hard-liners] against the 'reformers,' as alleged by certain people abroad, wouldn't it mean that [Deng] had launched an attack against himself?" the writer Dai Yannian asked almost facetiously. Although Dai would doubtless have disagreed, this, in fact, appeared to be exactly Deng's modus operandi in the winter of 1987.

Chinese everywhere watched closely for some telltale sign in Deng's position that might indicate which aspect of his hybrid political views, and which leadership faction, would finally become ascendant in this highly unstable political situation. For it was true that even as Hu Yaobang was being dismissed and the three intellectuals were being expelled from the Party amidst a flood of proto-Maoist rhetoric, signals continued to surface that indicated the possibility of yet another midcourse pro-reform correction. (As former Chinese President Liu Shaoqi observed, before his own political star waned and he died alone in prison during the Cultural Revolution, "Running the country is like piloting an aircraft. You go left, then you go right—and there you are! You've arrived at socialism.") So as early as January 12, four days before Hu Yaobang's fall, Premier Zhao Ziyang had met with Ferenc Havasi, a visiting Politburo member from Hungary, and announced that the unrest in China "would definitely not affect the line and goal of the Party," nor would it "change our policy of respecting knowledge, treasuring talented people, and giving full play to the enthusiasm and creativeness of intellectuals in socialist construction." He also hastened to stress to China's intellectual community that the campaign against bourgeois liberalization (using the expression himself for the first time in public) would not develop into a "political movement" with the kind of "leftist" practices that had been common during the Cultural Revolution.

Even as diehard hard-liners like Peng Zhen demanded "complete loyalty" to the Party and continued to rail against heretics "who think Marxism is obsolete and cannot solve the realistic questions facing us," Zhao Ziyang quietly signalled that he intended to go about the task of protecting the existing reforms and the open door policies by setting limits to the new political campaign. And such a position, it was assumed in China, could not possibly have been taken without the tacit backing of Deng.

The next day, when Deng himself met Noboru Takeshita, Secretary General of Japan's Liberal-Democratic Party, he dropped a few important clues of his own, affirming that China's "current policy of reform and opening to the outside world" would not be affected by any political upheaval. This, too, was an important signal, because it suggested that the campaigns against bourgeois liberalization and wholesale Westernization—which had obviously entered China through Deng's "open door"—did not presuppose a retreat into Maoist autarky, any more than the limited punishments of Hu, Fang, Wang, and Liu would represent a return to the extreme forms of persecution characteristic of earlier political campaigns. At the time, however, the failure of the hard-line counter-attack was still anything but clear, especially to those beleaguered intellectuals and reformers who were taking the brunt of it. Only as the weeks and months progressed did the clues dropped by Deng and Zhao begin to add up and to form a clear trend.

Speaking before a group of nervous engineers on January 17, Vice-Premier Li Peng, who was known to have certain sympathies with such hard-liners as Chen Yun, said that rumors circulating to the effect that the Party was going to make intellectuals the target of the anti-bourgeois-liberalization drive were "sheer slander and calumny," and that the Party still had "full confidence" in China's intelligentsia. It was later reported that Li had also issued orders decreeing that only the State Council could dismiss university heads, lest provincial leaders misinterpret the sacking of Guan Weiyan and Fang Lizhi and go on political housecleaning rampages of their own in search of "little Fang Lizhis."

On January 20, when Deng Xiaoping met in Beijing with Robert Mugabe, Premier of Zimbabwe, he acknowledged that China's previous reform efforts were "aimed too high, were excessively fast, and were out of touch with Chinese realities," but he insisted that China "should not create obstacles by staying aloof from the world." He went on to say that if there had been any shortcomings in the policy of opening up to the outside world, it was simply that China's door had not been opened wide enough.

Six days later, while addressing a national conference of provincial governors and mayors, Zhao Ziyang declared that the struggle against bourgeois liberalization should not take place in either rural areas or the economic sphere. On January 29, when he met with other Party leaders in the Great Hall of the People to celebrate the Chinese New Year, he gave his first televised, nationwide address since taking over from Hu Yaobang as Acting Party General Secretary. After making the obligatory references to opposing bourgeois liberalization so that China might "build socialism with Chinese characteristics," he got right to the heart of the matter. There were two basic points to be observed, he said. "One is upholding the Four Cardinal Principles, and the other is upholding the principles of carrying out reform, opening to the outside world, and invigorating the domestic economy." Then, putting political rhetoric aside, Zhao told the Chinese people that because they would "encounter great difficulties and problems in turning such a poor country into an affluent one," there was no alternative but to "concentrate our energies on construction."

But, he asked, "how can we possibly do so if there is not stability? There is hope for China only if the political and economic situation is stable. Can we possibly carry out reform and construction in a situation like that of the 'Cultural Revolution,' during which we all suffered? I should say that even if one city or one province was chaotic, let alone the whole country, nobody would have peace, and nothing could be accomplished." Here Zhao seemed to be alluding to what he viewed as the disruptive effects both of the student demonstrations and of the counter-attack of the hard-liners.

Underlining the importance of the Communist Party in China's future construction, Zhao mentioned that "a high degree of democracy" was a goal in building "a socialist country" (the first time that a major leader had publicly raised the issue of democracy since the student demonstrations). Yet, Zhao quickly added, "if the necessary conditions are not there, blind pursuit of certain forms may not help us realize democracy." Finally, addressing the obvious fears of intellectuals, Zhao declared, "On behalf of the Party Central Committee, let me take the responsibility for assuring you: There will be no political movement. . . . This project [the anti-bourgeois liberalization, anti-wholesale Westernization campaign] should be carried out strictly within the Party, and especially within the political-ideological realm."

Although obviously a carefully balance performance that offered something to all the key players in the ongoing drama, Zhao's New Year's speech had the intended effect of beginning to reassure frightened Chinese of every stripe that there had not been a total policy coup at Party Central. Zhao's style was one of reason and pragmatism, and resembled in many ways that of Premier Zhou Enlai (whose practical, humanistic approach to crises made him a crucial partner for the politically supercharged Mao Zedong). Perhaps more important than Zhao's doubtless tenuous control over the ongoing intra-Party struggle was the way in which his public statements provided an ideological basis for other liberal reformers to begin to launch their own counter-counter-attacks in the media.

On February 2, for instance, a *Guangming Daily* article, referring to Zhao's speech, said in no uncertain terms: "Previous kinds of 'leftist' practices should absolutely be avoided. . . . Moreover, it is completely forbidden to use this struggle as a pretext to retaliate against or suppress the people's rightful criticism of shortcomings or errors in work."

Yet because the same papers were carrying both these reassurances on the durability of reform and Lei Feng hagiography, it was difficult to tell in which, if any, direction the leadership as a whole was moving. Often the Party simply sounded like someone caught in a heated and confused argument with itself. Moreover, Deng Xiaoping had still made no major statement of his own to clarify his position, with the exception of his few terse utterances to visiting dignitaries. For now he seemed inclined to remain out of the public spotlight, sending Zhao into the breach instead to reassure China that there was firm resistance to the demise of China's liberal economic reforms.

But limiting the hardline counter-attack was one thing, breaking it quite another. After all, student demonstrations—the very incarnation of the hard-liners' darkest warnings that if you liberalized too rapidly, you created chaos—had happened, sending a frisson of horror through the whole Party. In this sense the hard-liners had been more prescient than the reformers. And, imagining that their moment had come to roll back the excesses of the reform movement, they had counter-attacked in the hope of extending their power base within the Party among those still "red" members who stood to gain little from the changes implemented by Deng—whose futures would not be secure in the modernized, "expert," or technocratic China envisioned by the reformers.

So in the early months of 1987, with the political situation so confused and unstable, the liberal reformers were left to perform constant, delicate operations of damage control and rituals of propitiation, lest they alienate Deng and further antagonize their hard-line adversaries. They hoped that if they could muster the necessary patience, this political seizure would pass. For they must have realized the obvious, although no one dared utter it: Bourgeois liberalization and wholesale Westernization could hardly be expected to disappear when the very economic policies that had promoted them continued in full force.

Finally, on March 15, Zhao Ziyang, wearing a Western suit and tie, addressed the Fourteenth Session of the Standing Committee of the Sixth National People's Political Consultative Congress, a confederation of non–Communist Party organizations and individuals. While his haberdashery undoubtedly sent its own message to hard-liners, his speech proved an important milestone in the reformers' efforts to limit the political campaign of their adversaries. Although clearly counter-attacking, Zhao used the time-honored Chinese tactic of wrapping himself in the mantle of his opponent's policy. Like Senator George Aiken of Vermont, who once proposed that America's solution to the Indochinese war should simply be to proclaim victory and go home, Zhao Ziyang admitted that to build "socialism with Chinese character-istics" inherently implied combatting bourgeois liberalization. "Now that the incident is over," he hastened to add, "social life in those places where the student unrest occurred has returned to normal and the previously widespread ideological trend of bourgeois liberalization has been checked. As Comrade Deng Xiaoping pointed out recently, 'The trouble is over.' " Mirabile dictu, Zhao had rhetorically dispatched the political movement of the hard-liners simply by declaring it victorious.

Turning, then, to the almost forgotten subject of political reform, Zhao said, "No units and no leading cadres are permitted to suppress democracy under the pretext of 'opposing liberalization.' On the contrary, we must work hard to open many different channels of social dialogue and to improve democracy further. . . ." Although this was certainly not as emphatic a call for the democratization of Chinese political life as the country had grown accustomed to during the previous fall, Zhao's fleeting reference did let troubled allies of reform know that the subject had not been completely forgotten.

On March 23, when Deng Xiaoping met with Canada's Governor General, Jeanne Sauve, he dropped an even more important hint. He promised that a "tentative plan for political reform" that would "grant more decision-making power to grass-roots units" would be introduced in the fall at the Thirteenth Party Congress. As if to signal a symbolic end to the campaign against wholesale Westernization, the following week he appeared in a photo (transmitted around the world by Associated Press) at a tree-planting ceremony at the Temple of Heaven in Beijing. He held the hand of his seven-year-old granddaughter, Yang Yang, who was clad in a sweater adorned with a large, familiar cartoon figure. The sweater was inscribed in English with the words "Mickey Mouse."

Zhao Ziyang, taking his cue from Deng's apparent realignment with the liberal reformers, was a veritable gusher of liberal sentiment in the ensuing days. Giving speeches almost every other day, he sounded more and more like an impatient undertaker who was only too eager that a corpse be properly eulogized and then quickly removed from the premises.

When Zhao appeared to address deputies of the Fifth Session of the Sixth National People's Congress, on March 25, he not only praised the existing economic reforms but in the most explicit language to date reassured intellectuals: "In literary and artistic creation and in academic research, we should, in conformity with the relevant stipulations of the Constitution, continue to advocate freedom in creative and academic work, and the free exchange of views and criticism and counter-criticism; and we should encourage bold practice and exploration."

Perhaps more important was the fact that only two seats away from Zhao on the podium was Hu Yaobang, glumly making his first public appearance since his dismissal. He had fallen from official grace, but as China's propaganda organs were now careful to point out, neither he nor the three expelled intellectuals had actually been arrested. Indeed, as all China learned, through Hu's silent presence in photos and television news clips, he was still a member of the Political Bureau. And Fang Lizhi was working as a research fellow at the Beijing Observatory, Wang Ruowang was still a member of the Shanghai branch of the Chinese Writers' Associations, and Liu Binyan was still Vice-President of the Chinese Writers' Association.

By parading the defrocked Hu Yaobang at the National People's Congress, the reformers in the Party were in effect reminding Chinese that both Hu and reform were still alive and well. The fact that he was neither in jail nor dead was testimony that even during a period of counter-reaction, the hard-liners had not been able to sweep the whole Party back into the past. "Look!" the reformers seemed to be saying. "We have even reformed the system of purging!"

Although the leadership quarrels were far from over, and although the new Party pecking order was still to be decided at the Thirteenth Party Congress in October, as spring returned, China, too, appeared to be springing back to at least some semblance of its former free-wheeling self. Travelling around the country in May, I had the sense that the momentum of economic reform had not been seriously broken, as some people feared. The countryside, for instance, was awash with vast open markets. (By July, 1987, there were reportedly more than 70,000 of these, accounting for approximately 18 percent of China's retail sales.) More and more shops and stores had been privatized. Newsstands were still filled with racy tabloids. People's clothes were more chic than ever. China's TV channels were broadcasting a diet of disco, soap opera, foreign programs, fashion shows, dramas, and commercials. Instead of political slogans about Lei Feng, all I saw were billboard advertisements, including a nationwide campaign urging people to buy private insurance so that the government could get out from under its onerous welfare commitment. The campaign left the countryside festooned with ads that could only have horrified hard-liners. "Insurance Guarantees the Road to Riches," declared one, and "Take Out Some Insurance and Do Not Lose Once in a Thousand Disasters," declared another.

That same month the national media carried another, far bolder appeal of Zhao's for liberalization. This time, in a speech to senior propaganda officials and scholars, he attacked the "obsolete, static, and fossilized viewpoints" of certain unspecified groups in the Party, which many took to refer to Maoist hard-liners. Reform-minded young officials with close links to Zhao also came back to life. Once again they began advocating a more expanded role for China's incipient stock market system; they urged that the prices of more commodities (once fixed by the government) be allowed to float freely according to supply and demand; and they even called for labor and housing to be treated as "commodities" that could be freely traded on the "open market." Significantly, intellectuals also began talking again, albeit cautiously, about democracy.

On June 1, the sixty-sixth anniversary of the founding of the Chinese Communist Party, the Central Committee reprinted a speech Deng Xiaoping had given in 1980 on the reform of the Party and state leadership system. The next day, in an editorial entitled "Reform of the Political Structure Is the Order of the Day," the *People's Daily* hailed the speech as a "guiding document on the reform of the political structure." It called for the separation of the functions of the Party and government, for the transfer of power from the center to lower levels, and for reform of administrative and management systems throughout the whole country. Moreover, it once again stressed change in the political structure as the key catalyst of successful economic development.

Then, on June 12, when he met with Stefan Korosec, member of the Presidium of the Yugoslav Communist Party Central Committee, Deng made his clearest declaration yet about reform. "China is now carrying out a reform. I am all in favor of that. After years of practice, it turned out that the old stuff didn't work. In the past we copied foreign models mechanically, which only hampered the development of our productive forces, induced ideological rigidity, and kept people and grass-roots units from taking any initiative.

"We made some mistakes of our own as well, such as the Great Leap Forward and the Cultural Revolution, which were our own inventions. I would say that our major mistakes since 1957 have been 'leftist' ones."

After this introduction, Deng broached the thorny subject of changes in the country's political structure. "By reform, we mean something comprehensive, including reform of both the economic structure and the political structure and corresponding changes in all other areas. By the open door policy we mean both opening to all other countries, irrespective of their social systems, and opening at home, which means invigorating the domestic economy."

Promising that reform of China's political structure would involve democratization, he cautioned that it was still a "complicated issue," whose meaning "is not very clear." And lest Chinese jump to the conclusion that after a brief reversal a new, democratic millennium was now on the horizon, Deng hastened to add, "To reform our political structure, we can't copy the Western system, the capitalist system. We socialist countries have to work out the content of the reform and take the specific measures to implement it in light of our own practice and our own conditions . . . democracy is an important means of carrying out reform. The question is, how to put it into practice."

Although intellectuals were heartened by any mention of political reform, it was clear to anyone watching closely that Deng's notion of democracy was still light-years away from that of Fang's. Like Liang Qichao, Deng was still not advocating democracy for its own sake, but was trying instead to locate some detachable aspects of full bourgeois democracy that the Chinese might adopt to "stimulate people's initiative" toward greater production. "The main idea is to delegate power to lower levels," said Deng. "The reason our rural reform has been so successful is that we gave the peasants more power to make decisions, and that stimulated initiative. We are now applying this experience to all fields of work. When people's initiative is aroused, that's the best manifestation of democracy."

Deng's narrow interpretation notwithstanding, by mid-June the *People's Daily* was forcefully declaring, "People have the right to express their views and to debate others on an equal footing. We should try not to be either fossilized or liberalized in thinking, and to allow mistakes. No one should regard himself as orthodox and others as liberal, or vice versa. Only by tolerating different views can theoreticians unite their common ground of reform."

Of course, as a bloc within the Party, the hard-liners had not disappeared, but their power had been diminished, partially because it now seemed so much clearer that they had nothing to offer under the present circumstances and nowhere to go. While they clearly knew what they ideologically opposed, they had little cogent idea of what to put in its stead. A return to Maoism was literally impossible, particularly since with their cast of aging Party veterans they were devoid of dynamic new leadership. Whatever they imagined as an alternative to Deng and his reforms—if indeed they imagined anything at all besides continued attacks—their ideas never surfaced to the level of public discussion.

As a result of almost a decade of reform, China had acquired a momentum that, while capable of being temporarily disrupted, was, at least for now, all but unstoppable. However, as past struggles had shown, while the reformers might win victories over their opponents, such victories often proved to be only one more round in what already had been, and would surely continue to be, a long, drawn-out struggle.

By spring, one could sense the frustration the hard-liners felt over their latest thwarted effort. A speech by *Red Flag* editor in chief Xiong Fu, given at a closed meeting of editors and propaganda personnel during the second week of April, sounded more like a lamentation than a political proclamation. "Whenever I encounter people advocating abstract reason and supra-class humanitarianism, and flaunting 'self-existence,' 'self-worth,' and out-and-out capitalist, egotistic values; whenever I hear them propagandizing for existentialism, social Darwinism, Freudian psychology, and Nietzsche's philosophy of the *übermensch*, as well as women writers eulogizing sexual liberation and sexual freedom. . . . Whenever I encounter works full of sex and every form of base desire, which have fantastic plots that try to transcend space and time, which take ugliness and evil and regard them as beauty. . . . Whenever I see these things, hear these things, encounter these things, it is indeed like a nightmare, and I can only feel profoundly shocked. But I also feel alone, for I can hardly hear the sound of Marxism."

Bruised and resentful, the hard-liners hunkered down once again that summer, struggling to retain their political grip where they could, battling for key positions that would be designated at the upcoming Thirteenth Party Congress in the fall, and doubtless hoping for a new reformist disaster to provide yet another opportunity for them to launch an assault on the citadels of Party power.

PART

6

DISCO

DREAMS

The Economic Effects of the Crackdown

A recognition of how closely economics was connected to politics, and how upsetting Maoist rhetoric could be to China's sensitive new economy, seemed to lie at the heart of Deng Xiaoping and Zhao Ziyang's resolve to limit the hard-line political counter-attack. Past experience had shown that, like so many wary animals ready to pull back into their burrows at the slightest sign of danger, China's free-market entrepreneurs were extremely sensitive to—and wary foreign investors could easily be frightened away by—any political perturbations that smacked of Maoism.

In 1983–84, during Deng Liqun's patently anti-capitalist campaign against "spiritual pollution," Deng Xiaoping had already witnessed one recent occasion when political fears had startled foreign businessmen and had caused participants in China's growing private sector (which by now included almost all of agriculture) to withdraw money from banks, slow down production, delay consumption, and halt deal-making out of fear of a new movement against capitalism. It was as if the stokers of the engines of China's new, privatized economy had threatened to go on a work slowdown. The repercussions of the campaign had ultimately caused Deng to overrule hard-liners and to bring the entire political movement to a halt almost as rapidly as it had begun.

Believing that China's economic problems lay in an incompleteness rather than an excess of economic reform, Deng, having sent a clear warning signal to the students and intellectuals, now wished to send another warning signal to the burgeoning hard-liners to the effect that their campaign must be limited to "the spheres of politics and ideology" so that it would not spill disruptively into the marketplace.

Fearful of frightening independent-minded factory managers, rural entrepreneurs, and the members of model peasant "10,000-yuan households"—all of whom had helped double China's real wealth in less than a decade—Deng and Zhao had decided that boundary lines needed to be drawn. In his nationwide speech celebrating the Chinese New Year, Zhao, as already mentioned, told the Chinese people that the new political campaign would be rigorously limited to "within the Chinese Communist Party" and should "not be carried out in the countryside." Broadcast over Central Television to every city and small village in China, Zhao's speech provided critical reassurance to all those in China's expanding private sector that their productiveness and new wealth would not open them to criticism or charges later on of having "taken the capitalist road."

As understandable as it was that Deng wanted to protect his reforms, his policies still left one to wonder how bourgeois liberalization could be so intolerable to the Party rank and file and yet so acceptable to the citizenry at large. The idea that there were two different sets of political values, one for Party members and the other for ordinary Chinese, was reminiscent of "one country, two systems," Deng's unusual formula for taking over Hong Kong. This theoretically meant that when Hong Kong officially became a part of China in 1997, the people of the ex-colony would continue enjoying both capitalism and democracy, even though their "compatriots" across the vanished borderline would remain under socialism and the dictatorship of the proletariat. Although Deng's formula for dividing and ruling different segments of the Chinese population with different policies was ingenious, its contradictions were obvious, and there was, moreover, no proof that it would work. In the case of the current political campaign, it was doubly perplexing that the very group of people whom the Party was exempting were the prosperous entrepreneurs and wealthy peasants—namely, members of China's new bourgeoisie—against whom the Revolution had originally been directed, while those within the Party were to be subjected to much more rigorous Communist standards.

But if Deng could protect the private economy from the hardliners' meddling by limiting the political campaign to the Party, the state-run sector, which, in effect, was run by the Party itself, was more problematic. For many key reformist economic measures affecting this side of the economy had begun to come under fire that winter. The State Council, for instance, decided to hold up a move that would have shot life into China's young stock and bond exchanges by allowing capital-hungry state enterprises to sell off assets in the form of shares. The leasing of state-owned enterprises and stores to private collectives and independent managers—a phenomenon called the "contract system," which had swept China in the past several years—was also under scrutiny. An enterprise reform law, which would have freed state-run industries from the suffocating grip of local Party cadres and put control into the hands of technocrats and managers (a move reformers held to be crucial to the success of their economic program) was shelved by Peng Zhen at the National People's Congress. Many private and collective entrepreneurs, whose business practices existed in a shadowland between the legal and the illegal, were alarmed by reports of a crackdown on "economic crime." For instance, the Shuguang Metals Factory (in the economically freewheeling city of Wenzhou in Zhejiang province, which had been a reformist model of how entrepreneurial energy and market mechanisms could create prosperity) was exposed in the press for having engaged in kickbacks and bribes on its way to economic success.

By spring, 1987, however, it became apparent that the containment vessel Deng and Zhao had rushed to construct around China's reformed economy had by and large served them well. Foreign investors did not seem unduly alarmed, and after some slowdowns and signs of hesitancy, the country's domestic economy had appeared to more or less shrug off the hard-liners' threat. In May, Ren Zhonglin, Director of the State Administration for Business and Commerce, declared that "individual economic activity had become an indispensable part of China's socialist economy and a necessity for the country's economic life." He then proudly announced that after faltering slightly in the beginning of the year, China's private businesses and free market economy (which by midyear included approximately 18 million individually operated business enterprises) were booming. Not only was the private sector of the economy as vibrant as ever in the countryside, but in the cities, too, after a brief moment of hesitancy, entrepreneurs had raced pellmell on their way to personal prosperity. Bureaus were set up to place domestics in the houses of China's urban elite. Private-car sales were up. (There was now a grand total of eighteen hundred in Beijing alone.) The sale and leasing of urban real estate for residential and commercial use was booming. Tourists, who had hardly even been aware of the political commotion the previous winter, continued to flood into China. Hangzhou and Wuhan became China's sixth and seventh cities to open stock markets. A six-day bodybuilding tournament, which doubtless further fueled the country's burgeoning physical culture postcard industry, opened in Beijing. And perhaps most symbolic of all, that spring and summer, the People's Republic of China held its first international advertising congress.

|||||||||||||||||||||||||||||||||||

· —— Advertising Comes ——————————————— ·
to the Great Hall
of the People

Nothing could have demonstrated the growing confidence of the liberal reformers more clearly than an envelope that arrived at my home in April. "PRIVATE AND CONFIDENTIAL: A personal message from the Premier of China" was printed on its outside. Opening it, I found that it contained not a confidential letter, but a piece of promotional literature similar to those that daily cram my mailbox from magazines, political groups, sweepstakes, orphanages, and companies selling mail-order leisure suits. The crimson brochure was emblazoned with a headline in bold white lettering that asked, "HOW DO YOU GAIN ENTRY INTO THE BIGGEST POTENTIAL MARKET IN THE WORLD?"

Reading on, I found that the answer to this provocative question was quite simple. All I had to do was attend the Beijing '87 International Advertising and Marketing Congress being held from June 16 to June 20 in the Great Hall of the People in the Chinese capital.

"China—the biggest, most dynamic advertising market in the world—welcomes you to talk business," the brochure informed me. Just below this tease, I spotted two color photos, one showing several Chinese women in Mao suits standing in front of a billboard advertising the clothing of Yves Saint Laurent (transliterated in Chinese to *Yifu San Loulang*), and the other showing a man in a Mao cap walking past a huge outdoor advertisement in downtown Beijing that was imprinted with an enormous green American Express credit card and the word "Welcome."

Half wondering whether this was not just an elaborate spoof by *National Lampoon*, I kept reading until I found the actual message from China's Premier Zhao Ziyang: ". . . On behalf of the Chinese government, I warmly welcome our friends in the advertising community throughout the world, and I sincerely hope that this congress will contribute to . . . cooperation and . . . dialogue."

In case the stamp of approval of China's Premier and Acting Party General Secretary did not provide enough "name recognition" for potential foreign participants, there was an accompanying letter heralding the attendance of such advertising movers and shakers as Ted Turner, president of Turner Broadcasting, Dr. Fernao Bracher, governor of the Central Bank of Brazil, Roger Enrico, president of PepsiCo, as well as chairmen, presidents, and vice-presidents of Unilever, Nestlé, Colgate, McCann-Erickson, AT&T, J. Walter Thompson, and other name-brand multinationals and ad agencies. All told, 123 speakers were scheduled to address such topics as "The importance of advertising and marketing within China's open door policy," "What China's advertising industry is looking for in foreign partners," and "How best to use market research . . . for an advertising campaign, concept testing, retesting, and campaign evaluation." There was also to be the "presentation of a fictional advertising campaign illustrating how an image campaign for China would have a beneficial effect on the image of its products."

A number of weeks after I received my "invitation," Xu Xin, chairman of the China National Advertising Association for Foreign Economic Relations and Trade (which was co-sponsoring the congress along with the London-based trade journal *South Magazine*), enthusiastically noted, "Our original estimate of 350 Chinese delegates and 700 foreign delegates appears to have been too conservative. . . . We sent 700 invitations abroad, but 869 have already come back, even though the registration fee has been raised from $950 to $1,680."

Ticking off the names of well-known multinationals like a proud talk-show host announcing a power-packed lineup of guests, Xu went on to observe that even though the congress was being pitched toward the Third World, organizers had nonetheless succeeded in attracting as delegates numerous high-ranking corporate executives from such "first world" countries as the United States, Britain, Japan, Canada, Spain, West Germany, France, Sweden, and Italy.

The idea of thousands of Chinese cryptocapitalists in Western suits and ties holding meetings with foreign corporate moguls on direct marketing, public relations, and consumer survey techniques in the auditorium of the Great Hall of the People, where Chinese Communist Party congresses and Central Committee plenums are held, took some getting used to. Nevertheless, more than anything I had seen, read, or experienced in China that spring, this single piece of junk mail put the hard-line counter-attack into perspective. If an international advertising congress could be held in the Great Hall of the People even after the upheavals of the previous winter, the momentum behind Deng's reforms looked to be virtually unstoppable.

Until Deng turned the rudder of the Chinese Revolution, in late 1978, the only thing one saw even approaching an ad in China were huge red billboards inscribed with white characters quoting from the works of Marx, Lenin, Engels, Stalin, and Mao. One of the first steps in China's long march from propaganda to advertising came in 1979, when the Swiss watch company Rado pioneered a corporate ad program in the People's Republic of China. It filled the windows of select state-owned stores in Shanghai with colorful cardboard cutouts and revolving displays featuring fashionable blond European models wearing svelte Swiss-designed timepieces. So intriguing did Chinese find these new ads that throngs of onlookers often stood on the sidewalks gazing in at them with the absorption of an audience enthralled by a thrilling new film.

Spurred on by a growing awareness that there was money to be made and power to be garnered through advertising, the *Yangcheng Evening News* in Canton, the city that had so often in the past led the way for China into the modern commercial world, began running ads—small classified announcements that nonetheless stood out like splashes of color in a drab post-Mao newspaper. Cautiously, other papers followed suit, but it was not until Beijing Radio began broadcasting commercials and Central Chinese Television (CCTV) began accepting spots that the ad age in the sense that we know it in the West took off. These early broadcast commercials were basically simple announcements telling potential buyers the names of products and where they could be bought. Graphics usually consisted of little more than a still photo of a factory gate or a lifeless shot of the product. A voice-over would intone the name of the enterprise and how to make an inquiry. Instead of being interspersed throughout programs, as they are in the United States, these ads were usually bunched together at the end of a show, so that they formed a mini-program of their own. These matter-of-fact efforts, like electronic bulletin boards, were intended more to inform than to sell.

What gave the indigenous advertising world its first cosmopolitan boost was the introduction of foreign TV commercials, replete with color, computer graphics, and sophisticated camera work. Lured on by a thirst for foreign currency to fuel its Four Modernizations, media outlets in the early eighties began to accept foreign as well as domestic advertisers. But since few of the products foreigners wished to advertise could actually be sold in China because of restrictive protectionist tariffs, there was a good deal of reticence among foreign firms about launching expensive ad campaigns. There were, however, a few foreign CEOs interested in establishing an early position in what they saw as a potentially vast future market (the first foreign commercial was one for the Westinghouse Corporation), a still unfulfilled dream they shared with several generations of Western businessmen extending back over a hundred years.

The arrival on TV of these slickly produced foreign commercials opened up for Chinese a sudden, influential window on capitalist selling techniques. In fact, long cut off from the outside world, Chinese often watched these foreign spots with greater interest than the commercial-free Chinese programs that followed.

In 1982 an advertising breakthrough of sorts occurred when CBS Productions began negotiations with CCTV and finally signed an agreement trading sixty-odd hours of American programming for 320 minutes of commercial airtime on China's only nationwide TV network. The rights to such shows as *Muggable Mary: Street Cop*, a four-part animated Dr. Seuss Special, *Count Basie in Concert*, several segments of *Sixty Minutes*, a National Basketball Association game, and the Tournament of Roses Parade went to CCTV, while CBS got the right to air commercial messages all across China from such American corporations as Procter & Gamble, Boeing, Kodak, IBM, Stauffer Chemical, and the Weyerhauser Paper Co. Following CBS in 1986 was Lorimar-Telepictures, producers of *Dallas* and *Falcon Crest*, which signed an agreement making 7,500 hours of American TV programming available to Shanghai Television in return for commercial time that it too was entitled to sell to American advertisers. By 1987, MGM/UA, Paramount Pictures Corp., and Universal Studios had formed a joint distribution venture to bring even more United States television programming to China in return for commercial time on CCTV.

To serve this rapidly developing market, foreign advertising agencies also began to move into China. In 1979 the Japanese firm Dentsu Incorporated and McCann-Erickson set up in-country offices. They were followed by two more major United States agencies, Young & Rubicam and Ogilvy & Mather. All were hoping to catch the updraft of what looked to be a rapidly growing worldwide trade with the world's most populous country. Although doing business with China's sluggish bureaucracy was still an unpredictable and often infuriating task, foreign companies looked optimistically at the experience of Japan, which had spent a great deal of money and energy in very successfully promoting its products to the Chinese. By 1987 over 87 percent of China's color televisions, 68 percent of its refrigerators, and 63 percent of its vehicles were Japanese imports.

The appearance of high-gloss foreign commercials had an immediate effect on local Chinese enterprises, jarring indigenous captains of commerce and industry into recognizing how they, too, might more effectively promote their own goods and services. As a result of Deng's new economic policies stressing competition and market mechanisms over government subsidies and state control, managers were increasingly thrown back on their own devices and therefore anxious to find new ways to boost sales. And so, as almost every feature of the economic and political landscape had begun to change, advertising quickly became an important aspect of China's domestic market. Whereas in 1980 there had been less than ten state-run Chinese advertising agency offices in all of China, by 1987 there were close to seven thousand. Between 1979 and 1985 domestic Chinese advertising revenues more than doubled each year, reaching $220 million in 1986, of which $14.9 million were revenues from foreign avertisers. By the end of 1986, the China Advertising United Corporation boasted a network of offices in over twenty-five Chinese cities. That same year, the country's first multinational joint venture in the field of advertising, DYR Advertising Limited—a cooperative arrangement between Japan's Dentsu Incorporated, the American firm of Young & Rubicam, the China United Trading Company (New York), and the China International Advertising Corporation—was set up, and by the following year it boasted such clients as Holiday Inn, Colgate-Palmolive, Unisys, Siemens, and Japan Airlines. By 1987, China's 81,000 ad industry employees were doing business with 966 Chinese newspapers, 1,788 magazines, 300 radio stations, and 360 television stations, which the Chinese Ministry of Radio, Film, and Television estimated reached more than 68 percent of China's billion-plus population. These were the kind of mass market statistics that ad men could only dream of in the outside world.

By the mid-eighties, almost everywhere one turned in China one saw and heard ads. Far from being limited to electronic- and print-media outlets, they were ubiquitous. The post office issued regulations allowing envelopes to be plastered with ads. Tickets to such national shrines as the Palace Museum in the Forbidden City were printed with commercials for Japanese cars that claimed that Chinese have "A smiling friend from far away in Mitsubishi." Ads instead of political slogans bloomed on walls, chimneys, and trees. They proliferated in buses, boats, trains, and planes, as well as on the tops of buildings. They were blasted over loudspeakers and played in theaters before films. One of the most recent escalations involved three hundred new phone booths in Canton which were constructed specifically so that they could display ads—a project that was the brainchild of a Sino-Canadian cooperative venture.

More and more foreign companies moved in to secure a position in China's new marketplace. By the middle of 1987, General Foods had begun pitching its Maxwell House Instant Coffee and had plans to introduce its synthetic orange drink, Tang (which had nothing to do with the Chinese dynasty), to the Chinese masses. Not to be outdone, Nabisco was also joining the fray, as was Tambrands, makers of Tampax tampons, and Colgate-Palmolive, makers of Colgate toothpaste. China, which had once been an advertising void, was now exploding with ads. Even politically stodgy publications like the official Communist Party newspaper, the *People's Daily*, the Party's main theoretical organ, *Red Flag*, and the very proper English-language weekly, the *Beijing Review*, had long since begun giving space to commercials for such products as Blue Sky toothpaste, Wuxi Air compressors, Leaf brand tote bags, and Flying Pigeon bicycles. In 1986, China sold $228 million worth of advertising, almost 40 percent more than the previous year.

"The results, so far, have been impressively effective," Jia Yubin, Secretary of the recently established China National Advertising Association, said of the developing industry, going on to note that new ad campaigns had helped many ailing businesses rebound by increasing "name recognition" and boosting "consumer choice."

The idea of a state-owned enterprise having to please or even relate to the public had been an extremely remote one during China's Maoist phase, when the abstract idea of "serving the people" definitely had not encompassed the notion of pleasing consumers, much less influencing them to buy more. But with China's new emphasis on production rather than politics, all this had radically changed, soon including even the field of public relations, which did not even appear in China until the first foreign joint-venture hotels began to open in the early nineteen-eighties. The Chinese were surprised to find that each of them had a "public relations manager." Since there had always been a shortage of hotel rooms in China, most Chinese wondered why anyone would want to waste money trying to curry favor among travelers. But, in 1983, a Chinese PR department appeared at the White Swan Hotel in Canton, and China's first PR firm opened its doors in Beijing. Then, as more foreign joint-venture hotels arrived, and more foreign businesses set up offices in China, creating an even more competitive environment, the idea of PR also began to spread like wildfire. While the whole notion of PR was, on the face of it, alien to the Chinese Communist system, it did share a common aspect with the Chinese phenomenon of *guanxi*, or connections, long the basis for getting things done in China. Simply put, the idea of *guanxi* is based on the assumption that you can only expect service from someone with whom you already have a connection. Effective *guanxi* presupposes knowing the right people and establishing a reciprocal but unofficial relationship involving the exchange of favors. So the notion that a factory, business, or enterprise should have a specially designated person whose job it was to cultivate these kinds of relationships and connections was one with which the Chinese had a certain natural affinity. "It's challenging work," Gui Zhipeng, Director of the Public Relations Department of the Shanghai No. 1 TV Factory, told a *China Daily* reporter. "How well you do in the job depends to a large extent on your ability to establish social contacts, and this has great appeal to young people."

By 1987, more than three hundred factories in the city of Shanghai alone had set up their own public relations departments. In an effort to make more state-run enterprises conscious of the need for PR, the city of Shanghai appointed former Mayor Wang Daohan as the honorary chairman of a new organization designed to "conduct research into public relations" on behalf of 134 government departments and businesses.

Canton, always strongly influenced by Hong Kong just across the border, became the de facto PR capital of China. Hundreds of large, medium, and even small-size enterprises such as restaurants, hotels, and private collective factories started to hire full-time PR managers. Articles began appearing in local newspapers extolling the marvelous powers of PR, as if public relations were a new wonder drug. For instance, under the tutelage of newly hired PR directors who began sponsoring sports matches and light-music concerts, managers at the Canton-based White Cloud Pharmaceutical Factory and the Ten Thousand Treasures Electrical Appliances Industrial Corporation reported that their sales had skyrocketed. The Household Chemical Factory in Shanghai was reportedly ecstatic over its 23 percent increase in cosmetics sales after PR specialists convinced them to sponsor beauty consultations and demonstrations of their products in factories, shops, hotels, and colleges.

"As a result of the economic reforms, businesses have become independent economic entities that must pay attention to public relations in a bid to build up good images, broaden their influence, and promote their economic performance," proclaimed the *Economic Daily*, China's most authoritative financial paper, while a writer in a new publication called *Market* indicated that "to become a qualified member of society every enterprise must engage in an effort to improve its image."

Not to be left behind, the official New China News Agency even got onto the PR bandwagon when, in 1986, it set up a new subsidiary called China Global Public Relations and then promptly signed an eight-year joint-venture agreement with the Burson-Marsteller Corporation, the largest international PR firm in the world. Other foreign PR giants like Hill & Knowlton also opened offices in China. Canton's Zhongshan University set up a PR research group as well as a PR night school. By the beginning of 1987, a national PR fraternity, the Public Relations Society of China, was founded by the *Economic Daily*. Soon thereafter it opened China's first in-service professional PR training classes.

In many ways, the four-day-long Beijing '87 International Advertising and Marketing Congress was the perfect culmination of China's advertising and PR revolution to date. When it opened, on June 16, organizers were already speaking of it as "the marketing event of the decade," while an article in the *China Daily* rhapsodically heralded China's new advertising age, proclaiming that "advertising, once cursed as a tool of capitalism, is now flourishing as a new industry and hailed as a promoter of the country's economic development."

When Jin Guiqi, chief of the Advertising Department of the State

Administration of Industry and Commerce, addressed the assembled delegates, he did not even mention Marxism–Leninism–Mao Zedong Thought. Instead he spoke of advertising as if it came from Scripture, proclaiming that "advertising has not only played an important role in promoting the country's production, marketing of goods, foreign trade, and in increasing the state revenue and the earnings of enterprises, but has also helped people to acquire more knowledge, to broaden their fields of vision, to cultivate better manners, and to display the new look of socialism."

If the acolytes of China's advertising age had any doubts about whether or not they were following the new "correct line," the appearance of Chinese President Li Xiannian himself to anoint the gathering with his official blessing must have been reassuring. He was followed in turn by Acting Premier Wan Li, who spoke of advertising as nothing less than an "indispensable element in the promotion of economic prosperity."

All that spring I listened for any discordant voice amidst this chorus of hosannas to the idea of Madison Avenue come to Beijing. The only faintly off-pitch note I caught was a slight expression of concern over the breakneck speed with which China was being visually ravaged by billboards and neon signs, particularly those of foreign corporations. In January, 1987, as the movement against bourgeois liberalization and wholesale Westernization hit high gear, the Beijing Municipal Government made a halfhearted gesture toward stemming the flood of foreign ads in prominent places by banning billboards and neon signs on tall buildings in certain key areas of the capital. However, nothing was done to limit other kinds of foreign advertisements. Although one might have thought that ads, combining as they did such concentrated doses of both capitalism and Western culture, would have been prime candidates for denunciation, no official attacks ever appeared that I saw. The bitter truth for the hard-liners may simply have been that there were now too many products to be sold, too much money to be made, and too much reliance on advertising as a component of China's newly developing market-oriented consumer economy to even consider scuttling it at this late date.

|||||||||||||
Disco
Dreams

Entering the Huating Sheraton Hotel, one passes from the lusterless, gray city of Shanghai into a dazzling cathedral of elegance lit with chandeliers whose light shimmers off polished stone floors and glitters in the jets of water from the banks of fountains in the towering lobby. In this country where factories often have to close down part-time because of power shortages, and where most families have no more than a few bulbs or fluorescent tubes to light their apartments, the Huating Sheraton was an anomaly of surplus illumination. Electric light streamed from every nook and cranny in such abundance that sometimes one could actually feel its warmth. The brightness, the cleanliness, the soft music emanating from unseen speakers, the desk clerks in crisp, dark morning coats and striped trousers, the zephyrs of warm air from the heating system—all made the hotel seem light-years away from the cold run-down city just outside its huge plate glass windows.

Because of an absence of local managers with adequate training and experience in running such ultramodern hotels, the Huating, although Chinese owned, was being managed by the Sheraton International Hotels chain. And like many of the other new, Western-designed and Western-run hotels then opening up in cities all over China, the Huating had become one of Shanghai's local tourist destinations. Knots of Mao-suited onlookers gathered out front, hands clasped behind their backs, watching with silent absorption as fashionably dressed foreigners came and went in their taxis and limousines. Then, as darkness fell and the hotel's outside floodlights came on, bathing the building in a luxuriant orange glow, the onlookers would gaze up with awe and reverence at the hotel's shining masonry facade and undulating rounded walls, its luxurious penthouse balconies stepped like rice paddies up the soaring sides of the building, and its futuristic elevators, one of which ascends and falls in an external glass shaft, like a bubble of shining mercury in an oversize thermometer.

A giant industrial mosaic fabricated out of millions of components gathered from every corner of the globe, the hotel was one of the very first large-scale manifestations of the contemporary foreign world in Shanghai. In this city whose physical features have hardly changed since the late nineteen-thirties, this singular hotel rose over the somber, graceless, low-lying buildings around it like a modern ocean liner in a harbor full of ragged fishing boats and barges. Already, other tall buildings were beginning to appear on the skyline, and undoubtedly soon enough the people of Shanghai would become so inured to their presence that they would hardly take notice. But in 1987 such hotels were still for most Chinese new and exciting dioramas of foreign life.

One day in March, while sitting in my room reading a newspaper article about the campaign against wholesale Westernization, I started compiling a list of where various objects in the room had come from. The TV set was from Japan, the soap from Ireland, the mattress and the movie on the closed circuit TV from the United States, the coffee urn from Italy, the coffee cup from Germany, the mixed nuts in the mini-bar from Singapore, and the miniature bottles of gin and whiskey from Great Britain; even the bottled water came from Hong Kong. With a sense of irritation, I wondered why nothing, not even the cups or the soap in this Chinese hotel room, could have come from China.

The answer lay in the fact that the Huating Sheraton was being billed as a first-class hotel, and the presumption in China was still that nothing made locally was up to first-class standards. Sitting in my completely Westernized room, in the middle of Shanghai, it seemed obvious to me that the manifest fear certain Chinese had of wholesale Westernization was, in part, a reaction not just against the fatal attraction so many other Chinese felt for things *yang*, or foreign, but the repulsion they often felt for things *zhong*, or Chinese—a reaction against the humiliating recognition that what was Chinese often could not stand up to what was foreign, in Chinese as well as foreign eyes.

In spite of official opprobrium, the tendency of many Chinese during this period of reform to slavishly worship things foreign was all too evident at the Huating Sheraton. The hotel was the toast of the town. It had a powerful fascination for young and old alike. Even Party members and city officials jumped at the chance to be taken to a meal there by a foreign counterpart. (Local Chinese were not welcome unless accompanied by a "foreign guest," even if they did have the requisite foreign exchange, without which nothing in the hotel could be bought.) The hotel, with its aura of Western glamour, ease, and elegance, was a new kind of liberated zone, a fragment of the modern world outside transplanted into the middle of Shanghai. In fact, it was as close as Chinese could hope to come to being "gold-plated" with foreignness right here at home. For foreign guests inside, it may have seemed like just another modern hotel, one whose workmanship was not even quite up to international standards, but for those Chinese looking in, it was an exotic embassy of the Western world sent to China to represent all that was most seductively foreign: fashion, style, stardom, graciousness, high-tech equipment, capitalism, freedom, and wealth.

For certain groups of young Chinese, the soul of this huge hotel complex was Nicole's, the world-class disco on the third floor, where at night the *thump-thump-thump* of an electric base reverberated through several floors of the building like the beat of a giant heart. It cast such a spell over Shanghai's "with-it" dance-crazed youth that even people who had never entered the hotel sometimes spoke of it with awe.

One night as I arrived back under the hotel's portico, the young cabdriver, who made his living team-driving a small, leased Romanian Dachia with a friend twenty-four hours a day, gazed reverently up at the third floor and said authoritatively, "That's the best disco in Shanghai, and probably all of China."

Several days later, a friend of mine brought a Chinese movie actress from the Shanghai Film Studio to lunch at the hotel. She wore high-heeled shoes, a lacy Chinese-made blouse, and tight leather pants, which, by 1987, had become all the rage. As we sat eating in the coffee shop, she announced with pride that she had actually already been dancing at Nicole's. "There's no other good place to go discoing in Shanghai," she mournfully told us. "Nicole's, that's where the fun is. The only problem is it's expensive and hard to get into if you're a Chinese."

As we talked about her life and career, it became clear that glamorous as they were by Chinese standards, they were still far from glamorous enough for her. She spoke about Nicole's as if it were a forbidden treasure room in a well-defended castle. She kept returning to the subject in a way that reminded me of those Western explorers who, at the turn of the century, so yearned to get to the forbidden city of Lhasa that after dreaming up elaborate ways to disguise themselves, even as Tibetan monks, they repeatedly tried to trek undetected through the Himalayas on foot.

She felt trapped by her life, she said, unsatisfied by the occasional movie she made and bored by the mandatory political study sessions at the studio on Saturdays. After lunch, she stopped by my friend's room "just for a look." She admired the private marble bathroom and the complimentary bottles of shampoo and hair conditioner with such rapture that my friend finally asked if she would not like to take a bath. Without hesitation she accepted the invitation, and for the next half hour we could hear her luxuriating in the tub, enjoying the sweet-smelling soap from Ireland, the large thick towels from the United States, and the inexhaustible supply of hot water, a luxury that not even the best Chinese apartment houses afford their tenants. When she left, it was with great reluctance, as if she were being banished from paradise.

Like pop music generally, discos in such hotels as the Huating Sheraton and all their accoutrements had become potent symbols of modernity and Western-ness, not just for this actress but for a growing segment of China's urban youth. By 1984, when the government allowed dance halls to open in China for the first time in thirty-five years, Chinese youth had embraced "couples dancing" with an almost delirious enthusiasm. On recent trips to Shanghai I had discovered that almost every hotel in the city held nightly dances (with stiff admission prices of 6 to 10 yuan). Young people, dressed so stylishly that it was possible to imagine one was in Hong Kong or Taipei, flocked to these new socialist pleasure domes, almost all of which were drab old halls from the thirties cheered up only by incongruous strings of Christmas tree lights. At least they featured live bands, never mind that they played time-warped disco versions of "Jingle Bells" and Stephen Foster spirituals. The fact that this mix often sounded more like circus music than dance music hardly bothered the youths ardently gyrating about the floor, dancing *di-si-ke* ("disco"), *yao-bai-wu* ("rock and roll"), *ji-ta-ba* ("jitterbug"), *tan-ge* ("tango"), *lun-ba* ("rhumba"), *wa-er-si* ("waltz"), and the *fu-ke-si-si-bu* ("fox-trot"). Sometimes boys danced with boys, and girls with girls, displaying a kind of innocence unimaginable in the United States; and they went about this newly rehabilitated form of recreation with a sensual abandon that contrasted starkly with the stiffness with which youths used to perform the "loyalty dances" of Maoist times.

What was even more surprising was that dancing had emerged largely unscathed by the hard-line counter-attack on decadent Western culture in the winter of 1987. Whereas one might have assumed that disco culture would be looked upon as the epitome of things bourgeois and Western, the hard-liners' campaign appeared not to have touched this "high tide of dancing." If anything, the tide rose only higher during these confusing months.

Perhaps recognizing how dance halls were helping in their own small way to "invigorate the economy," in March the Party even lifted a long-standing but largely ineffective ban on what they had called "underground ballrooms." By November, 1987, Canton alone was reported to be host to over five hundred such ballrooms and seventy tea rooms featuring music, several of which had reputedly become hangouts for China's nascent gay community. The beach resort city Qingdao bloomed with dancing spots. Even some small county cities now claimed to have six or seven dance halls as Chinese of all ages turned en masse to this new form of diversion. At the same time that the Party was purging members for their dalliance with Western ideologies, it carefully overlooked millions of other Chinese who were equally infatuated with imported culture. If this revival of dancing was an example of China's double vision, it also served as a testimony to the efforts of reformers like Zhao Ziyang not to let the campaign against Westernization spill out of the Party into everyday life.

In some cities, Party officials did more, however, than simply tolerate Western dancing; they often seemed eager to promote it. Over the Chinese New Year (at the end of January) not only did dance halls do a runaway business, but many government institutions held "dance parties" as well. Perhaps they were only too happy to see young people dancing instead of agitating and demonstrating for democracy. In fact, by the spring of 1987 official newspapers had even begun running articles proclaiming the wondrous effects of disco. This led to an unlikely dissonance in the press: One page would feature an article on the virtues of "bitter struggle" and of youths retempering their socialist spirit by "going down" to the countryside to labor side by side with the peasants; an adjacent page would have an article proclaiming the virtues of disco.

"Young and Old Dance Away Their Spare Time," read a headline in the *China Daily*. The article that followed dealt with dancing as if it were on the verge of becoming a new kind of post-Maoist compulsory activity. "Things have happened in many places that might have bewildered many Chinese a few years ago. Freshmen in the Beijing Youth Institute of Politics are now required to attend the college's ballroom dancing lectures," it noted matter-of-factly.

In an example of what came to be a veritable genre of articles extolling disco for the elderly, another article in the *China Daily* proclaimed, "Disco Lessons Keep Old People Young," and told how the Huangpu District Old People's Society in Shanghai had begun to hold disco classes. "Several years ago, disco in China interested very few young citizens and was deemed indecent by most others, especially the old," said fifty-five-year-old dance coach Ge Meihua, who led the classes at the Old People's Society. "Now it is popular among city folk and is fashionable in the countryside. We hope the courses may rouse the elderly's interest in disco music and dance, thereby enriching their lives and making their families more harmonious."

Another testimonial to disco, carried by the New China News Agency from Shenyang, was entitled "Dancing Helps Old Folks to Feel Young Again." "I was so depressed I thought that there was no point in living and that I would soon die," it quoted a retired worker from the Shenyang No. 3 Machine Tools Plant as saying. However, after attending several of the dance hall sessions at the Xiaobaihua Dance Hall, which opened at the unusual hour of seven-thirty every morning, he declared himself reborn because he had found "a wonderful new pastime in dancing . . . [and] made new friends."

In another, follow-up article, the *China Daily* reported on a new dance emporium called the Lilac Garden Ballroom that had opened in Shanghai in March and was offering daily disco galas for retired Party cadres, from nine to eleven each morning. According to the paper, the ballroom had turned at least one sixty-seven-year-old retired senior municipal official into a "disco addict."

"At first, I was in doubt about teaching veteran cadres to disco dance," said sixty-one-year-old Lu Hongbing, who organized this disco cabaret for retired cadres. "I thought that they would not accept it because of their rank. But now you see how lively they are. Disco has gained in popularity among them. Not only have the ordinary pensioners joined the disco world, but also veteran revolutionaries."

Were Lei Feng to reappear miraculously, I wondered as I read the article, would he, too, now rise at dawn to follow the Party's new line and join in these early morning disco celebrations? Perhaps—if one were to judge by another former soldier, sixty-six-year-old Shan Ruliang from Manchuria, who had fought in World War II. Shan observed of his hometown in the *China Daily's* Letters to the Editor column: "In Stalin Park along the Songhua River in Harbin, people can easily find groups of retirees from fifty to sixty years old accompanied by recorded music demonstrating their newly forged dance form, 'old men's disco,' swaying, rocking, and stretching their arms and legs skillfully, just like well-trained dancers on stage."

Such reports raised the possibility that those foreign tourists who had gone all the way to China in the hope of catching a glimpse of traditional Chinese life, would look out their hotel windows in the morning and, see not old-timers performing their daily rituals of *taiqi*, but phalanxes of discoing grandfathers and grandmothers with bound feet.

While disco may have been largely viewed as a form of exercise for elderly people trapped in cramped, airless living spaces, it was for China's youth something more. The mystique of disco as the consummate expression of all that was exciting, modern, and foreign was nourished not only by what Chinese were seeing in movies and on television about life abroad, particularly in Hong Kong (where disco was practically a religion), but by the presence of those few Olympic-size discos like Nicole's that were actually situated in China. In fact, such dancing places were fast becoming a regulation part of all the Western-style hotels now opening to meet the demand of ever increasing numbers of foreign businessmen and tourists. In Beijing, there was the Cosmos Club at the Great Wall Sheraton, Juliana's at the Lido Holiday Inn, the Xanadu at the Shangri-La Hotel, and the Glasshouse at the Kunlun Hotel, which ran ads proclaiming, "Latest Sounds, Latest Lighting, Disco Night Fever!" Canton, Xiamen, Chongqing, Xi'an, Tianjin, Nanjing, and Wuhan all had new hotels with discos. With Ramada Inns, Hyatt Hotels, Sheraton Inns, and Holiday Inns (which even ran a hotel in Lhasa) all now proliferating in China, the disco-ization of the People's Republic was proceeding apace. As living symbols of modernity in a country where modernization had replaced revolution as an animating ideal, discos, with their strobe lights, high-tech sound systems, up-to-date music, and svelte cosmopolitan styling, proved irresistible.

Gone were the days when China's youths spent their every waking hour going to political study meetings, reading their Little Red Books and working as volunteer laborers in order to learn from "the workers, peasants, and soldiers." Having caught a few fleeting reflections of the outside world through books, magazines, television, and films, these youths now wanted more exciting, cosmopolitan forms of entertainment.

The degree to which discos as metaphors for modernity, stylishness, and excitement had become embedded in China's youth consciousness was illustrated by an article in the *Guangming Daily* which reported on a get-together organized by the Tianjin Communist Youth League to discuss with a group of university students what the image of Chinese youth ought be in the nineteen-eighties. It recounted how one student had announced with perfect seriousness that his ideal of a contemporary student Party member could be expressed by the formula "Party member = progress + disco." The article commented: "His explanation was that 'progress' was something achieved according to the standards of the Party, and that 'disco' was a metaphor for practitioners and leaders of modern life-styles."

The society's inability to animate its own young people with goals both more self-referential and capable of providing the stuff from which higher aspirations and dreams could be fashioned seemed to be tragic and dangerous. So culturally enfeebled and idealistically bankrupt had China become as a result of its repeated attack on itself that there was virtually no homegrown force short of massive control and oppression to stand in the way of the unimpeded progress of Western pop phenomena like disco. In this sense, the hard-liners who now so ardently opposed bourgeois liberalization and wholesale Westernization had identified a very real problem. If Western consumer culture ends up being simply taken over, lock, stock, and barrel—without any strong Chinese critical element or input involved in the process—China will, as the hard-liners fear, become little more than a second- or third-rate imitation of the West and Japan. But what the hard-liners refused to acknowledge about the situation was that the vacuum into which these "polluting" outside influences were rushing was of their own making.

For many Chinese youths, each Western disco was like an intense beam of dazzling light entering a dark room through a crack in a door left slightly ajar. Each was a rare connecting rod between the mythologized Western world outside (as remote and as forbidden for most of them as life beyond the grave) and their own unexciting lives. But unlike television and films, which merely reflected this seductive foreign reality, discos, and the hotels in which they resided, were its actual embodiment. They were shards of a world that the hard-line Maoists scarcely knew; and what became clear by the summer of 1987 was that their attempts to banish it from the imaginations of their people, and to reimpose some truncated version of the old Maoist order, had come too late.

||||||||||||||||||||||||
· —— Fang, Wang, —————————————————————— ·
and Liu
Reappear

Once purged from the Party, Fang Lizhi, Liu Binyan, and Wang
Ruowang disappeared for a while from public view, although hardly
from the consciousness of Chinese intellectuals. For long after their
actual expulsion, Party propaganda against them kept their names
alive. Of the three, Fang came in for the most frequent and strenuous
criticism, being accused of having almost singlehandedly incited the
nationwide student demonstrations. The activities of all three men
were severely limited, but they were allowed to receive friends, to
continue their work, to attend select public functions, and, in Fang's
case, even to go abroad for a scientific meeting. But they remained in
a sort of limbo as the contending factions within the Party waged their
slow-motion struggle for ideological supremacy and political power.
Whereas the hard-liners would have liked nothing better than to
silence these men forever, the reform faction, as fearful as ever of
alienating other intellectuals from the cause of modernization, strove
to limit the attack against them—to show that even though they had
been expelled from the Party, they would not be hounded, persecuted,
or physically isolated as others had been in the past. In fact, in the
months that followed, as the three began to reappear occasionally in
public, the official press went to great lengths to announce these events.
Sounding almost like ornithological journals delighted to deliver
reassuring bulletins about the sightings of rare, endangered species of
birds, Party papers began flashing news items on the activities of Fang,
Liu, and Wang, as if to say, "Fear not! Our new style of purging is
much more humane than it was in former times."

The press announced, for instance, that Wang Ruowang had been
spotted at a February gathering sponsored by the Shanghai branch of

the Chinese Writers' Association, an official organization in which, the article took great pains to remind readers, Wang still retained membership.

Liu Binyan's appearance was reported at several literary get-togethers during Chinese New Year and at that winter's Lantern Festival. It was also generally known that he had written a three-point statement of self-defense for circulation among high Party officials. According to those who saw a copy, Liu had stubbornly refused to make a self-criticism, strongly denied that he had "gone against" the Communist Party, and accused his hard-line critics of having taken controversial sections of his writing out of context in order to attack him. Moreover, it was said that he had requested no foreign or Chinese journalist be allowed to interview him; and even though supporters from the provinces had begun making pilgrimages to his office at the *People's Daily*, offering him gifts, money, and support, he assiduously avoided the public eye. Nursing a chronic back ailment, perhaps fearing a more severe crackdown, or possibly hoping to demonstrate anew his continuing loyalty to China's socialist revolution, he retreated into silence.

In the summer of 1987, when he was invited to the twentieth-anniversary gathering of the Iowa International Writers Conference in the United States (he had attended a session once before in 1982), his request to leave China was denied by the government. A letter that he had written to a friend did, however, appear in the Hong Kong–based magazine *The Nineties* and gave some indication of his state of mind. He wrote: "While some thought the 'incident' was a loss for me, the overwhelming majority of people I know felt that it was actually a very good thing; that I gained much more than I lost. . . . [But] right now it is not my inclination to get into arguments. . . . Because of all the recent trouble, the times are still inhospitable for me, so for some time in the future I shall just busy myself with reading. . . . In fact, now I've even reached the point where I am no longer so eager to see my situation reverse itself again, because then I would only become busier than before. I would become deprived of the opportunity I now have to study and to prepare for the future. So, it's perfectly acceptable to me for things to be the way they are."

Liu Binyan had made his remonstrations. Now, like the official Qu Yuan in the fourth century B.C. who remained loyal even after being sent into exile for having pointed up the errors of his ruler (and whom Chinese still revere), Liu accepted his banishment from the Party without overt resistance, perhaps dreaming of the day when he might once again be rehabilitated.

Fang Lizhi, however, chose another route. Somewhat younger, more Westernized, much more confrontational in manner, and no longer bound by any deep-rooted commitment to Marxism, Fang continued to play a unique cat-and-mouse game with the Party throughout the spring. Although he was allowed to teach and see friends, he was explicitly forbidden to rendezvous with any Western journalists. But with Fang the Party had a dilemma that it did not have with either Liu or Wang. Fang had already made frequent trips abroad and had gained some notoriety in foreign scientific circles. In fact, after his expulsion, when Westerners in Beijing began to refer to him as China's Sakharov (an implicit rebuke to China for its pretensions that it was more open than the Soviet Union), some began speculating as to whether he might not become China's first Nobel laureate.

There was another factor that made Fang's situation unique. When he was forced to leave Hefei, he also had to forfeit the seat he had just won in the fall elections for the local district People's Congress. However, his wife, Li Shuxian, who taught physics at Beida, had also won a seat—in Haidian, the district in the capital in which many universities are situated—garnering the most votes of the four candidates running. Taking advantage of her new celebrity status, she told foreign reporters that she felt the Party had been wrong to discharge her husband and that, in due course, history would "prove that he was right." In the months that followed, Li Shuxian came to serve as a kind of local people's advocate, not only speaking out openly about the injustice of her husband's situation, but championing human rights and protesting on behalf of her student constituents, who were frequently harassed with unannounced searches of their dormitories and sometimes even detentions by security guards.

Well aware of Fang's unique situation, the Party adopted a divide-and-rule strategy: Fang would be given a relatively large amount of freedom in his scientific activities, but in the political realm he would be constrained, so that he would be unable to continue polluting the minds of China's youth with his appeals for freedom and democracy.

On February 28 Fang made his first post-purge public appearance in Beijing when he showed up at the Fourth National Congress of the Chinese Physics Society to deliver a paper entitled "Progress in Modern Cosmology." His debut was widely reported in the Chinese press, as was the fact that the meeting was chaired by none other than his old friend and comrade-in-arms Guan Weiyan (ex-President of the University of Science and Technology). Clearly, this was an all too self-conscious attempt by the Party to reassure scientists that there was now life after purgatory.

"Over the past two months, only Fang Lizhi and two others have been criticized by name and expelled from the Party. No extreme policy has been adopted against them," noted the *Beijing Review*, in an effort to underscore the Party's new leniency. "They have been given an opportunity to bring their special skills into play. Fang Lizhi continues to be a member of the Chinese Academy of Sciences, and he was recently made a research fellow at the Beijing Observatory. The two writers Wang Ruowang and Liu Binyan recently appeared at get-togethers of literary and artistic circles in Shanghai and Beijing. . . . In the history of the Party, there have been instances when intellectuals were persecuted. But these were regarded as mistakes of bad policies. . . . The status of intellectuals has [now] been changed, and they are acknowledged as part of the working class. . . . In order to enforce Party discipline, it is never too late to expel a few members who oppose its line. However, the struggle against bourgeois liberalization will not affect the Party's policy toward intellectuals."

Lest anyone misunderstand these advertisements of tolerance to mean that all was forgiven, the day after Fang's first public appearance in Beijing the *Guangming Daily* took pains to remind intellectuals that Fang was still persona non grata, and then, for good measure, it ripped into him once more for having criticized Vice-Mayor Zhang Baifa's 1985 junket to the United States to attend a conference on syncrotron accelerators.

In June, however, after Fang's application to go abroad had been approved by Zhao Ziyang himself, Fang was briefly allowed to leave China to take part in the annual meeting of the International Center of Theoretical Physics being held in Trieste. He was refused permission, however, to go on to Great Britain for a conference commemorating the three hundredth anniversary of the publication of Isaac Newton's *Principia*. No sooner had Fang gotten out of China than he was descended upon by hopeful interviewers. Far from holding back, Fang expounded to them on his political views as fearlessly as he had the past fall.

When *Der Spiegel* correspondent Tiziano Terzani met with him in Italy and asked him what his next political target would be, Fang answered with one word: "Marxism." When Terzani appeared surprised by his boldness, Fang remarked, "That Marxism no longer has any worth is a truth that cannot be denied. . . . It is a thing of the past; useful to understand problems of the last century, but not those of today. . . . It is like a worn-out dress that should be discarded." When asked what successes he would attribute to the Chinese Communist Revolution, Fang replied, "In China the Communist Party has never had any success. Over the last thirty years it has produced no positive results. . . . That is why the desire for a reformation is so strong; why the faith in the Party, especially among young people, has disappeared. . . . In China, the Party wants not only to manage politics but to have everything under its control as well, including the way people think and live. . . . To create a real economic democracy in China it must diminish this political control. But that is precisely what the Party fears."

When asked by Lu Keng from the overseas Chinese newspaper *Queens Daily*, why he had been allowed to go abroad while Liu Binyan was kept at home, Fang replied facetiously, "The country apparently needs to learn from the West only in science and technology, but not in the humanities." Then he went on to reiterate his belief that the Chinese Constitution must prevail over the Party, and that China's future lay in striving for "freedom of speech and freedom of the press, among other freedoms that are provided for by this Constitution. For only freedom of speech will be able to break the tyranny of a 'one-Party voice' and bring about the realization of political pluralism."

Surprisingly enough, after Fang's return to China, there were no immediate political repercussions from his outspoken interviews. Indeed, by summer, politically speaking, China seemed to be circling back to where it had been a year earlier, when public discussions of democracy and political reform had been allowed to reach a crescendo. Although most Chinese were aware that intense jockeying for power was going on within the upper echelons of the leadership at the seaside Party retreat at Beidaihe in anticipation of the upcoming Thirteenth Party Congress, for the moment the crisis of the past winter had eased. Reassured by Zhao Ziyang's promise that there would be no more Party expulsions, China's intellectuals once again began to relax. But like the aftershock of an earthquake, a new tremor soon hit.

On August 1, Hu Qiaomu (one of the main architects of the recent hard-liner counter-attack) made a surprise visit to the home of the well-known playwright and Vice-President of the Federation of Literary and Art Circles, Wu Zuguang. Without allowing Wu to speak, Hu read him aloud a decision from the Central Commission on Discipline and Inspection, the Party's disciplinary body, listing Wu's political transgressions and calling for his resignation from the Party. Wu's alleged crimes were being "flippant" about his Party membership, "promoting bourgeois liberalization," and "violating the Party's regulations." Wu was told that if he did not quit the Party voluntarily, his name would be "expunged" (*chuming*), a punishment that supposedly did not carry the same odium as outright expulsion but still accomplished the same end.

Wu's real crime, however, was that like Fang, Liu, and Wang, he had a habit of speaking his mind. For instance, the previous December, just as the student demonstrations were breaking out, he had published a piece in the *Yangcheng Evening News* entitled, "Censorship of Theatrical Works Ought to Be Abolished," in which he compared the censorious nature of the People's Republic to that of its historical arch-opponent, the Nationalist regime of Chiang Kai-shek. "What on earth is the purpose of exercising censorship over literature and art at every level and 'flagrantly interfering' in them?" asked Wu. Such a policy "is actuated by the mentality of fear; by fearing and not believing in the masses. . . . How can we turn out good works if . . . there is a system of censorship under the manipulation of a handful of people hanging over the heads of writers and artists, and if, bound hand and foot, artists always have to be thinking about how their works can pass inspection? . . . How happy and delightful it will be if this absurd mental burden is one day lifted!"

When I later talked with Wu, a short, affable, seventy-year-old quintessential Beijing gentleman, I asked him about the outcome of his meeting with Hu Qiaomu, whom Wu had ridiculed during the 1983–84 movement against spiritual pollution. (He had said, "If it is beyond our ability to clean up the pollution of air and water, how can we hope to take on spiritual pollution?") A look that mixed bewilderment and humor crossed Wu's face, and he replied, "Well, I didn't resist. Actually, I only became a Party member again in 1980. And, anyway, my wife was at first very upset by what seemed to be happening, fearing I had again brought catastrophe down on our heads. [Wu had been branded a rightist in 1957.] So I didn't want to cause her any more anxiety and agreed to resign willingly. Anyway, I'm not really the Party type. And now that I am out, I must tell you that I feel much freer to say and do what I want."

Also swept up in this bizarre do-it-yourself-style purge, in which the victim was asked to save the Party effort and embarrassment by purging himself, was Wang Ruoshui, a political theorist and former deputy editor in chief of the *People's Daily*. Wang, too, had been a target in the campaign against spiritual pollution, because he had dared suggest that socialism could just as readily breed human alienation as capitalism. When asked to resign in the summer of 1987, he had defiantly refused, and when he was threatened with ouster, he reportedly retorted, "I don't care."

Three other intellectuals—Sun Changjiang, deputy editor of the *Technology Daily*, and Zhang Xianyang and Su Shaozhi, both from the Chinese Academy of Social Sciences' Institute of Marxism–Leninism–Mao Zedong Thought—were pressured to resign from the Party. Su was also removed from his job as the Director of the Institute for allowing publication of works in periodicals under his control which allegedly opposed the Four Cardinal Principles. Su, who had gained quite a reputation for his bold reinterpretations of Marxism as a reformist doctrine, was also known to be a person to whom Zhao Ziyang frequently turned for canonical justification of his economic reforms. So to attack Su, in particular, meant indirectly to attack Zhao himself and his whole reformist program.

"It is a very bad practice when Party leaders act as if they are God Almighty; as if they know everything and have expertise in every field, whether academic, theoretical, or cultural. This practice is a resistant tumor inherited from feudal totalitarianism," Su had told a political reform conference in September, 1986. He had then gone on to decry the dogmatic nature of Stalinized Marxism, calling on Chinese "to search for freedom that is beneficial to political reform," to resist being "afraid of criticism and opinions," and instead to "encourage discussions about political reform" as a new "kind of creative activity."

In his book *Democratization and Reform*, which Party hard-liners had tried to suppress, Su rejected the notion that "socialist societies have entered the mature stage and have acquired some measure of communism." He suggested instead that China was actually only "at the first stage of socialism," that it was still "immature in every respect," and that it was thus both logical and necessary for China now to embrace "varied" modes of ownership and "different social elements." He attacked the rigid, doctrinaire attitudes of the Party, claiming that "in order to rethink socialism, it is necessary to re-examine Marxism," and he criticized the kind of "cultural autocracy" whose hallmarks were "accusing people abusively" and "attacking people at will" that China had endured.

"Democracy is our ideal and should be guaranteed in our political system," he openly declared. "The relationship between the Party and law must be clarified. Which will dominate? It can only be one of the two. Since the Constitution and the law are made by the people's representatives, and since the Party serves the people, the Party must therefore without exception operate within the limits of the Constitution and the law. The independence of the legislature and of the judiciary should be the sine qua nons in the reform of the political system."

From the start, this latest, modified purge was strangely out of synch with the generally optimistic reform-minded mood that had gradually reasserted itself that summer. Indeed, as it later turned out, Zhao Ziyang had not only vigorously opposed the outright expulsion of these Party intellectuals, but had hoped to minimize its impact as much as possible by refusing to announce it in the press.

If nothing else, the event served as a reminder of how divided the Chinese leadership still was, and how, even when the liberal reformers manifestly had the upper hand, the hard-liners were still able to wage disruptive rear guard actions. Occurring in such proximity to the Thirteenth Party Congress, to be held that October—when the future leadership of the country would be decided—the August "purge" left Chinese deeply apprehensive that Deng Xiaoping, who had said he wished to retire "before his brain got confused," would be no more successful than previous Chinese leaders in overcoming intra-Party factionalism and arranging for an orderly succession of power to a new generation of leadership.

|||||||||||||||||
· —— The Circle ——————————— ·
Comes
Around

By the fall of 1987, it had become clearer than ever that the various punitive measures taken against Party intellectuals were more in the nature of a wrist slapping than a full-fledged purge. In fact, the supreme paradox of the hard-liners' attempts to silence their opposition was that they ended up only lending their opponents more status than ever within China, and attracting instantaneous international interest to the very men whose ideas they wished to stifle. Not only was the foreign press suddenly writing adulatory accounts of these courageous Chinese defenders of freedom of speech and democracy, but the intellectuals themselves were suddenly besieged with invitations to go abroad to attend conferences, become visiting scholars at foreign universities, and even write books. What the hard-liners seemed to have incompletely accounted for was the voracious appetite of the West for Communist bloc intellectuals stamped with the imprimatur of Party persecution. As the political climate once again warmed up that fall, and with the behind-the-scenes support of certain key reform leaders, these already lionized intellectuals began to leave China for tours abroad, where they were treated like heroes. Wu Zuguang and Liu Xinwu (who had been restored to his post as editor of *People's Literature* in September) arrived in October at the twentieth-anniversary gathering of the Iowa International Writers Conference, to be greeted with cheers and applause by several hundred Chinese students. Yan Jiaqi, whose book on the Cultural Revolution had been so controversial the previous year and who had appeared on the hard-liner hit list of rightist intellectuals, was invited to be a visiting scholar at the University of Michigan. Liu Binyan, after being unable to go to Iowa, later received permission to go to Harvard University to become a Nieman Fellow and also won a lucrative book contract with an American publisher for a forthcoming autobiography. Fang Lizhi received invitations to be a visiting scholar from Cambridge University as well as from several American universities and had his collected speeches published in Hong Kong and Taiwan.

When I saw Fang that fall in Beijing, I was surprised by the freedom with which he was allowed to socialize and go about his academic life. It was true that he had been forbidden to make political speeches or give interviews to the press, that his phone was bugged, and that his movements were closely watched; but it was also true that he was able to continue a busy life in the capital, teaching, attending scientific meetings, and even meeting privately with friends, including some foreigners.

There was one occasion in particular that illustrated the surprisingly permissive post-crackdown policy of the Party toward Fang. Late in September, after dining with Fang and Li Shuxian at one of the capital's Western hotels, my wife and I introduced them to NBC anchorman Tom Brokaw, who was in Beijing for the network's week-long broadcast on China. As it happened, just the day before, Brokaw had interviewed Zhao Ziyang, who had spoken about Fang's situation at some length in what appeared to be an effort to reassure the outside world that Fang and other Chinese intellectuals would not have their freedom circumscribed any further. Upon meeting Fang, Brokaw asked him if he would like to screen the tape of the interview, which was not scheduled to be shown on Chinese television.

In what was surely one of the most unusual experiences of my many years following events in China, we soon found ourselves sitting in an NBC screening room, watching China's Premier and Acting Chinese Communist Party General Secretary, Zhao Ziyang, speak to China's number-one dissident via an American-network news video interview. Even stranger than the implausible situation itself was what Zhao was actually saying about Fang.

"Recently some Communist Party members were expelled from the Party, while others were persuaded to leave the Party," Zhao told Brokaw amiably while taking periodic swigs from a glass of Qingdao beer which he kept on a table beside him during the interview. "Maybe some people in the U.S. view this as a crackdown, as oppression against intellectuals; I do not agree. . . . I think probably you are already familiar with the name of Mr. Fang Lizhi." As Zhao spoke his name, I glanced over at Fang, who was sitting bolt upright as if at attention. He had a slight smile on his lips, a somewhat nonplussed expression on his face, and was utterly absorbed in what Zhao was saying. "He is a professor and a very accomplished physicist. Over the last few years he has made many remarks and speeches and written articles criticizing the Chinese government and the policies of our Party. Sometimes he has even referred to the leadership in our country. He delivered such speeches at universities and also at other places. But he is still working in a very important post, and not long ago he even went abroad for an international academic conference. Moreover, recently he gave an interview to two journalists from Taiwan. [These first journalists to visit the mainland from Taiwan arrived in September, 1987.] But he still maintains his original position and ideas. He was a Party member in the past. However, since he has such beliefs, he could no longer remain a Communist Party member. However, he is still an intellectual and a scientist, and is, moreover, respected for this. As such, he is still able to play his role in scientific and technological areas."

Going on to draw a distinction between the obligations of intellectuals who are Party members and those who are not, Zhao said, "If one joins the Party, one has to observe the regulations, the Party Constitution, and the Party program. . . . If someone cannot observe them, he will be asked to leave. . . . I think the Party itself should have the freedom to decide whether someone should remain in or not. But when intellectuals leave the Party, they will still be respected and will still be able to play their own roles in their own [professional] capacities. I don't think you could call this a crackdown."

Zhao spoke with confidence and conviction, and his words seemed so reassuring that it was difficult to remember that he had already spoken this way once before. Even though he had given his word the previous winter that Party harassment of intellectuals would cease, another wave of punitive action had nonetheless followed that summer.

Although heartened by Zhao's speech and doubtless also by the way the Party reformers had managed to bring China back from what had appeared to some as the brink of an abyss, Fang had hardly become more compromising in his attitude about the need for democracy in China. When I asked him what his own generation might leave by way of a legacy to China's youth, he replied simply, "That communism doesn't work. Although one cannot say that every sentence of Marxism-Leninism is wrong, one must admit that its basics are incorrect."

"Are there any Marxist true believers left in the Party?" I asked.

"They are very few. The whole atmosphere in China now is very bad. There is no morality or religion, or anyone taking care of our moral education. Formerly, the Party did this to some extent, but now belief in the Party and Marxism has literally collapsed. When you ask young people what they believe in, they tell you that they don't know. They have lost confidence in contemporary Chinese culture. They have nothing to be proud of. Except for those young people who are still idealistic because they have started to turn to democracy, there is a cultural and political vacuum."

"Do you put any hope in the Party's reform-minded leaders?" I queried.

"Perhaps there are a few who are idealistic, but on the whole they are primarily concerned with the question of power."

When I continued to press Fang on whether he truly doubted there was any hope for reform from within, he finally relented a bit. "Even if the leaders are not sincere, we must accept that this is the way things are going to be," he said. "One cannot say that success is absolutely impossible. . . . But for now, since the Chinese Communist Party is all there is in power, and there are no other democratic channels open, we can only allow these leaders to lead . . . and hope for the success of the reformers."

Then, brightening somewhat, he added, "The Chinese Communist Party now finds itself in a curious kind of competition with Gorbachev and his idea of glasnost. Both socialist countries now seem to be vying with each other to see which one can be most open, and by analogy, most modern. China's Party leaders do not want to seem to be outdone by Gorbachev, particularly since some people have likened my situation to that of the Soviet physicist Andrei Sakharov, and his situation has now improved so greatly. As far as I am concerned, this kind of competition is not only a very good thing for me, but for Chinese intellectuals and China in general. The hard reality is that there is no way now to get the Chinese Communist Party out of power. To try to replace them, or even to convince them to adopt some other political system is impossible. This is the difference between China and the West, where opponents can aspire to replace certain leaders completely. So presently, most Chinese feel that the only way to move forward is to hope that the Communist Party will be able to change its direction and do well by the country. Maybe the next generation will use different tactics and changed forms, but this will be up to them. Right now, such things are impossible."

By the time the Thirteenth Party Congress opened, on October 25, 1987, Fang's somber assessment of the chances of meaningful reform from within the Party seemed far more extreme than they had a few months earlier. In a masterful display of intra-Party diplomacy, Deng Xiaoping had, by agreeing to retire himself, managed to convince most of the aging hard-line leaders to withdraw from the front lines of Party leadership with him. Moreover, he had managed to calm the competing factions within the Party in a way that, at least for now, appeared to have left the hard-liners accepting a new leadership lineup in which the liberal reformers were clearly the ascendant force.

After a 160-piece military brass band had opened the congress by blaring out the "Internationale," Zhao Ziyang, appearing relaxed and jovial, delivered his keynote speech, "Marching Down the Road of Socialism with Chinese Characteristics." For the first time in Party history there were also—besides the 1936 delegates attending the congress—more than 400 members of the foreign press, including one journalist from Taiwan, looking on as Zhao decried the kind of political campaigns and mass struggles with which the Party had in the past tried to catapult China into communism. He declared that "the basic criteria for considering all problems and evaluating all work is whether productive forces can be advanced." Echoing Su Shaozhi, Zhao proclaimed that China was still only at an "elementary stage of socialism," an interim period that would "last at least a hundred years" and in which a "mixed economy" with "heterogeneous economic elements" such as private enterprise, stocks and bonds, private ownership, and foreign capital should be "further expanded."

When the ballots of delegates for the Party's 285-member Central Committee were tabulated and it was learned that most of the hardliners had been either eliminated or had retired—including Deng Liqun, Wang Zhen, Peng Zhen, Chen Yun, Bo Yibo, Li Xiannian, and Hu Qiaomu—while Hu Yaobang, who had been allowed to attend the congress, was surprisingly reelected, reformers and intellectuals in China were in a celebratory mood. And when on the next day, it was announced that Zhao Ziyang had been officially appointed Party General Secretary, they were almost delirious. But it was still far from a complete sweep for the reformers. While Deng Xiaoping, in his deft retirement act, had used his considerable influence to make sure that the new leadership hierarchy would be balanced in favor of the reformers, he had also been careful not to exclude that large faction within the Party which, if it no longer deserved the name "hard-line," was still manifestly more conservative in its approach to reform than leaders like Zhao and his predecessor, Hu. It was in the powerful five-man Standing Committee of the Central Committee's eighteen-member Political Bureau that Deng made sure the actual political forces of the country would be more or less proportionately reflected. The liberal reformers were represented by Zhao Ziyang and Political Bureau member and former Hu Yaobang protégé Hu Qili; the hard-line-conservative wing of the Party was represented by two of its more moderate members, Vice-Premier Li Peng and head of the State Planning Commission, Yao Yilin, while a swing vote went to a relative newcomer, Political Bureau member Qiao Shi, who had close ties to both groups.

In spite of the fact that the new Standing Committee reflected a spectrum of political views, it was immediately obvious to Chinese, who had been able to watch parts of the congress on television, that its members represented a stark break with the past when a beaming Zhao, clad in a stylish blue pinstriped double-breasted suit and a maroon tie, appeared on camera at a reception in the Great Hall of the People with his four colleagues. Standing in front of hundreds of members of the foreign press, Zhao clasped his hands above his head like a triumphant athlete and declared, "Our goal is common prosperity." The five leaders (not one of whom wore a Mao suit) then proceeded to do something that Chinese Party leaders had never done before: They casually circulated around the room, chatting, joking, and clinking glasses together in toasts with awestruck members of the press, who immediately seized upon this unusual opportunity to fire spontaneous questions at China's new and garrulous Party chief.

"Is there freedom to air different views in China?" cried out one reporter.

"There is freedom to air different views in China, but not absolute freedom. There is no freedom in the absolute sense in any country," rejoined Zhao with an air of bemused confidence that suggested he was enjoying the exchange.

"What will the principal problem in China be in your opinion?" ventured a West German reporter.

"Reform," Zhao shot back. "Both political and economic structural reform. . . . The two are mutually complementary and require a process of gradual development."

"I'd like to raise a personal question," interjected a Japanese reporter. "The double-breasted suit you are wearing is very smart. Is it made in China?"

"All my clothes are made in China, and I hope you can file a report saying that Mr. Zhao's clothes are made in China and that they are all very beautiful," joked Zhao.

"As you conduct reform, some people have become well-to-do quickly . . . but some are lagging behind, and the gap is rather big. How are you going to deal with this problem?" asked another correspondent.

"It's true that situation exists," admitted Zhao, showing a candor uncharacteristic of the older generation of leaders. "But this is not our ultimate goal. Our goal is to see all people prosperous. The gap is inevitable during the process of reform. . . . Even when you walk you have to move one of your legs first."

On only one question did Zhao show any signs of evasiveness. "Do you think that the Party Congress signals the end of the conservatives [hard-liners], or do you think there are still problems ahead?" called out a reporter.

In what was the longest and most detailed of all his answers, Zhao admitted that "there may be some differing within the leadership on some specific issues, measures, and policies," but he rebuked those "foreign friends [who] think there is a reformist faction and a conservative [hard-line] faction in China and base their interpretation of the Chinese political situation on the assumed struggle between these factions." Then, in an oblique genuflection to democracy, he declared, "It is my opinion that some differing views among our leaders . . . may help make our decision-making process more democratic and scientific. They serve as an important guarantee that we will make fewer mistakes and avoid serious errors."

The *People's Daily* deliriously described the congress as a "new monument" and a "glowing sun." A few days later when I talked with Mr. Song, the intellectual who had been so gloomy and skeptical about reform in China the previous winter, he seemed energized by the outcome of the Congress and by Zhao's performance, and buoyed up with a new sense of optimism.

"We watched it on television," he said, his voice rising in a crescendo of enthusiasm. "It was very, very impressive. There has never been anything like it in China!"

Fang Lizhi, however, was a little less optimistic. After the Congress, he told the Hong Kong journal *Baixing Banyue Kan*, "It is true Zhao's report was very stirring. But in his time Mao Zedong made speeches that were even more stirring than this one. But speeches are simply not enough. One must never lose track of concrete reality."

A month later, on November 25, the leadership shuffle was completed when Li Peng, the fifty-eight-year-old Soviet-educated Vice-Premier and newly chosen Standing Committee member, was named Acting Premier, taking over the position from Zhao. By the end of 1987 the political climate in China had again changed dramatically. Just as in the previous fall when the vigorous debates on political reform and democracy had made it difficult to imagine a return to the politics of the Cultural Revolution, so, once again, it was not easy to conjure up in one's mind the kind of militant Maoist rhetoric (and the sense of foreboding it had produced) that had burst on the scene only the winter before.

Although at the end of 1987 the Party was still very reticent about raising the issue of democratization again, and although the official political climate was still less expansive than it had been just a year earlier, the political momentum seemed moving resolutely back in the direction of openness. China appeared to be completing yet another of its many full cycles. But at the same time that another political circle had been completed, the country had not returned to where it had begun a year earlier. China had hardly been changeless. Just as a waltzing couple continues to move laterally across the dance floor even as they spin around and around, China, too, fueled by the internal combustion of its own intra-Party contradictions, had been propelled into entirely new territory.

By surviving this latest cycle of political dialectics, the reform movement now seemed to be running deeper than ever. Perhaps when Deng Xiaoping, the first Chinese Communist leader to begin surrendering political power voluntarily (after the Thirteenth Party Congress, he maintained only one official position, as Chairman of the Central Military Commission, which controls China's Armed forces), finally passed from the scene, powerful adversaries of reform might rally their forces for another disruptive counter-attack. But with the baton of leadership formally in the hands of Zhao Ziyang for now, it seemed more unlikely than ever that reformist momentum could be halted.

But in China, where political surfaces have so often proved illusory, particularly for outsiders looking in, it was impossible to predict the outcome of China's latest reform effort with any certainty. Who, for instance, during the fall of 1986 could have foretold the events that were to have followed that winter? In fact, who during the long chaotic years of Mao's Cultural Revolution could have predicted the reform era of Deng Xiaoping?

As Mao himself was fond of pointing out in his treatises on political philosophy, there is often an unexpected unity between opposites. Just as Deng's practical reform-minded attitude had somehow survived the vicissitudes of the Cultural Revolution, so the ideas of Mao had proven to have their own kind of durability. They, too, had a way of re-emerging when one least expected them, just as Mao's own quotes had begun resurfacing on the walls of Beida.

||||||||||||||||||||||||||

Mao and Kentucky Fried Chicken

Driving through the bleak, urban landscape of Beijing on my way to Tian'anmen Square, it was hard for me to believe that thirty-seven years ago, when the Communists came to power, this city had been considered one of the most historic, most magically atmospheric capitals in Asia—or that only ten years ago, aflutter with red banners and studded with the heroic iconography of Maoist socialism, it had been viewed as the citadel of a worldwide proletarian revolution.

By 1987 it was no longer easy to discern what exactly the city's predominant characteristics were. Certainly it was no longer ancient in feeling, and almost nowhere did one see signs of the Revolution. More and more, it looked like just another Third World city lumbering gracelessly into the industrial age. Beijing, like China itself, now seemed to stand for nothing in particular. Just as the old revolutionary landmarks of Beijing—the enormous hirsute visages of Marx, Lenin, Engels, and Stalin, which stood for years in their king-size frames at the north end of Tian'anmen Square along Changan Boulevard; the crimson banners that used to festoon the streets; the immense red propaganda billboards emblazoned with quotations of Chairman Mao and once as seemingly fixed in their places as heavenly constellations—had now vanished, so, too, the main pillars of belief in Chinese communism had evanesced.

In the fall of 1987 one of the few portraits of Mao Zedong still displayed in public hung in Tian'anmen Square, above the main gate to the Forbidden City. Over the past decade almost all the other images of Mao, once so commonplace, had quietly disappeared from commune headquarters, factories, Party branch offices, and people's homes, until this lone portrait came to seem like the last survivor of an endangered species. This very public remnant of the cult of Maoism had by now gained such an obvious (if, for many, an unwelcome) symbolism that to take it down would have meant sending the world the all-too definitive message that China's Maoist Revolution was over. This would have been an intolerable message for the remaining hard-liners, who, if they could not have the fact, at least wanted to maintain the fiction of Mao's socialist revolution. And so, even though the reformers had been deemphasizing Mao more and more, the Party as a whole was still not yet ready to remove this last, highly visible image of its heroic founder from public view. In a cryptic compromise, the Party clung to Mao in theory even as it repudiated him in practice. To help create at least an illusion of consistency with its political past, the Party left this one, anomalous icon gazing out of its peeling frame long after the rest of the country had relieved itself of most other Mao memorabilia.

Just across the square, directly in the gaze of this famous portrait, lay another Maoist shrine, the massive edifice of Mao Zedong Memorial Hall, where the Great Helmsman's mortal remains lay embalmed beneath a crystal sarcophagus. As the most recent cycle in Chinese politics was coming to an end, some impulse drew me here. Perhaps sparked by the way in which the hard-line counter-attack of the previous winter harked back, however incompletely, to the Maoist era, perhaps by the confusion that I and so many Chinese had been feeling about the oscillations in political lines since Mao's death, or perhaps simply by the lightning-fast speed with which the country had been changing since I had first come to know it twelve years earlier, I found myself curious to visit the epicenter from which the shock waves of this waning revolution had once emanated.

In spite of the raw cold that morning in Tian'anmen Square, two long lines of people snaked out from the huge doors of the Memorial Hall across the vast square. As I came closer, I saw that the lines consisted mostly of factory workers and peasants from the provinces wearing so many layers of winter clothing—including not a few down-filled parkas and Western-style ski caps—that they looked almost like inflated plastic toys. Years ago, when I had last visited the mausoleum, an awed hush had descended on the faithful as soon as they took their places in line; now, however, they disported themselves with an almost raucous irreverence. They pushed, shoved, chattered away, smoked cigarettes, even ate snacks as they waited. Uniformed security guards barked at them with hoarse voices through bullhorns in a way that seemed designed more to manifest their own authority than to keep order.

The Memorial Hall itself, which occupies about 200,000 square feet of floor space and has a 100-foot-high double roof supported by forty-four enormous granite columns, is distinguished more by its bulkiness than its grace. Its elements of traditional Chinese, Stalinist kitsch, Greek revival, and Hollywood biblical architecture now inspired no awe. Instead, the stylistic confusion suddenly seemed like the perfect metaphor for China's ideological disorientation.

Positioned around the mausoleum were immense statues rendered in that heroic style of socialist realism—now slowly vanishing from the face of the earth—which featured phalanxes of the "broad revolutionary masses," their eyes resolute, brows furrowed with righteousness, fists clenched overhead in defiance, all straining forward either against unseen enemies or toward a rosy socialist future.

It was hard to imagine students demonstrating for democracy and human rights in the shadow of these graven images of wrathful proletarians, just as it was hard to reconcile the figures themselves with the actual masses lined up nearby in their brightly colored winter sportswear. Nor was it easy to grasp the fact that these people in line around me were the workers, peasants, and soldiers on whom Mao's revolution had once been built; that they were the "oppressed masses" who had joined the Red Army to fight Chiang Kai-shek, had gone through land reform, had "spat out their bitternesses" against oppressive landlords, fought in Korea, and been the backbone of the people's communes.

While Mao still lived, the mere suggestion of his name had often been enough to cow Chinese into an immediate, respectful silence. I remember in 1975 meeting one breathless young woman dockworker from Shanghai who came close to tears as she described how she had shaken the hand of someone who had actually shaken the hand of Chairman Mao. But those who had come to pay their respects to Chairman Mao in 1987 seemed no more reverential or somber as they approached his mortal remains than tourists visiting the Egyptian wing of a museum. Even here, Mao was clearly in the process of descending from the status of a deity to that of a famous, albeit dead, mortal. Still revered by older revolutionaries, he was for the younger generation hardly more than a figure from history. In fact, a survey conducted by the pro-Beijing Hong Kong newspaper, *Wenhui Daily*, revealed the surprising fact that only 22 percent of the secondary-school children it polled in China knew who Mao Zedong was.

Passing a sign on an iron gateway that unceremoniously announced

376 — *Discos and Democracy*

in both English and Chinese, "Please Do Not Smoke or Spit," we began to mount the white marble steps that led to the portico. Only now, as if everyone had caught the same silent command at once, a hush fell. By the time we entered the Great North Hall, where a second sign directed us with an equal lack of decorousness, "Please Take Off Hat and Keep Quiet," there was absolute silence.

Hats in hands, the visitors now seemed filled by a sudden sense of wonder as they gazed around the cavernous red-carpeted hall at the gargantuan embroidered landscape of mist and mountains or at the translucent seated figure of Mao himself. Unlike the grainy concrete statue at Beida, this Lincolnesque figure hewn from pristine white marble was bathed in electric light in such a way that it seemed to shine from within and to float like an apparition across the panorama of the landscape behind it.

We were now approaching the figurative center of the Chinese Revolution. Aware of their symbolic proximity to this once seemingly ultimate Chinese event, as well as to the man who had led it, the onlookers were overcome with what appeared to be a mixture of awe and fear, reflected in a certain stiffness of their bodies and the nervous way they looked first here, then there, not quite certain where it was appropriate to fix their gaze.

As we approached the back of the room, our single line was suddenly split in two by several brusque guards, and before we knew it we had entered the Hall for Paying Reverence, the heart of the mausoleum. There, in the middle of the room, attired in a gray suit and draped with a crimson and yellow Chinese flag, was Mao Zedong. As they filed past, the onlookers stared, mouths agape, unwilling to avert their eyes until the very last minute as the lines approached the white marble backdrop inscribed in gold relief with the salute: "Eternal glory to our great leader and teacher Chairman Mao Zedong."

Just as we were about to file out of the Hall for Paying Reverence, an old peasant several yards in front of me stopped and cast one last furtive glance over his shoulder, as if to make sure that what he had just seen was no apparition. While the old man was momentarily lost in his reverie, the constantly moving line backed up around him, until a guard suddenly hurried over, scolded him, and sent him on his way. For those short moments the old man spent gazing at Mao's waxy visage, I had a sense of how deeply, if subliminally embedded Mao and his momentous revolution still were in the Chinese people. Even though Chairman Mao, once referred to as the "red red sun" in the hearts of the Chinese people, had lost much credibility in the years since his death (particularly among the younger generation), he evidently still held a fascination for, if not necessarily a grip on, those older people who had spent their lives immersed in his revolution. Like the portrait that stubbornly continued to hang over Tian'anmen and the embalmed corpse behind us, Mao's thought, too, had proved surprisingly resistant to banishment. Just when one was tempted to believe that China had at last put its era of radical socialist revolution behind it, Mao's legacy had a way of resurfacing in the guise of Party hard-liners calling for a return to the spirit of Yan'an or the selfless devotion of Lei Feng. In ways that were not always apparent from outward appearances, Mao's influence lived on beneath the surface of things. Like an arsenal of mothballed warships that could be made combat-ready and thrown into the fray at short notice, Mao's thought endured as a powerful anti-reformist weapon. Whenever modernizers and reformers took China too far and too fast from Mao's revolutionary baseline, whenever class polarization grew too pronounced or Chinese youth became too flamboyantly Western or too militantly democratic, Mao's thought was there, ready to be reactivated as a countervailing force by those Party members who had come of age and entered the Party during his long tenure. Although many Chinese intellectuals may have grown beyond its reach, much of the rest of China was still susceptible to its suasion.

For the reformers, the problem of Mao Zedong's legacy was a profoundly difficult one, as the events of the past winter had shown, for what Mao and his revolution had stood for was in so many ways diametrically opposed to what the reformers were now proclaiming as an alternative. No matter how Deng or other Party theorists might manipulate quotes from Mao to rationalize their new pragmatism, in their hearts most Chinese knew there was an insoluble contradiction between the notions of revolution and reform. And no matter how hard the reformers tried to distance themselves from Mao, there was no easy escape since his thought was still officially part of the country's founding ideology. Try as the reformers might to start anew, Mao could not simply be jettisoned, like a used-up fuel tank on a booster rocket. In some basic sense Maoism had been transsubstantiated into every Chinese leader, even the reformers, since without his legacy the continued political domination of the Communist Party was unjustifiable, almost inconceivable. Even Deng Xiaoping, who had been dismissed twice by Mao, had defended him after his death and the fall of the Gang of Four. "On no account can we discard the banner of Mao Zedong Thought," he had said in 1978. "To do so would, in fact, be to negate the glorious history of our Party." On another occasion he had warned the Chinese people, "Concerning the errors of Comrade Mao Zedong, we must not overshoot the limit. Going to extremes and blackballing Mao Zedong is tantamount to blackballing our Party and our country."

Mao had become so intertwined with the identity of the Party that to abandon his legacy would have been the equivalent of ideological self-immolation. So, charging him with certain "leftist errors" and sometimes being "divorced from reality," the Party endeavored to preserve at least part of his legacy. Its solution, as in so much else, was to try to have it both ways at once: to recommend, as Deng had in 1979, that Chinese adopt the same 70/30 percent formula in regard to Mao that Mao himself had applied to Stalin, namely to declare that 70 percent of what he had done was correct, and 30 percent incorrect. In fact, Deng had said that he would be happy if history gave *him* such a favorable rating.

Another strategy for putting Mao safely away into storage without having to repudiate him completely was to divide his tenure up into good and bad periods. The years before 1957 were designated as those in which his policies had been largely "scientific" and "correct" and the years after 1957 as those when his policies were largely incorrect. But while the Party could use formulaic manipulations to subtly devalue his legacy without risking its outright obliteration, it could do no such thing with his Memorial Hall. The hall was no abstraction. It sat with utter concreteness at the very spiritual center of the country, pulsing as if it were radioactive. As a religious order might try to dilute the influence of a patron saint, whose memory is too inciting to the faithful, by adding other, more acceptable martyrs to its pantheon of the revered, so the Party decided to give Mao some fellow tenants in his Memorial Hall; it opened special, mini memorial rooms for three other revolutionary leaders: Zhou Enlai, Liu Shaoqi, and Zhu De. But the fact of the matter was that these new shrines were afterthoughts, rarely open, and in any event, not places the crowds flocking to the Memorial Hall had much interest in visiting.

In the Hall for Paying Reverence, lines of people moved relentlessly past Mao's bier as if they were on a conveyor belt. The whole process, from entrance to exit, took no more than a few minutes. Then, as if coming to the end of a subterranean amusement park ride, the lines of people were suddenly shuttled through the rear doors back into the blinding light of day. Here, beyond the scrutiny of the guards and with Mao's corpse just a memory, they dissolved into a disorderly swarm, spilling down the marble stairs and fanning out into a milling throng among a series of small shedlike structures that sat behind the hall. It was not until I got closer that I saw they were actually souvenir shops, part of a thriving marketplace where mobs of unruly people with fistfuls of money were trying to elbow their way toward window counters to buy official Chairman Mao Memorial Hall chopsticks, cigarettes, earrings, ashtrays, plastic flowers, cups, thermos bottles, key rings, thermometers, neckties, and cigarette holders, and to have souvenir snapshots taken of themselves with Chairman Mao's final resting place as a backdrop.

As I stood and watched this orgy of buying and selling, I wondered how many of the comrades around me could still recite any of the Mao quotes that most of them had doubtless been compelled to learn in the endless required study sessions of years past. Was anyone in this acquisitive throng still aware of Mao's 1957 warning that "there is still a bourgeoisie, and the remolding of the petit-bourgeoisie has only just started. The class struggle is by no means over. The class struggle between the proletariat and the bourgeoisie, the class struggle between the different political forces, and the class struggle in the ideological field between the proletariat and the bourgeoisie, will continue to be long and torturous and at times will even become very acute. The proletariat seeks to transform the world according to its own world outlook, and so does the bourgeoisie. In this respect, the question of which will win out, socialism or capitalism, is still not really settled."

The spectacle of these latter-day pilgrims snapping up useless gewgaws with reckless abandon made it hard not to conclude that the bourgeoisie had, at least for now, been victorious and that capitalism had triumphed over socialism. What made the scene so eerie was that although this one spot contained the most tightly packed collection of Mao imagery still remaining in China, there was virtually nothing for sale in the souvenir shops that had any relevance to the political significance of Mao Zedong as a revolutionary leader. This was business, plain and simple—at best, a sort of Chinese nostalgia industry. Like those parasitic forms of marine life that cluster and thrive around the outfall pipes of large cities, these small businesses had gathered here to commercially exploit the people spilling out of Mao's place of entombment.

The inside and outside of the mausoleum might as well have been in different galaxies, so that in passing from one to the other, I felt as I had when Mao was still alive and I first crossed the Lowu Bridge on the Chinese border back to the Hong Kong side years ago. Now, without even passing over a national frontier, I had made a journey no less monumental. I had gone from one side of China's divided political personality to the other: from politics to commerce. The only similarity between the two was the same hell-bent totalism with which each of these opposites had been enshrined as national policy in its own time.

As I stood in the middle of the souvenir area gazing up at the towering mausoleum, I tried for one instant to imagine the comic pandemonium that would have ensued had Mao suddenly reappeared on the steps above and, like a wrathful God, thundered his familiar prophecy down on the preoccupied consumers below: "In our country bourgeois and petit-bourgeois ideology, anti-Marxist ideology, will continue to exist for a long time. In the ideological field, the question of who will win the struggle between the proletariat and the bourgeoisie has really not been settled yet. We still have to wage a protracted struggle against bourgeois and petit-bourgeois ideology. It is wrong not to understand this and to give up the ideological struggle. All poisonous weeds, all ghosts and monsters, must be subjected to criticism; in no circumstances should they be allowed to spread unchecked."

But if the ghost of Mao had seemed to stalk the land the previous winter, by the end of the Thirteenth Party Congress, in the fall of 1987, the idea of a hard-line, never mind an outright Maiost revival, had come to seem an increasingly remote possibility. While it was true that hard-line and reformist forces had long been locked in a repetitive cycle of struggle, it was also true that in the process China had changed dramatically. Mao and all that he had stood for seemed more limited than ever to the confines of his Memorial Hall. In fact, that fall, just across Tian'anmen Square from Mao's final resting place, the world's largest branch of the Kentucky Fried Chicken fast-food restaurant chain opened, complete with pictures of the Statue of Liberty, a poster saying "America—Catch the Spirit," and the familiar menu of chicken, coleslaw, biscuits, mashed potatoes (called potato mud in Chinese), and gravy. And as if this new neighbor was not emblematic enough of the changes taking place in China, that December, officials at Beijing

Teachers' University, engaging in a bit of unmistakable symbolism, blew up the twenty-five-foot-high concrete statue of the Chairman which had stood at the center of its campus since the sixties to make way for a new library largely financed by a wealthy Hong Kong capitalist.

||||||||||||||||||||||||||||||||
· ——— Notes on ——————— ·
Translations and
Sources

In researching this book I relied heavily on English translations of press and broadcast reports published by the United States government in the "China Report" series of the Joint Publications Research Service, the Foreign Broadcast Information Series, "Daily Reports: The People's Republic of China" published by the National Technical Information Service, and the "Summary of World Broadcasts: The Far East—China," printed and published by the monitoring service of the BBC. I have also drawn heavily on articles published by Agence France Presse (Paris), *Asiaweek* (Hong Kong), *Beijing Daily* (Beijing), *Beijing Review* (Beijing), *China Daily* (Beijing), *China News Analysis* (Hong Kong), *China Spring* (New York), *Der Spiegel* (Hamburg), *Jiushi Niandai* (*The Nineties*) (Hong Kong), *Far Eastern Economic Review* (Hong Kong), *Guangming Daily* (Beijing), *Hong Kong Standard* (Hong Kong), *Inside China Mainland* (Taibei), *Jardine Fleming Ltd. China Research Monthly Newsletter* (Hong Kong), Kyodo News Agency (Tokyo), *Liberation Daily* (Shanghai), *Liberation Army Daily* (Beijing), *Red Flag* (Beijing), *Los Angeles Times* (Los Angeles), *Ming Pao* (Hong Kong), New China News Agency (Beijing), *New York Times* (New York), *People's Daily* (Beijing), *South China Morning Post* (Hong Kong), *Washington Post* (Washington), *Wen Hui Bao* (Shanghai), *Zheng Ming* (Hong Kong).

The translations of Fang Lizhi's speeches were done by J. A. Williams, Jeffery Ringwold, and William Wagenblast. Many of the sections from Liu Binyan's works and speeches were translated by James Feinerman with Perry Link, Nieh Hualing, and Michael S. Duke. Some sections of Wang Ruowang's work were done by Nieh Hualing and Deborah Rudolph.

I found the following English-language works to be of invaluable help: Michael S. Duke's *Blooming and Contending: Chinese Literature in the Post-Mao Era* and *Contemporary Chinese Literature: An Anthology of Post-Mao Fiction and Poetry*; R. Randle Edwards, Louis Henkin, and Andrew Nathan's *Human Rights in Contemporary China*; Roger Garside's *Coming Alive: China After Mao*; Merle Goldman's *China's Intellectuals: Advise and Dissent* and *Literary Dissent in Communist China*; Willy Wo-lap Lam's *Toward a Chinese-Style Socialism: An Assessment of Deng Xiaoping's Reforms*; Joseph Levenson's *Liang Ch'i-ch'ao: And the Mind of Modern China*; Perry Link's *People or Monsters?: Liu Binyan* and *Roses and Thorns: The Second Blooming of the Hundred Flowers in Chinese Fiction, 1979–80*; Andrew Nathan's *Chinese Democracy*; Nieh Hualing's *Literature of the Hundred Flowers*; James D. Seymour's *China Rights Annals 1*; and Judith Shapiro and Liang Heng's *Warm Winds, Cold Winds: Intellectual Life In China Today*.

ABOUT THE AUTHOR

Orville Schell is a noted China observer who has visited that country frequently over the past years. He has written for the *Atlantic Monthly*, the *New Yorker, Rolling Stone*, and the *New York Times* among other magazines and newspapers. He is the author of numerous books on China, the most recent of which is *To Get Rich Is Glorious: China in the 1980s*.